Praise for
The Bad Catholic's Guide:

John and Denise, a long-time Catholic journalist and a trained Continental chef, have done it again. They've ransacked 20 centuries, 5 continents, and their own disturbed imaginations to uncover the fun in faith—and dozens of delicious recipes for dinner, cocktails, and party punch. It's educational—and intoxicating!
—Angelo Matera, publisher/editor of Godspy.com and former CEO,
the *National Catholic Register*

What a great book. . . . As a non-Catholic I found it most educational and extremely funny. It is so refreshing in this politically correct era!
—Rabbi Abba Perelmuter, Shul By The Shore, Long Beach, California

All saints suffer one way or another, but there are no sad saints. As this book makes abundantly clear, some more than others had the gift of *laetitia* or earthly gladness which, by not being lived as an end in itself, points the way to "beatitude," or heavenly joy.
—Rev. George Rutler, author, theologian, host, Eternal Word Television Network.

The authors prove that irreverence is compatible with true piety as they gallop through Catholic ideas, anecdotes . . . and recipes. The book often rises to the level of laugh-out-loud funny and observes the Catholic scene with wit and insight.
—Michael Potemra, *National Review.*

Silly some of the time, respectful most of the time, and hilarious all of the time. Even the squirrel recipes sound delicious and will have me driving slower thru the red states, chumming for low cost snacks on the two lane all the way to Mardi Gras.
—Mario Batali, chef, host of *Mario Eats Italy,* and *Ciao America* on the Food Network,
author, *The Babbo Cookbook.*

Chesterton remarks somewhere that a Protestant typically says he is a good Protestant while a Catholic typically says he is a bad Catholic. Two young Catholics who manifestly love the Church make the most of that, offering a frequently hilarious, sometimes sophomoric, romp through the church year, the legends of the saints, and the oddments of Catholic sacramental practice. Recipes for the celebration of feasts and fantasies abound. The book will not be everybody's cup of tea—or, more aptly, pint of ale—but those who like this kind of thing will undoubtedly like it very much.

—*First Things* magazine.

Among the many memorable recipes are Smothered Squirrel, Easter Bunny Fricassee, Baby Jesus Cookies, Greek Flaming Cheese, Feta Cheese Cigarettes and Nun's Farts, a deep-fried pastry-type confection. And frankly, if reading the words "Nun's Farts" didn't make you giggle, at least a little bit, then you're probably not part of the demographic for this offbeat, entertaining book.

—William I. Lengeman III, Epicurean.com

D0469558

A sharp, loving excavation of Things Catholic via a trip through the liturgical year—and recipes…. It's heartfelt, satirical, and, we can't neglect to say, accurate in its presentation of the faith.

—Amy Wellborn, author, *The Catholic Woman's Book of Days*

The ideas outlined here for food and fun are zany, sophisticated, and delightful! How many guides to seasonal cooking urge their readers to flambé chickens, smother squirrels, put antidepressants in the punch and sell indulgences? Not nearly enough, if you ask me.

—Georges Briguet, Owner, Le Périgord, New York City.

Bad Catholics, beware. John Zmirak and Denise Matychowiak have a hidden agenda: to make you better Catholics. Beneath the puns, ribaldry, and hilariously apt (and no doubt delicious) feast-day recipes lie a profound reverence for—and knowledge of—the Church, her saints, her teachings, and her traditions.

—Jeffrey Rubin, former editor, *The Latin Mass* and *Sursum Corda* magazines

For 30 years, heavy-handed works of "humor" by disgruntled, lapsed-Catholic writers have been a dime a dozen. Thanks to John Zmirak and Denise Matychowiak's uproarious cornucopia of Catholic fun, now we can laugh ourselves up and out of that literary purgatory. Their sharp-witted irreverence seldom fails to amuse—because they know the Church so well, and love her so dearly."

—Thomas McArdle, former communications director,
The Catholic League for Civil and Religious Rights.

A wacky poke at Catholicism's rich and quirky traditions and doctrines yet refreshingly devoted to them at the same time. "Lord, to whom shall we go?" If you're in the habit of kissing bits of bone on velvet you'll "get" this book.

—Susan Lloyd, author, *Please Don't Drink the Holy Water!*

It isn't often that a book comes along that forces you to laugh as hard as it makes you believe—Mr. Zmirak and Miss Matychowiak have produced such a book. It is irreverent all right, but not toward Catholicism. Instead, it is a book that laughs its head off at the crazy world around us that denies the Faith. Because they believe in the Catholic religion, the authors feel no need to pretend belief in anything else—and everything comes in for a skewering, from modern notions of respectability to sheer bad taste. But mixed in with the banter is solid Church teaching, history, and custom. Oh yes—and the food and drink recipes are delicious. Brings home Belloc's dictum that "wherever the Catholic sun doth shine, there's laughter and music and good red wine." This book reminds us that where it doesn't, there aren't.

—Charles A. Coulombe, KCStS, author of *Vicars of Christ: A History of the Popes.*

If the authors had not given me a free copy of this book, I would have bought it, but I would have done it online or in disguise at a bookstore. I certainly will give it to many friends, but anonymously. Unfortunately, I still have remnants of a respectable reputation to preserve…. The authors' contribution to the "new evangelization" may not be exactly what the Holy Father and the bishops have in mind, but it is certainly based on the same point of departure: Christianity as a wondrous event.

—Msgr. Lorenzo Albacete, theologian and author, professor at the
John Paul II Institute for Studies in Marriage and Family

The *Bad* *Catholic's* Guide to *Wine, Whiskey* *& Song*

A Spirited Look at Catholic Life and Lore, from Apocalypse to Zinfandel

JOHN ZMIRAK
&
DENISE MATYCHOWIAK

A Crossroad Book
The Crossroad Publishing Company
New York

This book is respectfully dedicated to the men and women who served the authors as sources of inspiration and enlightenment over the formative decades of their professional and intellectual lives:

Pope Benedict XVI
Paula Wolfert
M.F.K. Fisher
"Weird Al" Yankovic

Ad augusta per angusta.
—*The Feast of St. John Bosco, 2007*

The Crossroad Publishing Company
16 Penn Plaza, Suite 1550, New York, NY 10001

Printed in the United States of America

Library of Congress Cataloging-in-Publication Data is available.
ISBN-13: 978-0-8245-2411-1
ISBN-10: 0-8245-2411-X

1 2 3 4 5 6 7 8 9 10   13 12 11 10 09 08 07

Contents

Introduction

Since the appearance of *The Bad Catholic's Guide to Good Living* in 2005, we have been deeply moved by reports of the impact made by our little guidebook to the Church's feasts, saints, and sacraments. We have been deluged (okay, that's not quite true—we have been *spritzed*) by grateful letters, appreciative emails, and hoarse, late night phone calls reporting the many ways in which readers have been motivated, edified, or profoundly disconcerted by the book. Parents have given it to their teens, hoping that the injection of humor between the cracks in the edifice of our Church would warm their young ones to embrace her doctrines, dogmas, and idiosyncrasies—parents who later thrilled to hear the snicker of youthful laughter coming from behind their teens' locked and barricaded doors. Seniors have sought out the book as a comfort in their golden years, and reported how its nostalgic humor recalled them to their childhoods—for instance, by inducing incontinence. Parents have written, reporting that their tweens found the book in the bathroom and developed a precocious interest in the Theology of the Body. One mother actually phoned us, to let us know that

> [n]ow my 10-year-old daughter keeps repeating the phrase *The pope urged men to slow down the rhythm of their own arousal, to more closely match their wives' arousal.* And she wants to know what it means. What the hell am I supposed to tell her?

We're grateful for these responses, and happy to know that the book is making an impact on people's families. (The family, as Pope John Paul II repeatedly reminded the world, is the basic unit of society.) As we prepare to dig even deeper into the life and lore of the Church in this new guide to beer, wine, and spirituality, we would like to share with the reader a few more of these notes elicited by *The Bad Catholic's Guide to Good Living.*

From a student in Steubenville, Ohio:

> At our school we have a student club that goes every year to Spring Break in Florida to evangelize on the beach. Modeling ourselves on Evangelical Christian groups, we witness to our walk of faith through Bible skits, praise songs, and the modesty of our clothing. Sometimes

we'll go up and sit next to groups from sororities and give them pamphlets about "Mary-like dress."

To tell the truth, we're not usually that successful. The college kids we approach are pretty non-responsive. Sometimes we get pelted with dried jellyfish.

But this year, after using your Bad Catholic's book as devotional reading, we decided to try an outreach that was more rooted in Catholic traditions, like the ones you wrote about. Specifically, the Good Friday custom from the Philippines of conducting a live (non-lethal!) crucifixion—with actual nails and everything! We tried that this year in Destin, and you wouldn't believe the size of the crowd we attracted—mostly guys, who usually are the ones pelting us with jellyfish. This time they didn't do that. Most of them got really, really quiet—except for one guy who was drunk who started yelling "Crucify him! Give us Barabbas!" Which made the whole thing even more biblical!

The Spring Breakers told us they'd never seen anything like that before in their lives, and that our skit had "changed the whole atmosphere on the beach." Thanks, guys!

From a pastor in Los Angeles:

At one point in your book you criticize the practice of pastors sitting in the sanctuary, while lay Eucharistic ministers distribute Communion in the Hand—and compare this to "handing out movie tickets" or something. Well, some of my parishioners got hold of your book and started quoting it and making trouble, complaining that we were treating the Host disrespectfully, yadda-yadda. . . . They ended up making such nuisances of themselves that I decided to respond to their concerns.

We stopped distributing Communion altogether, and now the ministers hand out movie tickets. The troublemakers stopped coming to the parish, and our weekly collection take has doubled. I hope you're happy now.

From a mom in Neceda, Wisconsin:

For going on three years our teenaged son, Ignaz, has been worrying us. He is obsessed with this music he calls "Black Metal," which is full of occult and even Satanic lyrics. He dresses all in black, fills his room with taxidermied house cats, and refers to himself as "Mr. Death."

Of course we are concerned. We took your book out of the library and read to him the section on St. Bartholomew Longo—the fellow who practiced Satanism for 15 years, before converting back to the Church and becoming an apostle of the Rosary.

Ignaz loved the story and promised us that if we give him just 12 more years, he will do the same. I told him, "Okey-dokey, Mr. Death, but we're marking our calendars!' And now our whole family gets along just so much better. I wanted to write in and say Thanks!

From a dad in Still River, Massachusetts:

My wife and I have three sons, aged 7, 9, and 10, who have been getting caught up in consumerism and the commercialism of Christmas, so we decided to teach them about the REAL St. Nicholas. You know, of Myra. You describe in your book how he found three murdered boys in a barrel and raised them from the dead—and that's how he got to be patron saint of children, pickles, and barrels. So I got hold of a barrel and convinced the boys to hide in it. I filled it part-way with brine, nailed the thing shut for a while, and left them in the basement for a few minutes.

I came back dressed as a fourth-century bishop, opened the thing up, and told them that St. Nicholas had raised them from the dead. Well, talk about a look of excitement and wonder on a child's face! Once they stopped crying and pulled themselves together, I explained to them about the Council of Nicaea and the Creed, and I can tell you it *really made an impression*. What's more, none of them want Christmas gifts this year. They all said that "Santa should stay away. Let him give our presents to the poor, or something." So they've learned a lesson about charity as well. You guys keep up the good work!

From a soul in Purgatory (via email):

All of us down here would like to thank you for reminding everyone about the Feast of All Souls and the plenary indulgences available for the Suffering Souls during that octave. You're really helping thin out the ranks down here, so we don't have such long lines for the exercise equipment. However, I feel compelled to point out that those indulgence certificates you reproduce in your book for hosts to sell to their guests at parties *are no longer valid*. In fact, they expired during the Renaissance. Please inform your readers—we've already had a few dozen souls arrive down here waving what they called "Get Out of Purgatory, Free" cards, and they were really, really disappointed. We couldn't even get them refunds.

There were many, many more such notes.

As we release this new book and watch it sink with a satisfying *plunk*, we look forward to seeing the ripples it makes. If Christ called us to be "fishers of men" (Matthew 4:19), you ought to think of the apologetics practiced in this series as fishing with dynamite.

The Authors
www.badcatholics.com

Absinthe and the Apocalypse

Absinthe was invented as a medicinal tonic in the ancient world. It was recommended by Hippocrates the physician as a cure for rheumatism, by Pythagoras the mystic as anesthesia for childbirth, and by Pliny the Elder as mouthwash. In its modern form, spiked with alcohol, absinthe is said to be the concoction of Dr. Pierre Ordinaire—a refugee from the Reign of Terror, who apparently decided to avenge himself on the revolutionary French by addicting their most talented writers to a green, brain-eating liqueur.

In the late-nineteenth century, after the grape phylloxera epidemic had destroyed two-thirds of the vineyards in Europe, the price of wine skyrocketed while its quality took a nose dive. So Bohemian artists turned to other beverages. Absinthe had several advantages: it was cheaper than wine, stronger than beer—and oh yes, it was a hallucinogen. Artists who wanted to expand their "vision" soon learned how to buy delusions by the glassful. The drink was most popular among the so-called "decadents"—most of them REALLY bad Catholics—such as Charles Baudelaire, Henri Toulose-Latrec, Paul Verlaine, and Ernest Dowson. A famous fan of the "Green Fairy" was the deathbed convert Oscar Wilde, who wrote of the drink: "A glass of absinthe is as poetical as anything in the world. What difference is there between a glass of absinthe and a sunset?" To which a doctor might reply, sunsets are not quite so toxic. We know this first hand. In the spirit of investigative journalism, one of the authors spent an evening downing authentic Sazeracs made with actual absinthe—and woke up 16 hours later convinced someone had shot off the back of his head. (This is more fun than it sounds.)

Absinthe's active ingredient is wormwood—that's right, the very substance which, according to St. John's Apocalypse, will fall from the heavens poisoning one-third of the seas. Kind of makes you wonder what gave people the idea to start drinking the stuff. . . .

The Apocalypse (or Revelation) is full of exquisite imagery and profound metaphors of the mysteries of the Christian faith. Written during one of the most savage Roman persecutions of the Church, this divinely inspired book holds out hope to Christians in times of affliction, promising that even the most universal catastrophe must yield, at last, to the regenerative power of God.

The book is popular today; it's the favorite spiritual uplift for a certain type of Protestant—for instance, those who keep track in their Covey Planners which neighbors and family members are "unsaved" and liable to be "left behind."[1] But

---

[1] "Red-state" Protestants are fond of bumper-stickers like "In Case of Rapture This Vehicle will be Driverless." This seems a little presumptuous to us; we prefer our own slogan: "I Brake for Apparitions of Mary."

many Catholics avert their eyes from this book of inspired Scripture, averring, "What the BLEEP does it *mean?*"

We're not exactly sure; maybe it means St. John was drinking absinthe. (That would explain all those references to man-eating locusts. . . .) The Apocalypse has been the source of endless misunderstandings over the centuries. When Church Fathers were deciding which books belonged in the Old and New Testament, this prophecy barely made the cut; prominent churchmen wondered if it was really divinely inspired, while St. Jerome famously called it "too trippy."[2] The skeptics were voted down, and had to settle for placing the Apocalypse at the very end of the Bible, no doubt in the hope that weary Catholics might never get that far. This plan backfired—lazy readers tend to skip to the end to find out how the story turns out. (Not to spoil things for you, but . . . *Jesus wins.*)

A careful reading of the Apocalypse reminds us that the early Church expected the Second Coming to hop along any day now, which is why St. Paul recommended people stay focused on God by embracing lifelong celibacy. (Might as well keep your bags packed and your pants zipped; the Old Testament calls this "girding thy loins," and it's not referring to pork.) However, as the months passed on into years and decades, with still no sign of the End, St. Paul dismissed the taxi and the Church got down to business, seeking to sanctify a world that wasn't going anywhere. But we have always kept in the back of our minds the fearful events warned of in the revelations given to St. John.

Throughout the centuries, theologians disputed over how literally to interpret the Apocalypse:

- Would there really be seven trumpets and seven seals, as Ingmar Bergman insisted?
- Should Christians ready themselves to encounter these seals—for instance, by stockpiling fish?
- What exactly was meant by the beast with seven heads and ten horns?

---

[2] A loose translation.

- Who was that "girl gone wild" riding on its back, dressed in LSU purple and gold with a go-cup "full of blasphemies?"

Early Protestants thought they knew. They identified the Beast with the Church that had baptized them, and the whore on its back with the pope. Catholic scholars replied that perhaps John was not predicting details of the future, but using metaphors from the present. When the Apocalypse was written, the Roman empire was a pagan tyranny that enslaved other nations, held gladiatorial "snuff" shows, and persecuted Christians—in fact, it had crucified Christ. Still, "millenarians" over the centuries took literally the notion that when the End Times came, the righteous Elect would rule the earth for a thousand years—an idea appropriated by an infamous Austrian paper-hanger.

The picture isn't pretty. It's tempting, in the face of so many misreadings of this almost incomprehensible book, to leave the darned thing to the biblical scholars and the Pentecostalists. But as the multitalented novelist and artist Michael O'Brien reminds us, the Church included the Apocalypse in the Scriptures for a reason:

> There is always a battle over every soul. Even if our times prove not to be the times toward which St. John's Revelation is pointing, each of us must go through a kind of small "a" apocalypse. Each of us certainly will be given a capital "R" revelation at the moment of our deaths when we experience our personal judgment, when all that we are, all that we have done or neglected to do will be revealed. The Greek word *apokalypsis* means a revealing or unveiling. During our lives in this world each of us will indeed face the beast, which is the devil, our ancient adversary, the enemy of our individual souls and of mankind as a whole. In some form or other we must learn to personally resist him and to overcome him in Christ.[3]

We draw more from the Apocalypse than anxiety for the future. In it we find the doctrine that we will all be resurrected in the flesh like Christ, and live with Him on an earth transformed into a New Jerusalem: "And God shall wipe away all tears from their eyes; and there shall be no more death, neither sorrow, nor crying, neither shall there be any more pain: for the former things are passed away. And he that sat upon the throne said, Behold, I make all things new." (Apocalypse 21: 4–5)

Still, the events preceding this happy outcome are grim enough that the average Christian hopes they are meant allegorically—or at least that he'll be long dead before (for instance) fire-breathing horses with serpents' tails kill 33 percent of the world's population. We don't need to see that, do you? Again, there are brother

---

[3] See Michael O'Brien, "Are We Living in Apocalyptic Times?" *www.studiobrien.com.*

Christians who disagree with us here. In 2004, we learned that born-again Christians in Texas[4] are trying to hurry things up a bit. As Rod Dreher reported in *National Review*, Evangelical cattle ranchers have been cooperating with radical rabbis in Israel who want to rebuild the Temple in Jerusalem—which cannot be reconsecrated without the sacrifice of a spotless red heifer. The rabbis couldn't find such a creature, so the Texans are helping to breed one—in the hope that this will hasten the arrival of the Antichrist, the end of the world, and the Second Coming. Since building the Temple would require blowing up the third-holiest mosque on earth—igniting a war between a billion Moslems and a nuclear Israel—the secular government of that country is understandably jittery. So are we. Wasn't it Christ Himself who warned of these days:

> Then let those who are in Judea flee to the mountains. Let no one on the roof of his house go down to take anything out of the house. Let no one in the field go back to get his cloak. How dreadful it will be in those days for pregnant women and nursing mothers! Pray that your flight will not take place in winter or on the Sabbath. For then there will be great distress, unequaled from the beginning of the world until now—and never to be equaled again. If those days had not been cut short, no one would survive, but for the sake of the elect those days will be shortened. (Matthew 24:16–22)

Let's take Him at His word—instead of trying to force His hand.

CELEBRATE: Prepare spiritually for the End Times—acclimatize yourself to the taste of wormwood by serving delicious (and possibly visionary) absinthe Apocalypsicles (see recipe).

---

[4] Where else?

Amaretto: His Madonna Brought Him a Bottle

This tasty Italian liqueur goes nicely with dessert, or in a variety of cocktails. It is most often drunk by the ladies while their dates gasp over a bourbon or single-malt. But men who are secure in their masculinity should never feel embarrassed about ordering it in a restaurant. Sure, the waiter may snigger, particularly after that series of strawberry daiquiris, and the Screaming Buddha you started with (why did it have to feature *so many* paper umbrellas?). But a real man won't be put off. If he wants to order a curvy little glass of a fruity Italian dessert drink, there's nobody alive that's going to stop him. He'll just tough out the scorn, smile rakishly, and take little delicate sips of almond liqueur while his lady friend looks on, admiring his confidence. Yes, that's what will happen . . . .

It will help if he can recount the sad, romantic tale which lies behind the invention of Amaretto. It seems that the first bottle of this smooth concoction was distilled in 1525 by a lovely Italian art model for a famous painter, Bernardino Luini. This pupil of Leonardo da Vinci had been hired to create a Madonna fresco to stand in the same church as "The Last Supper," Santa Maria delle Grazie, in Saronno. In search of a woman with the likeness of the sinless mother of God, Bernardino looked in the obvious place—the local tavern. Among the serving girls, Luini encountered a lovely, poised young Italian widow with whom to spend the next few months of up-close sketching and daubing. In the course of all this rather flattering attention, she fell for the dreamy Renaissance man who was painting her. But what could she offer this famous artist? She had no wealth to her name, no title, not much of a vocational history, and little more than a G.E.D. One day, as she haunted her parents' kitchen, she came up with an idea: she'd make for him a liquid distillation of her love. Improving on traditional recipes, this suddenly Marian tavern maid crafted an exquisite liqueur from apricot kernels, brandy, and herbs. She brought the artist the bottle of a drink she named "Amaretto," and offered him her heart. Luini thought it over—and took the bottle. (It may be that he was so used to thinking of her as the Virgin Mary that the whole thing struck him as creepy.) The widow was broken-hearted when he left. But seeing her own form and face as the Madonna, holding the Infant Jesus on the wall of a famous basilica must have been comforting—and may have worked like a sixteenth-century personal ad. In fact, with such a lovely countenance, and her skill at making drinks, we doubt the lady was lonely for very long.

Drinking Song #1: A Patriotic Tune

There's nothing that goes better with a fifth pitcher of pilsner or a sixth glass of champagne than a rousing song. Early on in the evening, you'll want a bawdy, rollicking round. But as the blessed beverage mutes the high spirits, and the consonants begin to slur, it's time to wax sentimental. Leave behind the suggestive limericks with rhymes like "Nantucket." Move on to strong melodies, with noble or sentimental themes that send the tears running down a beer-stained cheek. A surprising number of hymns fit the bill (and you'll find those lyrics scattered throughout the book). So of course do patriotic songs, which commemorate the greatness of one's native land.

We considered including American anthems, but we know how many Catholics feel queasy about the nation's Protestant origins. So in order to avoid offending anyone, for our first drinking song we'll offer the tune that has stirred the authors' hearts many a tipsy evening to love of country—the imperial anthem of the Habsburg monarchy. That exquisite Catholic kingdom, which gave the world Mozart, Metternich, and the Sacher Torte, was famous for its diversity and ethnic tolerance. This earned it Hitler's hatred, and made it the target of fanatical nationalists of every stripe. Perhaps its greatest legacy is the wry *Gemütlichkeit* which grew up among its citizens. This old joke sums it up: When things are falling down all around him, a Prussian will say "The situation is *serious*, but not desperate." An Austrian will say, "The situation is desperate, but not *serious*."

If you've read this far without hurling the book across the room, we know which side you're on.

Melody: "Austria," by Josef Haydn

The *Kaiserlied* (lyrics by Johann Gabriel Seidl, melody by Josef Haydn)

2.

Fromm und bieder, wahr und offen
Laßt für Recht und Pflicht uns stehn;
Laßt, wenns gilt, mit frohem Hoffen
Mutvoll in den Kampf uns gehn
Eingedenk der Lorbeerreiser
Die das Heer so oft sich wand
  Gut und Blut für unsern Kaiser,
  Gut und Blut fürs Vaterland!

3.

Was der Bürger Fleiß geschaffen
Schütze treu des Kaisers Kraft;
Mit des Geistes heitren Waffen
Siege Kunst und Wissenschaft!
Segen sei dem Land beschieden
Und sein Ruhm dem Segen gleich;
  Gottes Sonne strahl' in Frieden
  Auf ein glücklich Österreich!

4.

Laßt uns fest zusammenhalten,
In der Eintracht liegt die Macht;
Mit vereinter Kräfte Walten
Wird das Schwere leicht vollbracht,
Laßt uns Eins durch Brüderbande
Gleichem Ziel entgegengehn
      Heil dem Kaiser, Heil dem Lande,
      Österreich wird ewig stehn!

5.

An des Kaisers Seite waltet,
Ihm verwandt durch Stamm und Sinn,
Reich an Reiz, der nie veraltet,
Uns're holde Kaiserin.
Was als Glück zu höchst gepriesen
Ström' auf sie der Himmel aus:
      Heil Franz Josef, Heil Elisen,
      Segen Habsburgs ganzem Haus!

6.

Heil auch Öst'reichs Kaisersohne,
Froher Zukunft Unterpfand,
Seiner Eltern Freud' und Wonne,
Rudolf tönt's im ganzen Land,
Unsern Kronprinz Gott behüte,
Segne und beglücke ihn,
      Von der ersten Jugendblüthe
      Bis in fernste Zeiten hin.

7.

In Verbannung, fern den Landen
Weilst Du, Hoffnung Österreichs.
Otto, treu in festen Banden
Steh'n zu Dir wir felsengleich.
Dir, mein Kaiser, sei beschieden
Alter Ruhm und neues Glück!
      Bring den Völkern endlich Frieden,
      Kehr zur Heimat bald zurück!

Benedictine XVI

The liquor with the most obviously monastic name, Benedictine, is no longer made by monks—and thereon hangs our tale.[1] This delicious concoction was developed by St. Benedict's brethren at the Norman Abbey of Fecamb in 1510, as a cure for malaria. In those days before the microscope, learned men believed that this illness came from bad air (*mal-aria*); so why not fight it with wholesome, tasty spirits? This medicine probably didn't cure the patients, though it certainly cheered them up.

But good cheer was only a side effect of the monk's higher mission, as summed up by the acronym on the label, "DOM." Wine historian Desmond Seward reports that this stands for *Deo optimo maximo*, "to God the greatest good."

A delicious mixture of 27 different herbs and a brandy base, this liquor takes three years to prepare, and needs to age for another four before it is ready. But it's worth the wait; the end result is richly complex and inspiring, like the monks who gave it the name.

As the drink combines the leaves and blooms of field and fen to infuse a spirit, so St. Benedict yoked regular work and prayer to help men fuse with the Spirit. While the monks of the East might scorn and scourge the flesh, Benedict sought only to discipline it, to prune its passions and point it toward the Light. Monks of Benedict's order weren't known for burning pagan books—but patiently recopying them, in the confidence that the traces of wisdom they contained could nurture the growing body of Christendom.

Embracing the world while trying to redeem it isn't easy, and risks abound. Because their farms and vineyards were so well managed and scientific, the monks showed a disturbing propensity to get rich. Now there's nothing wrong with this—except when you've taken a vow of poverty. Then it sets tongues wagging. The spectacle of well-fed, sometimes tipsy monks lording over enormous estates began to seem absurd—like a 50-something Marxist professor grilling tofu in the suburbs, or Spinal Tap performing at Stonehenge. To men who'd come to take for granted the liberties and achievements of Christendom, and hoped that they could continue without the whole messy business about "Christ," the monks proved an easy target. During the French Revolution, mobs attacked the Feramp Abbey and burned it to

[1] Here, as throughout, we will trust it to wag the dog.

the ground.[2] The regime's bureaucrats set their chemists to work trying to recreate the liquor—with no success.

Likewise, post-Christian Europe seems unable to reproduce itself. (Here in America, it's only in the church-going regions that we find a positive birthrate.) It seems that without some notion of the afterlife, modern man won't even lift a finger (ahem) to breed.

In practice, drinking often does result in breeding; alcohol may be the ultimate reproductive lubricant; it overwhelms alike crabbed caution and interpersonal friction to ensure the continuance of the species. If distilled spirits can assist in creating eternal souls, then the tale of Benedictine itself gives us a glimmer of hope. Some 70 years after the Jacobins wrecked the Abbey of Fecamp, a secular official picking through the ruins came across the secret recipe for Benedictine once written down by the monks, and patiently recreated the drink. When Cardinal Joseph Ratzinger was elected pope in 2005, he looked for his name and inspiration to St. Benedict, and the formula which his monks used to revive a decrepit continent. In his first encyclical, *Deus Caritas Est,* the pope shares it with us. The secret is that in order to live a happy life on earth we must anchor our hopes in heaven—if only to counteract the human, all-too-human, tendency to fall short, to sputter and fail. With a sidelong glance at Europe's empty cradles, Benedict suggests that *eros* itself cannot remain healthy without the guidance and infusion of another form of love, *agape*. As the pope writes: "Eros, reduced to pure 'sex,' has become a commodity, a mere 'thing' to be bought and sold, or rather, man himself becomes a commodity. This is hardly man's great 'yes' to the body. On the contrary, he now considers his body and his sexuality as the purely material part of himself, to be used and ex-

---

[2] It's hard, even today, to conceive the kind of madness that would possess *Frenchmen* to burn down a liquor distillery. This alone might demonstrate the existence and activity of Satan. . . .

ploited at will. Nor does he see it as an arena for the exercise of his freedom, but as a mere object that he attempts, as he pleases, to make both enjoyable and harmless."

In the spiritual realm, whatever is harmless is also generally useless.[3] If you don't believe us, close this book immediately; call someone to whom you're fairly indifferent to join you at Appleby's for a pitcher of non-alcoholic beer. Now compare that to holding hands with a beloved spouse at Mass watching real wine turn into real blood. . . .

Bourbon and the Bourbons

Bourbon is a noble adaptation of traditional Irish and Scots whiskey, created by early settlers in Kentucky and Tennessee, using the corn which grew locally (instead of wheat, which didn't). Bourbon is a marvelous American creation, which stands as one of our three great contributions to world culture (the other two are the Blues and the Hollywood Production Code). So how did it end up being named for the royal house of France?

By accident of history. The French government of Louis XVI, still smarting from the British conquest of Canada and India, was eager to help the American colonists rebel against George III. Attempting to avenge his grandfather's defeat, good King Louis sent his best generals (including Lafayette), much of his fleet, and the better part of his shrinking treasury to the aid of General Washington.

With all due credit to Washington's prudence and statesmanship, the French pretty much won the war for us—as most Americans at the time

---

[3] Here we must choose between two authorities: St. John (Apocalypse 3:16: "So then because thou art lukewarm, and neither cold nor hot, I will spew thee out of my mouth") and Goldilocks ("'Ahhh, this porridge is just right,' she said happily and she ate it all up").

admitted. In gratitude, the Congress hung a portrait of King Louis in the Capitol, and legislatures across the 13 states gave French names to regions and cities—including Bourbon County, which constituted much of Kentucky, as Charles K. Cowder noted in *The Bourbon Country Reader* (July 1, 1996). Even when the vast county was broken up, the whiskey from the region kept the name.

And quite a famous name it was. The slippery politician Talleyrand once said of the French royal house of Bourbon that over two centuries, its members had "learned nothing, and forgotten nothing." Now this was not quite fair—for instance, the first Bourbon king, Henry IV, did *forget* his Protestant faith when he was offered the throne, while his descendant Louis XIV *learned* valuable repression skills in his youth, which he later employed against the creepy heresy of Jansenism.

In brief, the Jansenists taught that death began at conception. Eternal death. Men are spawned irredeemably corrupt, and can only be saved if God overpowers them[4] and forces them to be good—which He does very rarely, essentially cherry-picking a few souls to save from the whole human race. The rest of us, including unbaptized infants, will slide into eternal fire—and we will *deserve* it. In fact, those of us who were relatively virtuous but didn't get the right card in the salvation bingo will be punished more savagely than outright sinners—for impersonating the Saved. No, we're not making this up.

The great French thinker Pascal was convinced of this theory, and fought with all the power of his pen against the "lax" Jesuits who preferred to win over souls through "sensual" devotions such as the Sacred Heart, the rosary, and frequent reception of Communion. Jansenists warned that people should only receive the Eucharist if they were already completely detached from every sin, and spiritually pure enough that they were ready to fly up to heaven at any moment. To the Jesuits, this was like restricting medicine to the healthy.

Of course, nowadays, we see things the other way around. Ordinary sinners, repentant or not, go to Communion every week; only the spiritually rigorous show up for Confession. In the old days, at Sunday Mass you could spot the divorcees, pious drag queens,[5] spiritual doubters, and drunks because they didn't receive Communion. Instead, they knelt quietly, communing with God in their hearts. Today, this is a good way of spotting orthodox believers. (Although it's probably not a good time to try meeting one. Sidling up beside an attractive young believer with downcast eyes, then whispering "Feeling scrupulous?" and winking will probably get you nowhere. Wait for the coffee hour.)

It's ironic that bourbon, a warm and welcoming beverage, was crafted by Scots-

---

[4] Think of the sex scene in an Ayn Rand novel—with God as the fiercely independent Architect and the human soul as a quivering Patricia Neal.

[5] Okay, these often were pretty easy to spot—for instance, by the beard growth showing through the white lace mantilla.

Irish émigrés, most of whom believed in the same Calvinist claptrap as the Jansenists. No wonder they distilled a drink that helps you forget—not just the fact that you're probably Hell-bound, but also your car keys, marital status, work deadlines, and maybe your name. Bourbon is just *that good*—and it goes down smoother than sometimes acrid whiskies. Its sweetness makes it more accessible to the fair sex, which perhaps explains how the Scots-Irish were able to reproduce so quickly, and overwhelm the Indians—to whom they sold this new liquor on the cheap, and who weren't as good at accurate shooting while stone drunk. You see, they were neither Scots nor Irish. . . .

Sadly, the rise of bourbon contributed to the fall of the Bourbons. Louis XVI's aid to American rebels caused the royal bankruptcy which finally broke the monarchy, and brought to power the craziest atheist intellectuals in France—where they have governed ever since. Therefore, every Bastille Day (July 14), we raise a glass of bourbon in honor of good King Louis XVI, who wrecked his own country to help found ours.

In doing so, we follow in the footsteps of our favorite American author, the Catholic novelist Walker Percy, who famously wrote of bourbon:

> What, after all, is the use of not having cancer, cirrhosis, and such, if a man comes home from work every day at five-thirty to the exurbs of Montclair or Memphis and there is the grass growing and the little family looking not quite at him but just past the side of his head, and there's Cronkite on the tube and the smell of pot roast in the living room, and inside the house and outside in the pretty exurb has settled the noxious particles and the sadness of the old dying Western world, and him thinking: "Jesus, is this it? Listening to Cronkite and the grass growing?"[6]

If you plug in "Bill O'Reilly" for "Cronkite," this observation will stand the test of time. But you'll need a couple of extra shots of bourbon to avoid shooting the television.

CELEBRATE: Since both the authors spent their formative years in the South, we're happy to offer a menu celebrating this uniquely American, Southern, sipping whiskey.

DRINK:

Mint Juleps—made with bourbon, of course.

---

[6]Walker Percy, "Potent Potables," *Signposts in a Strange Land*, ed. Patrick Samway (New York: Farrar Straus & Giroux, 1991).

Mint Julep

4–6 mint leaves and
Sprigs for garnish
1 tablespoon sugar

2 tablespoons water
4 ounces Wild Turkey Bourbon

In a cocktail shaker add mint, sugar, and water. With a pestle, muddle the mint and sugar together. The mint will release its fragrance.
  Add bourbon and crushed ice.
  Shake well and strain into glasses filled with ice.
  If possible use traditional silver mint julep cups.
  Garnish with mint.

Makes 2 cocktails

FOOD:

Romaine and Mixed Greens Salad with Sherry Vinaigrette
Bourbon Glazed Turkey (See recipe)
Yellow Corn Bread
Collard Greens
Bread Pudding with Hard Sauce

Bourbon-Glazed Turkey

5 pounds turkey wings and thighs

MARINADE:

1 cup brewed strong coffee
1 cup dry sherry
1 1/2 cups bourbon
1 tablespoon dried rosemary

3 cloves garlic, minced
1 teaspoon sea salt
Freshly ground black pepper

GLAZE:

3/4 cup bourbon
1/2 cup grade B maple syrup

2 tablespoons butter

Rinse and dry turkey. Place turkey in gallon-size Ziploc bag secured in a bowl or other container. Pour marinade ingredients over bird pieces. Close bag squeezing as much air out as possible. Refrigerate overnight, turning bag occasionally to evenly distribute ingredients.
  Preheat oven to 450 degrees.
  Remove turkey pieces from marinade.
  Roast for 30 minutes. Meanwhile, prepare glaze. Combine ingredients in small saucepan on low heat to melt butter. Lower oven temperature to 375 degrees and brush with glaze. Roast for another 1 1/2 hours, basting every half hour. Turn occasionally to brown evenly. Turkey will be dark golden and falling off the bone.

Serves 6

FUZZY MEMORIES AND TASTING NOTES

As part of the grueling research we selflessly undertook for this volume, the authors ventured out to their favorite barbecue and beer pub in New York City, the Waterfront Ale House, to conduct a rigidly scientific survey of bourbons. It began with good intentions. We even wore white lab coats. But somehow, after working our way through the bourbon menu, we ended up with little more than fuzzy memories of singing much too loud and a set of tasting notes hastily scrawled on notebook paper using Denise's burgundy lipstick. So these are results you can *trust*.

BAKER'S

107-proof, aged 7 years

We found this whiskey slightly acidic, even acrid. It is rich and smoky, with a slow burn, a long finish, and very little caramel. A real man's drink, it probably goes best with spicy Buffalo wings or Mexican food, a long maduro cigar, and videotapes of your favorite speeches by Malcolm X, Cesar Chavez, or Pat Buchanan.

BOOKER'S

Bottled at its natural proof between 121 and 127, aged 6–8 years

This liquor has a round, full flavor and a soft finish. Denise found it "gentle and velvety with an intriguing complex taste" that recalled "burnt toast." It's a comforting drink, with a long smooth finish, best suited to sipping straight while chatting with old friends or plotting acts of vengeance so elaborate you won't remember them in the morning.

BLANTON'S

93-proof

This whiskey comes in what looks like a big perfume bottle—with a jockey on top, so maybe it's eau-de-cologne for horses. And it's a drink to please the ladies. The first "single barrel" bourbon (compare to "single malt" scotch), this whiskey is very smooth and aromatic with no sharp edges, some heat, and notes of oak, vanilla, church incense, and toast. John found it a little too smooth and feminine, while Denise gushed that it is "not at all like eating nails."

WILD TURKEY

101-proof, aged 10 years

This bourbon's flavors are caramel and brown sugar, with notes of barbecue, and even fruity hints of apricot. John called it "sweet, potent, and palate cleansing." A stylish drink, it's well-suited to sipping on the porch. Named for the favorite hunting quarry of the distiller who developed it in 1949 after serving it to his friends on a shoot, this brand now sponsors the National Wild Turkey Federation, which works to preserve the native bird—so that tipsy vice presidents of future generations will have the chance to shoot at it wildly and hit their friends by mistake.

MAKER'S MARK

90-proof

This bourbon is made at the smallest and oldest still-working distillery in the country, which has been declared a National Historic Landmark. The recipe was developed by baking loaves of bread with the exact proportion of grain content for each proposed recipe. Its producers were aiming for an elegant, broadly popular alternative to the more "challenging" bottles on the market. The bourbon is lean and not terribly complex. Perhaps hysterical with drink, Denise denounced it as "simply pleasant."

KNOB CREEK

100-proof, aged 9 years

We agreed that this bourbon is at once smoky, masculine, harsh, medicinal—and very drinkable. (Perhaps this speaks to how much we'd been drinking.) This potent whiskey has a long finish which recalls a glass of sweet iced tea sipped after an especially shrewd Atlanta real estate deal in which you think you've snookered Ted Turner. Yeah, sure you did. Have another. . . .

BASIL HAYDEN

80-proof, aged 8 years

This treasure is a warm, spicy, smooth bourbon, whose peppery notes and gently smoky taste masks the alcoholic "kick." A great drink for new or skeptical bourbon drinkers, it goes down easy and calms the jagged nerves of the most high-strung, high-functioning ADD adult. (It might also work for kids instead of Ritalin, but we'll leave the testing to the FDA.) No surprise, it is John's favorite drink in the world.

....

Burgundy: Purple-Fingered Monks and the Niebelung

This region of France is the home of perhaps the nation's most famous wines; indeed, it was planted with grapes in ancient times by the Gauls and later the Romans, who esteemed its "Falernian" wine. The wines of this region are known for their great variety and distinctive flavors imparted by the "terroir"—the particularities of soil, shade, water and sun, which cannot be duplicated by high-tech, "laboratory" vintners. Burgundy is a patchwork of family wineries which bottle their own, and cooperatives which pool their grapes and sell them to larger producers. The resulting wines are complex and often sophisticated—in fact, authors have devoted whole books to analyzing subregions of Burgundy and their wines. A good rough outline of the region appears in the wonderful resource *Monks and Wine* by Desmond Seward:

> The red wines are grown on a long sequence of low hills, the first range being the Côte d'Or, which runs south-west from Fixin, just south of Dijon, almost to Chalon-sur-Saône; the Côte d'Or is divided into the

CARTE DE LA GAULE APRÈS L'INVASION.

Côte de Nuits and the Côte de Beaune. The greatest red burgundies come from these hills, which run for 36 miles. Farther south are other ranges which grow lesser but excellent wines, the Côte Chalonnaise, the Côte Mâconnaise, and the hills of the Beaujolais. However, some of the best white wines come from Chablis, north-west of the Côte d'Or, though the greatest white burgundies come from the Côte de Beaune.[7]

As Seward documents, we might not have any of these wines today without the hard work of pious monks. In the fifth century, as the western half of the Roman empire crumbled into chaos, this region was overrun by one of the fiercest tribes of barbarians ever to ravage a province. While they had nothing on the Vandals (who were so destructive they didn't even get to name a region) the Burgundians came originally from Scandinavia—which would later give Europe the Vikings, and more importantly, Aquavit. The Burgundians began as friends of the loveable Huns, and used this alliance to grab themselves a big chunk of Gaul. As Arians (Christians who saw Jesus as less of a divine redeemer than a human over-achiever) they were alienated from the subject population of peace-loving, Roman-ized Gauls. In time, the Romans bought off the tribe, won them over to orthodox Catholicism, and named them "allies." The Burgundians took turns aiding the Ro-mans and betraying them, until the empire finally expired in 476. The tribe's ex-ploits lived on in the legends of the *Niebelungenlied*, which Richard Wagner transformed into the longest, most pointy-helmeted operas in history. If these sto-ries are to be believed, the Burgundians spent entirely too much time in pursuit of magic rings, cloaks of invisibility, and mystical swords forged by subterranean

dwarves to take proper care of the vineyards.

This task they left to the monks of St. Benedict's order, whose communities had spread northward from Italy, carrying with them their founder's ethos of "work as prayer." Wherever they went, they took up the humble tasks disdained alike by Roman gentlemen and barbarian chieftains—recopying ancient manuscripts, replanting neglected fields, developing new forms of agriculture, and generally serving as the Dark Age equivalent of business incubators and vo-tech schools. They also became the stewards of the ancient art of wine-making—

[7] Desmond Seward, *Monks and Wine*, (New York: Crown Publishers, 1979), p. 37.

although the Benedictine Rule restricted them to only a half-pint of the beverage daily. The monks, Seward reminds us, were doing more than providing themselves altar and table wine; they were acting according to the biblical prophecy of Amos: "They shall build the waste cities, and inhabit them; and they shall plant vineyards, and drink the wine thereof." Some of the finest varieties were developed on monastery property and produced by Benedictines for over one thousand years, until the French Revolution—when all such land was seized by a newly omnipotent state, sold off cheap to capitalists, and the proceeds used in waging war.

And war has raged through the province many times over the centuries—since Burgundy was long ruled by a line of independence-minded dukes. Playing the French kings off against the English, aiming at forging a nation of their own, the Dukes of Burgundy once ruled the beer drinkers of Brussels and the sausage-eating Alsatians, as well as the grape-squashers of Lyons. Its dukes successively betrayed the King of France, tried to conquer Switzerland (big mistake), and burned Joan of Arc at the stake (bad PR), before their lands were inherited by the Habsburgs (don't you hate when that happens?).

Conflict still roils Burgundy, although today it is between the old-line, family wine-makers and modern corporate producers who bring American technology and tastes to the fields once tended by black-robed celibates who spent their evenings in song and prayer. This struggle was documented in the immensely interesting indie film *Mondovino* (**see Terroir**), which pulled back the covers to show the strange bedfellows involved: Communist mayors siding with local aristocrats in defense of tradition, against American entrepreneurs who hire French movie actors to appear on billboards for their corporate wineries. The whole thing is a royal (and stereo-typically French) *mêlée*, which will only be resolved when France's emerging Islamic majority gets together to outlaw the entire industry, replacing Burgundy's wine-shops with hookah-pipe cafes. So let's enjoy the wine while we can.

CELEBRATE: Serve up some of the fine wines of Burgundy, paired with the courses on this authentic regional menu:

Scallops with Wild Mushrooms and Truffle
Pouilly Fuisse

Rabbit with Dijon Mustard
Roasted Potatoes, Carrots, Shallots
Gevrey Chambertin

Burgundian Spice Bread
Epoisses, Montrachet Cheeses
Crémant de Bourgogne

BEAUNE, HOSPICES DE:
A WINE AUCTION FOR CHRIST

Just as the Christian Church was one of the first institutions in the West to undermine slavery (by treating all believers as spiritually equal) and infanticide (by rescuing infants who'd been left out by their parents to die), so it pioneered in care for the sick and for strangers. Early Christians set up the first "hospices" to shelter refugees, invalids, abandoned children, and old people. As early as 436, the Council of Carthage directed every bishop to create these refuges, funding them out of the Church's purse. Religious orders and pious laymen followed this example; to this day, the monks of St. Benedict's order are commanded by their Rule to accept any traveler "as if he were Christ" and offer him hospitality. In practice, this means that scrungy stoners traveling Europe with little more than a Eurail pass and a knapsack can show up at places like Solesmes and lay claim to "three hots and a cot."[8] Then again, nobody ever called Christianity a pragmatic faith. . . .

One of the most famous of these shelters in Europe is known as the Hospice de Beaune. It was founded in 1443 by husband-and-wife team Nicolas Rolin and Guigone de Salins to serve the poor of Burgundy—a province that lay in smoking ruins after a decades-long, three-sided conflict between the local duke, and the kings of England and France. (We just have to ask: Which part of starting a "Hundred Years' War" seemed like a good idea at the time?)

The Hospice was staffed with nuns, and the neighboring lands were turned over to the Church. On it, the guardians of the Hospice produce some of the finest wine in the world—which once a year, on the third Sunday in November, is auctioned off to fund the care of the sick and the poor year-round. This custom has continued for more than 500 years (with occasional interruptions by blood-crazed, anti-clerical mobs), and today is one of the most festive events in the wine world. The city fills up with connoisseurs (and their checkbooks), who huddle together under the ancient eaves of what looks like a guild hall, and the auction is timed by the burning of three candles. When the last one gutters out, everyone has to leave. The medieval hospital still stands as an architectural jewel—though the sick are now cared

---

[8] If you care to try this yourself, Google "Benedictines on the Web" and draw up your itinerary accordingly. But be prepared to bunk next to a lot of prayerful, sleepless celibates.

for in a more high-tech, if less picturesque facility. Few sites on earth so perfectly combine in one place everything that is delightful about old Christendom: love for God in the form of the poor is yoked to enjoyment of the beauties of His creation, and the cultivation of one of mankind's highest arts. But we'll let the founder speak for himself. As he wrote in his deed of gift:

> I, Nicolas Rolin . . . recognizing the grace and the belongings which God, source of all good, has gratified me; from now on, for ever and irrevocably, I found, construct, and date in the town of Beaune, in the diocese of Autun, a hospital to receive, serve and house the sick poor, with a chapel in honor of God the Almighty and of His glorious mother the virgin Mary, in memory of and to venerate Saint Anthony, abbot, dedicated to him and his name, to give it the belongings which God bestowed upon me.[9]

---

[9] Thanks to *www.vin-et-tradition.com* for translating this.

Calvados and the Shakespeare Code

This apple brandy takes its name from the region of Normandy where it has been distilled for centuries. Besides its potent warmth, the liquor's enticing aroma lights up a room, and helps dispel the garlic scent lingering on the hostess's breath, just in time for dessert. Gourmets with bigger travel budgets than ours who have savored the drink in its native clime say that true Normans use the drink to make "le trou Normand"—a space in the sated stomach for just one more course—which makes us a little nervous. As fans of Monty Python's *The Meaning of Life*, we remember the explosive power of a single "wafer thin mint." But still, we love Calvados, and prefer to use it to end the meal, rather than start it all over again.

We're also fond of the legend telling how this liquor got its name—and here's where Mother Church dips her toe in the drink. In May 1588, the mighty King Philip II of Spain launched his Armada of 130 ships and 19,000 men, intent on invading England. Even though Philip had once reigned as nominal King of England—during the short, unhappy life of Queen Mary I—historians do not think he intended to annex the island to his vast empire, which stretched from Spain to Peru, from Mexico to the Philippines. Instead, it's believed he intended to depose Elizabeth I, who was persecuting Catholics as traitors. Elizabeth's spymaster Sir Francis Walsingham had set up the apparatus for a virtual police state, attempting to suppress what was still the religion of a majority of Englishmen—including, scholars suggest, William Shakespeare. (Read Clare Asquith's *Shadowplay* for an intriguing account of the Bard's coded Catholic references in his plays.) By replacing her with a pro-Spanish Catholic ruler, Philip would ease his conscience about his former English subjects, win the gratitude of an often hostile pope, and complete the conquest of the Protestant Netherlands. (His own record of persecution there rivaled Elizabeth's at home.) He would also quell the pesky English pirates who raided his gold shipments from the Americas.

Tragically, the Armada foundered in bad weather and was torn to pieces by smaller English ships and fireboats—ensuring that

England would suffer another 400 years of suet pudding and Protestantism. The surviving galleons were scattered by the winds, and some ended up as far away as Ireland—where gallant Spaniards were welcomed by milky-cheeked lasses, and sired the so-called "black Irish." One of the ships, *El Calvador*, landed on the Norman coast north of Caen, and in garbled form gave the region its name, Calvados. Now this strikes us as mildly puzzling, rather like the inhabitants of the Alaskan coast christening their region "Exxon Valdez," but with a local drink this good, we're not going to argue with them.

Chartreuse: The Secret Sauce

The liqueur Chartreuse makes an ideal digestif (like an aperitif, but the opposite), serving as a seal on a rich, festive meal. The potent spirit—the better, "green" variety is 110-proof—makes further drinking unnecessary and further eating unthinkable, lulling the sated diners into a warm, desultory chatter that trails off into drowsy farewells.

It seems fitting that one of the most complex and mysterious liqueurs in the world is crafted at a medieval monastery by the strictest religious order in the Church. Named for the mother house (La Grand Chartreuse) of the austere Carthusians, the liqueur gets its pale green color from 130 local herbs and flowers collected by the monks and distilled behind the stone walls of the cloister. The formula has never been written down; it is passed along verbally to three trusted monks.

When one of these men dies, the survivors whisper the secret to his replacement. And no, the three monks never travel on the same airplane.

In fact, they hardly travel at all; the Carthusians are the quintessential contemplative (as opposed to active) order. These monks lead lives quite similar to the Desert Fathers of early Christianity. Each lives in a cell by himself, and says most prayers of the Divine Office by himself—gathering with his fellow monks just twice a day, and conversing with them only twice a week. In a sense, you might call the Carthusians the most "Eastern" of Western religious; even their architecture suggests a Zen simplicity, recalling the precincts of a Japanese monastery more closely than the elaborate piles built by the worldly wise Jesuits or festive Franciscans. Founded by St. Bruno in 1084, the Carthusians come in both sexes and from many lands, but once they join they descend into a well of solitude, "alone with the Alone."

Unlike most religious orders that have slogged through so many centuries, the Carthusians never sowed their wild oats. You won't find jolly Carthusians romping through Chaucer's pages, or fat ones depicted in tapestries quaffing ale. The only Carthusians to emerge from their cells in England were those dragged out in 1535 by Henry VIII for refusing to accept his divorce—and tortured to death for their faith. Pope Innocent once wrote that the order "need not be reformed, for it has never been deformed." The Carthusian spirit approaches perfection—which for most of us is best consumed in small doses, out of little, hand-blown glasses.

....

Châteauneuf du Pape: Pope Fictions

This spicy, dense variety of wine is usually red, and typically excellent. Once obscure, the wine was championed by Robert Parker of *Wine Spectator* (whom observers have dubbed the "pope of wine") and is now deservedly popular. The wine's name refers to "the pope's new chateau," often bearing the papal keys on its label. In fact, this does not refer to Robert Parker, but actual pontiffs. If you're wondering why the pope *needed* a new chateau . . . well therein hangs a tale.

Châteauneuf du Pape hails from a region of France near Avignon, and was first produced on the vast estates once held by the popes—which for some 70 years served them as gilded cages. In the thirteenth and fourteenth centuries the real power-struggle in Europe was fought between the papacy and the kings of France. As rulers of the largest and richest Christian kingdom, the French kings sought to micromanage the local Church and tap into its wealth. Fighting for the Church's spiritual independence, popes countered that they held the right to judge any king, or even depose him. This conflict between the sacred and profane powers reached its height when Pope Boniface VIII overplayed his hand; in just two years, he declared that it "is necessary for salvation that every living creature be under submission to the Roman pontiff," and excommunicated King Philip IV. Since Boniface threatened his throne, Philip decided to topple Boniface from his; the king sent a band of thugs to kidnap the pope and demanded that he resign.[1] Boniface was mortified—literally. The pope died three days later, a broken man. His successors were subject for the next 70 years to the whims of French kings. Philip forced Pope Benedict XI to try Boniface VIII posthumously for heresy, then decided in 1305 to move the entire papacy, lock, stock, and Bibles, to Avignon.

Once removed from chaotic Rome to exile in France, these caged popes were helpless to prevent the French king from persecuting and looting the innocent Knights Templar (**see Templars**). These pontiffs (not one of whom would be canonized) concentrated on accumulating wealth and keeping the king happy. Indeed, the worst abuses which would be condemned during the Reformation date from this period, when the Holy See was captive to secular monarchs and motives.

It took the heroic exertions of a self-taught theologian and mystic, St. Catherine of Siena, to convince one pope, Gregory XI, to move the papacy back to Rome in 1378. The French kings responded by starting a schism, suborning French cardinals to elect their own candidates as "popes." At last there were three men running around in tiaras, each claiming to be the Vicar of Christ. Devout people differed about which one was legit; there are canonized saints who lived and died loyal to men the Church now calls imposters. At one point it looked as if Church councils would arrogate the right to judge and depose the pope, threatening Catholicism with the specter of parliamentary democracy. (If this appeals to you, we invite you to watch the House of Commons debating on BBC.)

Pastorally speaking, none of this was really helpful. Indeed, the Reformation could never have caught fire as it did without 100 years or so of papal scandals. And without the Reformation there would be no Rev. Pat Robertson, or Rev. Jesse Jackson. So you can see how we're a tad ambivalent, as we enjoy a glass of this splendid stuff, about the papal keys on the label. It makes us feel like yellow-dog Democrats

---

[1] His predecessor, the saintly Celestine V had also resigned; for different reasons, Dante placed both these popes in Hell.

who come across an old copy of *Cigar Aficionado*, with a cover featuring Monica Lewinsky.

CELEBRATE: Serve up the story of this longest-lasting of clerical scandals along with a bottle or two of Châteauneuf du Pape, and a traditional dinner from the environs of Avignon, such as one of the mediocre captive popes might have enjoyed. Here's a menu that would have kept Pope John XXII fat and happy:

Pissaladiere
Flat bread with melted onions, anchovies, and olives

Daube d'Avignon
Lamb, herb, and vegetable stew

Banon with Walnuts
An ancient raw goat's milk cheese wrapped in chestnut leaves

Chocolate Tart with a Citrus Herb Sauce

Christmas Ale and Lemon-Eid

Christmas Ale is for people who find Guinness a little wimpy. Strong, heavy, with more than a touch of syrup, it tends to be more alcoholic than most other beers (with the exception of the potent barley wine). Brewed deep in Advent to be enjoyed with the feasts of the Christmas season, it is best made by Trappists, like the monks who produce the marvelous Corsendonc. To emphasize its festive

quality, monastic brewers infuse this beer with spices such as cardamom, cinnamon, nutmeg, and clove—essentially bottling the flavors and aromas of deep winter. The drink makes a fine accompaniment to a leg of lamb, turkey, or (best of all) roasted goose, standing up to any combination of seasonings . . . with the possible exception of curry. If for some reason you're greeting your Nativity guests with something like Goat Vindaloo,

we don't recommend Christmas Ale. We suspect that the Christians of India, whose faith is said to descend from the Apostle Thomas, accompany their fiery celebrations of the faraway King the Magi found with crisp lagers such as Kingfisher or Taj Mahal—or with the heady homebrews made from rice popular in northern India. This beer is so tasty and potent that elephants regularly raid Indian villages to rummage for casks of the stuff. But we digress. . . .

Because the beer is so very appropriate to the particular season and its reason—the entry of God into the flesh—we can't help regretting a piece of political correctness that has dropped into the brew. Many breweries have begun to shy away from the mention of "Christmas" in the title, afraid that the very name of Christ is enough to drive away their customers or turn the beer green. Instead, they unchristen their drinks "holiday," "Yule," or worst of all "winter solstice" beer. To which we answer: Of course! The reason all of us are gathered together with relatives we normally and studiously avoid and buying heaps of gifts from China, is to celebrate . . . the darkest, grimmest time of year, the virtual disappearance of the sun into a pile of snow and slush. And that fellow camping it up in red, with the long white beard? He's just a Siberian shaman. (This was the actual explanation given by a spokesman for Wal Mart as to why the store won't mention Christmas: one more reason not to shop there.)

What a pile of drunken elephants' poop. It's Christmas time, okay? Get over it. Open up a nice bottle of Christmas Ale, pony up with the gifts, and get yourself to Mass for a change. Join the rest of your neighbors in a tipsy rendition of "Silent Night," and be grateful you aren't a Zoroastrian. Their Satan is as powerful as their Creator, and to celebrate their holidays they have to jump through a bonfire. Count your blessings.

CELEBRATE: There's nothing wrong with reaching out to your non-Christian neighbors—or those who mark other holidays as well. Why not bring your Jewish friends a bottle of tasty Arkan vodka from Israel, and help them whip up "Channukahpolitans"? You can mark the Moslem winter holiday of Eid ul-Fitr, which ends their fasting month of Ramadan, with an abstemious jug of Pink Lemon-Eid—spiced up with pine nuts and rosewater, for a delightful Arabian touch. Or swing by a black pal's house with a fifth of "Kwanzaa Courvoisier." He won't turn you away. Nor would we.

Pink Lemon-Eid

Use only fully ripe and in-season strawberries.

1/2 cup strawberry water, chilled
1/2 cup lemon juice
2 cups sparkling water

1/4 teaspoon rosewater
1 tablespoon pine nuts
1/4 cup turbinado sugar

Fill pitcher with ice and combine ingredients.
Stir vigorously to dissolve sugar.
Pour into tall glasses filled with ice.
Serves 2

Strawberry Water:

1 pint strawberries

1/4 cup sugar

Hull strawberries. Place together with sugar in a heavy nonreactive pot.
   Cover with plastic wrap.
   Cook for 1 hour over lowest possible heat.
   Turn off heat and allow to steep 1/2 hour.
   Strain into a glass container through a muslin-lined strainer.
   Do not press down on berries. (Allow 30 minutes to an hour to capture all the liquid.) Chill until ready to use.
   The strained berries are delicious in yogurt or ice cream.

Yields 1/2 cup

Cider: O Happy Fall!

We all know that the Fall of man occurred when Eve took a bite of the fruit from the Tree of Knowledge, and Adam "supported" her in her decision. Of course, as soon as God came to confront him about this, Adam squirmed and blamed his wife. This is the first recorded instance of codependent behavior. What a passive-aggressive wuss our forefather and patriarch proved to be—setting the example for every weak leader, bumbling administrator, and inattentive parent in subsequent millennia. Just listen to Adam's wheedling tone: "The woman you put here with me—she gave me some fruit from the tree, and I ate it." (Genesis 3:12) Biblical scholars agree that Adam said this in a nasal whine, like the character in *Office Space* who mutters: "I believe you have my stapler. . . ." And Adam wasn't finished. As the film documents, he went on to say:

And I said, I don't care if they lay me off either, because I told, I told Bill that if they move my desk one more time, then, then I'm, I'm quitting, I'm going to quit. And, and I told Don too, because they've moved my desk four times already this year, and I used to be over by the window, and I could see the squirrels, and they were merry, but then they switched from the Swingline to the Boston stapler, but I kept my Swingline stapler because it didn't bind up as much, and I kept the staples for the Swingline stapler and it's not okay because if they take my stapler then I'll set the building on fire. . . .

No wonder God had Security escort him from the Garden. We're lucky He didn't turn Adam back into a bonobo and have done with it.

From the Middle Ages on, most Western art has depicted Adam's blunder-fruit as an apple. Given the geography of the Bible, this seems pretty unlikely. Whatever we mean when we speak of the Garden of Eden—whether we credit Genesis, which says the Garden was watered by rivers that flowed to Ethiopia and Assyria, or modern anthropology, which traces the first men to Africa—there's one thing we know for sure: There weren't any apple trees (**see Forbidden Fruit**). Plenty of pomegranates, figs, grapes, even citrons—but none of the lush apple orchards that grow across Europe. But it was in the wintry north of the old Continent that most illuminated manuscripts of the Bible were made, by monks who spoke Latin and knew how to appreciate a pun. Since the botanical name for apple trees includes the word *malus*—also a form of the Latin word for evil—it must have occurred to the brothers who lovingly inscribed the sacred story that this was a clever way to make a point. If you've never worked on a publishing deadline and had to scramble for an illustration, don't judge these monks too harshly.

The fruit's unfortunate associations never stopped local Christians from enjoying apples. The fruit is delicious fresh, stores better than most, and stands up well to drying. Not all apples are tasty straight from the tree; many varieties are tart or even sour. When these unsavory apples are mashed and fermented, the process concentrates the sugar into the delightful beverage, cider. This drink was made for centuries across pre-Christian Europe, but we owe its current name to St. Jerome, who called the stuff *sicera*.[2] In French that word became *cidre*, which the Normans brought into English and later misspelled as "cider." Since monks did a better job of tending orchards than, say, bands of roaming Vandals, monasteries tended to end up owning all the orchards.

Popular from Scotland to Spain, cider comes in many varieties depending on which fruit is used (pears are also popular), but cider-makers agree that the best drink comes from the tartest apples. And here's where the theology comes in.

The Church's Easter Liturgy includes a line referring to Adam's screw-up:

> O happy fault! (*felix culpa*) O necessary sin of Adam, which has won for us so great a redeemer.

Now this passage has always puzzled us. It raises some serious questions like: Are we actually better off today than we'd be if Adam and Eve had never sinned? St. Thomas Aquinas, who wrote that line of the Liturgy, echoed the teaching of St. Paul, who taught: "For if by one man's offence death reigned by one; much more they which receive abundance of grace and of the gift of righteousness shall reign in life by one, Jesus Christ." (Romans 5:17) From St. Ambrose on, theologians have taught that life as adopted sons of God is higher and better than the easy joys lavished on Adam and Eve—which they clearly didn't know how to spend, and squandered like pampered heirs with lax estate attorneys. Likewise, experience tells us that pleasures earned are more enjoyable than those we blunder into by sheer dumb luck. Perhaps the fact that we have to work against our fallen natures to follow Christ makes the attainment of holiness more meaningful than if it came to us as easily as to Adam.

But this seems to beg the question. We don't earn Grace; in fact, the very word comes from *gratia*, which refers to a gift, a special favor. Salvation is only possible because God agrees (while rolling His eyes) to overlook man's true deserts and invites back the Prodigal Son. In fact, He runs halfway down the road to meet this scraggly loser, and practically drags him into the house. So how exactly is this any different from the graces lavished on Adam? And what does it have to do with that six pack of Vermont Cider Jack sitting in our fridge?

Just this: Without God's taking those first steps down the road, we'd be lying by the side of it cadging strangers—perhaps with a crudely lettered sign saying: "Wasting my substance in riotous living. Won't you help?" Likewise, without an outside agent (**see Yeast**) to raise the spirit, a pile of mashed-up, aging apples would turn not into cider, but into a thick black mush that smelled like elephant

---

[2] Clarke's Commentary on the Bible cites the passage: "Any inebriating liquor is called sicera, whether made of corn, apples, honey, dates, or any other fruits." This reference is found in Jerome's *Epis. ad Nepot.*, his famed Epistle to the Nepotists.

poop—especially if after drinking too much cider you fell face-first into it.[3] But we're still not the active agents. At best, we must learn to cooperate with Grace, to "let go and let God"—lest He let go of us.

At this point, you might still wonder how exactly this is an improvement on the old Edenic status quo. Was it worth all the great expanse of human suffering and the grueling Passion of Christ, just to upgrade the human condition from one of total passivity before the Grace of God, to one of reluctant, fitful cooperation? Just how *felix* was that *culpa*?

If you're still not convinced, we really don't blame you. But we'd like to suggest you shift your focus just a little, to not focus so much on the human condition—let's be frank, anyone who ever so much as had hemorrhoids is likely to envy Adam—but on what God is doing. The beauty and goodness of Creation, affirmed in the Book of Genesis, is impressive enough on its own. From the vast reaches of the galaxies strung out through shimmering space to the intertwining complexity of ecosystems, or the brown-eyed adoring gaze of a beagle, we see in the non-human world enough to show us that God is loveable. But we don't know exactly how to love Him. Do we think of Him as a distant Watchmaker, applaud the craftsmanship, then pull the thing apart to find out how it works? (**see Loreto.**) The world of nature, viewed through simple reason, doesn't give us any clues. It's only the messy, convoluted narrative that comes to us through Revelation that unveils God's personality, and offers us Someone to love. That someone is Christ, and the love He showed in entering our life and sharing our death is vaster than the galaxies. If you think about it long enough, in the right frame of mind, you might just get giddy. You might start making playful analogies, thinking of how Adam's sour apple, which stuck in our throat, was pressed by the Cross, then fermented by Love. Are we waxing too poetic? It's just the cider talking.

---

[3] Don't ask.

MOSES BREAKING THE TWO TABLES OF STONE.

Loopholes in the Ten Commandments
#1: Thou Shalt Have No Other Gods Besides Me

Throughout this book, we'll offer the bad Catholic reader these little digressions, which don't really try to squirm out of obeying the Ten Commandments but to explain what they mean according to the mind of the Church—which isn't always what a fundamentalist would take away from a literal reading of the text in the Gideon he found on the motel bed stand, next to the remote control offering access to late-nite porn. (Male readers, please note: programming such as *White Trash Love Slaves Part 7* WILL show up on the bill you submit for your company expense report, so please protect your job and your soul by cracking that Bible instead. But make sure to check your private interpretations of Scripture against the Church's—or you might end up in worse shape altogether, heresy being the *ultimate* impure thought.)

The First Commandment, which forbids the worship of strange gods, seems obvious enough at first. If you call yourself a Christian or Jew, and you've also been secretly worshiping the fertility goddess Astarte, *cut it out!* Fertility goddesses are *so* 3000 years ago. Besides, that regular sacrifice of newborn infants Astarte demands raises some serious ethical questions. Speaking less literally, this commandment calls us to ask ourselves if we've been placing God (the One God) first in our lives—or keeping little shrines to money, power, pleasure, or pride, which we tend lovingly behind closed doors.

Arguments over the meaning of this commandment have marked Christian history since Jesus first hinted at, then outright proclaimed, His divinity (John 5:18)—to the surprise and horror of most of His contemporary Jews. The crime for which He was condemned to death was blasphemy, claiming equality with Yahweh, as few Jews had expected their Messiah to do. The split between those Jews who accepted this claim (such as the Apostles) and those who rejected it was what distinguished Christians from the rest of the worshipers at the Temple. Later on, in the fourth century, disputes about the developing doctrine of the Trinity caused the earliest schisms in the Church; Arians claimed that Jesus was not quite equal to the Father, while Sabellians insisted that God the Father had also suffered and died on the Cross. The orthodox formula established at the Council of Nicaea (three persons in one God) ended the question, without resolving what is an ineffable mystery.

Not everyone was satisfied with leaving the question there. One notable dissident was Mohammed, who proclaimed that he was reviving the ancient "religion of Abraham" corrupted by the Jews and Christians alike, but who regarded Jesus as the last and greatest prophet to come before himself. Scholars suggest that Mohammed was tapping into the "pure monotheist impulse" that motivated Jews before him, and Unitarians after him. But we've never met any Unitarians whom we found really "motivated," so perhaps this theory needs more work.

The human mind seems to be pulled in two directions on the question of monotheism—and anthropologists have traced the myriad developments of the religious impulse around the world. In *The Origin and Growth of Religion* (1931), the great priest-scholar Wilhelm Schmidt offered evidence from every primitive or ancient culture he had studied of a "primitive monotheism," traces of belief in some kind of unitary deity who was higher than the lesser gods of rain, fertility, or fire. Philosopher Jacques Maritain, drawing on this discovery, dubbed this creed "the religion of the Garden of Eden." For a variety of reasons—including the need to explain the disorder and evil found present in the world—in most of these cultures the One God faded into the background, regarded as too elevated to take an interest in human affairs. There He remains in Haitian Voodoo (**see Rum**), for instance, whose devotees focus their attention instead on the lesser gods who are willing—for enough rum—to pitch in and give men a hand.

If this reminds you of the Catholic devotion to Mary and the saints, you aren't alone. You can find little tracts devoted to the "paganism" of the "Antichrist Church of Rome" on the windshields of minivans at strip malls across America. But no serious Catholic offers to any saint, not even Our Lady, the adoration proper to God alone. Instead, we are simply asking them to pray with us and for us—just as Evangelical believers ask the Rev. Bob Tilton to pray with them. But Our Lady

doesn't ask for $1,000 in return for little sweaty prayer cloths that will help us win the lottery. . . .

The difference between Protestant and Catholic notions of the saints and their role is nicely illustrated by a story from Edith Nesbit's Edwardian memoir, *The Wouldbegoods*. It seems a friend of Nesbit's was visiting a cathedral currently occupied by Anglicans, and taking a tour. The docent explained that the room they were entering was called the Dean's Chapel, but had once been called the Lady Chapel, "in the wicked days when people used to worship the Virgin Mary." Puzzled, the visitor asked, "Do we nowadays worship the Dean?"

What we call the "cult" of the saints involves no idolatry or toxic Kool-Aid, but instead the belief that the Church is a spiritual family, in which the souls of the saved still play a role. They pray for us and inspire us, and we treasure their memories as examples. The craving which mankind seems to feel for a divine division of labor is satisfied (without falling into paganism) by the particular specialties these saints carry on, even in Heaven. Hence, St. Thérèse is patroness of missions, St. Jude of hopeless causes, and St. Vincent of Saragossa the patron saint of vinegar makers. The Church does not teach that their prayers can contradict the Providence of God, any more than you can change the results of a baseball game by booing. Especially when you're watching at home on TV. Unless you have a prayer towel.

Dionysos: The Sacred Grapes

Dionysos, the Greek god of wine and drunkenness (known to residents of ancient Rome and New Orleans's French Quarter as Bacchus), was for some reason one of the lesser gods. He played no part in the *Iliad* or *The Odyssey*, and never lived on Olympus—preferring to caper about the vineyards of Hellas on his horny hooves, spreading joy and fertility through the villages, generously dispensing the ancient equivalent of "beer goggles." (If you've ever compared the lithe and flawless maidens and *kouri* from antiquity to the modern Greeks of, say, Astoria, Queens, you know that even the sculptors must have been wearing them.) One of the more charming stories about Dionysos reports that he was so exquisitely handsome that a band of Greek sailors tried to kidnap him as their (ahem) "mascot," but he turned them into dolphins—which may explain why dolphins sometimes make advances swimmers find "inappropriate."

Like the drink he dispensed, Dionysos had his dark side. If he was invoked as the god who liberated men and women from social constraints (such as tunics), he was also dreaded as the bringer of frenzy and madness. His female devotees (known in Latin as *Bacchantes*) were the original "girls gone wild." But they took off more than their tops; these empowered women religious would roam the countryside in drunken bands, encountering goats, deer, and unlucky travelers whom they would tear limb from limb, and serve with a hearty red—such as Mavrodafni, which also goes well with dessert.

In the late-nineteenth century, scholarly skeptics such as Sir James Frazer attempted to explain away the uniqueness of Christianity by finding precedents for its practices among the pagan cults. Unsurprisingly, they looked to the cannibalistic custom of the Bacchantes as the origin of the Eucharist. We must admit the close resemblance: whenever we attend a bloodless offering of bread and wine conducted by a celibate Irishman, our thoughts turn to gangs of naked Greek women, roaring drunk, gouging

flesh out of passersby with their fingernails. It's positively distracting, some Sundays.

When Christ instituted the Eucharist, it shocked the Apostles and Pharisees—but He was indeed tapping into a mysterious aspect of our psyche, the desire to offer sacrifice. The Covenant of Abraham was sealed when that patriarch offered his son to Yahweh—rendered bloodless only by a miracle. Most of the gentile peoples surrounding Israel did practice human sacrifice, believing that human blood was the only way to propitiate the gods. The Hebrews themselves would slaughter bulls instead—by the hundreds at the Temple in Jerusalem. Genesis reports that "Moses took the blood, and sprinkled it on the people, and said, Behold the blood of the covenant, which the LORD hath made with you concerning all these words." (Exodus 24:8) Catholic anthropologist René Girard theorizes that the craving for ritual violence is reinforced by our nature and culture alike, and that only the single sacrifice of Christ (repeated in an unbloody fashion at the Mass) can interrupt the cyclical savagery that marks human societies. This sets us to thinking: Perhaps all British soccer games should begin with a liturgy. In the spirit of Vatican II, it could be translated from the Latin into Cockney "rhyming slang" as below:[1]

---

[1] Our thanks to the creators of the Cockney Rhyming Slang Generator (*www.whoohoo.co.uk*). We've run entire encyclicals through this program, and found the results quite edifying.

Latin	English	Cockney
P. Introibo ad altare Dei	P. I will go to the altar of God.	P. I will Scapa Fla ter the bloomin' altar of god.
S. Ad Deum qui laetificat juventutem meam.	S. To God, the joy of my youth.	S. To God, the joy of me youf.
P. Judica me, Deus, et discerne causam meam de gente non sancta: ab homine iniquo et doloso erue me.	P. Do me justice, O God, and fight my fight against an unholy people, rescue me from the wicked and deceitful man.	P. Do me justice, o God, and Read and Write for me against an unholy people, rescue me from the wicked and deceitful geeza.
S. Quia tu es, Deus, fortitudo mea: quare me repulisti, et quare tristis incedo, dum affligit me inimicus?	S. For Thou, O God, art my strength, why hast Thou forsaken me? And why do I go about in sadness, while the enemy harasses me?	S. For thou, o god, 'rt me strengf, why 'ast thou forsaken me? and why do I Scapa Fla abaht in sadness, while the bleedin' enemy 'arasses me?

CELEBRATE: You can tap into the primal appeal of Dionysos without turning into Hannibal Lector by serving a hearty Greek feast of roasted goat that can be eaten with a strong red wine and ten fingers. . . .

Grilled Goat with Retsina

We purchase our goat hind quarters at a local Greek butcher. You can special-order yours from any decent butcher.

2-1/2 pounds goat meat,
    cut into 2-inch pieces
Coarse ground black pepper
1 tablespoon sel gris
1 tablespoon sumac
1/4 cup olive oil
4 cups retsina

1 yellow onion, cut into thin half-moons
10 cloves garlic, finely sliced
1-1/2 tablespoons dried wild Neapolitan
    oregano
3 stalks rosemary
Fine sea salt

In a nonreactive dish, season goat meat with pepper, salt, and sumac. Pour in retsina and olive oil. Add onion, garlic, and herbs. Stir to evenly distribute ingredients. Marinate for 2 to 4 hours.

Prepare grill.

Pour marinade into small pot and set on grill to reduce.

Grill meat for 10–12 minutes on each side. Meat will be slightly charred and a reddish gold. Brush with marinade several times.

Strain marinade and serve with goat.

Serves 4

....

Dom Perignon: Champagne and Caritas are **Always** *Appropriate*

It's widely believed among wine enthusiasts that champagne was invented by a French monk of the Order of St. Benedict, Dom Pierre Perignon, born in 1640, who at age 28 earned the prestigious job of cellarmaster at the Abbey of Hautvillers. A master vintner, Perignon blended the juice of different grapes, performed the first "blind" taste tests in recorded history, and experimented with how much sugar to add. Experts point out that we have records of sparkling wines from a century before Dom Perignon, so it's likely that the good monk merely perfected the beverage—and found a way to keep it safe. The "second fermentation," which occurs in the juice of certain grapes, produces a natural carbonation that makes the

wine bubbly, delightful, and dangerous. When they held such wine, ordinary corked bottles tended to burst—like the "old wineskins" of which our Lord spoke (Luke 5:33–39)—with disastrous results. One bottle often set off a chain reaction of explosions and shattered glass. Historians agree that Dom Perignon perfected the first effective champagne cork (complete with wire cage), which made bottling the beverage practical.

Except that champagne is never really practical. A glass of champagne, served in the right spirit, is always something quixotic, fine, and fair. The delicate balance of sweet and dry, the tap-dance of bubbles against the palate, and the gentle tipsiness wafting through the blood. . . it's no surprise that champagne is called the beverage of love. It's fitting, then, that the Church had a hand in its creation; conversely, champagne may have led to the conception of more new Catholics than any other drink in history.

But champagne evokes more sorts of love than only eros. There are many kinds of love, and champagne resembles each of them in its way—and none more than the highest love, *agape* or *caritas*, which St. Paul praised so poetically in 1 Corinthians 13, and Pope Benedict XVI analyzed so perceptively in his first encyclical. As caritas is the best response to any situation, so champagne may be served with any meal. Like caritas, it is always appropriate.

Caritas	Champagne
Love is patient, love is kind.	Every kind of champagne is patiently crafted.
It does not envy, it does not boast, it is not proud.	A gentle flavor, never assertive.
It is not rude, it is not self-seeking, it is not easily angered, it keeps no record of wrongs.	May be served even with spicy foods.
Does not delight in evil but rejoices with the truth.	If drunk in sufficient quantities, it inspires people to blurt out the truth.
It always protects, always trusts, always hopes, always perseveres. Love never fails.	Can last for decades if properly stored.

CELEBRATE: Serve up a dinner for a few select friends employing the beverage of caritas, and try throughout dinner—just this one time—not to engage in uncharitable gossip about others who weren't invited. Come on, just try it once. To see how it feels . . .

Sole in Champagne Sauce

4 6-ounce sole fillets	Butter
Sea salt	Grapeseed oil
Freshly ground black pepper	Champagne sauce
Flour, on a plate for dredging fish	

Rinse and pat dry sole. Season fish with salt and pepper. Heat a large heavy skillet over medium heat; then add equal parts butter and oil to reach a depth of about 1/4 inch. Dredge fillets through flour, coating evenly. Shake to remove excess.

Add fillets to hot pan and cook until golden on each side. They will be cooked through at this point.

Serve hot with sauce and reserved garlic chives.

Pass around the extra sauce.

Serves 4

CHAMPAGNE SAUCE

1 tablespoon grapeseed oil	1 tablespoon white peppercorns
3 cups finely sliced leeks	1 cup clam juice
1-1/2 cups plus 1 tablespoon	8 ounces white mushrooms
finely sliced garlic chives	1 cup cream
(1 tablespoon reserved for garnish)	Sea salt
1 750 ml bottle champagne	Freshly ground white pepper
1 bay leaf	4 tablespoons butter, chilled and cubed

Heat grapeseed oil in large heavy-bottomed pot. Add leeks and sauté until just turning translucent. Add garlic chives and continue sautéing. Pour in champagne; add bay leaf and peppercorns. Cook over medium heat about 15 minutes, until reduced by half.

Next add clam juice and mushrooms. Return to a simmer and reduce by half. Finally add cream. Reduce again, simmering for about 30 minutes. Sauce should be somewhat thick. Now strain through a chinois or other fine strainer. Do not press down on solids.

Return sauce to heat and reduce a bit more if needed.

Season to taste and whisk in butter a bit at a time.

Keep warm while preparing fish.

··

Drambuie: The King Across the Water

This is the drink of exiled kings and the Scots who love them. The drink was aptly named in Gaelic *an dram buidleach* or "the drink that satisfies," and we agree. It makes a warm and complex cocktail, or on the rocks caps off an evening meal—even if you aren't eating haggis. This distillation of whiskey, heather, honey, and herbs was crafted for Charles Edward Stuart—the dashing Young Pretender, the legitimate heir to the British throne whose grandfather had been chased out of the country for keeping true to the Catholic faith. After failing to retake the throne, Charles Edward fled for his life to the Isle of Skye—and left the secret formula for the whiskey with his loyal hosts, whose descendants still brew the liquor today. Since the drink made the Mackinnon clan's fortune, the family is probably just as glad his cause was lost.

According to Jeremy Watson of the *Scotsman*, Drambuie became most popular in the 1950s with the vogue for the "Rusty Nail"—a cocktail which infused the singing voice of Frank Sinatra and Sammy Davis, Jr., and still keeps the liver of the late Dean Martin miraculously incorrupt. Watson reports that the liquor is newly popular among young Britons. The dating habits of the Bridget Jones generation predispose them to a drink with the aura of romantic failure.

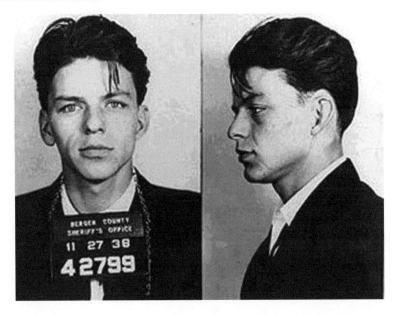

And what a failure it was. Indeed, the Stuarts had been trying and failing to rule England on and off for almost 100 years. In 1640, under the Stuart Charles I, the country had erupted in a civil war between low-church Puritans, led by Oliver Cromwell, who favored a parliamentary oligarchy, and an alliance of Anglicans and Catholics who fought for the king. It ended with the 1649 judicial murder of Charles I, whose sons Charles and James fled to France. In ten years, a literally puritanical dictatorship of Parliament closed theaters, banned Maypoles and cancelled Christmas (too "papist"). In 1660, the English decided they preferred Divine Right to the Christian Right, and invited the princes back.

Charles II returned to take the throne—bringing with him a bride and a younger brother who were both Roman Catholics. The grateful English did not make too much of this, until it became clear that James would inherit the throne—and that he intended to restore to Catholics their civil rights. Under laws that James enacted when he took the throne, for the first time in over 100 years Catholics could serve in Parliament and the Army, and attend Oxford and Cambridge. Even though James extended the same rights to members of every faith, the populace believed he intended far more: to convert all England back to Catholicism by force. (It didn't help that James's ally and former host, Louis XIV, had resumed persecuting Protestants in 1685, over the fierce objections of the pope.) By this time, a century of royal propaganda had succeeded in convincing Englishmen that belonging to their national church—a mishmash of semi-Protestant beliefs in Catholic costumes—was essential to remaining a patriotic Englishman. Roman Catholics were dangerous traitors for preferring the Church of Christ's foundation to that of Henry's erection. Worst of all, because they obeyed an Italian pope, they were essentially *foreign*.

The taint of "Papistry" was so profound that leading Englishmen conspired to replace their native-born king with his Dutch son-in-law, William of Orange. The usurper arrived on November 5, 1688 at the head of a kind of Protestant "international brigade." James II was betrayed by his army commander and defeated in Ireland at the Battle of the Boyne. He departed for France, to father sons and plan their return.

After a series of gallant, impossible attempts to invade Britain, rouse the loyal Scots to their cause, and retake the throne, the Stuarts made their last bid for power in 1746—and came painfully close to succeeding. Sailing in from exile in France, James's grandson Charles Edward and his followers won several early battles. Scots Highlanders in their tartans drove back the redcoats at Prestonpans in a matter of minutes, sending England into a panic as the Jacobite armies came within 120 miles of London. Then, in good Catholic fashion, they started squabbling, wasting precious time that allowed the English forces to gather and chase them north. The final defeat of the Jacobite cause took place at Culloden, where Charles Edward's gallant Highlanders were crushed by the Duke of Cumberland's seasoned regular troops. After the battle, the ruthless Cumberland ordered that the wounded "traitors" be killed, and unleashed a massacre of Highland civilians—slaying women and children alike, and banning such customs as the wearing of tartans and kilts. It wasn't until 80 years later, when Sir Walter Scott's novels reminded Britons of the beauties of old Scots culture, that kilts and tartans would be revived—as nostalgic gestures.

Charles Edward's defeat ushered in 100 years of British kings who spoke English as a second language, and who reigned mostly as puppets of Parliament—but who were, at least, Protestant. To this day, the House of Windsor[2] can boast of that—if little else.

CELEBRATE: To accompany this Highland drink we suggest the following Scottish menu, accompanied by the tough-guy cocktail, the Rusty Nail.

If you're a fan of legitimate British kings or American popular standards, you have ample reason to savor the drink favored by Jacobites and the "Rat Pack." You can carry on an old Scots tradition by clinking your glasses over a glass of water—as Scotsmen loyal to Charles Edward did to toast "to the King" across the waters. Or, carry on an old custom of Sinatra's by grabbing the blackjack dealer who called you a "dago" and punching his lights out. The knucklehead.

Butterhead Lettuce with Champagne Vinaigrette
Drambuie Smoked Cod (see recipe)
Creamy Garlic New Potatoes
Sautéed Arugula and Shallots
Drambuie Butter-Glazed Carrots
Strawberries with Lavender and Black Pepper

Drambuie Smoked Cod

This cod is a cinch to make with a stovetop smoker. If you have a large outdoor smoker by all means use it, but for city dwellers these are a Godsend.

1 pound cod fillet	Dried lavender sprigs
1/2 cup coarse sea salt	Summer savory
1/2 cup honey	2 tablespoons oak chips
1/2 cup Drambuie	

Make sure all the bones have been removed from the cod; rinse under cold water.

Combine salt, honey, Drambuie, lavender, and savory. Rub mixture into fish and place in a nonreactive container. Chill for at least 2 hours.

---

[2] The real name of the dynasty is Saxe-Coburg-Gotha, but during World War I the monarchs took the name "Windsor" in an attempt to assimilate.

Rinse cod under cold water to gently remove marinade. Place on smoker rack over drip tray; refrigerate for 30 minutes.

Place oak chips in bottom of smoker, following manufacturer's directions. Insert rack and tray with cod and turn heat to medium. Cook over medium heat. As soon as the first wisp of smoke appears, close the lid tightly.

Smoke for 15 minutes. Turn off heat and let sit 5 minutes. Remove to platter and serve.

Serves 2

Rusty Nail

4 ounces Drambuie	3 lemon twists
4 ounces Scotch	

Combine Drambuie, Scotch, and lemon twists in a cocktail shaker. Fill with crushed ice.

Shake and strain into Old-Fashion glasses filled with ice.

Makes 2 cocktails

Drinking Song #2: A Nostalgic Tune

A friend of ours—a well-known Catholic apologist and mixologist—is descended from a family who took part in most major wars over the past 300 years—on the losing side. His French and Austrian forebears fought for Charles I and James II against the Protestants, Louis XV against the English, George III against the Americans, Louis XVI against the Jacobins, the Confederacy against the Yankees, and Kaiser Franz Josef against the Serbs. It took until World War II for the family to pick a winner, but our friend has no regrets: "We were always on the right side," he insists, "and besides, it's the losers who usually write the best songs."

One of our favorite songs for a lost cause is the Jacobite anthem "Will Ye No Come Back Again."

Will Ye No Come Back Again

Bon - nie Char-lie's now a - wa', Safe - ly owre the friend - ly main; Mo-ny a heart will break i' twa, Should he no'come back a-gain. Will ye no come back a-gain? Will ye no come back a-gain? Bet-ter lo'ed ye can-na be, Will ye no come back a-gain?

2. Mony a traitor 'mange the isles
Brak the band o' nature's laws;
Mony a traitor wi' his wiles,
Sought to wear his life awa'.
Refrain:

3. Many a gallant sodger gaught,
Mony a gallant chief did fa,
Death itself were dearly bought,
A' for Scotland's king and law.
Refrain:

4. Whene'er I hear the blackbird sing,
Unto the evening sinking down,
Or merl that makes the wood to ring,
To me they hae nae other sound.
Refrain:

5. Sweet the lav'rock's note and lang,
Lilting wildly up the glen;
And aye the o'erworld o' he sang,
"Will he no' come back again?"
Refrain:

Easter Beer: Miracles . . . and Yeast

It wasn't so long ago that Lent was a serious business. Catholics who marked the season prior to Vatican II will recall complex rules of fast and abstinence, which forbade meat on Wednesdays as well as Fridays, and on the eves of major holy days. Indeed, it was only in the twentieth century, by special papal indult, that Catholics were reluctantly permitted cheese. Less rigorous rules applied in Advent, which was (curiously) deemed a season of penance rather than shopping. Things were even stricter during the Middle Ages when married couples were expected to sleep separately for 40 days (excluding Sundays—which today would just wreak havoc with Natural Family Planning).

Indeed, children born at Christmas time, nine months after Lent, were frowned upon by the superstitious as the fruit of their parents' sin. Such strict rules, of monastic origin, still apply to Eastern Rite and Eastern Orthodox Christians.[1]

While some of this seems excessive to us today, it did serve the purpose of emphasizing each sinner's solidarity with Jesus' fasting in the desert. It prepared us to take Holy Week seriously. And it made Easter something more than an uptick on the sales charts of the milk-chocolate industry. Instead, it was like the last day at a very bad school—a feast of liberation, an end to dreary rules, celibacy, and fish-sticks. You can see why this would inspire the brewing of Easter Beer. The monks themselves were often the ones tending the barrels. Among the breweries of monastic origin or ownership, which still produce a special Easter brew, are the Belgian St-Feuillien, St. Bernardus, and Grimbergen. Like Christmas Ale, Easter beers are often flavored with spices or hints of fruit, but they are lighter and simpler, more like the lagers with which Americans are (all too) familiar. They go well with a roast pork, ham, or

---

[1] Then again, in the Christian East there is not the same concept of "mortal sin," so most people simply ignore them. Catholics of Irish descent or schooling realize that occasions of mortal sin lie at every bend in the road, like IEDs in liberated Iraq—so we tread carefully, shoot first, and ask questions later.

Easter Bunny Fricassee (for recipe, see our previous book, a guide to the liturgical calendar and saints, *The Bad Catholic's Guide to Good Living*).

There's a deeper level at which it makes perfect sense to brew a special batch to celebrate the Resurrection. We find this insight in "Christ, a Quickening Spirit," an Easter sermon preached by that most sober Christian, John Henry Newman. There Newman points out that Jesus was not raised by the Father from the dead, or newly infused (as at His conception) by the Holy Ghost. In fact, Jesus was *immune to death*. It could claim Him for a little while, long enough for Him to descend into the underworld and "harrow Hell," reclaiming for Heaven the souls of all the just men who'd lived before Him. But as Newman wrote:

> St. Peter says, that it "was not possible that He should be holden of death:"(Ps. 16:10. Acts 2: 24, 27) as if there were some hidden inherent vigour in Him, which secured His manhood from dissolution. The greatest infliction of pain and violence could only destroy its powers for a season; but nothing could make it decay . . . immortal even in His mortal nature, clear from all infection of the forbidden fruit, so far as to be sinless and incorruptible. Therefore, though He was liable to death, "it was impossible He should be holden" of it. Death might overpower, but it could not keep possession; "it had no dominion over Him." (Romans 6: 9) He was, in the words of the text, "the Living among the dead."

At this point, you might be wondering what all this has to do with beer. The answer is yeast (**see Yeast**). That miraculous microorganism is responsible for turning a bucket of grain and water into beloved brew. Without it, nothing happens—there's no inherent power in malt or barley to ferment itself. You need yeast to raise the spirit. Christ Himself compared the soul to a grain of wheat (John 12:24), and the Kingdom of Heaven to yeast (Luke 13:21). This yeast is the Gospel, which Jesus didn't need to hear, as He didn't require outside help to rise from the dead. We, on the other hand, need all the help we can get.

Eau de Vie: A Curious Perversion of the Spanish

Perhaps the most venerable type of liqueur in Europe is the eau de vie, whose name is a French rendition of the Latin *aqua vitæ* (water of life). Folklorist E. Cobham Brewer calls this etymology "a curious perversion of the Spanish *acqua di vite* (water or juice of the vine), rendered by the monks into *aqua vitæ* instead of *aqua vitis.*" But if you've ever tasted one, you know that the mendicants were onto

something. They invented eaux originally as medicines to combat scourges such as cholera. Along the way, the monks may have cured a few other ailments: there are records of a Danish eau de vie made from St. John's Wort—the natural counterpart to Prozac.

And a good eau de vie will surely lift your spirits. Made from pure, fresh fruit quickly distilled to keep the essential flavor, eaux de vie make the ideal end-of-dinner beverage, doing double duty both as a digestif and a dessert.

There are many different types of eaux, ranging from the reassuring to the raucous. Lady drinkers report that raspberry framboise is irresistible—and surprisingly potent. Over the centuries, it has led many a night of love across the line from prudence into passion. At the other end of the spectrum is throat-searing *grappa*, originally rendered from the skins of discarded grapes by smelly Alpine shepherds whom no women wanted. Thanks to machismo or through some miracle of marketing, this gritty liqueur evolved into a fashion statement, and is now offered in a dozen or more varieties (from moscato to chamomile), displayed in hand-blown glass on the top shelf of urban cocktail bars. There has been no recorded instance of a woman enjoying the stuff.

More approachable eaux include kirsch made from cherries, fraise from strawberries, marille made of apricots, and slivovitz—the fiery plum brandy which has fueled many useless Balkan wars. Some Quebecois desperate for an alternative to beer and Canadian whiskey have invented an eau made from maple syrup—which we bet goes great with crepes. But our favorite eau is Poire William, distilled from William pears, and sold in a bottle with a whole fruit inside. To make this "*poire prisonniere,*" French distillers actually hang empty bottles on the pear tree, so the fruit grows inside it. This sweet and complex liqueur has stilled many a late-night squabble between the authors. If this potion of peace could work for us, we wonder how it might benefit the world at large. Perhaps the stuff should be served at diplomatic functions, instead of water. Then again, since the pear was the medieval symbol of fecundity, one might want to be careful. Does the world really need the love-child of Kim Jong Il and Condoleeza Rice . . .?

....

Eggnog and the Incarnation

If you've read our entry on Christmas Ale, you already know why the coming of Christ into human flesh to save the human race from eternal death was a definite net "plus." But we cannot resist mentioning another beverage cooked up to celebrate the season marking the birth of the God-Man; the redeemer who knit together in a single mysterious Person both creator and the created. And that is eggnog.

The drink is of relatively recent vintage, but its roots lie (like every other good thing) in the Middle Ages. Medieval Englishmen used to drink something called "posset," a blend of Spanish sherry and milk, served (it's said) in wooden mugs called "noggins." Eggnog historian[2] W.J. Rayment suggests that when the drink came over to Colonial America, the sherry was replaced by cheaper and stronger rum called "grog". The result, writes Rayment, is that "a mixture of the two and eggnog was originally called 'egg and grog in a noggin.' This was a term that required shortening if ever there was one." We agree, and affirm it's worth each of the calories contained in a standard serving (approximately 7,300). The rich, luxuriant beverage is a dessert in its own right, which lets you save that fruitcake to use as rodent-proof insulation.

Too often, pious Catholics think of the Incarnation as simply the preface to the Passion—as in the slug line of the worthy Mel Gibson movie, which read: "Dying Was His Reason for Living." True enough, but it's only part of the picture. Had Jesus simply been an exquisitely holy man, His martyrdom would not have accomplished much. As countless theologians (especially St. Anselm) pointed out, it was only because of His divine nature that Jesus' sacrifice was "perfect" and efficacious. In the Renaissance—and since antiquity in the Christian East—theologians laid heavy emphasis on the significance of the Incarnation in itself, on "God becoming man so man may become God." By seamlessly weaving together (without confusing) human and divine persons, Jesus bound up the

----

[2] Ain't Google great?

gap that Adam's sin opened between earth and heaven. His self-sacrifice on the Cross was the crowning moment of that reunion, but it began with the Annunciation.

At about the same time Englishmen began mixing milk and sherry, theologians in the West were rediscovering this truth. As the learned Jesuit John W. O' Malley writes:

> "the mystery of the Incarnation tended to be seen as the central truth of Christianity and as being identified with the mystery of the Redemption. This was no novel idea. It was the basis for the theology of many of the Greek Fathers and is found also in Thomas Aquinas. But the idea was revived with a new emphasis in the Renaissance and tended in effect to place as much, if not more, redemptive efficacy on the moment of the incarnation in the Virgin's womb as in the suffering and death of Jesus on the cross. Humanity was saved, redeemed, at least inchoately, at the moment the Godhead assumed human flesh and became one with us. . . . [T]he liturgy of the Roman Rite prescribed that the celebrant and the entire congregation fall to its knees at only one point during the recitation of the ancient Creed—'*et incarnates est ex Maria Virgine, et homo factus est.*' The next phrase—'*crucifixus etiam pro nobis*' followed almost as an afterthought, a corollary, once the assembly had again returned to its feet." [3]

Nowadays, of course, few people genuflect at this part of the Creed (the authors do, but we're just obnoxious). Instead, since the rubric calls for a "profound and reverent bow," even at Christmas Mass the priest at best dips his head, while the laymen fish for change in their pockets. Thus, the saving significance of the Incarnation recedes into the shadows. And everyone gets non-alcoholic Eggnog Lattes™ at Starbucks.

CELEBRATE: Mark the miracle of the Virgin Birth by producing this wondrous beverage made exclusively from unfertilized eggs. If your friends don't get the theological significance, sit them down after you've had a few and explain the pun pedantically, and at great length. When they erupt in spontaneous laughter, you can stop.

---

[3] Cited in Leo Steinberg's art history, *The Sexuality of Christ in Renaissance Art and Modern Oblivion*, (Chicago: University of Chicago Press, 1996). This fascinating book explains why devout, perfectly orthodox Catholic painters in that period insisted on painting Jesus nude—to assert His real humanity and masculinity. Needless to say, the book has driven feminist theologians up the wall. In search of a neutered Christ, they're ready to paint loincloths on the frescos.

Eggnog

This recipe can be easily multiplied to serve a crowd. If making ahead, chill milk mixture and warm gently on stove. Make meringue at last minute.

2 cups milk
4 whole eggs
2 eggs, separated
1/4 cup sugar plus 2 tablespoons
   for meringue
1/4 teaspoon cinnamon

1/4 teaspoon allspice
1/4 teaspoon cloves
Pinch of sea salt
2 tablespoons Amontillado sherry
1/4 cup dark rum
Fresh nutmeg

In blender whirl milk, whole eggs, 2 yolks, sugar, and spices until smooth.

Transfer to heavy saucepan over medium heat. Stir with a wooden spoon until mixture just begins to thicken. Add sherry and rum, then strain through a sieve.

In a mixer beat 2 egg whites. Start on low speed. (A hand mixer can be used but a stand mixer such as Kitchenaid is superior in most all respects. One notable exception is the making of Italian meringue, in which the whites and sugar are mixed together on the stovetop.)

As whites become noticeably thicker, increase speed one notch at a time until the highest speed is reached. Allow whites to whisk for about one minute on each speed. The whites will form soft peaks and begin to pull away from the sides of bowl. Rain in the 2 tablespoons of sugar and continue mixing until stiff peaks form.

Fold meringue into strained milk and whisk lightly.

Grate nutmeg on top; ladle into mugs.

Makes 1 quart

....

Est Est Est—Quaffing with the Cardinals

Est Est Est is more than just a pizzeria in New Haven—though that is how we remember it. The restaurant takes its name from a variety of wine produced in Lazio, the countryside surrounding Rome. The wine itself is a light and fruity white, a bright accompaniment to such local specialties as Spaghetti Carbonara or Pasta e Ceci, a garlicky chickpea soup flavored with rosemary.

The wine gets its title from the glee it once provoked in a prince of the Church. It seems that around the year 1110, Johannes Fugger (either a

EST! EST!! EST!!!
di Montefiascone
DENOMINAZIONE DI ORIGINE CONTROLLATA
Descovo
PRODOTTO E IMBOTTIGLIATO ALL'ORIGINE DA
CANTINA DI MONTEFIASCONE
SOC COOP. a r.l. - MONTEFIASCONE - ITALIA
750 ml ℮   PRODUCE OF ITALY   11,5% vol

bishop or a cardinal, depending on who's telling the story) traveled to Rome to attend the coronation of the emperor Henry V.

Although Henry ruled mostly in Germany, to validate his election as Holy Roman Emperor, he needed to receive his crown in Rome from the hands of the pope. In return, popes usually strove to win independence from the government—for instance, the right to appoint bishops themselves, instead of settling for the cronies of local kings. This struggle between emperor and pope continued for centuries, weakening both institutions, laying the groundwork for the Reformation.[4]

Perhaps Cardinal Fugger was used to the finer things in life—or else had drunk one too many glasses of gut-churning moonshine—because he sent ahead a scout to serve as his personal "wine spectator." His steward, Martin, rode ahead of the prelate's entourage to sample the wines at local inns—and award the eleventh-century version of a Michelin "star." Over the door Martin chalked the single Latin word "EST," meaning "It's here!" As the cardinal made his way from inn to inn, he confirmed Martin's judgment, faithfully sampling a glass at each recommended spot. At the last tavern, in Montefiascone, Cardinal Fugger paused skeptically—

surely there had been some mistake, or it was time Martin switched to water. Because over the door of this pub were written not one "EST" but three. The prelate led his entourage inside and started sampling. By the end he was . . . shall we say, won over.

Cardinal Fugger bought up as much of the wine as the town could supply, and placed a standing order for annual deliveries. He even changed his will so that his body would be buried in Montefiascone, and left the town a small fortune as a bequest—on the condition that once a year, the locals would pour a cask of wine over his grave. Later on, the local bishop, after taking a swig, decided that this was a sinful waste. "Remember," he may have said, "the sober children in Arabia."[5] He changed the cardinal's will so that the wine would be given instead to the seminary—where he just happened to reside.

Another version of this legend has the poor cardinal drinking himself to death, and going to the grave with Martin's epitaph: *EST EST EST, PROPTER NIMIUM EST HIC JO DEUC, DOMINUS MEUS, MORTUUS EST.* Not very likely: Even an

---

[4] To understand the relation of Church and State in the Middle Ages, see either Christopher Dawson's *The Formation of Christendom* (1967), or any news report on the Republican Party and the Southern Baptist Convention.

[5] This is how we reprimand any friend who fails to finish a drink.

experienced drinker would have a hard time killing himself with wine, unless he jumped into a vat of the stuff and drowned. But the fact that locals came up with this morbid twist says something about the reputation higher clergy sometimes got as luxurious and decadent. In fact, the College of Cardinals was organized around 1170 by Pope Alexander III as a reform to end the corruption and coercion that once tainted papal elections. Before that time, local politicians, angry mobs, and emperors used to squabble over the throne—with generous input from well-armed "families" such as the Orsinis, the Colonnas, and the Gambinos. At one point in the tenth century, some noble women got into the act, winning the papal throne for their favorites—which led disgruntled misogynists to call this period the "pornocracy," which translates as "rule by whores." Centuries later, similar election critics would mock Florida's Katherine Harris for her makeup.

By handing the right to choose future popes to cardinals, the Church diminished but could not erase the influence of secular powers on the election of the most important man in the world. The cardinals themselves, scions of noble families, were used to worldly comforts—though many were also pious, and dozens earned the title of saint. Great cardinals over the centuries included the austere Franciscan Ximénez (1436–1517), who created the first multilingual Bible and championed the human dignity of Indians in Mexico; St. Robert Bellarmine (1542–1621), who denied the "divine right" of kings and insisted on the right of subjects to rebel; and Kung Pin-Mei (1901–2000), the first native Chinese Bishop of Shanghai, who spent almost 30 years in prison for insisting on religious freedom.

But cardinals and bishops didn't always appear in such a heroic light, especially in the Middle Ages. Having gained wealth and influence through a specialized education, they were the medieval equivalent of lawyers. As they rode their caparisoned mounts from one vaulting gothic cathedral to another, they must have seemed like the "jet-set" to the unlettered, mud-spattered peasants who watched them pass. No doubt, they'd turn to each other and mutter in Old English or Old French[6] snarky canon lawyer jokes such as the following:

Q: When canon lawyers die, wherefore art they interred 600 feet under ground?
A: Because deep down, they're really nice guys.

Q: Traveling upon the road, how canst one tell the difference between a dead skunk and a dead canon lawyer?
A: The vultures aren't gagging over the skunk.

Q: What call'st thou a wain full of canon lawyers tumbling over into a ravine?
A: A damned good start.

---

[6] Peasants couldn't afford the new ones.

CELEBRATE: Order a few bottles of the preferred Italian white of canon lawyers, and serve it with a favorite of the region where it's made—the delicious chickpea and macaroni concoction, Paste e Ceci.

Pasta e Ceci

CHICKPEAS:

1 pound dried chickpeas	1 pound baby carrots
2 stalks celery	6 cloves garlic
1 yellow onion, minced	Sprigs of rosemary and thyme tied together

SAUCE:

2 tablespoons olive oil	3 tablespoons tomato paste
6 garlic cloves, sliced	Sea salt and freshly ground pepper
1 tablespoon rosemary leaves, minced	

TO FINISH:

8 ounces ditalini	1/4 cup chopped parsley

Begin the night before by setting out the chickpeas to soak. The next day drain, rinse, and add to a roomy soup pot with water to cover; add vegetables and herbs. Bring to a boil; cover and simmer 1 to 2 hours until cooked but firm.

At this point remove and discard the celery and herbs. Use an immersion blender to partially puree the chickpeas; you should end up with a third of the peas pureed.

Prepare the sauce.

Heat olive oil with rosemary and garlic in small sauté pan. Cook until garlic is soft. Add tomato paste and fry for a few minutes. Add this to chickpeas and simmer briefly. Season with salt and generous turns of black pepper. Add up to a cup of water if needed. This is a thick soup but there should be enough liquid to cook the pasta. Bring to a boil. Add ditalini and cook until it's just shy of being done. Turn off heat. Cover and let rest for 15 minutes.

Garnish with parsley and serve with a drizzle of extra virgin olive oil.

Leftovers are delicious right out of the refrigerator.

Serves 6–8

Loopholes in the Ten Commandments
#2: Take Not the Name of the Lord in Vain

Since the dawn of human language, men have suspected that there is a mystical connection between a thing and the name by which it is called. In Norse and other mythologies, heroes and gods had hidden names, known only to them or those they trusted most—because to know a person's name was to have power over him, which one might abuse. In the Jewish tradition, God commanded His people not to abuse the names they had for Him—lest they take His fidelity and love for granted, and turn their worship to other gods or themselves. When Moses went to the mountaintop to receive the Ten Commandments, the Lord revealed to him what Jews ever after referred to as the "secret name" of God. Unlike the more generic terms Adonai and Elohim, which were used in everyday speech, this name was potent and sacred—and its use tightly restricted. As Jewish playwright

David Mamet writes in an essay, "Secret Names," "the most secret name of God, the Shem Ha Meforesh, could be uttered only by the high priest in the afternoon of Yom Kippur. He would alone enter the Holy of Holies, and there would say the name. He would have a rope tied around his ankle, so that, should he die while in the Holy of Holies, he could be gotten out. No one else, of course, being permitted to enter there." Those Levites may have been devout, but they were also eminently practical. So was Yahweh, Who perhaps restricted use of His name so the Hebrews wouldn't *kvetch*. After all, He does have a universe to run. . . .

Working from the sacred Name, the speculative rabbis who practiced the Kabbalah played upon its four letters (IHVH) to come up with 72 elaborations, each representing one of God's attributes or powers. For centuries, the secret teachings of the Kabbalah were reserved as a mystical practice to learned Jews—before they became a good luck charm for movie stars and pop singers.

There's an inherent tension in any personal religion between the desire to keep God on a pedestal—let's face it, who else really *belongs* there?—and the craving to clutch Him close. Striking this balance became exquisitely important with the coming of Christ, Who at one moment might be eating or fishing with His friends, and at another raising the dead and proclaiming His equality with the Father. What to *do* with such a person? Jewish etiquette books offered no advice. The Apostles had to come up with something new, which would balance intimacy and awe. By the time of St. Paul, as it sank in among the new Christians that Jesus was (1) really

God and (2) really gone, the saint could write his followers in Phillipi that "at the name of Jesus every knee should bow, of things in heaven, and things in earth, and things under the earth." (Philippians 2:10) Instead of keeping God's name secret, they sang it to the skies—and interpreted this commandment against blasphemy as meaning that Jesus' name (and God's other names) should be used mostly in prayer or petition. Until recent decades, every time the name of Jesus was mentioned at Mass, the priest, the servers, and the congregation would bow their heads. (We much prefer this pre-conciliar practice to the contemporary custom of simply yawning.)

Christian liturgy grew more formal over the centuries, but personal prayer was always practiced—most of it taken from the Hebrew psalms. However, another type of prayer grew up among pious folk, becoming popular in the Middle Ages— little expressions of devotion which one might whisper to one's self or under one's breath, such as "My lord and my God," or "Jesus, Mary and Joseph." In its simplest form, this became the "Jesus Prayer" practiced in the East, where monks tried to turn every breath into praise.

Such prayers were called pious "aspirations" (from the Latin *ad-spirare*, to breathe) or "ejaculations" (Latin: *ejaculari*, to throw out).[7] And there is surely something to the idea of carrying on a running conversation with the Lord, all through one's day—in order to cultivate what the great Msgr. Robert Hugh Benson called "the friendship of Christ." But like most things in this fallen world—such as the earthy connotations of theological terms—this cuts both ways. It's not a far step for most of us from saying the Jesus Prayer to shouting "JESUS!" when we stub our toes. Now we aren't the sort to make a big thing of "foul language"; expletives exist in every language for a reason. When you drop a casserole pan on your foot, or slam head first into a caribou, what else are you supposed to belt out—an aria? There has to be *something* you can shout when you're angry and trying to scare your kids into silence.

Sadly, in many Catholic countries, that something became something sacred. Most infamous are the Quebecois, who back when they worshiped Christ (instead of their dialect of French) developed an entire language of blasphemous expletives called *sacres*, such as "*Câlisse!*" (chalice), "*Tabernac!*" (tabernacle) and "*Sacristie!*" (sacristy). Now it's tempting to crack a French joke here (the Republican reader may insert his own, or recall one he memorized while listening to Sean Hannity), but this happens elsewhere as well. Even the English carried on into modern times some traces of medieval sacrilege. In Shakespeare's plays you'll hear characters shout out "Marry" (Mary), "Bloody" ("By Our Lady") or "Zounds!" (from "God's wounds!"). So this problem seems to be endemic.

---

[7] No we're not making that up. In 1980, one of the authors at age 16 sat biting his tongue as the saintly Fr. John Hardon, S.J., taught a class on the virtues of pious ejaculations. "It is best to accumulate hundreds of these each day," he explained. The author thought it best not even to try.

As an alternative, the Irish developed substitute expletives which sounded like blasphemies, but weren't—such as "Judas Priest" (instead of "Jesus Christ!"). But once these harmless alternatives began to form themselves into ear-bleeding heavy metal bands, this custom fell into disuse.

We'd like to suggest another approach. Shocking as it might be to the old ladies in the room (or in your head), there's really nothing sinful about using profanities, so long as you're not profaning something sacred. When you slam your fist into a wall for a good reason—for instance, while listening to a presidential speech—and you feel a knuckle break, don't vent your frustration by shouting the name of the incarnate Son of God. Or even the Quebecois word for Easter Candle (*ciarge*). It's also unacceptable to shout a string of racial epithets; depending on who's in the room, this might sin against charity or even prudence. But it's a venial sin at most to let out a string of words related to excretory or reproductive functions. Unless you're abashed at blaspheming the sacred name of BLEEP.

Forbidden Fruit:
We've Fallen and We Can't Get Up

In 1750, amateur botanist Rev. Griffith Hughes was poking around the wild flora of the British colony Barbados when he came across an unfamiliar fruit. It resembled the orange, but hung from a tree in clusters like grapes. Today we call it the grapefruit. But the imaginative Rev. Hughes, who'd found it on an island paradise, dubbed it "the Forbidden Fruit." In the twentieth century, natives of the island began to make a grapefruit brandy of the same evocative name—

which until recently was distributed by the same company that sells Chambord. Sadly, they no longer make the liqueur, which now remains as out of reach as the fruit that Adam sampled.

Of course, most of us grew up thinking that Adam and Eve ate an apple. But that's the result of a bad translation; however allegorically you choose to read the Book of Genesis, there's almost zero chance that early man lived in the temperate zone where apple trees grew. Medieval theologians actually argued about which fruit hung from the forbidden tree; most leaned towards the fig because of its abundance of seeds and overtly sexual shape. (Just cut one in half.) Here prudery trumped theology, since the Christian tradition does not hold that the sin of Adam and Eve had anything to do with sex. It was, rather, a sin of pride—a desire to be "like unto God." And not in a *good* way.

Some dour Eastern monks did argue that physical intercourse and sexual desire were imposed by God as a punishment for Original Sin, but happily married couples begged to differ. It's no surprise that it took an Italian, Tommaso D'Aquino (St. Thomas Aquinas) to argue that sexual pleasure was part of God's original plan—and in fact, that sex in paradise would have been even better. Our desires would have worked in perfect tandem with our reason, instead of warring against it, and physical attraction would follow from love, esteem and respect. (Today, of course, it works the other way around, but let's not get into that.) Suffice it to say, according to Thomistic exegesis of the Genesis, absent the Fall of man there'd be little demand for Viagra or fishnet stockings.

If you read on a little further in the Genesis narrative you come across an intriguing section that's rarely mentioned in homilies—no doubt because it's puzzling:

And the LORD God said, Behold, the man is become as one of us, to know good and evil: and now, lest he put forth his hand, and take also of the Tree of Life, and eat, and live for ever:

Therefore the LORD God sent him forth from the garden of Eden, to till the ground from whence he was taken.

So he drove out the man; and he placed at the east of the garden of Eden Cherubims, and a flaming sword which turned every way, to keep the way of the tree of life. (Genesis 3: 22–24).

One's first reaction on reading this passage is to wish that Adam had been more enterprising, and grabbed the second fruit that warded off death. No one who has lost a family member—much less died himself—can disagree. The least Adam could have done was try to clean up his mess, and grab for us from the Tree of Life a fistful of eternity.

But would that really have been a good thing? To live forever in our sinful state, unredeemed and cut off from God. . . . The Genesis passage suggests that God found this prospect appalling, that man would have become a species of demon, roaming

the earth like the Serpent who recruited us. Dante and C.S. Lewis depict the netherworld as a kind of infernal pyramid scheme, a nightmare of hierarchical power relations which never ends. Without the great equalizer Death, tyrants could reign forever and no one could escape. We would have our Hell on earth.

Likewise, ideologies promising an earthly Heaven always end in blood and squalor. While we're well within our rights to try to make our brief sojourns here as pleasant as possible—perhaps through social reform, backrubs, and the occasional cocktail—fallen man is prone to overreach, and try by any means necessary to recreate a Garden of Eden, either in society or in private life. Whether it's the mirage of a "socialist paradise," the "life-extending promise of stem-cell technology," or merely a big bowl of hash, all these attempts to grasp the Fruit of Life are all doomed to fail. Just ask that angel over there—the one with the flaming sword.

Frangelico: Faith and Hazelnuts

This delicious Italian liqueur is made from toasted hazelnuts, and flavored with vanilla berries, coffee, cocoa, and even a bit of rhubarb. It goes well before or after dinner—though it's sweet enough to render dessert negotiable. Frangelico was first sold commercially in the 1980s, and quickly established itself as a staple on every bar shelf, thanks to its evocative name and packaging. The distillers even put the liqueur in a bottle shaped like a friar, belted by a real hemp rope.

The drink, which is named for the saint, is not quite as unique as its namesake. In fact, it is but one fine example of the rural drinks produced in Italian villages up and down the geographical spiky boot (**see Amaretto**). Frangelico is made in Canale, located at just about the shinbone. But the saint for whom the drink is named hailed from Fiesole, which is rather closer to the quadriceps.

Fra Angelico Giovanni da Fiesole may not have drunk much hazelnut hooch, but he would have worn a rope to complete his habit. After joining the Dominicans in 1418 at age 23, Fra Angelico took up the task of "illuminating" Bibles and prayer books with tiny miniatures, then moved on to painting scenes on the walls of churches. He paid frequent visits to Assisi, home of the Franciscans, and may have studied painting under Giotto. Fra Angelico's own work soon garnered him fame—and would have made him rich, if not for that pesky vow of poverty. He was summoned by the Medicis to Florence, and commissioned to paint the Convent of San Marco, now one of his most famous works.

But this acclaim never turned his head. Fra Angelico indulged in none of the typical vices we associate with artists: absinthe-drinking, frantic gambling, ear-mailing. His female models, if he used them, went unmolested. When offered by the pope the plum assignment of Archbishop of Florence, the friar turned it down. The art historian Vasari reports that Fra Angelico began every painting with prayer, insisting "To paint Christ, you must *live* Christ." He was canonized a saint by Pope John Paul II in 1982, and named the patron of painters. (For a sample of his work, see Fra Angelico's portrait of Peter Martyr, above.)

Fra Angelico is perhaps the most beloved and bragged-about member of the Order of Preachers (Dominicans). That order was founded by St. Dominic in 1216 to win back the heretical Albigensians, who embraced ideals of radical poverty and population control. These premature Malthusians believed that the material world itself was evil, and are said to have originated the popular phrase, "This isn't the kind of world into which I'd want to bring a child."[1] Dominic organized his friars to practice a similar poverty, while preaching the goodness of Creation. Fra Angelico's paintings, with their eloquent use of flowers, light, and wild nature, argue the same point silently. Of course, a glass of Frangelico after a plate of *osso buco* is all the argument some of us need.

CELEBRATE: Test out our theological argument which renders superfluous the artwork of Fra Angelico. Serve up this delightful Florentine specialty to some friends, and ask them if they still suspect that the universe was created by a malevolent Demiurge. We think they'll be convinced.

Osso Buco

6 veal osso buco, each tied around the middle	3 cloves garlic, minced
	1 cup white wine
Sea salt and freshly ground pepper	1 cup veal or chicken stock
Flour	1-1/2 cups canned Italian plum
2 tablespoons olive oil	tomatoes, chopped with juice
3 tablespoons butter	1 teaspoon fresh thyme leaves,
1 yellow onion, chopped	chopped
2 carrots, chopped	1 bay leaf
1 stalk celery, chopped	1 tablespoon chopped parsley

Preheat oven to 350 degrees.

Use a heavy-bottomed pot that can just accommodate all the veal shanks in one layer.

Season veal and dredge in flour, shake off excess.

Heat oil and butter in pan until hot, bubbles from butter will subside. Add veal and brown well on all sides. Remove veal and set aside.

---

[1] When someone says this, it's fun to ask them: "Well into what kind of a world would you *want* to bring a child?" The answer usually boils down to something like, "The kind of world where I could afford a Filipina nanny, then boarding school."

Sauté vegetables until just tender.

Return veal to pot along with remaining ingredients. Season lightly. Sauce will reduce and concentrate flavors. Stock should come two-thirds of the way up to the top of the veal. Bring to a simmer. Cover and place in lower portion of oven.

Cook 1 1/2 to 2 hours turning several times. Add a bit more stock if needed. The meat will be very tender and sauce thickened when ready. Adjust seasoning. Remove twine and serve with sauce and gremolata sprinkled on top.

Serves 6

GREMOLATA:

1/4 cup chopped parsley   2 cloves garlic, minced
2 teaspoons zested lemon peel

Combine all ingredients.

Drinking Song #3: A Snarky Song

One of our favorite drinking songs in the world is the catalogue of philosophers and their alleged drinking habits concocted by Monty Python's Flying Circus, as sung by the faculty of the University of Woolloomooloo. Yes, that's a real place, but it's not a real university, and the song is one of the funniest we've come across. It's republished all over the Internet. We were planning to reprint it here, but as old Robbie Burns once said, "The best-laid plans o' mice and men gang aft aglay."

What was it that ganged our aft? Well, if you're a fan of trivia, you might know that law books are still chock full of archaic regulations dating from centuries past, which legislatures never got around to repealing. For instance, in Florida, men aren't allowed to wear strapless gowns. In California, you can't shoot animals from a moving vehicle—except for whales. You can't drive barefoot in Alabama.

And apparently, in the state of New

York, you can't just take someone else's copyrighted material and pawn it off as your own. To which we say, "P-shaw!"

However, our publisher's legal staff has informed us that "P-shaw!" is not an all-purpose defense against suits alleging copyright infringement, so in lieu of hunting down the British loons who own this little ditty and asking permission, we decided it was easier simply to write a parody. The "parody privilege" was affirmed by the U.S. Supreme Court in *Campbell v. Acuff-Rose Music, Inc.* (1994), which ruled that our Founders intended the First Amendment to protect the right of 2 Live Crew to turn Roy Orbison's "Pretty Woman" into a rap song about a "big hairy woman." And we'd like to thank the court. We're sure that's exactly what James Madison had in mind.

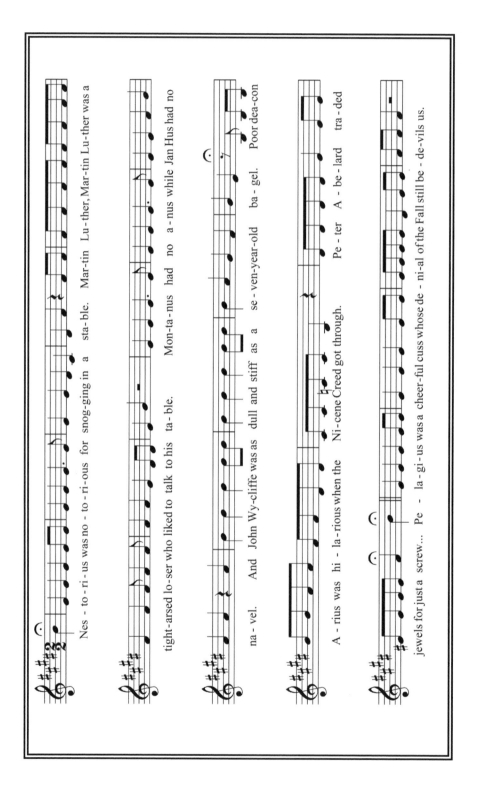

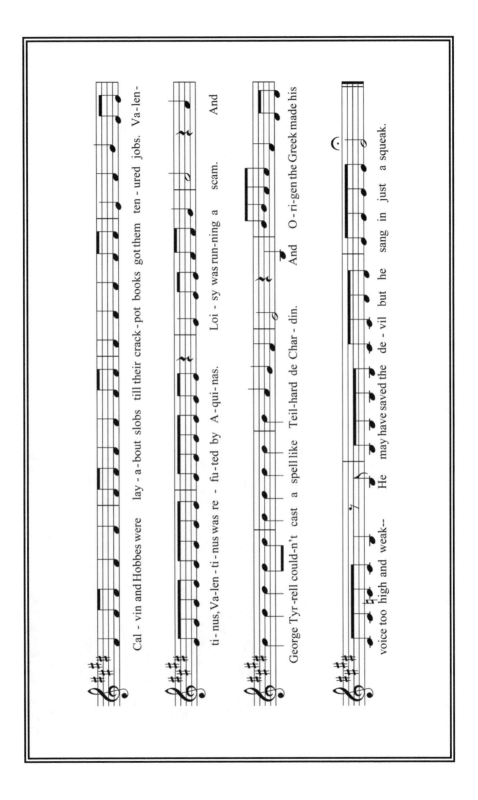

Gewurztraminer:
The Alsatians Need Better Neighbors

The folk of Alsace-Lorraine have a fascinating culture and history. As a borderland between two once-great European powers, they partake in the rich cultural traditions of the German Rhineland and of France. In these regions you'll find both good German sausage and fine French wines, sophisticated Gallic recipes and frothy Teutonic brews. One of the finest products made today in this region is Gewurztraminer —a light wine with floral tones, one of the few whites that goes well with meat dishes (especially hot cuisines, including, incongruously, Thai). As the incomparable resource Epicurious.com describes the wine, "The German word *gewürtz* means 'spiced,' and these wines are known for their crisp, spicy attributes. They're highly fragrant, with flavor characteristics of litchis, roses (or flowers in general), and spices such as cloves and nutmeg." In other words, it's essentially a German wine, now mostly made in France.

But then, the incessant mixture of the incompatible is a running theme in the region. Its people have kept alive medieval dialects which exist nowhere else, and their blend of Latin and Germanic folkways is perhaps the last trace remaining of the great Frankish empire created by Charlemagne, whose capital stood at Aix-la-Chappelle (Aachen). That empire allowed for the rebirth of high culture in the West after the fall of the western Roman empire, a renaissance led by the scholarly monk Alcuin. Charlemagne built so many churches, endowed so many monasteries, and brought peace to so many once-chaotic lands that after his death the Church declared him "blessed." However, he killed just a few too many pagan Saxons to quite make the grade as a saint.

But serving as the seat of a once-powerful country at the crossroads of two great nations can be a mixed blessing—just ask the Poles. The cultural enrichment provided by neighboring Germany and France frequently came to Alsace and Lorraine in the form of invading armies from one or both. Up through the seventeenth century, the region was a relatively peaceful region of the (German-speaking) Holy Roman Empire, with much of its territory controlled by prince-bishops. These ecclesiastical rulers were not exactly pacifists; like Pope Julius II, they sometimes were compelled to defend their territories by force. But they were always careful to obey canon law, which forbade clergymen to carry swords. Instead, they'd wield a mace.[1] The territory eventually became part of the prosperous, culturally diverse[2] Duchy of Burgundy—and fell into the lap of the Habsburgs after one of their many strategic weddings.

However, neither mace-wielding bishops nor marriage-minded Habsburgs could hold back the conquering French. It was in part to seize this wealthy region that French kings fought for the Protestants in the Thirty Years' War. In its aftermath, the grasping Louis XIV, who'd humbled the pope and reduced his nation's once-proud nobles to cringing commode-polishers at Versailles, annexed most of the provinces to France. When the rigid, centralized kingdom crumbled in 1789, most Alsatians and Lorrainers resented the utopian revolutionaries who came to power, and sided with the German and Austrian forces that tried to restore the monarchy. For this, many residents lost their homes and were forced to emigrate. By the time all the wars provoked by the Revolution and its heir Napoleon had ended, the region was exhausted—and divided over which neighbors it hated the most, the Germans or the French. When the dunderheaded Napoleon III provoked a war with Prussia in 1870, France was quickly crushed and plunged into chaos; the Paris Commune, applauded by Karl Marx, murdered dozens of clergy and religious, including the Archbishop of Paris. Anti-clerical forces came to the fore in France, where they still dominate today.

A newly united Germany "took back" Alsace and Lorraine, and thousands of French speakers left—including Alfred Dreyfus, whose loyalty to France would later be repaid by a sentence on Devil's Island, when he was falsely accused of spying for the Germans whom he'd fled. The German Kaiser, for his part, began persecuting Germany's (and Alsace-Lorraine's) Catholics, whom he saw as loyal to a foreign ruler. Meanwhile, the pope was a virtual prisoner of the Vatican, overrun by the forces of a hostile Kingdom of Italy. All in all, the 1870s may have been even worse for the Church than the 1970s . . . hard as that might be to believe.

One reason the French marched so eagerly into World War I was the hunger to avenge their 1870 defeat and take back these "lost" provinces. After three years of grinding slaughter and futility, by 1917 the warring powers were lurching towards a negotiated peace proposed by Pope Benedict XV and St. Karl I, the Austrian em-

---

[1] Ceremonial maces such as those carried by university presidents—and until Vatican II, by ceremonial guards appointed to cardinals—carry on this tradition. In our judgment, this detail of Church history is not so much scandalous as really cool.

[2] In the *positive* sense.

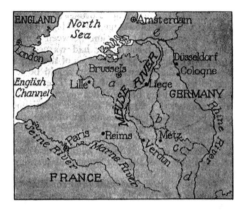

peror. Such a peace might have blocked the rise to power of the Bolsheviks (and other fanatics elsewhere), but it was prevented by Woodrow Wilson, who treasured a messianic vision to impose American-style democracy on foreign lands. [3] Wilson threw his campaign peace promises to the wind and America's men onto the Marne, ensuring the ultimate victory of the Anglo-French Entente. Bewildered by these events, the folk of Alsace-Lorraine saw in the post-war chaos an opportunity to get free of both the Germans and the French. In 1918, when the Kaiser abdicated, the locals declared themselves the Republic of Alsace and Lorraine, under the slogan "Not German, Not French, Not Neutral." This nation lasted only a week—then French troops marched in. We note that its short-lived government was led by the president of the beer-brewers union.

Wilson's idealism, French *realpolitik*, and a continued British blockade of starving Germany combined to create the lop-sided Treaty of Versailles. Anyone who has seen "Hogan's Heroes" knows what happened next.

Gin: This Liquor Left England Shaken, Not Stirred

Gin is one drink that no one is likely to associate with monks. In pure form, the stuff evokes Hogarth drawings like "Gin Lane" (pictured) and Dickens novels, full of sodden beggars sprawling in the gutter. However, add a single drop of dry vermouth and an olive, and Oliver Twist disappears, replaced by Sean Connery in a dinner jacket. It's funny how the mind works—especially when it's infused by a crisp, grain liquor flavored with juniper.

Gin was first developed commercially by a Dutch chemist at the University of Leyden named Franciscus de la Boe, as a tonic for indigestion. The drink (called "Genever") quickly became popular among the local Calvinists at war with Spain, offering them what the Spaniards sneeringly called "Dutch courage." This liquid spunk won out over Spanish silver, leaving the Dutch vastly wealthier than their onetime masters in Madrid. (It would take centuries for economists to figure out that precious metals did not constitute wealth so much as *currency*, so that import-

---

[3] Sound familiar? For the real story behind America's blundering entry into WWI, see *The War for Righteousness: Progressive Christianity, the Great War, and the Rise of the Messianic Nation* by Richard Gamble, (ISI Books: 2004).

ing huge quantities of silver from Peru achieved no more than printing boatloads of $100 bills. Massive inflation ruined the Spanish empire.)

Gin crossed the Channel with William of Orange, the Dutchman who usurped the British throne from the Catholic King James II (**see Drambuie**). Once in power, William encouraged Englishmen to make and drink gin, instead of wines and brandies from "enemy" Catholic countries such as France and Spain. Stronger than beer and cheaper than wine, gin soon became indispensable to the working class—which had been driven from the countryside into the cities by the "enclosure" of pastureland where their forefathers had tended sheep. The nobles, enriched by seizing land from Church-run abbeys, hospitals, and schools, got richer still by confiscating the grazing lands used by the poor.[4] According to the encyclopedic site Tastings.com:

> By the 1720s it was estimated that a quarter of the households in London were used for the production or sale of Gin. Mass drunkenness became a serious problem. The cartoonist Hogarth . . . shows a sign above a Gin shop that states, "Drunk for a penny/Dead drunk for twopence/Clean straw for Nothing."

It's widely believed that London's Scotland Yard, the first organized police force in the country's history, was founded to deal with the effects of mass gin consumption. No laws passed by Parliament could make much of a dent in gin drinking; it was hard to prohibit something so easy and cheap to make. During America's darkest years (1919–1933), it was gin (rather than, say, champagne) which our grandfathers made in their bathtubs.

But gin has its brighter side. If you travel through what is optimistically called the Developing World, you might notice a strange correlation: The places with the most democratic governments, most honest police, and fewest torture cellars per capita also turn out to be lands where gin and tonics are popular. This delightful drink, of course, was favored by British colonial officials, who used gin to kill the

---

[4] The new ruling class deflected popular discontent by stoking fears of "papist" plots—and riots aimed at the beleaguered English Catholics still clinging to their faith. In 1688, when William landed, mobs attacked the homes of Catholic citizens and embassies of Catholic nations.

TRAVEL

bitter taste of quinine—a drug that prevents malaria. Of all the colonial empires, the British was the most benevolent. Sure, they committed their share of abuses; just ask a Kenyan—or, if you've three hours to kill, an Irishman. However, compared with the record of other colonial powers, the British come off pretty well. They brought with them a preference for limited government, the rule of law, and maintaining order through negotiation rather than massacre. (Imagine how Gandhi's peaceful resistance would have fared against the Germans or the French.) This preference had deep roots in English culture—the same culture that made it possible for the United States to live up to its liberal constitution, as other young nations (such as Bolivar's Colombia) could not.

It has long been fashionable to associate this Anglo-Saxon love of liberty with Protestantism; the semi-official "Whig" view of history casts such intolerant Protestants as Elizabeth I, Oliver Cromwell, and William of Orange as heroes in the long march of freedom. America's founders certainly held this view; having drunk in the Whig theory with their mother's milk, they associated Catholicism with tyranny and Protestantism with limited government. Of course, the truth is more complicated. As intellectual historian Russell Kirk explains in *The Roots of American Order*, the "ancient liberties" cited by the likes of Jefferson and Franklin in fact dated not from the Reformation, but the Middle Ages. Nor were they unique to England, but existed in one form or another across Europe, from Spain and France to Germany, Switzerland, and the city-states of Italy. Limits to the arbitrary power of government such as parliaments, habeas corpus, trial by jury, and the right of rebellion against tyrannical kings all have their roots in the Common Law tradition—a synthesis of Church (Canon) law and feudal customs imported by the Germanic tribes who overwhelmed the Roman empire. It was only in the Renaissance that these ancient rights began to be questioned, by court intellectuals, funded by kings who sought greater power over their subjects. These "progressive" thinkers preferred everything classical to anything medieval; they touted the benefits of ancient Roman law, which allowed for no such limitations on the claims of monarchs. The "divine right" of kings asserted by King James I (and refuted by St. Robert Bellarmine) was the English manifestation of this "forward-looking" leap into ancient tyranny—which had become trendy all across Europe. Feudal lords, bishops, and popes resisted this drive towards centralized autocracy with mixed success—until the Reformation.

With Luther's revolt, monarchs suddenly had the option of seizing the Church's lands and wealth—again, in the name of progress. Those who exercised it became rich enough to cow the nobles and centralize power. Monarchs who remained Catholic could still wield this threat against the papacy, which feared losing more souls to the new religions. Kings demanded, and got, the right to name their own bishops, tax the Church, and squelch religious orders (such as the Jesuits) that insisted on the rights of subjects to resist abusive government. Ironically, it was in Protestant England that Roman law never quite caught on. The Anglican Church, born as a sad compromise with Caesar, was soon abandoned by the prosperous merchants of England's exploding seaports and manufactures—who adopted more radically Reformed theologies, such as Calvin's. To defend their right to resist the Anglican bishops and kings, these "dissenting" Protestants reached back to the Magna Carta and other medieval assertions of limited government—all of which dated from England's Catholic past, and partook of the Church's real teaching about the limits of governmental power. So it was a kinky irony when William of Orange landed in England with banners reading "The Liberties of England and the Protestant Religion I will maintain." In fact, those liberties were first invented by Catholics.

But then, so was gin. According to historian Davide Morena, of the Mattoni Drink Database, the first liquor based on juniper berries can be found in a series of recipes from twelfth-century Italy. It was made by monks.

CELEBRATE: Mark the stereotypical, icy WASP sensibility ushered in by William of Orange's victory with a dish of gin-laced grapefruit sorbet. If you really want to hammer home this historical point, you may substitute orange juice for grapefruit.

Salty Dog Sorbet

Use your favorite premium gin for this sorbet, which is good as an intermezzo, dessert, or cocktail.

2 large grapefruits, cut in half   1 cup powdered sugar
(remove seeds, if any)   1/4 cup + 2 tablespoons gin
1 cup orange juice

Squeeze grapefruit into measuring cup. Do not strain. Add orange juice to equal 3 cups.
    Pour into blender and whirl. Add sugar and whirl to dissolve. Lastly, add gin and blend.
    The flavor will be a bit strong to compensate for the dulling effect of freezing.
Chill for two hours.
    Turn in ice cream machine.

Makes 1 quart

Göttweig Abbey: Baroque Poverty in Wine Country

If you've ever known an Austrian (especially if you've dated one), you're familiar with their distinctive sensibility, their wry embrace of life as a paradox and a puzzle,[5] a quixotic journey best begun with tongue in cheek and Tabak in hand (**see Drinking Song #1**). Sometimes the Austrian spirit shades too far into cynicism for most Catholics' tastes—as in the plays of Arthur Schnitzler, the nudes of Egon Schiele, or the "Just So Stories" of Sigmund Freud. Still, you can't help loving a country that produced Franz Kafka, who reported that when he read aloud his Job-like tales of innocent weaklings persecuted by a cruel Providence—for instance, after being transformed into a giant cockroach—he and his friends would break up *laughing*. Only in Austria. . . .

It took almost 800 years of imperial history to produce the Austrian character, composed of equal parts white wine, dogma, and *Schadenfreude*. Through most of that time, the Habsburg dynasty used a small collection of German-speaking provinces as the basis of an empire which at one point ruled over Czechs, Slovaks, Hungarians, Poles, Ukrainians, Jews, Belgians, Croatians, Italians, Romanians, Turks, and even Aztecs. Except during ugly periods such as the Thirty Years' War, this empire was far more tolerant than most—allowing these cultures to flourish and intermingle, producing such wonderful hybrids as Baroque architecture, Jesuit theater, and Paprikaschnitzel. When the Reformation came, it's not surprising that a culture so accustomed to complexity was not won over by the grim simplifications offered by Luther and Calvin. In sticking to the apostolic Faith, and providing many thousands of the Jesuits who helped revive and restore it, the Austrians clung to the paradoxes they'd learn to treasure: divine grace *and* free will, the Bible *and* tradition, folk piety *and* enormous, ornate churches.

Such as the Abbey of Göttweig in the Wachau. This monastery stands incongruously atop a hill surrounded by almost empty countryside planted with vines. Even

---

[5] A busted Rubik's cube, to be specific. Erno Rubik was born in the Habsburg's second capitol, Budapest. Why are we not surprised?

though it now mainly draws tourists rather than pilgrims, it is still staffed by a dedicated corps of Benedictine monks who serve as parish clergy for the churches of the region. From the time of Charlemagne until the eighteenth century, monasteries such as Göttweig owned and tended the vineyards, planting grapes up almost impassable hillsides and nurturing a wide array of grapes, crafting varieties of wine still treasured by connoisseurs: Riesling, Grüner Veltliner, Yellow Muscatel, and Zweigelt.

Founded in 1072 by the Canons Regular, Göttweig managed by 1094 to become so lax that the local bishop imposed on its priests the Rule of St. Benedict, which includes vows of poverty, chastity, and obedience. Like most places guided by that devout but eminently practical Rule, the abbey flourished for centuries, becoming a center of learning, art, and culture. After another period of genteel decay in the 1500s, Göttweig ran out of monks,[6] and the place became uninhabited. Eager to fight the Reformation, the Habsburgs stepped in and restaffed the place, which soon became a center of the Catholic revival after the Council of Trent. When a fire destroyed the old medieval buildings in 1718, the monks reflected on the deeper meaning of the Benedictine spirit of poverty—and decided to build a new abbey based on the Spanish palace El Escorial. As the *Catholic Encyclopedia* notes, it was "a scheme so lavish that Abbot Gottfried was nearly deposed because of it."

While secularists may have sniped about the luxury of the building, the monks used their own money (much of it earned from wine-making) and constructed one of Europe's great architectural treasures—a building intended to give the common folk who came there to pray a glimpse of heavenly splendor. Artists, who otherwise would only have decorated the parlors of the elite, labored to illumine this church that would serve the poor, in the Baroque style designed to illustrate eternal truths in stained glass, marble, paint, and plaster. This mode of communicating religious truth was a far cry from what prevailed in Calvinist cities such as Geneva, where dour zealots had stripped the churches, smashed the stained glass, and painted over elaborate illustrations of the Gospel—leaving the city's temples whited sepulchers.

During the so-called Enlightenment, secularists and court intellectuals poured their contempt on monasteries and convents devoted to teaching "superstition" to the simple, and reciting "useless" prayers. They saw these institutions as Elmer Fudd viewed a live "wabbit"— a tasty meal for the taking. The Emperor Joseph II won praise from the irreligious likes of Voltaire by closing one-third of the monasteries in Austria-Hungary, expelling their priests, and stealing their land. The vine-

---

[6] There's a similar vocation crisis in Austria today. Take a glance at Klimt's women to see why celibacy must be a hard sell over there.

yards which monks had carefully tended were put up for sale, with the money going into the government's pocket.[7]

But the good work done by the monks did not go to waste. The complex varieties of grapes, and the scrupulous artistry put into growing and fermenting them was passed on to laymen—the very parishioners whom the monks served as priests. In the Wachau region surrounding Göttweig, the vineyards planted by Benedictines continue to flourish, in a variety of soils, and in combinations of depth, height, rainfall, sun, or shade that wine experts call "microclimates." Wachau is particularly known for the subtle variations in qualities of grapes which grow from one field to the next, and the complex combinations the wines grown there can achieve. In every glass of the local wine—on sale at the Göttweig gift shop, and served to retreatants—one can taste the love these long-dead monks lavished upon grape and ground.

CELEBRATE: Whether or not you enjoy Baroque architecture, you can sample one of the great hybrids born of Austrian culture by cooking up a dinner of Paprikaschnitzel, which enriches the Viennese style of cooking veal with a spicy sauce of peppers from Hungary. It goes beautifully with a bottle or two of white wine from the vineyards around the Göttweig Abbey, such as Domäne Wachau's Riesling "Terrassen" Federspiel, or Freie Weingartner's Grüner Veltliner.

Paprikaschnitzel

6–8 veal cutlets	1/2 cup chopped shallots
1/4 cup lemon juice	1 tablespoon sweet Hungarian paprika
Fine sea salt and freshly ground	1 cup chicken stock
black pepper	1/4 cup cream
3 tablespoons clarified butter	1/2 cup sour cream
Flour	Chopped parsley
1 tablespoon butter	

Marinate veal in lemon juice 10 to 15 minutes. In a large heavy- bottomed skillet heat butter. Season cutlets and dredge through flour. Gently shake off excess and slip into skillet.

Cook until browned on each side. Wipe out pan between batches except for the last one. The brown bits will be used in the sauce. Remove veal to baking sheet and keep warm in oven set to lowest temperature.

Add butter to pan and melt while stirring with a wooden spoon to loosen brown

---

[7] This rape of Church institutions is blandly described by historians as "secularization," a euphemism which was mirrored in the 1930s by the Nazis, who seized Jewish property and called it "Aryanization." Indeed, the book remains to be written on the commonalities between anti-Semitic and anti-clerical persecution.

bits. Add shallots. Cook until they begin to color and soften. Season with salt and pepper. Add paprika and stir to coat shallots. Cook for a few moments before adding stock. Start with 1/4 cup. Bring to a boil and reduce slightly before adding remaining stock. Reduce about 10 minutes. First add cream, then sour cream after reducing cream enough to coat the back of a wooden spoon.

Remove from heat. Adjust seasoning.

Arrange veal on serving platter. Spoon sauce over and sprinkle with parsley.

Serve with egg noodles or spaetzle.

Serves 4

Gout: A Gouty Man is Hard to Refine

The attentive reader will have noticed that we are not enamored of asceticism. All apart from the altar-smashing liturgical changes undertaken in its name, the aspect of the Second Vatican Council which troubles us the most is its "universal call to holiness." (*Lumen Gentium*, 32)[8] Read a certain way, this could mean that every layman is required to attain the spiritual heights once sensibly subcontracted to the clergy. And that, we fear, could lead to things like fasting and mortification, prac-

tices which (like chanting the Office and making Chartreuse) we prefer to leave to the professionals.

Nevertheless, in thinking about a disease like gout, we see that even worldliness can be taken too far. Look at Henry VIII. Just *look* at him (pictured). He barely fits in the frame.

As a young man, this son of the Tudor usurper Henry VII was slim, handsome, and learned. A consummately educated Renaissance man, Prince Henry was known for skillfully dancing the gavotte, writing poetry and even music. He composed an eloquent refutation of

[8] To learn more, visit *www.prosanctity.org*, the U.S. Web site of the International Pro-Sanctity Movement. Which raises the question—where are the Church's *anti*-sanctity organizations? We can think of a few, but we'd rather invite the reader to compile a list for himself.

Luther's Eucharistic heresies, really *earning* the title granted him by Pope Leo X, "Defender of the Faith." He must have seemed a candidate for philosopher-king, of the sort portrayed by Erasmus in his hopeful book, *The Education of a Christian Prince*.

Alas, Henry did not so much "grow in office" as *expand*. Spurning his cautious father's old advice, Henry bankrupted the Crown in foreign wars, enraged his subjects by raising taxes, and soon had to dismiss (and behead) the officials he'd appointed to squeeze more gold out of his subjects. Hungry for land, Henry annexed Wales and outlawed its language. Eager to control his subjects' lives, he imposed the death penalty for homosexuality and witchcraft. Henry's passion for hunting ended in a serious accident, which left him incapable of exercise—without diminishing his passion for fine food and wenching. The result was morbid obesity and a dose of syphilis—which he probably passed to the three wives he divorced and the two he beheaded, a wide variety of mistresses, and each of his children.

This illness no doubt helped kill off six of the seven children born to his first wife, the saintly Catherine of Aragon, leaving Henry with no male heir. The ever-pragmatic Henry decided to replace Catherine with someone young and fertile. He began the tortured negotiations with the Vatican portrayed in Shakespeare's least convincing play, *Henry VIII*, to gain an annulment. Under pressure from Catherine's nephew, the emperor Charles V, the Vatican refused Henry's request. Undaunted, Henry entered a bigamous marriage with his pregnant mistress, the 12-fingered Anne Boleyn—whose sister he'd seduced and infected years before. Enraged that any authority on earth dared naysay him, Henry decided to pull his kingdom out of the Catholic Church, and appoint himself the local pope. A compliant Parliament handed the churches over to the state, and declared any Englishman remaining loyal to the pope guilty of treason. Bewildered Carthusian monks were dragged out of their cells and burned at the stake, while humanists such as Cardinal John Fisher and Henry's old friend, Sir Thomas More, were publicly beheaded— and a persecution of the Church began which would continue (with short interruptions) for centuries.

Another motive which probably goaded Henry was hunger for gold; his Machiavellian ministers such as Thomas Cromwell looked hungrily at the savings compiled over centuries by monks and nuns at hundreds of abbeys across England. In one of the greatest acts of vandalism in Western history, Henry in 1535 ordered his ministers to travel the countryside closing monasteries, seizing their wealth, closing the schools and hospitals they ran for the poor (who had no other social support), even pulling the lead from the roofs of these magnificent buildings. As a result, dozens of historic structures such as Glastonbury Abbey simply collapsed, leaving only what Shakespeare called "Bare ruined choirs, where late the sweet birds sang."[9] Those "sweet birds" were the monks and friars who'd once sung in prayer, transcribed precious manuscripts, and even made wine.

Of course, Henry was too fond of wine and fine food, which may explain the gout that spelled the end of his dancing days. We say "may explain" because while we know what brings on syphilis and Anglicanism, the causes of gout are still in doubt. Even in Henry's day, however, the disease was associated with excessive consumption of wine and rich foods such as sweetbreads, kidneys, liver, brains, sardines, anchovies, and shellfish: all in Henry's diet, the diet of a king. These foods are, it turns out, high in uric acid—the substance which forms tiny crystals in the joints of a gouty man, typically beginning with his big toe.

As it progresses, gout can become crippling and intractable, like the schism Henry started to sate his appetites. Much as we hate to say it of a layman, Henry could have done with some mortification of the flesh, and fewer visits to the wine cellar. Even the Anglican apologist C.S. Lewis pictured the founder of his church roasting in Hell,[10] and it would seem sectarian for us to disagree.

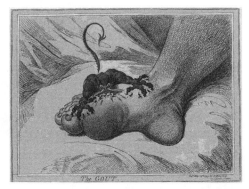

The GOUT.

The church fathered by Henry's reckless passions (especially its American, Episcopal branch) has since its founding been known for worldly coziness, and an extreme aversion to "extremism," by which the good Anglican fathers really meant "principle." Looking at the state of Henry's body at the end (some eyewitnesses claimed his corpse finally exploded), and of the Episcopal Church today, we draw a sobering lesson: Too much wine and wenching can lead not just to gout, but to lesbian bishops.

Now there's no reason to react to Henry's bloated toe by rushing into Puritanism. Just as every heresy has an equal, opposite error which results from overreacting to it, there's also an illness out there called "pseudo-gout" mirroring gout's symptoms, but is in fact an entirely different disease. Doctors don't know what

---

[9] One historian estimated that all the wealth Henry obtained by this rape of the Church he spent in a single year, on a failed campaign against France.

[10] From *The Screwtape Letters*: "Oh, to get one's teeth again into a Farinata, a Henry VIII, or even a Hitler! There was real crackling there; something to crunch; a rage, an egotism, a cruelty only just less robust than our own. It put up a delicious resistance to being devoured. It warmed your inwards when you'd got it down."

causes it, but we bet that it's brought on by drinking non-alcoholic wine and beer, and eating high-tech, low-fat substitutes for the fancy foods you really crave. The lesson we draw from all this is moderation in all things—even in one's pursuit of moderation.

Grapes, God, and the Vines of Sodom

If you research the treatment of grapes in the Bible, you'll find it full of references to wine making and wine. As soon as the waters receded from the Flood, Noah set about planting grapes. Throughout the Old Testament, when Yahweh offered encouragement to His people about the Promised Land—to keep them trudging through the desert, spurning idols—He reminded them that the land was fertile enough to sustain vineyards. After Moses sent scouts to see if a region was worth settling, they didn't bother bringing back sheaves of wheat:

> When they came to Nachal Eshkol, they cut a branch and a cluster of grapes, which two men carried on a frame. Because of the grape-cluster that the Israelites cut there, the place was named Cluster Valley. (Numbers 13: 23–24, pictured)

Wine was one of the offerings God required of Israelites at the Temple, and an essential element at Passover. This meant it was used at the Last Supper, which Catholics recall was the world's first Mass.[11] This teaches Christians that from the beginning one of God's greatest gifts to men has been the fruit of the vine—and we don't mean Raisinettes.

However, the ubiquity of wine making and drinking in Scripture makes some of our separated brethren squeamish. When the Church of God Bible Study ("the most popular Bible Study resource in the world") pointed out the biblical references above, and the author admitted to drinking a single glass of wine a day, he was

---

[11] Alas, it wasn't in Latin—but at least there weren't any altar girls.

flooded with angry letters from readers accusing him of sinful drunkenness. (Those readers must have a pretty low tolerance.) These abstemious Evangelicals argued that the Church of God was being too literal: the Bible authors really must have meant *unfermented grape juice.*

Which all goes to show that sometimes even fundamentalists often find themselves straying from the plain text of Scripture into the airy realm of allegory. Other passages where they feel compelled to do this include:

- "Take and eat; this is my body." (Matthew 26: 14–15)
- "You are Peter, and on this rock I will build my church" (Matthew 16: 18).

And the ever popular:

- "What God has joined together, let man not separate." (Matthew 19: 6)

On the other hand, the Bible does indeed warn against drunkenness and debauchery. For instance, in Deuteronomy 32:32, it is said of sinful Israelites that "their vine is of the vine of Sodom, and of the fields of Gomorrah." Bible scholars and oenophiles are divided over which varietal was produced in Sodom, but we're pretty convinced it was white Zinfandel.

....

Loopholes in the Ten Commandments #3: Remember the Sabbath Day, to Keep It Holy

This is one of those commandments harder to keep than it sounds. At first, it seems that God is simply cutting us a little slack, asking that we follow His example and rest on the seventh day. And on that day, we should remember to worship Him. In fact, the main reason for avoiding busy-ness on the Sabbath is to sanctify it, to set it aside like the lamb Abel saved for sacrifice, or the first-fruits offered by the Jews to the Lord.

But it wasn't long before the Israelites realized that resting once a week can turn out to be a lot of work. As time went on, the Lord got much more specific about what tasks he didn't want to see anybody performing on the Sabbath. It started with:

- No cooking.
- No plowing.
- No reaping.
- No lighting a cook fire.
- No gathering wood.
- No carrying burdens.
- No putting burdens onto animals.
- No bringing sheaves into the house.
- No buying or selling.
- No taking medicine before the Sabbath, if it will keep working on the Sabbath.
- No pressing grapes (this is getting serious!)
- No gathering manna which had fallen miraculously from the sky.
- No traveling, except to Temple.

And the penalty for violating any of these was death. (Exodus 31:14–15; Numbers 15:32–36)

Remembering what happened to cities like Sodom and wives like Lot's, the Pharisees who came to interpret the Law were prone to make these rules ever stricter, just to be on the safe side. In fact, as the *Catholic Encyclopedia* points out,

> At the time of the Machabees the faithful Jews allowed themselves to be massacred rather than fight on the Sabbath. . . . Under the influence of pharasaic rigorism a system of minute and burdensome regulations was elaborated, while the higher purpose of the Sabbath was lost sight of. The Mishna treatise Shabbath enumerates thirty-nine main heads of forbidden actions, each with subdivisions. Among the main heads are such trifling actions as weaving two threads, sewing two stitches, writing two letters, etc. To pluck two ears of wheat was considered as reaping, while to rub them was a species of threshing. . . . To carry an object of the weight of a fig was carrying a burden.

Very pious Orthodox Jews to this day maintain some version of this ancient rigor. We have friends who won't answer the phone, turn on a light, or tear a piece of toilet paper on the Sabbath—this means that for them a day's rest requires a bit of . . . planning.

One of the ways Jesus asserted His divinity was to flout the letter of the Law in favor of its spirit—for instance, by healing the sick on the sacred day, and proclaiming, "The Sabbath was made for man, not man for the Sabbath. The Son of Man is lord even of the Sabbath." (Mark 2:27–28) After His death, Jesus engaged in some really egregious Sabbath-breaking, spending Holy Saturday mucking around in the underworld to reclaim the souls of the just from Limbo, and take them to Heaven.

Jesus' most serious snub of the Sabbath, however, was His decision to raise himself from the dead on Sunday. Because Easter occurred on the first day of the week, the early Christians took that day, instead, as their Sabbath, in order to rest and meet for their Eucharistic meals. Indeed, they began to refer to Sunday as the "eighth" (or eternal) day.

Christian practice never attained the strictness of Jewish law concerning the Sabbath. However, we do honor its spirit. As the Catechism of the Catholic Church teaches: (#2172) "God's action is the model for human action. If God 'rested and was refreshed' on the seventh day, man too ought to 'rest' and should let others, especially the poor, 'be refreshed.' The Sabbath brings everyday work to a halt and provides a respite. It is a day of protest against the servitude of work and the worship of money." An admirable sentiment. It's certainly appealing to hear that one has a religious obligation not to engage in servile (manual) labor on Sundays. Let the dead bury the dead, and let those leaves rake themselves.

It's a little less comforting to realize that we aren't supposed to cause *other people*[12] to do such labor on Sundays, either—lest we deny them the rest to which they have a right. Precisely for this reason, the Church has always supported laws restricting what kind of businesses can operate on Sundays. For those Americans who include consumerism and capitalism as part of their creed, this can cause a crisis of conscience. Think of it as a tiny martyrdom, every time you have to spend your Saturday working on the yard. Remind yourself, "I'm just like St. Thomas More. . . ."

The other part of this commandment seems like a slam-dunk: Get to Mass. Even lackluster Catholics should be able to manage that. In the bad old "pre-conciliar" days, most American papists did; in 1958, 74 percent of U.S. Catholics attended Sunday Mass. After 30 years of renewal, that number had dropped to 58 percent. There's really no excuse for this. Some dissenting Catholics complain that they feel disaffected by a Church whose doctrines have not been updated to suit the times; conversely, when the priest stopped facing the altar, some traditionalists stopped darkening the door. We can't endorse either view. As far as we're concerned, if God took the trouble to create the universe, become a man and die to redeem it, the least you could do is to acknowledge Him. (As any Jewish dad would say, "Some gratitude would be *nice*. That's all I'm asking. . . .")

It's not as if you had to make a pilgrimage to Jerusalem ("though a visit from time to time would be *nice*"). The Church is a worldwide organization with low prices, friendly service, and outlets located conveniently near you. Think of it as Wal Mart. Or better yet, a dollar store—since that's how much most Americans

---

[12]Yes, this does include underpaid Mexicans.

typically drop in the collection. If more of us did the math to figure out that this adds up to a whopping 52 bucks a year, we might think through whether this really covers our share of the Holy Water bill—much less the living costs of the underpaid priest, the light bill, or the deficit run by the parish's struggling school. How's this for a church reform: Any employed American who can afford cable TV should up his weekly collection cash to something like $20, or the cost of spending 45 minutes not at church but at Chili's. At least in church the staff don't have to wear "flair."

Agoston Haraszthy:
Call Him Johnny Grapeseed

Willie Nelson once wrote that his "heroes have always been cowboys." We hate to disagree with Willie on anything, but our heroes have always been European aristocrats. Not the pasty-faced jet-trash you encounter nowadays snorting heroin in the Hamptons, but old heroes of culture and Catholicism like Alexis de Tocqueville, Klaus von Stauffenberg—and Agoston Haraszthy, the Hungarian count who came here in 1840 and virtually created the wine industries in two American states—California and Wisconsin.

Yes, Wisconsin. That was the first spot where Haraszthy settled and attempted to plant European grapes from a much warmer climate. Frosty winters killed most of his plants, and Haraszthy sensibly switched to brewing beer. But his heart was still set on wine. He looked for balmier shores, which he soon found in California, newly conquered by the U.S. from Mexico. Haraszthy must have been something of a swashbuckler; he so impressed the locals of San Diego County that they elected him their very first sheriff. (Indeed, we first learned about Haraszthy from the San Diego Sheriff's Department, which is justly proud of its gun-toting, grape-pressing founder.) As the San Diego sheriffs boast:

> After settling in San Diego, Haraszthy studied soil conditions and learned much about the flora and suitable cultivation in the arid climate of the region. He learned about the Mission grape which he was surprised to find was of true European origin. He noted defects in the quality of the wine and he became convinced that plantings of nobler varieties could be commercially viable. He sensed that by planting vines brought directly from Europe he could realize his old dream of producing wine of a quality that could compete with good Hungarian

and other European wines. It was here in San Diego that he first began to preach that good wine can only be made from good grapes.

The grapevines Haraszthy was working with had been planted three hundred years before by Franciscans who founded the missions; indeed, just before fumbling its war against the U.S. and losing half its territory, the Mexican government managed to steal these buildings and vineyards from the unarmed friars. So now the estates were up for grabs. Haraszthy bought some old mission land and planted new European grapevines, including now-famous varietals (**see Zinfandel**).

However, this time the climate proved too warm, so Haraszthy moved north. Attracted to the legacy of the friars, Haraszthy purchased a plot near the Mission Dolores in San Francisco in 1853. There he started greenhouses, nurturing plants from Europe. Eventually, he settled in the Sonoma Valley, where he planted some 80,000 vines, creating the first commercially viable winery in California. This makes Haraszthy a very important American—as if he'd been the man to introduce cotton to Mississippi. Except without the slaves.

Haraszthy came to an heroic, if unhappy end. After losing much of his winery in a fire, the intrepid aristocrat looked for greener pastures in Nicaragua, where he started a sugar plantation. After losing his wife to yellow fever, Haraszthy was disconsolate, and decided to return to California. On the way, his boat sank, and he was eaten by a crocodile. We'd like to see a cowboy top *that*.

....

Highballs and High Society

When it comes to such complex topics as theology and mixology, misconceptions breed like mayflies. Few laymen could explain how a Church founded by an itinerant carpenter ended up allied with aristocrats, so they assume it's faintly scandalous. If we don't understand the history and social teachings of our Church, we know even less about the drinks we're mixing. We're confused at once about high theology, high society, and highballs.

Where there's a vacuum of fact, legends rush in. For instance, Catholics somehow get the idea that the Church believes in absolute, global equality—except that it took us almost 2,000 years to realize this. Or we

imagine that any drink served in a short glass is a proper highball. Few of us realize the true price exacted by our ignorance, until we're flummoxed in an argument with a Stalinist, or a dinner guest gags on our "innovative" cocktail of Galliano and grapefruit juice.

Now, if you've read our book on the saints (*The Bad Catholic's Guide to Good Living*), you'll see that we've nothing against the recreational use of legends. While we prefer medieval folktales involving martyrs' tongues that go on preaching long after they're beheaded (St. Livinus, feast day Nov. 12), in a pinch an urban legend will do. In fact, they can make one's day. What could be more delightful than to learn (by email, of course) that:

- Public restrooms across the country are infested by venomous "two-striped telamonia spiders" lurking beneath the seats.
- A teenage girl in California went swimming and got impregnated by octopus eggs.
- Toilets flush counterclockwise in Australia.
- Drinking Visine can cause diarrhea.
- Jesus married Mary Magdalene and fathered a race of French petty kings, but Opus Dei is killing nuns to cover it up.

To all of which we say, "Would that it were true . . ."

We would especially like to believe the theories of David Icke,[1] a former British soccer player who "discovered" the fact that the world has been dominated, for the *past 10,000 years,* by a race of alien lizard-men who can take on human form. According to Icke, keeping up a human appearance is hard work, and if you stare at George Bush, or Queen Elizabeth, long enough, eventually you can get a glimpse of lizard. Or if you want a shortcut, Icke suggests, there's a surefire way of seeing the lizard-men: Just drop a little LSD. That's right, this wonder drug can pierce the veil of reptilian illusion . . . *which is precisely why it's illegal!* In case you were wondering. Icke's theory, of course, casts Church history in a fascinating, innovative light. (For instance, he argues that Jesus had a long, darting tongue.)

Some people seem to spend much of their time disseminating such stories (you probably know a few, and have learned how to block their emails). Others (as puzzlingly) devote themselves to debunking these stories. The entertaining Web site, Snopes.com, is a virtual Wikipedia of misinformation, arranged conveniently by categories. The next time an ex-fiance sends you a warning about the lizard-men, before you invest in reptile repellent we suggest you check with Snopes.

If contemporary Americans are a little too credulous about the rumors they pass along, they're entirely too promiscuous about the drinks they mix and serve. There

---

[1] David Icke, *The Biggest Secret* (The Isle of Wight: Bridge of Love Publications, 1999). We can't recommend this book highly enough—it's much funnier than anything we'll ever write.

are entire categories of cocktails whose names alone induce the gag reflex, such as "Sex on the Beach," "Dirty Girl Scout," and others we'd rather not name. (One rhymes with "gourd spasm.") If you live near a university, you probably pass by shops where the once-delightful daiquiri has been jazzed up into a nearly toxic Slushy, and is served to coeds from enormous, whirring machines that dispense drinks with names like the "Horizontal Freshman." Call us prudes, but we do not approve.

In fact, a proper highball is made in only one way: with equal parts rye whiskey and ginger ale, in a tall glass full of ice. Acceptable variations include substituting scotch for rye or club soda for ginger ale. This is enough for us, and should suffice for anybody. Sorry, but we feel we have to be strict about this. Good people, don't you realize that *our country is at war?*

Likewise, we'd like to narrow the range of debate over Church teaching on equality and hierarchy to exclude the most egregious sorts of nonsense. For starters, the theory once popular on the far Right in France, which asserted that the Church existed precisely in order to suppress the destructive, anti-social egalitarianism found . . . in the Gospels. At one point, many leading Catholic intellectuals (including a young Jacques Maritain) subscribed to this notion, which was propounded by the extreme royalist Charles Maurras. The movement he led, the Action Française, was at one point the largest pro-Catholic political force in France—which goes to show how desperate the Church's situation has been in that country since along about 1789. In 1927, the movement and its leader were condemned by Pope Pius XI.

Embracing the opposite error are the partisans of Liberation Theology, a baptized Marxist theory which once dominated Church circles in Latin America and Western Europe. (For some reason, we can't think why, it never caught on in Eastern Europe, and took rather a nose-dive after 1989.) This theory, still popular in watered-down form in certain circles on the Catholic left, asserts that Jesus' saving mission largely consisted in the attempt to transform society and abolish economic and social inequalities—establishing a Kingdom of Christ that was, indeed, "of this world."

We find a more balanced view in the writings of Pope Leo XIII. In paragraph 22 of his most famous encyclical, *Rerum Novarum*, Pope Leo teaches that the prosperous are indeed obliged by charity (not justice) to share with the needy. "True, no one is commanded to distribute to others that which is required for his own needs and those of his household; nor even to give away what is reasonably required to keep up becomingly his condition in life, 'for no one ought to live other than becomingly.' But, when what necessity demands has been supplied, and one's standing fairly taken thought for, it becomes a duty to give to the indigent out of what remains over." In other words, prosperous people, social classes, or countries are not obliged to abolish inequality. Wealthy Catholics need not give away so much that they become middle- or working-class, and prosperous nations need not transfer their "surplus" GNP to the developing world. Indeed, secular economists such as Milton Friedman have demonstrated the perverse effects of careless foreign aid—which frequently devastates local business, and retards the economic development of countries.

But this is no argument for complacency in the face of grinding poverty. Pope Leo goes on to write "But the laws and judgments of men must yield place to the laws and judgments of Christ the true God, who in many ways urges on His followers the practice of almsgiving—'It is more blessed to give than to receive' and who will count a kindness done or refused to the poor as done or refused to Himself—'As long as you did it to one of My least brethren you did it to Me.'" This tells that in the Divine Economy, there are few more prudent investments than money wisely given to help the poor, especially when it helps them attain self-sufficiency and dignity.[2] Think of it as stockpiling "cups of cold water" (Matthew 10:42) in the divine refrigerator. As the old saying goes, give a man a drink, and he drinks for a day. Teach him to make a drink, and he drinks for the rest of his life.

··

Hospitality: Crashing with the Benedictines

If you've read this far, you know that we are big fans of the Benedictines. They united the Eastern asceticism of solitary monks like Simon Stilites, who lived for decades on a pillar, with a practical, Western concern that every Christian serve the community. In most of their monasteries, this amounts to a daily round of activities combining spiritual reflection with useful labor. Their founder, St. Benedict (480–543) asserted the holiness of everyday work, adopting the motto *"Ora et Labora."* As he wrote in Chapter 48 of his founding Rule: "Idleness is the enemy of the soul; and therefore the brethren ought to be employed in manual labor at certain times, at others, in devout reading." If you've any friends who spent time as a

---

[2] One of our favorite charities can be found at Gardenharvest.org; it collects money to buy oxen, cows, goats, sheep, and chickens for needy farmers around the world. Come on, pony up, and give the gift of a goat!

Benedictine monk or nun, they'll tell you that their founder wasn't kidding. Whatever you might have seen in romantic English paintings, Benedictines don't spend much time in Gothic gardens gazing mistily into the distance. They're too busy mopping floors, preparing food, shearing sheep, making soap or gathering grapes—when they're not getting up in the middle of the night to sing and pray.

We can't concretely measure the effects of all that prayer (though double-blind laboratory studies are underway),[3] but the fruits of Benedictine work are all around us—especially in our libraries. During the Dark Ages, Benedictine monks and nuns were the only people interested in recopying the basic texts of Western civilization. So if you had to read Thucydides in college, you have long-dead, anonymous Benedictines to thank. The order also pioneered new methods of farming to help millions avoid starvation, so perhaps it's responsible for overpopulation, too. Religious orders developed Europe's first universities, so if you lose money betting on college football—again, you can blame the monks. Indeed, without the Benedictines and other orders they inspired, Europe might have turned into something very different. It might look more like Libya.

But perhaps the most attractive aspect of the Benedictine spirit is its religious embrace of hospitality. Living as he did in the ashes of a Roman empire overrun by barbarians, Benedict knew that the communities he founded would be islands of order, and decreed that they serve as safe havens for strangers. Indeed, the saint thought this important enough that he wrote it into his Rule:

> Let all guests who arrive be received as Christ, because He will say: "I was a stranger and you took Me in" (Mt 25:35). And let due honor be shown to all, especially to those "of the household of the faith" (Gal 6:10) and to wayfarers. . . . In the greeting let all humility be shown to the guests, whether coming or going; with the head bowed down or the whole body prostrate on the ground, let Christ be adored in them as He is also received." (Chapter 53)

Even in today's overcivilized Western Europe, Benedictines still offer such a welcome. This means that at ancient abbeys across the continent, any shaggy stranger

---

[3] No, they aren't.

with a knapsack full of Lacan and a Eurail pass can crash for several days at a time with a group of almost silent celibates in robes, so long as he doesn't disrupt the community (for instance, by trying to "share" his dissertation). It happens more often than you'd think.

This spirit of hospitality manifests itself in a wide variety of ways, at different communities. For example, the monastery of Andechs in Bavaria—endowed by that glorious lunatic King Ludwig I—operates a profitable farm. The monks make the modest claim that Andechs "is a place where the monastic life and modern economic thinking go hand-in-hand." Andechs Benedictines offer their guests fine food and locally crafted beer, boasting that their Bräustüberl and Klostergasthof, offer "the cultivated hospitality which is keeping with the centuries-old Benedictine tradition. In these traditional facilities and on the Beer Terrace, the gastronomic wellbeing of guests from around the world is attended to. . . . Today visitors from all over the world enjoy the hearty beers and delicious Bavarian foods within the tradition-laden walls of the Andechs Bräustüberl." These enterprising monks even stage an annual symposium on "Art and Beer." Now *that's* Bavarian.

A very different approach to Benedictine welcome can be found at Camillus House, a homeless shelter in Miami-Dade County, Florida. Founded in 1960 by the Little Brothers of the Good Shepherd, Camillus House provides a whole range of social services to impoverished residents and new immigrants, inspired by "the deeply held belief that every human being is precious in the eyes of the Lord and deserves love, respect, and a chance to live a dignified life." Like the monks at Andechs, the dedicated staff at Camillus House cite St. Benedict's Rule as their inspiration—though we doubt they offer guests the same quality of beer.

If you'd like to spend a few nights as a guest of the brethren, check out the useful guides to monasteries that carry on St. Benedict's tradition at *www. monasteriesofitaly.com*; here you'll find guides to hospitable cloisters in Italy, France, and Spain.

Hotter Than Hell: The Burning Question

Call us superstitious, but we don't like to joke about things like roasting in Hell for all eternity. And we're not that fond of schnapps. At one of our parties, we're as likely to serve the cocktail called "Hotter Than Hell" as we are to pass around a can of Cheez Whiz for guests to spray in their mouths, and wash down with a Budweiser as they sit around watching NASCAR. Still, like the editors of the *Oxford English Dictionary*, we aim here for encyclopedic completeness, so here's how to make "Hotter Than Hell":

> Mix up two kinds of schnapps, Rumple Minze and Goldschlager, over ice.

Ah, the banality of evil. . . .

There's another schnapps which by itself evokes the condition of perdition: DeKuyper's Hot Damn, a cinnamon drink that cloys the tongue and burns the

throat. (Who's hogging the Cheez Whiz? Come *on!*)

But the very fact that people feel driven to make up drinks expressing bravado on the subject of damnation suggests that it even makes atheists a little nervous. That childless vegan couple in front of you going 54 mph in the fast lane in the Volvo hybrid with the Darwin fish and the pro-abortion bumper sticker—these people don't just believe but hope, devoutly *hope*, that God does not exist. That death is simply a Doors song: "The End."

Thinking about souls in Hell, we're tempted to agree.[4]

The existence of Hell is a doctrine taught by the Church at the highest levels of authority, based on numerous statements in the New Testament from Jesus' own lips, so it's not going anywhere. Ingenious theologians have tried at various times to "nuance" this hideous reality to the point of disappearance, but they could never quite manage it. Like the rock band KISS (who recorded the goofball song, "Hotter Than Hell"), whenever you think that Hell might finally break up, it always launches a comeback tour.

---

[4]Just tempted, mind you. . . .

The Church Father Origen speculated that God's will to save sinners and His mercy are so great, even the Devil and his angels will someday be reconciled. This optimistic opinion was condemned by an ecumenical council. More recently, the great theologian Hans Urs von Balthasar (made a cardinal by Pope John Paul II) wrote a profoundly appealing book, *Dare We Hope That All Men Are Saved?*, which argues that we may—that the statements in the Gospel asserting God's will to redeem all mankind counterbalance warnings of the state where the "worm dieth not, and the fire is not quenched." (Mark 9:44) We hope he's right, but we're not entirely convinced. So you might say we *dare to hope* that we might dare hope.

Such a theory at least proves a corrective to the brand of Catholicism some older people might remember—and which James Joyce portrayed in his autobiographical *A Portrait of the Artist as a Young Man*. Theologians and popular (extremely popular!) preachers for centuries assumed as a matter of course that few souls would ever be saved, while the bulk of humanity was sure to end up as a "*massa damnata.*" The Church and the Sacraments were essentially a means of sewage reclamation, by which a tiny proportion of souls might be rescued and put to good use. To this day, if you happen to know the wrong sort of people, you're likely to get from them encouraging email forwards such as the sermon by St. Leonard of Maurice, "The Fewness of the Saved," asserting:

> The Bible also tells us that *only two Hebrews out of two million* entered the Promised Land after going out of Egypt, and that *only four* escaped the fire of Sodom and the other burning cities that perished with it. All of this means that the number of the damned who will be cast into fire like straw is *far greater* than that of the saved. . . .

What's striking, at least to us, is the *glee* with which our dour friends pass on this prognostication, as if it proved to them that they were right to abandon their local parish, and join that schismatic chapel behind the laundromat that dispenses anti-Semitic pamphlets. Or worse, it suggests that they agree with those critics of von Balthasar who lambasted the learned Fr. Richard Neuhaus, when he too dared hope. As Neuhaus wrote:

A different and much more troubling objection is that it makes no sense to be a Christian if, in fact, one can be saved without being a Christian. In this view, the damnation of others, maybe of most others, is essentially related to the reason for being a Christian. The joy of our salvation is contingent upon the misery of their damnation. . . . Such a perverse view is also more than a little like that of the laborers in the vineyard who complained that those who came at the last hour received the same reward as those who had worked all day.[5]

Now you needn't buy von Balthasar's whole hog, and believe that no one is likely to be damned, to find the traditional theories regarding Hell a little puzzling. When apologists such as C.S. Lewis offer arguments for the possibility of damnation, they make a great deal of sense: Surely God does not force His mercy upon us. A soul that genuinely refuses the offer of spiritual matrimony with Christ will not be abducted and held in a harem. If we believe, with the Church, that Divine Grace is resistible, we must hold that souls can indeed be damned—even though the Church has never officially taught that any human beings have joined the devil in Hell. Still, it seems pretty likely.

If you think of someone like Hitler (or, if you prefer, the railroad executive who tore down New York's Penn Station) persevering in his sins to the very end, frozen in hatred of entire peoples (or Beaux Arts buildings), it's easy to imagine him hardening his heart against the offer of repentance. Conceived of this way, as a grim choice made out of pride in the teeth of mercy, it's possible to make sense of the idea of Hell. So far, so good.

But now comes what we must regretfully call the bait-and-switch. Once you have accepted this argument for the possibility that hardened moral criminals can fight their way into Hell, the reasons for people going there seem to multiply. You can end up in the eternal microwave for any unrepented mortal sin—spanning everything from blasphemies committed against the Blessed Sacrament by mobs of murderous anarchists to a teenaged boy's impure thoughts. What began as a fitting end for genocidal tyrants is soon invoked as the punishment due a lusty unmarried couple who "went too far" before their car was buried in a mudslide. Unless, of course, they achieved perfect contrition[6] on the way down. And perfect contrition, as St. Leonard reminds us, is virtually impossible to achieve. Particularly during a mudslide.

Thinking this way about God and His justice makes it harder to love Him, we have to say—and suggests that for most of the human race, the Good News of

[5]Fr. Richard Neuhaus, "Will All Be Saved?", *First Things* (August/September, 2001).
[6] A hatred for one's sin entirely unmotivated by fear of punishment, but only by a pure love of God.

Christianity is really the worst news in history. As a wag once had it, "We regret to inform you that Christ is risen."

But this is not the end of the story. The Church has loosened the screws on all of us by invoking the insights of psychology to explain why many objectively mortal sins, particularly those committed out of frailty rather than pride, may in practice be viewed more forgivingly by God, Who sees in our hearts and knows our true culpability. For this reason, the Church has stopped denying Christian burial to poor souls who died by suicide. By extension, we're encouraged to offer mercy generously, and ask for it continually. The Divine Mercy devotion revealed to St. Faustina paints a rather encouraging picture of the Divine Economy—not quite so much like a potato famine, where we're fighting for mouthfuls of grass.

What is more, there is warrant in Scripture itself for a hopeful attitude about the salvation of the many. As Fr. Neuhaus writes:

> With respect to all the faithful departed, we are invited to have a generous expectation, "that you may not grieve as others do who have no hope" (1 Thessalonians 4:13). Moreover, there is plenty of room for the saved in the New Jerusalem, which we are told is approximately fifteen hundred miles in height, breadth, and length (Revelation 21:16). That's a city of a size that would cover more than half the continental U.S., and it will be more than a thousand miles high. It would seem there is ample space for everybody to be saved. (Where people who don't like cities will go, I don't know.) The details may not be meant literally, of course, but the picture of a well-populated heaven can, I think, be trusted.

We dare hope he's right.

CELEBRATE: Sometimes it's a fine line we tread between the opposite errors of despair and presumption. On the one hand, we can't be sure we will be saved, but if we think about this fact too much we might conclude that we can't. Or squirm out from under that feeling by focusing on how many other people we're pretty darned sure are damned. Instead, we suggest throwing oneself on God's mercy—then laughing at the devil (St. Thomas More assured us Satan hates that) by throwing up some slaughtered squid that plays on his name.

Balsamic Caesar Salad (see recipe)

Calamari Fra Diavolo (see recipe)

Devil Fruit and Mango Tart

Calamari Fra Diavolo

Maras biber is a Turkish sun-dried pepper with medium heat with a sweet after-taste.

1 tablespoon olive oil
1 small yellow onion, chopped
6 cloves garlic, smashed
2 heads fennel, finely chopped
3 carrots, diced
Pinch each crushed red pepper flakes,
    cayenne, *maras biber* and
    smoked paprika*
2 cups white wine

1 14-ounce can Italian plum tomatoes—
    the liquid only
1 tablespoon dried wild oregano
1/4 cup basil leaves, sliced
Salt and freshly ground black pepper
    to taste
2 pounds calamari
Pasta

Heat oil in pan. Cook onions until soft and add garlic then fennel. After a few minutes add carrots. Sauté together about 3 minutes and add spices. Toss all together. Pour in wine and simmer for 5 minutes. Add tomato liquid and oregano. Simmer, stirring occasionally until most of the liquid has cooked away. Stir in basil leaves and salt and pepper.

Meanwhile prepare calamari. Fish mongers sell them cleaned but you will normally still need to do a bit of work. Under cold running water feel inside each body to pull out the cartilage; cut into rings. Remove sharp pointy beak from tentacles and cut into quarters.

Stir into sauce. Stir to heat evenly and cook just until rings turn white. This shouldn't take much more than 2 minutes.

Toss with perciatelli or other long tubular pasta.

Serves 4–6

Balsamic Caesar Salad Dressing

4 ounces anchovy with capers
6 cloves garlic
Pepper to taste
2 tablespoons balsamic vinegar

2 tablespoons red wine vinegar
Juice of 2 lemons
1 egg plus 2 yolks
1 cup extra virgin olive oil

Combine everything except the oil in the bowl of a food processor. Puree to a smooth paste.

Add oil in a thin stream. Add up to 2 tablespoons water as needed.

Infusions: Of Virtues and Vodka

Oscar Wilde once quipped that life imitates art. Just so, it seems to us that theology mirrors oenology. Without some outside agent (yeast), a dull lump of aging grains or grapes won't turn into anything but mush; likewise, without some outside prompting (Grace) the fallen human soul will never turn towards God. Likewise, without some mixture or infusion, vodka has very little taste—in fact, it's designed that way (**see Vodka**). Vodka makers pride themselves on producing drinks which they boast are "solid," "pure," and "pristine." All of this reminds us of the natural virtues described by Aristotle and Aquinas:

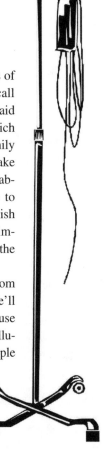

- Justice
- Temperance
- Fortitude
- Prudence

It's easiest to think of these qualities as habits built up by years of training and practice— the reason why some theologians call them the "acquired" virtues. Catholic thinkers have always laid heavy stress on the importance of these habits of character, which are essential to the functioning of society—from a happy family all the way up to an orderly country. Taken together, they make the difference between, say, Australia and Albania. In their absence, good impulses go astray and blessings from God go to waste. This is why St. Thomas insists that Grace does not abolish but builds on, or perfects, human nature. Of the four, the most important (if you're a Republican, think of it as "the decider") is the governing virtue, prudence.

These good habits may keep your home or homeland from turning hellish, but none of them will get you to Heaven. We'll emphasize this point for you English-speakers out there because our entire culture since the "Enlightenment" is built on the illusion that somehow they will. In what other culture could people possibly say, with a straight face, that "cleanliness is next to godliness"? Tell that to Simon Stilites or Francis of Assisi—or for that matter, to the Apostles. As we read the New Testament, it was the Pharisees who were always ragging Christ for His seedy-looking disciples—

and not the other way round. The two nattiest characters in the Gospel, and the most "effective" in a Stephen Covey sense, were doubtless Pilate and Caiaphas. And Judas never missed a meeting.

No, to break out beyond the bounds of mortal, human existence, you need what we call the "infused virtues" of Faith, Hope, and Charity. As one Jesuit theologian wrote way back in 1908:

> [N]o amount of virtue acquired by mere effort of nature will ever take a man to heaven, or win for him any reward there. Heaven means the vision of God, and that vision is simply out of range of all creatures' unaided strivings. The vision of God is not due either to the dignity or to the natural merits of any creature that God can possibly create, let alone man. It is a pure grace and gratuitous favour done to any creature who attains it.[1]

The gift of Faith amounts to a willing acceptance of things unseen, as suggested by the arguments and evidence offered by the Church. It amounts to believing what God has told us about Himself—sometimes, admittedly, over a cell phone with lousy coverage. (The entire twentieth century was something of a dropped call.)

The virtue of Hope is what separates us from the demons who "also believe but tremble." (James 2:19) If when you read the Gospel or the Catechism it all seems to you terribly, hideously *plausible*, it's time to start begging God for the gift of Hope. When he saw, really *saw* the divinity of Christ, dapper Judas committed sui-

---

[1] Found in Rev. Joseph Rickaby's classic *Four Square: The Cardinal Virtues*, Chapter 12. The whole book is available online, and well worth the fortitude required to read it onscreen.

cide; fishy Peter repented. Each had betrayed his master, but one of them had Hope.[2]

Charity (**see Champagne**) is the habit of loving God, one's neighbor, and one's self. If you have neighbors (or selves) like ours, you'll understand why it requires direct, divine intervention.

CELEBRATE: If only God can infuse the sterile soul with Faith, Hope and Charity, we can imitate His saving work in the vital matter of vodka. While on its own a glass of this distilled grain alcohol is little more than a means of hammering the prefrontal cortex into submission, with a little intervention from above, you can transform it into a tasty, fruity infusion. Just take a fifth of vodka—you needn't use anything expensive, although our favorite brand is Luksusowa, a Polish brand made in the original way, from potatoes—and pour it into a decanter, and then fill it up with fruit. After a few weeks the fruit will have flavored the vodka, and the vodka inspired the fruit.

To hammer home the theological point of this exercise, we suggest you infuse one batch for each of the infused virtues:

Faith Infusion: 750 ml. Luksusowa, plus 11 mustard seeds
Hope Infusion: 750 ml. Luksusowa, plus seeds of three pomegranates
Charity Infusion: 750 ml. Luksusowa, plus hips of one dozen red roses

The results will be both delicious and instructive.

Intemperance and the Intolerant

While several million Americans do suffer from what is now recognized as a disease—addiction to alcohol (**see Temperance**), it was once a far more serious social problem. When cheap corn whiskey and rum replaced beer and wine as the drinks of choice, many Americans essentially crawled into the bottle. By 1830, the average adult was consuming the equivalent of 7.1 gallons of pure alcohol per year (compared to 2.1 gallons in 2000). Now this might not sound like much to someone from Poland or Russia, where some men drink that much at a single wedding, but few Americans are as hardy as we Slavs.

In the nineteenth century, working-class people lived unprotected by any workplace laws. Their only solace was often at the saloon, where laborers went straight

---

[2] Hope as defined here theologically is distinct from the "high hopes" that allowed a "little old ant" to "move that rubber tree plant." Said hopes were more akin to "ambition," which is morally neutral, dependent upon its object. Sinatra never really told us where he was moving the rubber tree plant. Though perhaps he was moving it closer to God, in which case. . . .

from hazardous factories or mines, stumbling home later on to beat their wives. The plight of working families led trade unionists and early feminists such as Susan B. Anthony to favor the "Temperance" movement.[3] In the religious arena, an upsurge in distinctly Methodist piety led devout Christians to look askance at Jesus' miracle at Cana and publish bowdlerized Bibles with all references to wine discreetly removed. Meanwhile, unscrupulous politicians in big cities would grease the wheels of their political machines with liquor, herding large numbers of voters on election day straight from the saloon to the voting booth. These tipsy electors posed a grave political threat to America's native Protestants, which helped get the newly founded Republican Party (and soon the Klu Klux Klan) organized and on board. All in all, quite a winning Christian coalition.

Even that inveterate friend of the grape, the Catholic Church, spoke eloquently of the need to moderate alcohol consumption—particularly among its newly arrived Italian, German, and Irish flocks. The clear and constant Church teaching on the virtue of temperance was built up by St. Thomas on a solid foundation in Aristotle. According to the 1917 *Catholic Encyclopedia*, temperance is:

> the righteous habit which makes a man govern his natural appetite for pleasures of the senses in accordance with the norm prescribed by reason. In one sense temperance may be regarded as a characteristic of all the moral virtues; the moderation it enjoins is central to each of them. It is also according to St. Thomas (II-II:141:2) a special virtue. Thus, it is the virtue which bridles concupiscence or which controls the yearning for pleasures and delights which most powerfully attract the human heart.

For instance, a roll in the hay or another pitcher of Pilsner. The Church itself gave birth to organizations[4] intended to curb the abuse of alcohol, restraining it both

---

[3] Susan B. Anthony was also an activist against abortion, which she saw as the medical exploitation of women. But you won't read about that in *Ms.* magazine.

[4] For instance, the admirable Irish organization the Pioneers (*www.pioneertotal.ie*), which urges pious Irishmen to foreswear alcohol altogether—not as something evil, but as one of the great goods in life which they renounce to offer God glory, set an example, and make reparation for the excessive drinking of others. An admirable aspiration, reminiscent of religious poverty or celibacy—and every bit as attractive.

through the use of reason and the mortification of the flesh. By the turn of the twentieth century such awareness campaigns had succeeded in cutting American alcohol consumption from 7.1 gallons per year to 1.6. The problem seemed largely solved.

However, the "Temperance Movement" had grown itself intemperate. Its leaders were no longer content to diminish or restrain the abuse of alcohol; they wanted to ban it altogether. Indeed, the reforming zeal of upright Protestant women such as Carrie Nation (pictured) began to spread to a wide variety of causes, from closing saloons to imposing "democracy" around the world, and encouraging "eugenic" birth control. As feminist scholar Carol Mattingly documents in her *Water Drops from Women Writers: A Temperance Reader*: "The temperance movement was the largest single organizing force for women in American history, uniting and empowering women seeking to enact social change."[5]

Many of the same Progressive activists who campaigned for Prohibition and U.S. entry into World War I would later turn their zeal to requiring I.Q. tests and mandatory sterilization of "idiots" and "imbeciles." If you think the Religious Right is unsavory, try the Religious Left some time. It tastes a lot like . . . Woodrow Wilson.[6]

---

[5] Sends an icy chill down your spine, doesn't it?

[6] Or corn flakes. For fun, read up on the history of John Harvey Kellogg. This self-taught Protestant preacher, temperance activist, and food crank (he invented the cereal named for himself, and touted it as a cure for most diseases), was a popular guest at the Race Betterment Conference, where he complained that the teeming masses of (mostly Catholic) immigrants had turned the U.S. into "a great stock farm, breeding mongrels." To learn more about this movement, see *Blessed Are the Barren: The Social Policy of Planned Parenthood,* by Robert G. Marshall and Charles A. Donovan (San Francisco: Ignatius Press, 1991).

By 1919, enough Americans had quaffed the righteousness cocktail to vote in the Eighteenth Amendment—outlawing alcohol in every state, just barely leaving a loophole for Eucharistic wine. (Even the whiskey-making Canadians briefly banned the stuff—though the Quebecois rebelled within a year and revoked the law.)

The Church's reaction was swift and certain. America's bishops condemned Prohibition as unjust and said we need not obey it. G.K. Chesterton wrote an entire novel, *The Flying Inn,* devoted to ridiculing such laws. More succinctly, he wrote in an essay entitled "American Morals": "Prohibition is sometimes praised for its simplicity; on these lines it may be equally condemned for its savagery." The great Thomist philosopher Charles de Koninck warned: "Prohibition is not a solution, for it is contrary to a natural right, which, if violated, will not be slow to avenge itself."

As they usually do, events proved the Thomists right. When Americans awoke from their rectitude binge, the long hangover that followed saw law-breaking on an unprecedented scale, as ordinary citizens learned to hold their country's statutes in contempt. The massive demand for illegal liquor fueled the first emergence of organized crime in America as billions of 1920's dollars flowed to Al Capone and Meyer Lansky—instead of the beer-brewers, vintners, and small-scale distillers who'd been bankrupted by the law. Indeed, American beer-making never really recovered; when Prohibition was finally repealed in 1933, only half the breweries in the U.S. ever reopened. Taking their place were the mass-production mills that churned out the tasteless likes of Coors and Budweiser, instead of the diverse and well-crafted beers brought here by German immigrants. Those people had enough problems—their ethnic clubs, charities, and even their language had been outlawed during World War I. Ain't Progress great?

Today, alcoholism has been replaced as our leading public health threat by obesity. If our ancestors tried to pickle themselves in liquor, we are instead embalming ourselves with Big Macs, Little Debbies, and 64-ounce Big Gulps® full of sugary Coke. And somewhere in America, probably in the basement of a megachurch, well-meaning women are forming a movement to outlaw food.

••

The Irish and the Cream Thereof

We aren't breaking any news by noting that most Irish are fond of a pint or two. The sheer abundance of excellent Irish beers, drinking songs, and temperance organizations speaks for itself. Of course, we cannot fail to mention Irish whiskey, a drink unique to the island, used in making that delightfully sweet concoction, Irish Cream. The most prominent brand of Irish Cream is Bailey's but others include Carolan's, and the evocatively named St. Brendan's—dubbed for the monk who *re-*

ally discovered America, sailing across the Atlantic in an oak bark *currach* in the sixth century. And if you don't believe *that*, buddy boy, it's time we stepped outside to settle this like lads. . . .

In one sense, Irish Cream embodies the correct approach to drinking; it tastes lovely, emits a gentle buzz, and is virtually impossible to abuse. If you tried to get drunk on the stuff, you'd barf long before you had a chance to start a fistfight over the Sligo Rovers or the Kennedys. Irish Cream serves equally well as an ice-breaker with that lass you met on *irishsingles network.com*, and as the last drink you two may share at your wedding reception. It packs enough protein that, in a pinch, it could even serve at the honeymoon for breakfast. The drink is at once sturdy and sweet, just like the Irish-Americans we know.

But America's Irish were not always seen this way. In fact, they once appeared to Americans as a menace to public order and democracy—and not just once a year, during the St. Patrick's Day Parade.

From the 1820s on through the 1870s, thousands of Irish emigrants sailed annually to escape the repression and poverty imposed upon them by the English. As William Stern wrote in a famous article,[7] in occupied Ireland, Catholics were

> barred from ever owning a house worth more than five pounds or holding a commission in the army or navy. Catholics could neither run schools nor give their children a Catholic education. Priests had to be licensed by the government, which allowed only a few in the country. Any Catholic son could seize his father's property by becoming a Protestant.

Even the slums of New York and Boston sounded promising by comparison. As the Irish families climbed out of steerage and "coffin ships," they raised the suspicions of natives and nativists—who feared the influx into a pristinely Protestant America of millions of loyal "papists." Prominent Americans from John Quincy

---

[7] William Stern, "How Dagger John Saved New York's Irish," *City Journal* (Spring 1997).

Adams to John Calhoun asked aloud if these ragged emigrants were the vanguard of "Romish tyranny." To make matters worse, when the Potato Famine devastated Ireland in the 1840s, the influx became a torrent of millions—and the immigrants disembarked in an appalling state to seek shelter under bleak conditions. As Stern described the new arrivals:

> In New York they took up residence in homes intended for single families, which were subdivided into tiny apartments. Cellars became dwellings, as did attics three feet high, without sunlight or ventilation, where whole families slept in one bed. Shanties sprang up in alleys. Without running water, cleanliness was impossible; sewage piled up in backyard privies, and rats abounded. Cholera broke out constantly in Irish wards. Observers have noted that no Americans before or since have lived in worse conditions than the New York Irish of the mid-nineteenth century.

Illiteracy, alcoholism, and prostitution were rampant. The Irish indeed formed America's first underclass—and set some natives (such as the anti-Catholic cartoonist Thomas Nast) to wondering whether they were some inferior sub-species of *homo sapiens*.

What saved the Irish from this desperate situation, as Stern documents, was neither a government program nor a guerilla movement. Instead it was the efforts of the local Catholic Church led by the intrepid and bellicose Archbishop "Dagger" John Hughes.

Born in 1797 to a poor farmer in county Tyrone, Hughes had seen oppression up close. Stern notes that after Hughes's sister Mary died: "English law barred the local Catholic priest from entering the cemetery gates to preside at her burial; the best he could do was to scoop up a handful of dirt, bless it, and hand it to Hughes to sprinkle on the grave." The family left for Maryland soon after. There the young John worked as a stonemason building a seminary—and discovered his own vocation to the priesthood. The local (French-speaking!) pastor gave little encouragement to this strapping but unlearned lad. Fortunately, he met with St. Elizabeth Seton, who used her influence to gain his admittance to Mount St. Mary's—which still trains priests today. Hughes was appalled by the hostility he encountered in America, where hatred of Catholics was growing—even as Britain was repealing most restrictions on the Church. In Philadelphia, the first city where Hughes ministered, nativist organizations armed themselves with rifles and cannons—while Catholics were disarmed by the police. (In 1844, the Philadelphia nativists rioted, burning three churches and many Catholic homes, killing 13.) Hughes traveled the country debating ministers who accused impoverished immigrants of conspiring to impose the Inquisition in America, winning a worldwide reputation—and appointment in 1838 as Archbishop of New York.

Hughes fought fire with fire—organizing armed groups of Irishmen to defend his churches from arson at the hands of Protestant mobs—but he fought poverty through compassion. And not the nanny-state, non-judgmental kind which nowadays hands out condoms to schoolkids and free needles to addicts. Hughes used his parishes to start a chain of Catholic schools, which would drill the ragamuffin children of recently starving laborers in useful trades and the Catechism, and universities such as Fordham to teach the liberal arts. At their churches, his pastors preached purity and penance. They'd dispense food and clothes to needy workmen—but only after sniffing their breath for the scent of whiskey. Young women who wanted the nuns to find them work had to keep a blameless good name. Orphans and the sick could find shelter in Church-run homes.

Soon, the once-destitute Irish re-formed themselves into a healthy working class. As Stern documents, the tough love of good priests like Hughes and the nuns who staffed the schools, in a single generation pulled an entire people out of penury—and into the NYPD.

So whenever we drink Irish Cream, or go to Mass at Old St. Patrick's Cathedral (which John Hughes built) we remember Dagger John, truly the Cream of the Irish.

....

Izarra: Almond Liqueur of the Fighting Basques

If you're craving something with a little more kick than Bailey's, it's worth hunting down a bottle of Izarra. It's a sweet liqueur made in the French Basque city of Bayonne, and like Chartreuse, comes in two varieties, yellow and green. The green Izarra is a complex concoction of 48 herbs plucked from the mountainsides of the Pyrenees and tastes like 48-proof peppermint candy. By comparison, the yellow Izarra is simple, incorporating a mere 32 herbs with an almond flavor. The natives

mix the stuff with gin or bake it into candies, but it's popular all over the Continent—just like the beret, which the Basques invented.

What's not so well-loved in modern Europe are the Catholic faith and regional freedoms to which the Basques have clung for over 1500 years. As Unified Eurocrats impose postmodern paganism and draconian regulations on cheese—twin evils which always march together—they threaten the national identities and faith of historic peoples from Pamplona to Poland.

Similar to the Irish, the Basques have suffered, only worse, and stuck to their guns. If the Hibernian fight for freedom has been widely remembered in story and song (notably on the jukeboxes of every bar from Boston to Woodside, Queens), too few of us know the history of these fiercely faithful folk of the Pyrenees who fought to keep their culture from being swallowed by nearby empires.

The Basques were living in Europe before anyone else showed up. Their own legends suggest that they've pretty much stayed put since the Stone Age. Some anthropologists speculate that they descend from the first Cro-Magnon men to invade Europe and claim it from the Neanderthals—who appear in Basque folklore as the "jentilak."[8]

In the sixth century, B.C., the Basques viewed with grave alarm the sudden influx of the Celts. When the Romans arrived, they adopted the hardy Basques as allies. In the wake of that empire's fall, Charlemagne attempted to unify Western Europe and met his only defeat at the hands of the Basques—a battle immortalized in the Song of Roland, as you might remember if you'd done your reading freshman year.

The Basque[9] homeland today straddles the border between France and Spain. It once made up the Kingdom of Navarre, whose capital was the bull-fighting town of Pamplona. When Christianity came to Spain, it seeped into Basque country more slowly but went rather deeper; the Basques took longer to join the Church than most Iberians, but have also proved slower to leave it. The most famous Basque in Church history is Ignatius Loyola, founder of the Society of Jesus (the Jesuits). If

---

[8] Literally, "big, hairy guy who lives in the woods." We might just say "Sasquatch."
[9] Or "Euzkadi" in their own language—a non Indo-European tongue full of twisters such as "puxika" (balloon), "txirrindula" (bicycle), "pinpilinpauxa" (butterfly), and "sakakortxo" (corkscrew).

you've ever read his biography or attempted his Spiritual Exercises, you'll see why the Basques are such a formidable folk. We're glad they're on *our* side.

Indeed, the Basque country has served as a Catholic heartland in Spain over the centuries. In 711, when Spain was suddenly blessed with the richness of multicultural diversity, Navarre was one of the only territories to remain unconquered by the Moors. This rugged independence set the tone for Basque history from the Arab invasion up through ETA.[10] Even when the Kingdom of Navarre and other Basque regions were divvied up between the expansionist empires of France and Spain, the Basque towns retained a wide array of liberties that restricted these foreign kings' power to tax and tyrannize. These traditional rights were called *fueros*, and the Basques treated them as their Constitution. In fact, they were Justice Scalia-style originalists—they clung to every jot and tittle, insisting on the traditional readings of the text, refusing the demands of modernizing monarchs who wanted to impose alien customs and tongues. The American founder John Adams, desperate to find some historical precedent for our constitutional system, pointed to the Basques and their *fueros* as examples where medieval liberties had survived outside Switzerland and England.

Maybe Adams shouldn't have called attention to them, because the *fueros* soon came under attack. The rationalizing autocrats who seized control of France in the Revolution tore up the *fueros* of the Basques in France, and later Napoleon occupied the Spanish sections along with the rest of that peninsula. After the Bourbon kings returned to power, technocrats attempted to suppress the *fueros* in Spain in order to extend state control over the Church. This tore the country in half and provoked the "Carlist" wars—after Prince Carlos, who claimed the throne as champion of the Church and of Basque liberties. Most of Europe's great powers intervened to support the anti-clerical modernizers, and in 1837, after almost seven years of war, the Carlist cause was crushed. Ten years later, the Basques rebelled again, and lost again. The victorious liberals revoked most of the regional rights the Basques had treasured for over 1,000 years.

What liberties the Basques had left were threatened again in 1936. In a stereotypically Spanish cascade of ironies, the virulently anti-Catholic Spanish Republic—allied with that great friend of ethnic minorities, Josef Stalin—restored some autonomy to the pious Basques. Meanwhile, the conservative Spaniards who rose in defense of the Church insisted on a centralized Spain. This meant that devout Basques fought on the same side of the Spanish Civil War as the anarchists who massacred priests and nuns in Valencia, while Spanish bishops prayed for the victory of authoritarian generals whose German allies bombed Basque towns such as Guernica. An ugly war all around ending badly for the Basques: A victorious General Franco revoked all regional rights once held by Basques and attempted to extirpate even their ancient language. More militant Basques began to resist through the terrorist movement ETA;

---

[10] The Basque separatist guerrilla group which has only recently laid down its arms. We hope.

others attempted quietly to conserve their culture, while pioneering movements to implement Catholic social teaching. Indeed, it was in the Basque regions that priests and clergy worked together to blunt the harshness of modern capitalist practice by establishing business cooperatives such as those of Mondragon. These worker-owned corporations offered health care, low-cost loans, and job security, along with family-friendly business practices—all inspired by the Church's vision of social justice, to be found in Leo XIII's *Rerum Novarum* (**see Highballs**).

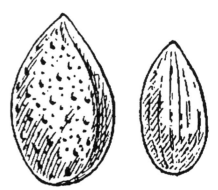

Almond with and without its shell

CELEBRATE: Commemorate the spirit of the Basques by serving it with a traditional regional menu like this:

Fried Sardines with Lemon

Roasted Red Bell Pepper Soup

Hake in Green Sauce (see recipe)

Asparagus

Roasted Potatoes

Green Salad with Sherry Vinaigrette

Spanish Cheese Plate
Featuring Petite Basque, Idiazabal, Bleu des Basques, and Etorki
with Quince Paste, Marcona Almonds, and Bittersweet Chocolate

---

Hake in Green Sauce

4 6-ounce hake fillets, with skin
Salt and freshly ground pepper
6 tablespoons extra virgin olive oil
1/4 cup chopped parsley

6 cloves garlic, sliced
1 cup white wine
1 cup frozen peas, thawed

Pat fish dry and season.

Heat oil and garlic in roomy sauté pan over low heat until garlic begins to turn light golden. Add half of the parsley and fish, skin side up (service side down). Swirl oil in pan to gently overlap flesh of fish for about 5 minutes. Flesh will turn white. Turn over with flexible metal spatula. Allow to sit for 1 minute before swirling pot again. Add stock in a thin drizzle, continue to swirl; add peas and remaining parsley after about 10 minutes. Cook another 3 minutes.

Remove fish to platter. Adjust seasoning for sauce and pour over. Serve immediately.

Serves 4

....

Loopholes to the Ten Commandments:
#4: Honor Your Father and Your Mother

If you come from a certain kind of family, you may have learned when you were young to resent this commandment—which some parents tend to trundle out only when they're trying to impose some particularly irrational whim. For instance, when they insist on turning off your classical music so they can listen to Guy Lombardo during dinner, or they decide to seize your college fund to pay their gambling debts/buy a bass boat/make bail.[11] Misused this way, this commandment amounts to nothing more than "Because I said so!" backed up by hellfire.

Of course, there are good comebacks to which a well-catechized Catholic child can always resort. Here are our favorites:

- "Well, Mom, the Bible also says 'Wife, obey thy husband.' When you start obeying him, I'll obey you."
- "Okay Dad. It also says that you have to obey legitimate authority— which includes not cheating on your taxes. Want me to call the IRS to ask them?"

And:

- "You always told me I was adopted.[12] I'll go find my real parents and obey them."

------

[11] Not that this happened to us. In fact, we categorically deny it. *Categorically.*
[12] Except that you weren't.

However, there are indeed many instances where the duty to obey and honor one's parents does apply. Depending on one's age (and mental age), one does owe deference to the wishes of the parent who's trooping off every day to deliver mail so he can buy you all that Chef Boyardee and pay the tuition at Most Precious Blood so you don't get stabbed in public school.

In the ancient world, the authority of parents (okay, of the father) extended much further than it does today. The Roman notion of *paterfamilias* was so extensive that it granted a father the right to snuff out a rebellious son.[13] In the Old Testament, the punishment prescribed for rebellious children was stoning. While scholars tell us that this penalty was rarely if ever inflicted, that hasn't stopped a group of modern-day fundamentalists from trying to revive it. The Calvinist movement that calls itself "Christian Reconstructionist" favors the enactment of Old Testament regulations like this into civil law. In his notable essay, "Stoning Disobedient Children," contemporary pastor Rev. William Einwechter advocates that modern Americans consider . . . doing just that. But only after a fair trial before "the magistrates." So that's okay then.

It was, in fact, the Church that began to undermine the radical authority fathers once wielded over their children. Early Christians, who chose a religious vocation or the priesthood over a marriage their father had arranged, died by the hundreds in the Colosseum. As the Church climbed out of the catacombs, it was careful to insist upon the right of young people to choose their own vocation or their spouse. While feudal lords often ignored it, canon law insists that a forced marriage is simply invalid. The interests of the family could never override a person's liberty to choose his or her state of life. When a parent's (or a bureaucrat's) command conflicts with the moral law, one is obliged (respectfully) to disobey. This astounding political innovation struck patriarchal societies encountered by missionaries as yet one more reason to . . . kill all the Christians. And they did, with great enthusiasm and technical creativity, from Uganda to Vietnam. This enriched our calendar honoring hundreds of holy martyrs whose stories you shouldn't read over dinner.

If the family once had too much cohesion, nowadays it has too little. One needn't follow Rev. Einwechter to the rockpile in order to regret the decay of the familial bond. Indeed, the collapse of the extended family into its unstable "nuclear" core has threatened the very cohesion of society, and vastly increased the reach of the State into private life—as Uncle Sam takes over neglected tasks such as child care, sex education, and support of the aged. Increasingly, the family has ceased to be the "basic unit of society" (as Church teaching insists), to be replaced by atomized individuals facing each other and the State armed only with abstract "rights" and sometimes attorneys (though faced with a family stoning, a kid probably needs one).

The Church has always been aware of this danger, which is why our social

---

[13] The Romans weren't pro-snuff; they were just pro-choice.

teaching is centered on the doctrine of "subsidiarity." Whatever social activity can be performed by families should remain with them; only where they fail should private agencies step in. Where they cannot manage, then local government should get involved. If a necessary task exceeds the grasp of your city or town, the regional authorities should get involved. It is only as a last resort that the federal government should insert itself—since it is by definition the least responsive to voters, and the most susceptible to abuse. This bottom-up view of authority has underpinned Catholic attitudes toward the State—though grasping kings and revolutionaries have ever resented it. The entire Jesuit order was once suppressed, largely because its priests insisted on teaching this doctrine—against the "rational," "modern" autocracies favored by *philosophes*. Although you wouldn't know it from standard textbooks, most "reformers" throughout history have been power-hungry cranks. When they win, their disciples write the history.

Even though a doctrinal truth or political principle does not always lie smack dab in the center between two polar extremes, it usually strikes a balance between them. We must live with the paradox posed by two opposing mysteries which coexist—like the claims of parental authority and the spiritual freedom of the child, or the authority granted the government by God and the citizen's right to flout unjust laws, such as Prohibition (**see Intemperance**). As Chesterton wrote, the Church's annoying insistence on looking at both sides of every question has infuriated the simplifiers and ideologues of every generation—and guaranteed that Catholics will never run out of opportunities for martyrdom. It's the gift that keeps on giving.

Drinking Song #4: A Sacred Song

When you're gathered with a group of friends and a case of beer or wine, if conversation begins to ebb, sooner or later someone's likely to get the bright idea of watching a DVD, probably some goofball comedy like *Dodgeball*. Great movie, bad idea. You may start off laughing together and nudging each other in the ribs, but since alcohol hits different people at varying paces, some of you will get active and antsy, while others will nod off to sleep, and the evening will end in catastrophe—perhaps in a quarrel, or worse, in some unwanted "heart to heart" talk where one of you bares his soul to the group. And that's really not something anyone wants to see. Save it for the priest behind the confessional screen: He's paid to listen.

Instead of drowning your camaraderie in the rewritten jokes of some underpaid Hollywood screenwriter, it's far better to cook up some group activity—something *other* than a drinking game. In our experience, there's nothing better than gathering everyone for a song. Those with strong, clear voices will carry the tune; your

friends who croak like frogs or squeak like weasels will serve for comic relief, and the effort of staying in tune and sticking to the lyrics will keep everyone awake. What's more, as Aristotle noticed, the best way to be happy (or to have fun) is, ironically, not to search for happiness or amusement. (That usually amounts to "trying too hard," and typically ends in something like an Adam Sandler movie.) Instead, we find happiness by trying to be good, and have fun by trying to do something together—even something as silly as staying in tune through a drinking song.

We suggest you start with something funny to get the group in the mood. You might also put on one (just one) old rock song to which everybody knows (or thinks he knows) the lyrics, like Don McLean's authentic classic "American Pie." That will serve as a smooth segue to a slightly more sentimental tune (**see Song #2: "Will Ye No Come Back Again"**). If that puts people in a patriotic mood, move on to a tune that stirs the heart to love of country (**see Song #1: "The Kaiserlied"**). Remember, at the heart of every love,[14] including the love of friends, beats the love of God. Our connection to the Creator is what makes it possible for us to treasure any kind of selfless or self-giving love, whether it's aimed towards a spouse, a starving stranger, or that puppy in the window. So it makes sense to give your song-session with friends a touch of gravitas by including at least one classic hymn. For those who grew up Catholic, it will transport them back to childhood, reminding them of parents who may have passed, or long-forgotten friends.

---

14 Okay, maybe not one's love for revenge or shopping.

One of our favorite old hymns is the sonorous and singable "Faith of Our Fathers." It was penned by the great English convert Frederick William Faber (1814–1863). Faber had been raised a strict Calvinist; his uncle was a well-known anti-Catholic author and Oxford don. But when he went to that university, young Faber encountered men such as John Henry Newman, who sought to rediscover the apostolic and Catholic roots remaining in Anglicanism. At first this meant simple things, like bringing back incense and other Sacramentals ("smells and bells"). A fondness for lace and pageantry attracted some unlikely characters to "high church" circles—including a group of priests who gave each other . . . female nicknames. Ahem.

But the solid research and argument undertaken by priests like Newman and other members of the Oxford Movement helped bring back long-abandoned practices like Eucharistic Adoration and Confession. Indeed, papers like *Punch* helped whip up a scandal about that Sacrament—warning Victorian men that priests' advice might undermine their authority over their wives.

The Oxfordians made their best arguments in a series called "Tracts for the Times," which won for the group the label "Tractarians." In 1841, Newman wrote the last and most famous "Tract 90," declaring a strong, implicit case for Roman Catholicism. Newman's new ideas got him repudiated by the authorities at Oxford—who rightly saw him as ripe for crossing the Tiber. He did so, in 1845—and Frederick William Faber joined the Catholic Church just a month later. Like Newman, he gave up a comfortable income at a posh Anglican parish to start from scratch in an English church that was made up mostly of recent Irish immigrants, whom natives viewed as hooligans. Like Newman, Faber heard himself being called a "traitor" to his Protestant forefathers. To answer such accusations, Faber wrote a hymn recalling the sacrifices of England's Catholic martyrs, such as Thomas More, John Fisher, and the Carthusians burned alive by Henry VIII. It's still one of our favorite sacred songs, and it would make a nice finale to any gathering of faithful friends:

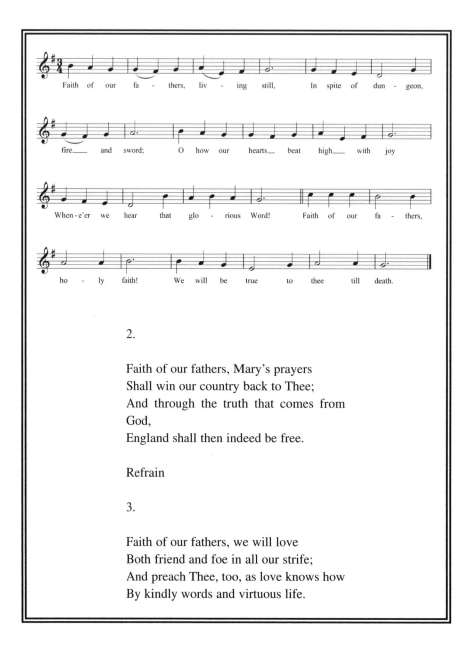

Faith of our fa - thers, liv - ing still, In spite of dun - geon,
fire___ and sword; O how our hearts___ beat high___ with joy
When-e'er we hear that glo - rious Word! Faith of our fa - thers,
ho - ly faith! We will be true to thee till death.

2.

Faith of our fathers, Mary's prayers
Shall win our country back to Thee;
And through the truth that comes from
God,
England shall then indeed be free.

Refrain

3.

Faith of our fathers, we will love
Both friend and foe in all our strife;
And preach Thee, too, as love knows how
By kindly words and virtuous life.

In the prose vein, Father Faber once wrote that, "Kindness has converted more sinners than zeal, eloquence, or learning." And fate has mostly been kind to his song, which is popular even in Protestant churches—though they usually delete that awkward mention of mother Mary. Alas, well-meaning Catholic modernizers are not always quite so kind. The liturgical magazine *Adoremus* reports that the 2002 edition of the *Seasonal Missalette* has added a new, feminist verse to the song:

> Our mothers, too, oppressed and wronged
> Still lived their faith with dignity;
> Their brave example gives us strength
> To work for justice ceaselessly.

While we appreciate the sentiment, that verse would have made our moms break up laughing. Loudly. In church.

Jagermeister: The Talking Jesus Deer

We all know the story. Every child learns on his mother's knee the tale behind Jagermeister, the liquor depicting a deer and a crucifix on the label. The story goes something like this:

St. Hubert was once a dissolute duke who spent all his spare hours slaughtering deer. So fond was Hubert of hunting that he neglected his feudal duties, his wife, and even his Faith. Things went from bad to worse when he decided to keep on hunting all through Lent—which in medieval Aquitaine simply wasn't the "done thing." But then you knew that.

One Good Friday at noon, as pious folk knelt in Church to mark the hours Jesus spent on the Cross, Hubert spotted the largest, finest buck he'd ever seen. He rode after the wondrous beast until he cornered it . . . and between the antlers appeared a crucified Jewish carpenter. Even worse, the tiny Jesus began to talk.[1] It started, in fact, to kvetch:

"Hubert, unless you turn to the Lord, and lead a holy life, you shall quickly go down to hell."

It is not recorded whether Hubert soiled his shorts, but he did drop to his knees. He wheeled his horse around and galloped home—then made the mistake of telling his wife. She died soon afterward, and poor Hubert became a monk. . . .

This isn't a self-help book, but if we might proffer some unsolicited advice: When something of this sort happens, it's probably best to keep it to yourself. Likewise, if you find yourself abducted from your Iowa cornfield by the almond-eyed Grey Men and awake with an abraded colon—just carry that one with you to the grave. The little woman is not going to "understand."

If the Virgin Mary appears in the mold on your tortilla, just say a prayer of gratitude and for God's sake *eat the thing*, unless you really want a broadcast truck from Telemundo parked for six weeks recording the crowds of pilgrims on your lawn. If the apparition starts curing people, you can kiss your garden goodbye: It's going to fill up with discarded crutches, artificial limbs, and thank-you notes written in Tagalog. Try reselling the place after that. You might as well hang up your day job and concentrate on making a profit on the gift shop.

Here's a hint in case that happens: Think down-market. Don't get all pretentious and Episcopalian by trying to market tastefully carved renderings of St. Bede made

---

[1] Don't you hate when that happens?

out of sandstone; they simply won't move. Stick to trinkets made in China[2] out of plastic that glow in the dark. One of our favorite items, sold at the Shrine of the Immaculate Conception in Washington, D.C., is a Holy Family Bike Reflector. Keep in mind that this gift shop refuses to sell our books, because they're "tasteless."

At least one marketing genius must have been involved in the cult of St. Hubert, as he was quickly adopted as patron saint by hunters all across Europe who seemed to have . . . missed the point of his story. Still, we can't help loving a saint who (as we noted in our other book) is used as a pretext for once a year filling up parish churches with howling beagles. We need more saints like that.

Our research has revealed that Jagermeister contains 56 herbs and plants, and was first produced in Wolfenbuttel, Germany, in 1935—making it one of the few good things to come out of that country in that period. While it's the only drink of its kind to become widely popular in the States, the liqueur is quite similar to the local "medicinal" liquors produced in villages all over Europe. One of us was going up the Alps (by car) in Appenzell, Switzerland and started to get sick from the altitude. The driver knew exactly what to do. He turned off to the nearest inn and fetched a glass of "our distinctive local liqueur." It tasted almost exactly like Jagermeister, and did the trick.

---

2 Strange, isn't it, how at Catholic gift shops most of the items were produced in a country where the Faith is illegal and bishops rot in prison?

If you've had a hearty hunter's dinner like the one we suggest here, you ought to top it off with a potent digestif like Jagermeister—or whatever comparable cordial is produced in your Alpine village.

CELEBRATE: Tell St. Hubert's story as you serve up this savory entrée to your family. Make sure to explain to your kids: "*No,* we're not eating Bambi. *No,* this isn't the talking Jesus deer. Now eat. Damn it, eat! Do you want me to give it to the dog, and let you go hungry? *Do you???*"

Venison St. Hubert

This traditional French treatment can also be applied to beef. Denise used to prepare filet mignon in this manner at Louis XVI Restaurant in New Orleans's French Quarter.

MARINADE:

1 750-ml bottle of red wine
1 onion, chopped
2 shallots, chopped
1 head garlic, crushed
2 stalks celery, chopped

2 carrots, chopped
2 sprigs each parsley, thyme, rosemary, tarragon
3 juniper berries
1 tablespoon black peppercorns

SAUCE:

1/4 cup brandy
1 cup veal demi-glace
1 heaping tablespoon red currant jelly

Salt and freshly ground pepper
1 tablespoon butter, room temperature

VENISON:

4 8-ounce venison tenderloin fillets
Salt and freshly ground pepper

Butter

Combine all marinade ingredients and add venison. Cover and refrigerate 24 to 48 hours.

Remove from marinade and pat dry. Season and sear on all sides in hot pan with just enough butter to brown the meat. Cook to just above rare. Meat will continue to cook from carryover heat while the sauce is cooking. It should be medium rare for service.

Deglaze the pan with brandy, tipping it towards the flame to catch fire. The alcohol will burn off and the flame will die within seconds. Add the demi-glace and bring to a boil. Stir with a wooden spoon to liberate any bits on the bottom. Reduce slightly and add jelly. Cook a few more moments to incorporate sauce; season with salt and pepper. Swirl in butter to give body and richness to sauce. Pour over plated venison.

Serves 4

Jeremiah Weed: Official Bourbon of the Book of Lamentations

You've probably never heard of this hard-edged brand of low-priced bourbon, and for darn good reason: It is almost unavailable, except on Air Force bases. But U.S. fighter pilots go through the stuff like airplane fuel, and some concede it tastes pretty much the same. As one airman wrote online of the drink: "Weed is one of those things you wonder why any-one would consume! However, after you choke down the first one you try another. After three to four, it becomes strangely pleasant and smooth. . . . It's one of those creepy drinks that sneaks up on you long after you thought you had it licked, and inexplicably erases all memory of the evening."

Jeremiah Weed has been adopted as the semi-official liquor of Amer-ica's fighter pilots, who drink it on special occasions out of spent can-non shells—though none can ex-plain exactly why. The closest thing to a trustworthy account appears in C. R. Anderegg's memoir *Sierra Hotel*, where he writes of pilots who came to a desert saloon after checking out the site where one of them had crashed a plane. At a nearby bar, they convinced the bearded bar-tender to join them in a drinking game called "Afterburners", which involves slam-ming back shots of whiskey set on fire. . . . And you don't want to hear the rest. It involves singed flesh, a blazing beard, and penitent pilots purchasing a case of cheap bourbon from a bartender who was headed for the burn ward. And thus began a tradition.[3] Our pilots have been choking down the stuff ever since.

By inscrutable Providence or happy accident, this bourbon shares a name with one of the Old Testament's greatest prophets, whose message warned of fire and war (though he didn't mention crashing F-16s, at least in the Douay-Rheims Catholic translation). Jeremiah taught in the seventh century B.C., at a time when the Jewish nation occupied a unique position: It stood like a deer in the headlights in the middle of the road.

Once a major power in the region under kings David and Solomon, the Jewish

---

[3] You think this one is silly? The maniple, worn over a priest's arm at Mass until Vatican II, began as a kind of sweat-rag which he used to wipe his forehead. With the rise of air-conditioning, the Council Fa-thers deemed these vestments superfluous, and ordered them sold to vintage clothes shops.

kingdom had torn itself apart in civil wars and lapsed from strict religious practice—despite a series of increasingly irritable prophets. To make things worse, the remaining land of Judah lay smack dab between two aggressive empires.

The prophets whom God sent to the people carried a two-fold message, which can be boiled down to this: "Go to Temple—and don't provoke the goyim!" Again and again, the prophets of Israel countered the claims of ambitious kings and zealous nationalists (think of them as the first neocons), whose plans for national greatness entailed risky and needless wars. In fact, the Hebrew prophets were the precursors of the Christian critique of conquest. While the Church has never advocated outright pacifism, beginning with St. Augustine it has developed increasingly strict criteria by which to judge the causes and conduct of war. The Just War tradition specified that Christians should only take part in a war if it is

- In a good cause,[4] to repel aggression or protect the innocent.
- Waged by legitimate authorities.
- Reasonably likely to succeed.
- Unlikely, proportionately, to cause more harm than good.
- The last resort after attempted negotiations.
- Waged with the minimum force necessary, making every attempt to protect civilians.

These criteria take all the fun out of war—banning naked land-grabs, empire building, torture, mass-rape, fire-bombing cities, and the use of America's 10,000 or so nukes for pretty much anything at all. Since the Just War tradition is such a buzz-kill, Christians of a certain kind often argue it away (**see Loophole to the Fifth Commandment**) as cleverly as a canon lawyer wangling an annulment for a Kennedy.

Sadly, the kings and people of Israel did something similar. They disdained their peacenik prophets, and instead marched off to disaster in places we now call Lebanon and Iraq. This suggests to us that certain current politicians eager to re-make the Middle East do indeed read their Bible. They just don't understand it.

By Jeremiah's time, the rump Jewish kingdom called Judah was a subject ally of the rising empire of Babylon. Judah had to pay tribute, but its people could live untroubled, and Jerusalem's Temple was left untouched. Jeremiah's message mirrored that of previous prophets: He urged the Israelites to leave well enough alone. Instead of allying with one pagan kingdom—and provoking the others—or "arming for peace," the Jews should concentrate on pleasing God. He alone had given them their kingdom in the first place, and only He could save it. But Judah's ruling class were not keen to listen; it didn't help that Jeremiah's idea of tact included phrases like "You have polluted the land with your whoring and wickedness." (Jeremiah,

---

4 No, "revenge," "a presidential sex scandal" or "an upcoming election" don't count.

3:2) Eager to throw off the yoke of Babylon, Judah's king cut off the tribute and allied with the bumbling king of Egypt who promised to bail the Israelites out. "Fat chance," said Jeremiah.[5]

Jeremiah wandered the countryside, often two steps ahead of a lynch mob, warning the people and king that their policies would bring on disaster: "I will even give them into the hand of their enemies, and into the hand of them that seek their life: and their dead bodies shall be for meat unto the fowls of the heaven, and to the beasts of the earth," to be specific. (Jeremiah 34:20)

For his candor, Jeremiah was locked in chains, chased from town to town, and condemned as a traitor who did not support the troops. When the Babylonians did indeed invade, destroy Jerusalem, level the Temple, and lead almost all the Jews off to slavery in exile, those who were left behind dragged Jeremiah off to Egypt—where they would finally pay him back for his prescience by stoning him to death.

From all this, we draw a message for today: When politicians propose a war, *get behind it.* Don't ask if it's just, wise, or winnable—or even which country it is against. Just put that yellow ribbon sticker on your car, hunker down, and support the president. It beats getting stoned in Egypt.

Of course, that's cold comfort to the brave souls who'll have to fly combat missions over Pyongyang, Persia, or Paris. It's your duty at least to pray for them—and maybe send a case of Jeremiah Weed.

Joan of Arc: The Soldier, the Saint, the Beer

Some of the best beers in France bear the name of the greatest woman in the history of France—and perhaps of Europe—Jeanne (or Joan) of Arc. She's also our favorite saint. Beer expert Michael Jackson's lavishly illustrated handbook, *The Great Beer Guide,* highlights three distinctive brews from the Jeanne D'Arc Brewery in northern France:

---

[5] Our own, contemporary translation.

- Ambre des Flandres, with a "peppery start and a grainy, figgy palate, with a big, dry finish."
- Belzebuth, incongruously named for the devil,[6] which Jackson calls "smooth, almost candyish, with peppery alcohol flavors" and a "spicy, surprising dryness."
- Grain d'Orge, which he calls "slightly nutty" and "slightly smoky."

Another brewery, La Lorraine, makes its beer in De Gombervaux not far from one of Joan's old forts, and used her image (pictured) in 1893 to advertise its brew to Frenchmen still smarting from their country's defeat by Germany (**see Gewurztraminer**). This is none too surprising; the figure of Joan has been invoked by French patriots for centuries, as an emblem of *La Patrie Française*. This young girl died condemned as a heretic and witch—and worst of all, as a woman who persisted in unbiblical fashion in wearing men's clothes.[7] Long regarded by locals as a saint, she was only officially canonized in 1920. This helped seal a truce between Church and State forged on the fields of World War I, after the vicious persecution of the clergy begun by the Third Republic in 1905.

Speaking of combat in France, if there's one war that we can say with supernatural certainty was just, it was Joan's campaign to throw out the English and end the Hundred Years' War. This war began in 1328, when the French king died heirless, and the English King Edward III—who boasted more French royal blood than English—claimed the throne. Since the monarchs had relatively little power outside their personal domains, and authority was decentralized among the provinces, the question of who got to call himself "king" over

---

6 Perhaps a reference to the fact that Joan's closest lieutenant, Gilles de Rais, tormented by grief after her execution, became a Satanist and serial killer and then repented with spectacular sincerity on the scaffold—a story recounted in J.K. Huysman's brilliant, creepy novel *La Bas*. Yeah, we're sure that's what these brewers had in mind.

7 No we're not kidding. For an accurate, heart-rending depiction of her trial and condemnation by a kangaroo court, see perhaps the greatest film ever made: *The Passion of Joan of Arc* (1928). Once considered lost, a single copy of this classic was found in the closet of a Danish insane asylum, and is now available at Blockbuster.

the independent-minded Duke of Burgundy, for instance, was pretty much academic. It certainly wasn't serious enough to merit turning loose bands of heavily armored knights—the medieval equivalent of a panzer division—to burn, rape, and pillage their way through the peasantry.

But that's not how King Edward saw it: What he saw was a throne with his name on it, in a much richer kingdom than England, left vulnerable by divisions among its nobles. So he launched a war that continued, with ups and downs for each side, for almost a century. It bankrupted both kingdoms, divided the Church, and cut a swathe of devastation through France—where all the fighting took place. The English adopted a scorched-earth policy, destroying any region they could not hold—burning farms, towns, and fields, leaving the bewildered peasants to starve. According to some accounts, one out of four people in France died as a result of this war.

By 1425, the war was at a hopeless impasse. Thanks to the victorious campaigns of Kenneth Branagh,[8] the king of England claimed the French throne for himself. But the new king, Henry VI, was a hapless kid whose scheming regents were busy provoking a civil war at home. Still, English armies swarmed all over France, swilling beer, forcing peasants to make them porkpies, and pointing longbows at anything that moved. The divided French mostly hid in the walled cities they still controlled, while their uncrowned Dauphin sat around waiting for divine intervention.

And it wasn't slow in coming. That spring, the thirteen-year-old daughter of a peasant in Domremy began to hear voices claiming to be three famous saints:

- St. Margaret, whom legend tells was swallowed by a dragon—but coughed out unhurt. For her pains, this virgin was named the patroness of childbirth.
- St. Catherine, an untutored girl who confronted a Roman emperor, demanding he stop persecuting Christians—then bested his court philosophers in a theology debate.
- St. Michael the Archangel, commander of the Heavenly Host.

In medieval France, these were names to conjure with, and Joan was duly impressed. Besides the usual religious advice apparitions dispense—"Go to Mass more often," "Make reparation for the sins of others," and "Don't open a gift shop here," they had another, more dangerous message: Joan was to rouse the armies of France and lead them into battle.

A smart girl, Joan was understandably skeptical. Every time these spirits showed up, she marched straight off to her confessor to run their messages by

---

[8] Some purists will insist the war was in fact led by Lawrence Olivier, but this is a liquor dictionary, not a history book.

him—just in case. (We advise any reader who hears the voices of such saints to do the same.[9]) She fasted and prayed. She discussed her new career plan with her parents. She argued with the spirits for almost three years. "I am a poor girl; I do not know how to ride or fight," she told the spirits. They answered: "It is God who commands it."

She must travel to see the Dauphin, and convince him to march into battle. She must raise the siege of Orleans—one of France's last free cities—and arrange for the conquest of Reims. It was only there that the Dauphin could be anointed as the true king of France. Once he was crowned, the English would see that their cause was lost, and would slink back through the Chunnel. Or something like that—the voices hadn't been too specific on how events would shake out. But they were dead clear that Joan was the one to make it all happen. At last, Joan obeyed. She found some friendly noblemen to conduct her, in drag, through enemy territory to visit the Dauphin.

The modern reader might wonder why jaded aristocrats would listen to a girl like Joan, whose military experience was slim (ROTC was not mandated for French shepherdesses until the 1980s). It helps to know that there was a popular legend abroad in France, which promised that at the nation's moment of greatest need, a young virgin from near Lorraine would be called by God to save the country. This legend was variously attributed to the Venerable Bede, the wizard Merlin, and a fortune cookie opened by Marco Polo, but the French were so desperate after decades of war that they were ready to believe in just about anything—even in Joan. At first, the Dauphin's courtiers sneered at her because—well, because they were French. They mocked her accent, and pretended not to understand her. But the Dauphin found her intelligent, utterly sincere, and finally convincing. Because the legend specified a virgin, the Dauphin sent Joan to a local Ob-Gyn for a checkup. She passed this test,[10] and got the job.

And what a job it was. At age 17, Joan set out to rouse the dispirited armies of France and lead them against the fearsome English military machine, whose longbows had mowed down Gallic armies like machine guns at Crécy (1346) and Agincourt (1415). But Joan's charisma raised the morale of the weary veterans, and her tactics were brilliant. Believing that they were doing God's work, the French managed in just over a week to drive away the English forces besieging Orleans. The victory seemed miraculous. Before each combat, Joan would exhort her troops to confess their sins (she provided priests) and spare the enemy wounded.[11] Afterwards, she would travel the field with clergy in tow, to dispense

---

[9] Especially St. Michael—a notorious prankster!

[10] This point was more important than one might think. It was also widely believed that a virgin could not be possessed by the Devil—which is the story the English spread about Joan. In Shakespeare's *Henry VI*, he depicts poor Joan as a witch, and a randy one.

[11] Instead of energetically slitting their throats—as Henry V had done.

absolution to dying French and English soldiers alike. Joan never carried a sword, only a banner; her force was moral and intellectual, and it carried the day. Joan was hurt several times in battle—she got hit in the head once by a cannon ball—but never left the field.

After several more battles, the Dauphin was convinced the coast was clear, and he traveled to Reims, where he was crowned king. His armies began to prevail across France—but not fast enough for Joan. She wanted the war concluded so rebuilding could begin, and she clashed with the new king's cautious advisors, whom she urged to capture Paris. For reasons that still puzzle historians, the king lost interest in the young girl sent from God to save his throne, and sat on his hands. Joan set off on her own to raise an army and take the capital. In a skirmish, she was captured by the forces of the Duke of Burgundy—who controlled the town of Vichy, and fought for the English. The duke offered her to the highest bidder. The French king didn't bother offering a ransom, so she was sent to the English.

Once in captivity, Joan was treated like a sorcerer and a heretic, by soldiers and pet clergymen eager to discredit her mission. In violation of Church law, she was guarded by male soldiers, one of whom tried to rape her. The bishop who served the English, Cauchon of Beauvais, summoned theologians from the University of Paris to interrogate her for heresy—which people took seriously in those days. (It was the medieval equivalent of a hate crime.) Despite a total lack of evidence, Cauchon went ahead with the trial, refusing to pass on Joan's appeal to the pope. The learned bishops and professors spent weeks grilling the illiterate girl, posing complex theological questions designed to trip her up. But she never wavered—in fact, her ability to answer these men with perfect orthodoxy and sincerity began to strike some of them as miraculous. More than one of these theologians came around to believing in her.

But these academics knew where their bread was buttered, and the outcome of the trial had been decided in advance. Joan was condemned to be burned at the stake for heresy and witchcraft. At one point, just before her execution, she panicked and signed a confession to save her life. But she retracted it the very next day, explaining simply "I signed because I was afraid!" On May 30, 1431, Joan was burned alive, and her body pulverized to make sure there would be no relics. It was only in 1456, after Joan's family had appealed to the pope, that the Vatican conducted another trial which vindicated her, describing her as a martyr, and implicating Cauchon himself as a heretic.

The English were soon driven out of France, and the war concluded. But Joan's story still maddens dogmatic secularists, who have searched for every possible explanation for her visions except the obvious one: that they were authentic. The hack filmmaker Luc Besson made a movie about her in 1999 called *The Messenger*, starring his distinctly non-virginal girlfriend Milla Jovavic, who portrayed young Joan as a deranged killing machine in the body of an underwear model. Researchers have suggested that Joan had a brain tumor, was schizophrenic, or hallucinated from the side-effects of drinking unpasteurized milk.[12] None of them can explain how a demented teenager could command armies, sway kings, and beat Europe's leading theologians in arguments (shades of St. Catherine here).

One thing is certain: Had the English held onto France, that country's most popular drink would not be red wine but lager beer—though probably nothing as good as Jeanne d'Arc's Grain d'Orge. And they'd drink it *warm*.

....

Jubilee: Get Out of Debt, Free!

There's something in the human heart that craves a party. Whether you're a band of cavemen jumping up and down and grunting over a newly killed wildebeest, or a crowd of LSU DKEs cheering a victory for the Tigers—and in our experience, it's

sometimes too hard to tell the difference—you know what it means to mark a jubilee. But you might not know where we get the word, or how it relates to wine making, brewing, ancient Jewish debt-collection, Catholic theology, bankruptcy law, or Gulf-Coast handfishing. Knowledge is just too specialized these days, and it's hard to keep all those connections straight. But that's where we come in.

The original meaning of jubilee referred to a very specific sort of celebration, with its roots deep in the ever-festive Book of Leviticus. The name probably comes from the Hebrew word "jobel," meaning "ram's horn," the instrument the rabbis would blow to signify the beginning of a feast. (In the hands of Catholics, this word was probably conflated with the Latin "jubilo," to shout.)

In Leviticus 25, the Lord told the Jews that just as every seventh day they must give themselves and their servants a break, so every seventh year they must allow the land to rest: No reaping, harvesting, planting, or pruning that year. This "Sabbath year" would allow the earth to replenish itself and the crops to run to seed—a thoroughly sensible measure in a climate like Palestine's. But the Lord had more in mind than soil erosion; He also saw the danger of social classes forming, which

---

[12] Considering how well the French have fought since they started boiling their milk, maybe this last theory deserves a second thought.

might divide His people. So every seventh year, whoever had bought someone else's land would have to give it back, no charge. Likewise, all debts were canceled and all Hebrew slaves were set free. As God reminded the Israelites: "The land shall not be sold for ever: for the land is mine, for ye are strangers and sojourners with me." (Leviticus 25:23)

What is more, after seven cycles of seven years each, a really *big* Sabbath celebration must be held in the forty-ninth year, which the Jews called their Jubilee—and which they associated with Yahweh forgetting the people's sins. To this day, religious Jews still blow the ram's horn once a year, after Yom Kippur, to mark God's promise of forgiveness.

This custom of remitting all debts and returning all land never caught on among the Christians. Like the ban on shellfish and the whole circumcision thing, it seemed like more trouble than it was worth. But the Church retained the spiritual message underlying this celebration—the idea that God might, out of sheer generosity, dispense with the punishment due for sins, so long as we had repented them. The doctrine of Purgatory has its roots in the early Church. Ever since our forefathers squatted in the catacombs, Christians have been praying for the souls of the dead. Now let's think this through for a moment: If (as most Protestants believe) a soul at the moment of death is either damned or saved, and headed straight for Heaven or Hell, these early Christians were wasting their time. Then again, they were also baptizing infants, invoking saints, praying to Mary for intercession, using incense and venerating the Eucharist, so maybe it's best not to bother about them at all, and admit that the Christian Church was founded not by Christ but Martin Luther,[13] and has

---

[13] When confronted with biblical evidence (in Macchabees) that ancient Jews had also prayed for the dead, Luther tossed that book, and 11 other inconvenient documents, out of the canon of Scripture. The Pharisees had done the same thing in the first century, discarding the sacred books most often quoted by early Christians—now called by Protestants the "Apocrypha," which is Greek for "embarrassing stuff."

only existed since 1517. Since it was a bunch of relic-polishing bishops who compiled the Bible itself (and decided which books were inspired, and which were not), we ought to skip that, too. That's one solution.

This isn't the place to explain in depth the Church's doctrine on Purgatory or indulgences. You can find that in our other book, *The Bad Catholic's Guide to Good Living*, pp. 174–179. (On p. 180 we include a handy clip-and-copy indulgence certificate, suitable for framing or sale.) Suffice it to say that when you commit a sin, it's like getting off at the wrong exit on I-10, en route from New Orleans to Baton Rouge. Contrition is that sick feeling you get when you realize you're lost in LaPlace. Repentance is the moment when you pull up in front of Cretin Homes,[14] smack yourself in the head, and make an illegal U-turn across Airline Highway. That's like going to Confession. Now you're headed in the right direction, but you're still farther from God (or Tiger Stadium) than you were before, so you have to backtrack. If you don't backtrack in this life, you'll have to do it once you're dead—but your friends can help you by praying for you, obtaining what is called an "indulgence." It's like sending a traffic helicopter to escort you all the way to the 50 yard line. You can call that help in yourself, by earning indulgences through works of charity or prayer. Does this all make sense now? We thought it would.

In the Jubilee Year, the pope essentially sends out his own pontifical chopper to give each of us a lift. He extends a special indulgence, reducing or eliminating the punishment due in Purgatory, to any penitent sinner who makes a pilgrimage to Rome to visit several holy places—and to anyone who can't make it to Rome, who'll make a similar pilgrimage to designated churches in his area. Just as the Jews were called to the Temple in Jerusalem for prayer on special occasions (such as their Jubilee), so Christians are summoned to our holy places. Since ours is a universal rather than a national religion, our sites of pilgrimage are scattered across the world—although the Jubilee, like the Faith, centers on the one-time seat of St. Peter, in Rome.

The first Christian Jubilee for which we have a reliable record was announced for the year 1300 by Pope Boniface VIII: Bad pope, good idea. Boniface was by all accounts a grasping, power-hungry pontiff. In proclaiming his holy year of Jubilee, he no doubt wished to flood Rome with visitors to fill his empty coffers; he was at war with several secular kings who wished to turn the papacy into their puppet (**see Châteauneuf du Pape**). Regardless of his mixed motives, his Jubilee and each one described by witnesses in subsequent centuries (at regular intervals of 50 or 25

---

[14] A real subdivision on Airline Highway, built, it's said, by a Sicilian family with the unfortunate name of "Cretini," which in Italian means "idiots." They came to the U.S., made good in real estate development, and changed their name to Cretin—which means "idiot" in English. The thing about this book: We don't make anything up. We don't have to.

years) served as a kind of tent-revival for the Church, reminding Christians of their unity amid diversity, of God's generous mercy, and the broadening effects of travel.

Pilgrims descended on Rome from all over Europe in the Jubilee Year—as they did in 2000, when Pope John Paul II celebrated the millennial Holy Year. In accord with a 700-year-old tradition, the pope used a tiny hammer to break down a bricked up "Holy Door" symbolic of the gates of God's abundant mercy, which would flow through the city and the world throughout the year.

Christians of different countries and continents, religious of many orders, and people who prayed in Chinese, Ukrainian, even Latin mixed in the streets of the Universal City in 2000, summoned not by a film festival or even a soccer match, but by the promise that God would forget their sins and remember why He bothered to create them in the first place: Because He loves them. We'd say that's worth a plane ticket (especially if you're flying Jet Blue—they offer each passenger cable TV, including reruns of *24*: Go Jack Bauer!).

The Jewish and later Christian custom of celebrating a Jubilee taps into our innate desire to sanctify time as well as space. We designate holy places, and mark sacred times—like the Sabbath, or Sabbath Year, or Jubilee—by associating them with special graces offered by God, or that we offer each other. An example is the forgiveness of debt offered to debtors who declare bankruptcy. In past centuries, those who could not repay their loans were thrown in debtors' prisons until—well, until they could pay. This begged the question of how they were expected to scrounge up the money while they sat behind bars; the practice recalled the medieval custom of holding war prisoners hostage until their relatives or friends coughed up (**see Joan of Arc**). In the nineteenth and early twentieth century, more humane bankruptcy laws were passed, which allowed those truly unable to remit money they'd borrowed to repay only part of it—or sometimes none at all. After a period of time, a bankrupt would be permitted to rebuild his credit, and win a fresh start; in good Old Testament fashion, lawmakers set that period at seven years. Of course, those laws were sometimes abused, and have recently come under assault by credit card companies, who succeeded in lobbying[15] Congress to tighten the laws. If they had their way, such companies would cheerfully indenture for life their hapless borrowers, some of whom they hooked on easy credit through mass-mailed credit cards sent on their eighteenth birthdays—and again once or twice a week for the next decade or so. (College students have reported being offered six-figure lines of credit.) Having made risky investments in loaning cash to teenagers, these companies now want the ground rules changed, to retroactively eliminate their risk—and enlist the government as their debt collection service. Nice work, if you can get it. To companies that dream of reviving medieval practices such as serfdom, we'd like to suggest another venerable practice: How about some good,

---

[15] Bribing.

old-fashioned usury laws? With interest limited to five or six percent, most people would probably be able to repay their debts without going bankrupt. Or to debtors' prison. But we digress. . . .

The idea of turning anniversaries into sacred events is not uniquely Christian, but thoroughly human. The Romans marked the important milestones in the history of their city. But time had a different meaning for pagans than it does for Christians and Jews. While we do mark the cyclical passage of the week by celebrating Sabbath, and the turn of the centuries through things like the Jubilee, we also see time quite differently. The Greek philosophers agreed with Hindus and Buddhists that time is purely cyclical, a wheel upon which we spin like a roulette ball, from which we may at best hope to escape. But time itself can never be redeemed; indeed, it is the very phenomenon from which we hope, perhaps in vain, to be freed. With God's revelation to the Jews and His Incarnation in Christ, time took on a radically different dimension, as eternity erupted into it. For believers in the Bible, time is an arrow shooting forward from the Creation of the world to the coming (or Second Coming) of the Messiah, Who will sanctify both time and space, in a new Creation that will last for all eternity.

This is heady stuff—like the beers we sometimes brew to mark the little milestones in our own lives. One Jubilee beer was made by the post-Soviet brewing company Baltika, to mark the three-hundredth anniversary of its home city, St. Petersburg, and the tenth anniversary of the brewery's existence. Its Jubilee Beer #10 is a malty brew, characterized by one connoisseur on BeerAdvocate.com as possessing "an almost syrupy sweetness . . . rather like a Slurpee that has melted." We tried to get hold of this beer in order to taste it. But we didn't try very hard.

What sounds like a better beverage is the Xavier Golden Jubilee Wine from Navarra, Spain. That city is the birthplace of St. Francis Xavier, the great apostle of East Asia, and the wine was commissioned by the Xavier School, a Jesuit academy in downtown Manila. It was founded in 1950 by missionaries expelled by Mao from China, but it carries on teaching the Faith in Chinese and to Chinese—a people whom Francis Xavier labored mightily to convert. To mark the fiftieth anniversary of the school, and the five hundredth anniversary of St. Francis's birth (1506), the school commissioned the Estate of La Serna Real to produce this special vintage. To try some, contact the school at *wine@xs.edu.ph.*

Perhaps the most unlikely place for the Jubilee tradition to pop up is in Mobile Bay on the American Gulf Coast. Each summer, its residents are treated to a windfall that seems to come from heaven, in the form of seafood. Off the coast of Fairhope, Alabama, and neighboring towns, the water currents are such that several times a year, thousands of flounder, blue crabs, stingrays, eels, and shrimp will suddenly wash up near the shore, half-stunned from lack of oxygen. These fish just hang out in the water for 10 hours or so, unable to move, until the currents change, then swim away. Unless, of course, a clear-eyed resident happens to notice them. If he does, he will run through the streets (or pick up his cellphone) shouting "Jubilee! Jubilee!" This will summon all the townspeople, who have learned to keep their buckets and ice chests handy. Soon hundreds of hungry Southerners will crowd the beach, singing songs and picking up the compliant fish by the handful. What will follow is a festive all-night fish fry on the beach, as Alabamans feast like ancient Israelites on manna in the desert. If we recall that the fish is an ancient symbol of Christ, this Gulf Coast tradition takes on a certain . . . theological significance. Pass the tartar sauce.

Kahlua and the Problem of Ecclesiastical Land Reform

One of the best-loved liqueurs in the world is the Mexican concoction Kahlua. Even though it was only invented after World War II, and didn't reach the U.S. until the early 1960s, it has become the second most popular brand of liqueur in the world. This delicious coffee drink embodies the complex, happy confusion of life lived under the sun.[1] It is made from fermented sugar cane—like rum—but it's also spiked with vodka. The alcohol makes it relaxing, but the caffeine perks you up. In fact, you think you're sober enough to drive. But the Breathalyzer will say you aren't. And so on.

Likewise, the role of the Church in Mexico over the centuries has been packed with paradox. The missionaries first arrived with rapacious Spanish conquistadors, and marched behind them seeking converts. In the minds of the natives, this put the priests on the side of the invader. But as soon as the Spanish got control, the priests went around baptizing and catechizing everyone in sight—so they couldn't be enslaved. They forced the Spanish Crown to declare the Indians fully human, and allow them to keep their land. The Church used its moral authority to sequester almost half the property in Mexico, much of which it administered as communal farms. It set up missions, hospitals, and schools—including the first university in

the Western Hemisphere, the University of Mexico in 1551 (that arriviste Harvard dates from 1636).

Modern "diversity" addicts now mourn the spread of Christianity in Mexico—which replaced the native Aztec religion. They deplore as "genocide" the destruction of that elaborate pagan cult—which did leave behind some fascinating friezes

---

[1] This confusion will all be cleared up, and everything that has happened in mortal life made blisteringly clear, at the General Resurrection, when "all flesh" will be gathered before Christ the Judge and our every sin revealed, but we're happy to wait.

and highly aerobic ziggurats for post-Christian ecotourists to climb while they're on sabbatical. The Aztecs didn't use armies of nuns to drill kids in catechism, and never bothered with bingo.

But if you look closely, you'll notice a running theme in much of Aztec art: Serving man—in a zesty sauce. The friezes are full of pictures of prisoners of war, tied up by priests with knives, who are cutting out their hearts. And those nifty pyramids? They were all equipped with channels to drain off whole swimming pools of human blood. Read the records of the Aztec priests to find recipes for human flesh flavored with chili peppers; it turns out that a main source of protein for the Mexican upper class was . . . the Mexican lower class.

Now we all know how obnoxious "foodies" can be. At busy diners, they interrogate the waitress about the cheese on their tuna melt. They scrutinize a Thai take-out menu like a pre-nup, and question the freshness of the lemon-grass. When they eat soul food in Harlem, they bring their own fleur-de-sel. Just imagine an entire country run by people like this, with a taste for human flesh. So let's cut Cortes some slack.

But not too much. He and his followers were largely the dregs of Spain, land-pirates hungry for power. To such men, the priests were a dangerous nuisance. If you dreamt of owning a vast *hacienda* manned by compliant Indians gathering *agave* while you drank *rioja* in the shade, the last thing you wanted was a Jesuit making trouble—teaching them to read, and luring them off to some commune where they'd get to keep their crops. Leading thinkers in Spain and Mexico began to explore the whole "Enlightenment" thing—particularly the part about suppressing the Jesuits, then seizing the Church's lands and selling them to the highest bidder. By the mid-nineteenth century, the lily-white descendants of the original conquerors had become big fans of the Separation of Church and State. If they'd had an ACLU, they would have joined it. Instead, they joined the Masons.[2]

The white elites kept their control of Mexico when the Spanish empire fell apart in 1821, but still chafed under the Church's restraints. "Reformers" eager for land (they call it "land reform") got their chance in 1854, when they found an Indian willing to take up their cause—Benito Juarez, an embittered ex-believer. Taking office in a new "liberal" junta that replaced the scoundrel Santa Anna, Juarez began a crusade to strip the Church of its position in Mexico, and seize its lands. In 1857, he spearheaded laws that expelled all religious orders, made marriage a secular contract, and declared it a crime to take religious vows. Priests and nuns could go to prison for wearing their habit outdoors. The junta granted complete religious

---

[2] Masonic groups, largely harmless in England and America—like Ralph Kramden's Loyal Order of Racoons—in Catholic countries became the nexus for underground atheism, and plots to persecute the Church. For this reason, Catholics are still forbidden to join them, on pain of being handed pamphlets by old Irish ladies. And excommunication.

freedom to Mexico's 137[3] Protestants—and seized the vast estates, which the Church had maintained on behalf of the Indians. These were sold to friends of the regime. All this provoked a series of civil wars—and a tragically farcical attempt by Napoleon III to install a Habsburg prince as Emperor of Mexico[4]— which only ended in 1876, when the dictator Porifirio Diaz stopped enforcing the anti-Catholic edicts.[5] But the rich kept the land. As they always seem to do.

CELEBRATE: You can mark the heroic struggle of the Church to evangelize and champion the Indians—or, if you prefer, the heroic struggle of Mexican liberals to secularize and impoverish them—by making a tasty dessert to serve with a nice glass of Kahlua: Mexican "Hot" Chocolate Ice Cream:

Mexican Hot Chocolate Ice Cream

In this case it is imperative to use the specific coconut milk asked for. Nothing else is as creamy and flavorful. The other ingredients can be found in the Mexican section of most grocers.

2 14-ounce cans Roland organic
  coconut milk
3 sticks Mexican cinnamon

5 small squares Luker bitter chocolate
3 ounces panela, an unrefined sugar
1/4 cup water

Heat coconut milk.

Meanwhile singe cinnamon. Find an old metal pan that you don't care too much about. Separate layers of the bark to expose as much as possible. Now you get to use a blow torch. You could also use a fancy crème brulee torch from a kitchen shop. Simply torch the stuff. Do not catch it on fire. It will turn black and some of the edges will glow red. The kitchen will fill with warm aromas. This bit of pyrotechnics releases the essential oils. Add to coconut milk.

On the lowest simmer allow the flavors to meld. Add chocolate and sugar.

Dissolve all before adding water. Taste for flavor balance. If you like very sweet desserts add another ounce panela.

Whirl in a blender and pass through a strainer. Chill overnight before turning in an ice cream machine.

Makes 1 quart

[3] An informal headcount, perhaps inflated.
[4] The holiday of Cinco de Mayo marked by *émigré* Azatlan nationalists in San Diego and Texas fratboys alike, celebrates a victory by Juarez's anti-Catholic allies over the French armies of poor Maximilian— a well-meaning liberal who would die before a firing squad. That's pretty much what happens to well-meaning liberals in Mexico.
[5] These would be revived, with bloody results, in 1924 (**see Tequila**).

Klosterneuburg: The Canons of Quality

Have you ever wondered why we call certain centuries "Dark Ages" (roughly 500–1000 A.D.)? It's not as if the sun did not come out for 500 years—that only happens in England. The continent wasn't shrouded in London fog or L.A. smog. In fact, the population had plummeted thanks to famine and plague: It was an eco-friendly age. Global warming was not a problem, as very few Westerners emitted carbon—except perhaps when their bodies, impaled by invading Ostrogoths, decayed. Most buildings relied on natural heat and lighting—open fireplaces where skinny goats could roast on spits, and narrow slits in the thick stone walls built to keep out the Vikings. It was a simpler time, where most folk worked from home; indeed, they lived and usually died within a day's donkey ride of the spot where they'd been conceived—often in a large, communal bed that held the entire family. Which might have made conception awkward. Or so you'd think. But that's where wine came in.

The problem was that people were forgetting how to make the stuff. To raise a crop of grapes, crush it to juice, age it in barrels, and mix up various vintages to produce a worthy beverage requires patience, skill, and stability—not qualities abundant in Europe for 500 years, when our barbarian[6] ancestors were using Roman ruins as urinals and scrolls of Heracleitus for t.p. These wandering bands of Germans and Slavs were not well-versed in viticulture, but were satisfied to chug down that comparatively cheap and easy beverage, beer. Meanwhile, in the civilized Mediterranean, the armies of Islam were conquering ancient Christian countries from Syria to Spain, and ripping up vines which had grown there since the days of Abraham. The future for wine did not look bright. Indeed, the first recorded use of the term "Dark Ages" occurs in the July/August, 476 issue of *Wine Spectator*, with the headline: "Collapse of Roman Empire Threatens Dark Age for Latium Chianti."[7]

In such dark times, Christian monks kept alive the ancient traditions of winemaking, and introduced new techniques that raised the quality and productivity of vineyards across the continent. In most cases, the evidence has vanished from sight, since money-hungry monarchs or power-mad mobs confiscated the lands once belonging to the monks—though sometimes the corporations now running the vineyards will slap Friar Tuck on the label.

But at one monastery in Austria, Klosterneuburg near Vienna, you can visit a thriving religious community, which still makes fine wine—and sets the standards of quality for the country. Founded in 1114, Klosterneuburg has been staffed since

---

[6] Our apologies to any of the 32 million direct descendants of Ghengis Khan who are reading this book. Had your great-great-great-great grandfather had his way, Christianity would not exist. Neither would books. Hey, at least he tried. . . .

[7] Cf. documentary evidence in our private archives.

1133 by Augustinian Canons Regular.[8] This isn't exactly a religious order in the same sense as the Benedictines or Franciscans. Instead, it's a rule of life designed for priests based on the customs St. Augustine observed among the Christians of fifth-century Milan, which they in turn traced back to the Apostles. This leads Augustinians to claim that theirs is the oldest mode of religious life in the Church. (Of course, the Carmelites say that their order was really "founded" by the Prophet Elias. But since they're mostly vowed to silence,[9] they don't say this very loudly.)

The Augustinian way of life entails living in common, praying the Divine Office[10] several times a day, avoiding accumulated wealth, and serving as parish clergy. As the monks of Klosterneuburg themselves describe their Rule: "This life is essentially priestly, focused on perfecting the priesthood according to the Evangelical Counsels, monastic discipline and the solemn celebration of the liturgy."

In the turbulent centuries before the great rebirth of learning we call the High Middle Ages, it was only the monks and clergy who kept alive such ancient technologies as wine-making, and quaint old customs like literacy. The rest of the population was far too busy scraping out a living from the soil, or riding around on horseback extorting chickens from the peasants. The monasteries stood as oases of learning and logic—like the time-out box at a hockey game. Yeah, just exactly like that.

While many of Austria's monasteries (**see Göttweig**) were over the centuries burned by invading Lutherans, Turks, or Frenchmen, and the survivors seized by the state, by some miracle of Providence—or the judicious use of bribes—Klosterneuburg survived intact. Perhaps its wines were too well-beloved to permit

---

[8] Beware of the Canons Irregular, who claim to offer similar service at a "discount." In our experience, you get what you pray for.

[9] On their home page, the Discalced Carmelite Sisters of Port Tobacco, Maryland, even host a silent auction.

[10] Contrary to urban legend, this does not refer to a suite of rooms at the Vatican, but rather to an ancient compilation of prayers, spiritual readings, songs, and implausibly austere advice recited daily by priests and religious throughout the Church—when they're not serving the poor, making wine, or calling Bingo numbers.

even the most anti-clerical emperor to kill this golden goose. But the canons of Klosterneuburg did more than stomp on grapes and slap on labels. They developed new techniques for producing better wine. According to the wine-loving scientists of the International Conference on Laser Probing, who met at Klosterneuburg in 2006:

> With the increasing importance of wines to Klosterneuburg Monastery came the responsibility not only to preserve but also to develop their quality. As a consequence, the Klosterneuburg Monastery founded the world's first School for Oenology in 1860, encouraging an increasingly professional understanding of wine growing and making. The combined experience and expertise of the monastery and the school further boosted production quality of a unique assortment of wine varietals. Nowadays, wines from typical Austrian varietals such as Grüner Veltliner and St. Laurent as well as from widely grown grapes such as Riesling and Pinot Noir are produced to the highest international standards at the Klosterneuburg Monastery.

As the Laser Probers[11] go on to say, it was at this Oenology school that the monks developed the wine standard still used throughout Austria, the Klosterneuburger Mostwaage scale. This scale classifies wines by their sugar content, measured by how ripe the grapes are when they are picked. As Robin Garr of the *30 Second Wine Advisor* (July 21, 2006) reports, the richest wines are called

> "Smaragd" (which means "emerald" and is also the name of a local emerald-green lizard). The lightest wines from the least-ripe grapes . . . are called "Steinfeder" (literally "stone feather," a kind of grass). And the in-between category . . . is "Federspiel" (meaning "falconry").

It's heartwarming to think that the wine rules in Austria are made not by technicians or bureaucrats, but celibate scholastics in cassocks, and that they're named for local lizards. Somehow, it makes each glass of white taste that much better.

Klosterneuburg still thrives, thank you very much, with new vocations coming in from the U.S., Norway, and even Vietnam. The monks are considering expansion—in fact, they are hoping to open an American branch of Klosterneuburg, to offer us a bracing dose of Augustinian spirituality. Which we'd greet with gladness—so long as they bring along the Gothic architecture. And the wine.

---

[11] Coming to abduct you soon, at a cornfield near you.

Loopholes to the Ten Commandments
#5: Thou Shalt Not Kill

The Church's teaching, while grounded in eternal truths of Natural Law and the injunctions of divine Revelation, has also evolved historically to meet new circumstances, address new challenges, and make life even tougher for bad Catholics like us. This process, which the Ven. John Newman called the "development of doctrine," explains how previously unclear or imperfectly expressed

teachings have become more explicit, sophisticated, and nuanced over centuries. Such development is not unique to the Christian tradition; in fact, it has its roots in the Jewish tradition of midrash, whereby rabbis would debate the true meaning, applicability, and significance of the laws of the Torah. Typically, these debates would end up making the laws even stricter. For example, the seemingly modest divine command "Thou shalt not seethe a kid in his mother's milk" (Deut. 14:21) was probably meant to forbid Israelites from taking part in a pagan ritual featuring this dish. But the law metastasized over the centuries to include ever more prohibitions—to really, really make sure there was no mixing of meat and milk—until at last Kosher kitchens on the Upper West Side use two sets of sinks and refrigerators, one for dairy and one for flesh.

But sometimes the process works the other way, as commentators examine divine laws and find the limits of their true application—or what we like to call the "loopholes." For instance, "Thou Shalt Not Kill." Sounds pretty straightforward, right? If taken absolutely literally, it would seem to imply pacifism, vegetarianism, and any number of other evils. Happily, the rabbis of the Old Testament and theologians of the New came up with quite a variety of circumstances in which killing might well be necessary. For instance, in what the Church calls a "just war," (**see Jeremiah Weed**). Another exception to this commandment occurs in the case of capital punishment, which the Church supported for millennia—sometimes, as in the case of witches and heretics, with a tad too much enthusiasm. Traditionally, the Church allowed for the state to execute criminals for a variety of reasons—primarily, in order to defend the community from the violence committed by an outlaw, but also in order to enact on earth the just retribution for sin. Essentially, this meant that the State, as God's designated authority on earth, had the right to demand an eye for an eye, a tooth for a tooth.

In his encyclical *Evangelium Vitae*, and in the revised edition of the new Catechism of the Catholic Church, Pope John Paul II tried to sew up this loophole. He left out the second reason for capital punishment—the enactment of justice—and only allowed for executions in the rare circumstances where criminals could not be safely held in prison: for instance, in countries where drug lords or terrorists are likely to escape.

Pope John Paul's attempt to nudge along this particular development of doctrine has met with mixed reviews. Some progressive Catholics think it does not go far enough, while traditionalists complain that the pope has set himself up against St. Thomas Aquinas, 1500 years of tradition, and the long history of papal executioners who served the Papal States. (Vatican City had the death penalty on the books until 1968.) But there's one point all of them are missing: The potential conflict between this development and the spirit of Vatican II. Most observers agree that the Council was meant to open the Church to the modern world; this was the clear intent of *Gaudium et Spes*, which Cardinal Wotyjla himself helped to write.

But if there is one thing for which the twentieth century will be remembered, it will be for its enthusiastic embrace of capital punishment—for almost any crime, or none at all. In his essay "Death By Government," scholar R. J. Rummel points out that "during the first eighty-eight years of this century, almost 170,000,000 men, women, and children have been shot, beaten, tortured, knifed,

burned, starved, frozen, crushed, or worked to death; or buried alive, drowned, hung, bombed, or killed in any other of the myriad ways governments have inflicted death on unarmed, helpless citizens or foreigners."

And here Pope John Paul II stands, rejecting the voice of modernity, trying to impose yet another medieval superstition. . . . It's enough to test one's faith.

Lambic and the Laity

The most celebrated beers of Belgium are the monastic brews made by Trappists and other orders (**see Ales**). Yet this elite of spiritual brewmasters is but one small part of that nation's Catholic life and beer making. As in any other country, these higher pursuits have always had to rest on a solid foundation among the laymen—ordinary folk who wed and work, who regularly raise both families and a glass or two. In his letter *Christifideles Laici*, Pope John Paul II compared Catholic laymen to "the laborers in the vineyard mentioned in Matthew's Gospel." (Matthew 20:1–2) Christ might just as well have spoken instead of brewers gathering hops. Had Our Lord been addressing Belgians.

In that curious, bicultural country,[1] the proudest culinary product of any description is neither wine nor cheese but beer. Belgium produces hundreds of different varieties, most of them distinctive and complex—and meant to be drunk in a particular type of glass. Visit the home of any Belgian, and you'll find an entire cabinet devoted to beer glasses of dozens of different shapes.[2] And the beer that evokes

---

[1] The two main linguistic groups in Belgium are the French-speaking Walloons and the Dutch-speaking Flemish. They are woven together by an historic Catholic Faith, a love of beer, a profound mutual hatred of each other.

[2] It's telling that the country's national symbol is the Manneken-Pis, a bronze statue of a little boy taking a whiz. This emblem is widely used in tourist brochures, where it sends out the unspoken message to underage college students: "Hey Americans, come to Belgium: *We don't card.*"

the image of ordinary, pious Belgian laymen who kept the Church alive for centuries is not the carefully crafted ale created by celibate contemplatives, but the rough and ready beverage known as lambic. Elite brews such as lagers, ales, and stouts are made with special varieties of yeasts (**see Yeast**) maintained by brewers' guilds or brewmaster monks—and passed along to novices like the Rule and traditions of a religious order. Indeed, many guilds had elaborate, pseudo-liturgical initiation rites—stonemasons, for example, whose quirky traditions later gave birth to the Freemasons and a world of trouble.

But lambic production has always relied on wild yeasts and bacteria, which float through the Belgian air or survive in casks from last year's beer. Often made at home by peasants or laborers, lambic was not strong enough to cause a work-stoppage, like higher-proof ales such as Chimay. Instead, lambic was a cheap and pleasant beverage with a complex taste. In contrast to German beers, which are governed by creepy-sounding medieval "purity laws,"[3] lambics are made in messy cellars, where beermakers let dust and cobwebs form on the barrels to help encourage the right mix of up to 86 different microbes in the

brew. Made with older hops that serve as natural preservatives and keep the beer from spoiling, lambics are often dry, and even a little sour. Resourceful Belgian peasants made the best of a bitter beer—by dosing the finished lambic with ripe, fresh fruit or syrup. Popular lambics today include cherry, apple, peach, and grape. Our favorite is Lindeman's *Framboise*, made with raspberries, which we've nicknamed "beer for girls." Even women who swear they hate the very smell of beer—perhaps because it evokes sundry boozehounds they used to date and the associated restraining orders—will happily down a tankard or two of *framboise,* the beer equivalent of a frozen daiquiri.

Just like the little critters that give rise to lambic, the yeast of Faith most commonly grows not in the stark environs of a convent, but in a messy, distinctly non-celibate house full of laymen. Indeed, the Church's vitality stands or falls with the faithfulness of the ordinary churchgoer. Not every Church leader in the past 2,000 years has appreciated this fact. No less a saint than Jerome, the translator of the Bible, once made the snarky comment, "I praise wedlock, I praise marriage: but it is because they produce virgins." It's this kind of self-serving comment that lights a fire among anti-clerical mobs, on their way to burn down

---

[3] The term sounds even worse in German: **Rienhietsgobot**. Do you really want the **Reinheitpolizei** knocking down your door? Nor do we.

historic cathedrals. But a strong current of respect for the activity of lay Catholics has always existed among the great theologians. In the Renaissance, it was laymen who spearheaded the *devotio moderna*, a movement to encourage ordinary Christians to study the Bible, examine their consciences, and more deeply assimilate the truths of the Faith. The spirituality of two great thinkers who would likely have detested each other, Erasmus of Rotterdam and Ignatius Loyola, both emerged from this lay-led movement—with its roots in the Low Countries, where lambic reigned supreme.

Over centuries, ordinary laymen as much as clergy helped keep the Flemish and Walloon regions faithful to the Church—not an easy task, given the area's history. For some 300 years, the Catholic parts of the Low Countries (which later made up Belgium) had to fight the expansionist, Calvinist Dutch. Their Catholic faith kept most Belgians loyal to the Habsburgs—which left them on the losing side of the Thirty Years' War. In 1648, the conquering Dutch cut off the port of Antwerp from the sea, crippling its economy. Politically, the Catholics of the area found themselves traded back and forth like pawns—awarded now to Spain, now to Austria, then invaded by Revolutionary France, which persecuted the Church. In fact, the Jacobins expelled so many priests from the region that laymen used to gather in the barns they used for harvesting hops to celebrate a "blind Mass"—a prayer service with neither priest nor Eucharist. When the French were finally driven out after Waterloo, the hapless residents found themselves ruled by the Dutch, who promptly passed laws restricting the Church's freedom to run schools. Rising to the occasion, Catholic laymen led a successful revolt in 1830—and created the independent Kingdom of Belgium.

When secularizing liberals came to power in Belgium in 1860, and tried to clamp down on Catholic education, it was a lay movement, the *Fédération des Cercles Catholiques*, which led the fight to keep the State from hobbling the Church. The laity worked against these anti-clerical laws, inspired by songs such as "They are not going to have . . . the beautiful souls of children." One eyewitness wrote:

> Almost every Catholic meeting which I attended at that time was a fiery furnace for the souls, from which a torrent of sparks and flames of holy enthusiasm was generated; a powerful forge, in which the armaments were hardened for a battle for the Cross which now threatened from all sides.[4]

It was of laymen like this whom Pius XII spoke when he said that "The Faithful, more precisely the lay faithful, find themselves on the front lines of the Church's life."

---

[4] Cf. S.N. Kalyvas, *The Rise of Christian Democracy in Europe* (Ithaca: Cornell University Press, 1966), as cited by John Rao in "All Borrowed Armor Chokes Us," *Seattle Catholic* (July 9, 2005).

Of course, the lay faithful in Belgium aren't quite what they used to be. For all the emphasis placed on the role of the laity at Vatican II—where Dutch and Belgian bishops helped write (or trash and rewrite) major documents—the faith of such folk since then has gone as flat as a glass of lambic left out for 40 years. Mass attendance has plummeted, and recent papal visits to the Low Countries have been attended by small crowds of faithful—and plenty of protestors, hurling condoms at the clergy. Perhaps the faith of layfolk flourishes best when the priests seems to tolerate us reluctantly, rather than making a big fuss about how we "are Church." That's more pressure than most of us can handle. Our creaky, sometimes superstitious faith is more like wild yeast, which prospers when it's left to itself, with plenty of cobwebs and bacteria.

CELEBRATE: Honor the special sacrifices made by the clergy and religious who make possible the middling Sacramental lives of puttering laymen like you and me. Invite a priest, brother, or nun over for a posh dinner at your home. (If they're like the priests we know in New York City, they earn about $20,000 per year and are on call almost 24/7.) Use as the pretext the feast of whichever saint occurs on the evening you find most convenient, and serve up one of the tasty menus you'll find throughout this book. Then serve up this powerfully pleasurable dessert made of Raspberry Lambic and vanilla ice cream, which (fittingly) takes very little effort to prepare. Remind this clerical guest, "While most of us laymen may be lukewarm, this float is frosty cold."

Raspberry Lambic Float

Of course it sounds great. It tastes even better than it sounds. If frat boys were to discover this drink, no father would let his daughter go off to college.

1 750-ml bottle Lindeman's Framboise Lambic
 Fresh Raspberries
2 pints Haagen-Dazs vanilla ice cream

Chill 4 tall glasses. Place several raspberries in the bottom of each glass, then three scoops ice cream. Slowly pour in lambic. Garnish with more raspberries.
    There will be extra raspberries and ice cream, but since when is that a problem?
    Serve with long spoons and straws.

Makes 4 servings

Late-Harvest Wines: Deathbed Converts Welcome

If you don't happen to be a cork-dork,[5] you might never have heard of late-harvest wines. If so, that's a shame, since these wines are especially appealing, even to those of us who can't tell a pinot grigio from a pineapple. Late-harvest wines are sweet, fruity, and fun—that's why they're usually served with dessert. Examples include riesling, spätlese, sauterne, and the exotic ice-wine—made from bunches of grapes that have frozen on the vine (pictured). Late-harvest grapes are left in the field long after all others have been gathered in the hope that they will undergo what vintners call "noble rot." There's a grape fungus called *botrytis cinerea*, which

Photo by Dominic Rivard

drains the grapes of water and concentrates their natural sugar—leaving a kind of raisin, which when fermented turns into a rich, lively drink to wash down your profiteroles or sorbet. Or to drown a quarrel over dinner in a sweet and tipsy haze.

There's at least one passage in the New Testament referring to late-harvest wine, albeit allegorically. One of the most intriguing—and to some, infuriating—of Jesus' parables is the tale of the laborers in the vineyard. Since we'll be doing a close textual analysis, we've included the whole story below:

> For the kingdom of heaven is like unto a man that is an householder, which went out early in the morning to hire labourers into his vineyard.
>
> And when he had agreed with the labourers for a penny a day, he sent them into his vineyard.
>
> And he went out about the third hour, and saw others standing idle in the marketplace,
>
> And said unto them; Go ye also into the vineyard, and whatsoever is right I will give you. And they went their way.
>
> Again he went out about the sixth and ninth hour, and did likewise.
>
> And about the eleventh hour he went out, and found others standing idle, and saith unto them, Why stand ye here all the day idle?
>
> They say unto him, Because no man hath hired us. He saith unto

---

[5] The oh-so-self-deprecating nickname adopted by chianti-gargling, cork-sniffing wine snobs. If you've ever been a waiter, you know what these folks are really called. It rhymes with "fast moles."

them, Go ye also into the vineyard; and whatsoever is right, that shall ye receive.

So when even was come, the lord of the vineyard saith unto his steward, Call the labourers, and give them their hire, beginning from the last unto the first.

And when they came that were hired about the eleventh hour, they received every man a penny.

But when the first came, they supposed that they should have received more; and they likewise received every man a penny.

And when they had received it, they murmured against the goodman of the house,

Saying, These last have wrought but one hour, and thou hast made them equal unto us, which have borne the burden and heat of the day.

But he answered one of them, and said, Friend, I do thee no wrong: didst not thou agree with me for a penny?

Take that thine is, and go thy way: I will give unto this last, even as unto thee.

Is it not lawful for me to do what I will with mine own? Is thine eye evil, because I am good?

So the last shall be first, and the first last: for many be called, but few chosen. (Matthew 20:1–16)

Biblical interpreters, known as "hermeneuts," have been quarreling about how to read this passage for centuries. The first question to arise, of course, is why Jesus

spoke in Elizabethan English. Scholars have not yet resolved this mystery, but there are deeper issues at stake—such as what the passage really means. Some see this parable as a heads-up from Jesus to His Jewish disciples, letting them know that the late-coming *goyim* would be offered the same mercy as the Chosen Folks.[6] Others saw it as a warning to the devout of either Covenant that the Lord would welcome late harvesters, lost sheep, and prodigal sons with open arms—so that they'd better get with the whole "mercy program."

We'd like to propose another reading: Perhaps Our Lord was thinking of late-harvest grapes, which are gathered at the eleventh hour, just before winter. While

---

[6] Kinky Friedman's term, which we picked up from his delightful anthem "We Reserve the Right to Refuse Service to You." Thanks, Kinkster—we voted for you. And we don't even live in Texas!

these grapes render less juice, the wine they make is sweeter and fetches a higher price. It's possible that the "goodman of the house" in this parable was at once merciful and savvy; he knew that the grapes brought in at the end would more than repay his penny, since they'd end up inside a $27 bottle of Château d'Yquem.

Before you laugh this off, consider that the grapes gathered might be a metaphor for souls, and these late-harvest grapes might refer to late or deathbed converts—while the "noble rot" that perfects such grapes might be the very sins they committed before their conversion. Our Lord repeatedly speaks of the "joy in heaven" evoked by lost sheep found, and the history of the Church has been enriched immeasurably by those who accepted the Faith only in their last years or even hours. Famous examples include the poet Wallace Stevens, the actor John Wayne, the playwright Oscar Wilde, and the artist Aubrey Beardsley (see Beardsley's illustration for Wilde's great play on the death of St. John the Baptist, *Salome*, pictured).

Perhaps the most important deathbed convert for the earthly mission of the Church was the Emperor Constantine. This son of a saint (Helena) was for most of

his life no saint himself. As he fought a bloody war for control of the Empire, however, he did see a vision of the Cross, with the slogan *"in hoc signe vincet"* ("in this sign, conquer"). As a man who knew how to take a hint, Constantine adopted the hitherto-scorned emblem of convicted criminals as his standard, and rapidly gained the throne. In gratitude to whatever Higher Power had granted him victory, he repealed the laws that had kept Christians locked in the catacombs. Finding among the Christians the noblest remnants of a faded Roman republican virtue, he began to favor the Church openly. Within a few years, he was building grand basilicas, mediating doctrinal disputes, and presiding over the Council of Nicaea, which affirmed the divinity of Christ—*all before he'd even been baptized.*

Why did he wait? That's easy: Baptism wipes away every sin, however mortal, and all attendant time in Purgatory, too. It's a like a presidential pardon, which clears away all legal liability for

A) Bugging the Watergate Hotel (Richard Nixon, 1973)
B) Running guns to Islamic dictatorships to help fund Latin American death squads (Elliott Abrams, 1992)
C) Earning over $1.5 billion trading illegally with Iran, never paying taxes, then fleeing to Switzerland (Marc Rich, 2001)
D) Lying the U.S. into war (We'll get back to you on this.)

Both baptism and the presidential pardon are like a Get Out of Jail, Free, card—and you only get one of them. Once you use it, your sins start piling up again. And in Constantine's time, it wasn't clear how to get rid of them. The Sacrament of Confession was not widely practiced.

And Constantine was a realist. If baptism would wash his soul as white as snow, he knew that to keep his throne and hold the Empire together, he'd have to resort to some pretty questionable means—spraying that snowy soul a deep, warm yellow. So Constantine procrastinated. He didn't get baptized until after he'd taken care of his enemies and his empire, for instance by:

- Executing a rebellious son.
- Imposing confiscatory taxes on pain of torture.
- Driving a disloyal wife to suicide.

Now, some purists scorn the attempts of Christians to build Christendom, and prefer the rigor of the catacombs. We cordially invite them to pick up and move to someplace more hospitable to martyrs, such as Sudan. Thanks to Constantine, we got 1,000 years of Christian Europe—complete with cathedrals like Chartres, poets like Dante and Chaucer, and saints like Joan of Arc. It's true that Christendom has lost its lease (we hear it's being turned into a hookah pipe café), but it was fun while it lasted. We'll miss it.

In a similar vein, if Oscar Wilde had been a devout Catholic taking spiritual direction from, say, Cardinal Newman (a friend to whom he wrote decades before he converted) the world would be much poorer. No *Picture of Dorian Gray*, no *Salome*, and no *Importance of Being Earnest* would have passed muster with *that* confessor. Wilde still might have written the deeply Christian children's tale, "The Selfish Giant," but there's no way he would have garnered the . . . er, *experiences* which yielded the great *De Profundis* or "The Ballad of Reading Gaol."

Likewise, a pious Aubrey Beardsley would have abandoned his sexy, provocative prints—and applied that same weird, decadent style to holy cards. We shudder to think.

Most chillingly, had John Wayne entered the Church before his deathbed, he might have felt obliged to do more movies like *The Greatest Story Ever Told*, in which he played the soldier Longinus who pierced Christ's side—then saw the Light and drawled, "Truly, this man wuz the Son of Gawd." Thank heaven for such small mercies.

Loreto: The Holy House and the Skeptic

There's nothing here that relates directly to mixing drinks, so the single-minded reader may choose to skip ahead. We're discussing the Shrine of Loreto not for any liqueurs distilled on the grounds or grapes grown in its shadows, but because the miraculous story behind the shrine sounds rather like a drunk's tale—something an old man with oddly colored teeth would recount while you tried to flag down the bartender. Not that this means it isn't true. . . .

As we point out in *The Bad Catholic's Guide to Good Living*, many of these good people's stories ring strange to modern ears: elaborate executions worthy of Edgar Allen Poe, extraordinary penances that evoke the DSM-IV, and implausibly grand miracles out of 1950s Japanese sci-fi flicks. We won't know until the General Resurrection how many of these things

really, you know, *happened*. And then we'll be too busy squirming at the exposure of our sins, and gawking at sins of others. But even the most pious Catholics admit that some of these tales are the fruit of fancy, or grew in the telling. I mean, if God made this sort of thing happen in the past, why not now? If second-century martyrs could be burned, crucified, and drowned without dying, only succumbing when they were finally beheaded,[7] why doesn't this happen today in Sudan or Indonesia? On the other hand, the life of twentieth-century saint Padre Pio contained a laundry list of well-attested wonders, from soul-reading to apparitions in the clouds that warned off Allied B-17s. . . .

So on the question of particular miracles we remain, like the Church, agnostic. Aware of the danger of superstition—or diabolical charades—recent popes and bishops have erred on the side of skepticism. When told of wonder-cures worked at Lourdes, they send in atheist doctors to look for a natural explanation. Nuns and monks who claim that they hear the voice of God are sent straight to the neurologist. Most apparitions of Mary are chalked up to indigestion. The Church's attitude boils down to this: If God wants to perform a miracle, He'd better make His intentions crystal clear. Otherwise we're not buying it.

Given this sturdy, show-me papal stance, it's all the more surprising that repeated pontiffs have given credence to the most outrageous miracle ever claimed by any Catholic outside of a locked ward with no sharp objects: the Holy House of Loreto. In 1920, a thoroughly rational pope (Benedict XV), in full possession of his faculties, approved a special blessing for aircraft, invoking this shrine in Italy. It reads:

> O merciful God, You have consecrated the House of the Blessed Virgin Mary with the mystery of the Word Incarnate and placed it in the midst of your children. Pour forth your blessing on this vehicle so that those who take an aerial trip in it may happily reach their destination and return safely home under Mary's protection.

Because, you see, aircraft fly. *And so did . . . the house.*

The Holy House of Loreto, according to a centuries-old tradition, is the very house in which the Holy Family lived. That's right, the same bricks and mortar that surrounded St. Joseph, the Virgin Mary, and the child Jesus throughout His boyhood. Legend tells that the house was carried by angels from Palestine in 1291. It made a three-year layover in Dalmatia, before settling down in Loreto, near Ancona. The locals were deeply impressed, and spent the next 100 years building a basilica to house the house.

---

[7] The closest modern equivalent is Rasputin. And nobody considers him a saint. Except for some fanatically anti-Semitic Tsarist monks we once got stuck with for a weekend . . .but that's a whole 'nother story.

It's a humble little hut, made of stone that is found in the Holy Land, not in Italy. It measures only 31 feet by 16, but inside you'll find an altar with a black statue of the Madonna and child, and the inscription *Hic Verbum caro factum est*: The Word was made flesh *here*. Now, even if the Holy House is authentic, this isn't quite accurate: The Basilica of the Annunciation in Nazareth has a prior claim, since it's said to contain the home where Mary lived when Jesus was *conceived*. Still, the idea that this cottage in Italy was the place where Jesus toddled around and toyed with carpenter's tools is deeply impressive. It has attracted pilgrims for centuries, received the blessing of almost 50 popes—right down to John Paul II— and served as the site of innumerable miracles. Some of the greatest intellectuals in Western history paid tribute to the shrine and the cures which happened there—including saints Charles Borromeo, Francis de Sales, Ignatius Loyola, and the essayist Montaigne.

Others were skeptical. Renaissance humanists and Enlightenment *philosophes* were quick to mock the simple faith of folk who believed in houses flying around the Mediterranean. Thanks to modern research, which raised new questions about the house, the 1917 *Catholic Encyclopedia* hedged its bets, pointing out that no one in Nazareth ever complained that a Holy House had gone missing. Later researchers would offer a sane solution to the mystery of this house, which legend told was brought over by "*gli Angeli*." They turned up evidence that around 1291 a small house was shipped, stone by stone, from Palestine by a family named Angeli. So the aerodynamics of the house may result from an historical typo.

Of course popes are far from infallible when they discuss the veracity of miracles. Indeed, the Church's authority extends only to the realm of faith and morals, and the body of public Revelation that ended with the death of St. John the Apostle. The only historic events on which the pope can comment definitively are those. This means that Pope Pius XII was within his rights to define the dogma of Mary's Assumption—which took place during this time period. But he couldn't have announced, for instance, that Catholics must believe St. Francis got the stigmata, or that Joseph of Cupertino[8] could levitate. Likewise, later private revelations such as at Lourdes and Fatima may win official favor, but the Church can't vouch for them.

Still, few Catholics want to go through life accepting only the infallibly defined articles of faith (though a fair number like to cite them at every possible opportunity, and at great length, as you back away from them with a nervous smile). Most of us are happy enough to believe in any number of improbable tales, which are also unproveable and delightful—from St. Christopher carting baby Jesus around on his back to St. Nicholas dropping bags of gold down chimneys. The life of Faith requires a kind of balancing act, a tightwire walk between superstition and skepticism, centered on an openness to mystery.

---

[8] Patron saint of pilots.

The one philosopher in history who did the most to unsettle this classic tension was the French thinker René Descartes (1596–1650). Trained by the Jesuits and a faithful Catholic throughout his life, Descartes nevertheless led Western thought down a rabbit hole from which it has not yet emerged. Indeed, he may have single-handedly and unwittingly set off the Enlightenment. (That's a lot of Purgatory he's looking at; let's keep him in our prayers!) As a young philosopher, Descartes was tormented by the quest for radical certainty. At a time when the Christian world stood at point of sword—the Thirty Years' War was raging between Catholics and Protestants—Descartes looked for arguments that would resolve these bitter questions.

In vain. The fight between different sects of Christian could not be resolved by debating the Bible; its roots lay in centuries of messy history and circular debates.

Each group pointed to the same authorities, and came up with opposite answers.

Meanwhile, in the realm of secular science—where Descartes' true vocation lay—biologists were prone to accept the authority of ancient Greeks like Galen over the evidence of their eyes, and serious scientists dabbled in alchemy and magic. Worst of all for Descartes, most philosophers practiced scholasticism, relying on tradition and authority to bolster or base their arguments.

The young Descartes craved something plainer, a clean slate from which to begin the quest for knowledge on grounds of absolute certainty. At 23, this high-minded Frenchman hoped to reinvent the basis of all human knowledge. To paraphrase Martin Luther King, Jr.: He had a dream.

No—really. He had an actual *dream*. On November 10, 1619, Descartes went to bed with a low-grade fever. As he slept fitfully, he dreamt that he was asked to choose between two books—one a collection of poetry, and the other a dictionary. He had to pick the more reliable source. Descartes surprised himself by choosing the poems. Then he woke up.

Now when most of us have a puzzling dream, we either forget about it or call up a friend who owes us a favor and bore him with it for an hour. If we're Woody Allen, we pay an M.D. $150 to listen to it while grunting. But Descartes took this dream as a revelation, as a sword that cut through the knots tying up his mind. He knew, in a brilliant intuition, what this dream meant and what he must do.

Pen in hand, Descartes began to compose a philosophical system, which would not rely on the dry-as-dust, uncertain knowledge of the sort that washed up in dictionaries, but rather on the clarity and precision that came to poets. He decided the only source of certitude that could be found was the mind itself—the rational mind which looked at timeless truths like the principles of geometry. Indeed, he made geometry the model for every other science. Descartes adopted a principle of ruthless, radical doubt—rejecting out of hand every "truth" relying upon tradition, authority, or consensus. He began with the basic, unshakeable awareness: "I think, therefore I am." He even explored, and argued at length against, the idea that all life was a dream, fed into our brains by an "Evil Genius" or the Matrix.

In fact, Descartes did not even believe his lying eyes; he dismissed Aristotle and Aquinas for trusting sensory information. The level of certitude Descartes demanded went far beyond the dubious data collected by man's five imperfect senses. Critics such as Jacques Maritain (*The Dream of Descartes*, 1944) said that Descartes craved the knowledge only vouchsafed to angels. There's certainly something to that, since Descartes could not wrap his mind around why or how our souls are linked to our bodies; he described this arrangement unhappily as like a ghost trapped in a corpse. Animals, he decided, had no feelings, but were simply robots made of meat.[9] The goal of science, he said, was no longer the comprehension of the cosmos, but to "make man the master and possessor of nature." That is, instead of God.

One of the greatest modern Catholic novelists, Walker Percy, cited Descartes as the source of modern man's alienation. By rejecting the senses and devaluing the body, Descartes undermined the very notion of a Sacrament, and taught us to see ourselves primarily as minds—and our bodies as lumpy, smelly, imperfect tools. If we look at Christianity through a starkly Cartesian lens, the whole thing falls apart. Why would the Word become Flesh in the first place? And how would that be an improvement? Why trap God in flesh and blood, and box Him up in a tabernacle? Far better to imagine Him as a faraway Watchmaker, popping in the lithium battery a few billion years ago, then wearing it like a Swatch. The psychiatrist and convert Karl Stern pointed out, in his classic book, *The Flight from Woman*, that such a worldview could only have occurred to a young *man*—and one with serious issues about his mother. Stern suggests that ambivalence toward matter begins with anxiety towards one's *mater*.

We don't mean to reduce a great thinker's work to some petty neurosis, but we can't help suspecting that Stern and Maritain were on to something. Without Descartes' influence, it's hard to imagine a loudly Christian country like America scattered thick with infertility clinics and freezers full of embryos, languishing like tiny ghosts who are indeed trapped in machines.

Perhaps the most amazing part about Descartes' famous dream is the effect it had on his religious life: It sent him marching off happily to a famous Marian

---

[9] For this reason, the Body Shop refuses to stock the works of Descartes, since all their products bear the label "against animal testing."

shrine. So grateful was the young thinker for the private revelation which founded his philosophy, that upon waking up he vowed to make a pilgrimage. To thank God for starting him on the path towards absolute skepticism, Descartes went to visit . . . the flying House of Loreto.

So maybe Descartes was a tippler after all. To quote Monty Python: "Rene Descartes was a drunken fart/ I drink, therefore I am."

Malta: The Knights, Their Wars, Their Wines

We hate to spoil the romance of the grape, but most wine estates once run by monks or noble families are now in the hands of corporate vintners with publicly traded shares, human resource departments, and 401k plans. The closest connection to aristocracy or the Church most wines now keep is a coat of arms on the label.

However, a few fine wines are made to this day by one of the most delightfully anachronistic institutions in the Church—an order of military monks called the Knights of Malta. In Umbria, this order's Castello di Magione vineyards produce over 100,000 bottles every year of Colli di Trasimeno, at an old castle where the Knights once patrolled the walls. Another first-rate knightly wine is Kommende Mailberg, a white Grüner Veltliner produced at the order's castle in Austria, which can be ordered at any imaginative wine shop.

The Knights got named for Malta because that small, Mediterranean island was ruled for centuries by this distinctive religious order, the last group to carry on the spirit of the Crusades. It was founded around 1100 by a band of Italian merchants and a pious knight known only to history as Blessed Gerard. Its mission at first was simple: to open shelters in the Holy Land for Christian pilgrims who got sick with Levantine diseases, or caught one of the millions of arrows flying around the region at the time. Many elderly or sick Christians in fact took ship to Jerusalem intending to die there, in the town where (medievals believed) the General Resurrection would begin.[1]

Since these shelters offered hospitality, they were called "hospitals"—which is

---

[1] Nowadays old folk prepare for the possible heat of the afterlife by moving to the Sunbelt, giving Purgatory a healthy head start.

153

where we get the word—and the group that ran them was dubbed the Knights Hospitaller of Jerusalem. Unlike certain other medieval medical facilities, which will go nameless,[2] the Knights' shelters were compassionate and clean. Indeed, as Jonathan Riley-Smith, author of *The Oxford Illustrated History of the Crusades*, writes:

> A feature of their nursing was this: because every poor man and woman was Christ, he or she should have not just good treatment, but the best and most luxurious treatment possible. This was, of course, a religious imperative, but it was also the application of a basic nursing principle, taught in the greatest of the western medical schools at Salerno, that patients tended to get better if they were well-fed, clean, and comfortable.[3]

Riley also points out a surprising feature of this crusader estate: Its shelter welcomed sick Moslems and Jews on the same terms as Christians, even serving them halal and kosher food. As one Hospitaller document insisted, "Friends should be loved in God and enemies on account of God."

However, the time and place were far from peaceful, and the Knights were not slow to see that their charitable work required a paramilitary wing. The Latin Kingdom of Jerusalem was an island of Western influence in a hostile Islamic sea—like a medieval Baghdad Green Zone, except without CNN. At first, the Knights who agreed to carry the sword served simply as escorts to groups of pilgrims, but—boys being boys—they soon formed an army. By 1170, the Hospitallers were less focused on treating wounds than on inflicting them. They controlled seven enormous fortresses and more than 140 estates around the Holy Land, with thousands of manors scattered all across Europe, earning money for their foreign mission.

When Jerusalem fell to Saladin's Arab armies in 1187, most Christian armies declared victory and went home. The Hospitallers stuck around, conducting a kind of insurgency until 1291, when they fled to safety in Cyprus, and then to Rhodes—which they conquered in 1309, and governed until 1522. While they gave up dreams of reconquering Jerusalem, the Knights kept up a first-rate navy to suppress the Arab pirates who traded in white slaves. When Rhodes fell to the new Islamic superpower, the Ottomans, the Knights removed to Malta. They controlled that island until 1798, when French knights opened the gates to Napoleon's armies. After

---

[2] Okay, they won't: For instance, the London clinic called St. Mary's of Bethlehem, where mentally ill medieval Englishmen were locked away with no access to SSRIs or even standard psychoanalysis. Conditions there were so "interesting" that the place's name gave rise to the modern word "bedlam."

[3] Jonathan Riley-Smith, "The Military Orders: Their History and Continuing Relevance," a conference paper read at Emmanuel College, Cambridge, 2005, p. 9.

defeating Napoleon at Waterloo, the British saw no reason to turn this strategic spot over to an order of antiquated papists, so the Brits remained there until 1964, and the Knights remained in exile. That might have logically spelled the order's end, if logic had any say. But chivalry, faith, and institutional inertia spoke louder, and the Knights kept on recruiting and raising funds. With gentle nudging from various popes, the group switched from cannons to ceremonial swords, and rediscovered its founding mission: providing ambulances on battlefields, and opening hospitals for the poor.

Unlike some groups that fell prey to lurid scandals (**see Templars**) or were coopted by crafty kings, this order thrives today, with thousands of members around the world. There's a small priestly core surviving as the world's corps of warrior monks, and a large male membership of Knights[4] (dames may enroll as Dames). The organization still retains a unique status as a "sovereign order" with some of the rights of an independent state—keeping diplomats in 92 countries, and holding a seat at the U.N. It issues passports, mints coins, and maintains two post offices in Rome. As our friend, Knight of Malta Stephen Klimczuk, likes to recount, if you visit the order's palace on the Aventine Hill in Rome:

> You can look through a famous keyhole in the grand doors and see three sovereign entities—looking through the gardens of the Knights' extra-territorial compound through Italy to the dome of St Peter's in Vatican City. There is no other place on earth where one can do something like this.

Today, as Riley-Smith reports, the Knights of Malta and their Protestant off-

shoots boast nearly 50,000 members, 400,000 volunteers, and work in 150 countries—rivaling the Red Cross. The good work of the Knights is widely recognized; indeed, the Knights were among the first organized firefighters in the world, so when Irishmen in New York and Boston began volunteer fire brigades, they adopted the Maltese Cross as their emblem (pictured).[5]

To some, the do-gooding mission revived by the Knights—wiping noses and tending

---

[4] In his Cambridge lecture, Jonathan Riley-Smith distinguishes this papally erected military order from the Bay-area based Gay and Lesbian Knights of Malta (est. 1976), an "Old Guard Leather . . . adult social club that is dedicated to community service." These West Coast knights hew to a more contemporary creed than the Catholic Knights, and their costumes are strikingly different.

[5] If you've seen *Gangs of New York*, you know that some of these fire brigades also took up the sword—which they'd use on rival firemen, in fights over the right to fight a given fire.

wounds—might seem a sad fate for a group that once helped conquer Jerusalem and fought in the Battle of Lepanto. In an age when members of other faiths feel free to take up the sword on behalf of their beliefs, it irks a certain type of Christian that we are reduced to turning the other cheek. There's a craving among some muscular-minded Catholics to revive the militant spirit of the Templars and Knights of Malta, albeit with modern weapons. The Fraternity of St. Sebastian (*www.christiansoldiers.org*) seeks

> young men from any walks of life to be Christian Soldiers. There is equal need for experienced military and protective services men, active duty or retired, to volunteer to educate our recruits in the martial arts, weapons, reconnaissance, field medicine, communications, protective service, and a dozen other specialties.

These knights will volunteer to "serve as a force for the physical protection of bishops, priests, and missionaries." Besides spiritual formation, members will face Boot Camp and a year of Basic Training. After six years of service, they take vows of poverty, chastity, and obedience—and receive a title of knighthood.

As the group admits on its Web site, "this Fraternity has yet to be authorized."

CELEBRATE: Mark the Knights of Malta and their Hospitaller heritage by getting hold of some Colli di Trasimeno or Kommende Mailberg and serving it with this traditional Maltese dinner:

Bright Salad (see recipe)
Dolphin in a Piquant Sauce (see recipe)
Melted Onions and Summer Squash
Spongy Country Bread
Kannoli (the Maltese spelling!) and Coffee

Bright Salad

This is a very Mediterranean combination, perfect as a starter.

2 oranges, sectioned	Salt and freshly ground pepper
2 stalks celery, cut in half-moons	Pour of extra virgin olive oil
2 medium carrots, sliced into wheels	Splash of red wine vinegar
Handful of walnuts	

Toss all ingredients together and season.
   Set aside for flavors to meld.

Serves 2

Dolphin in a Piquant Sauce

No, the Maltese don't eat Flipper. There's a fish called the Dolphin which Maltese call "dorado," and American restaurateurs have wisely renamed Mahi Mahi. It doesn't sing, save drowning swimmers, or secretly rule the planet.

While hard to resist freshly made, this dish is meant to be served cold. Try to hold out until it reaches the right temperature.

2 8-ounce Mahi Mahi fillets
Flour
Olive oil
2 yellow onions sliced
1 tablespoon tomato paste
1 cup white wine plus more as needed

1 tablespoon red wine vinegar
1 tablespoon Sicilian olives, chopped
1 tablespoon Alfonso olives, chopped
1 tablespoon capers
Freshly ground black pepper

Dredge fillets in flour and set aside.

Pour enough oil in a cast iron pan to cover bottom. Over medium heat brown Flipper on each side. Make sure the fish is cooked all the way through. Set aside.

Meanwhile make sauce. Fry the onions in a saucepan with 1 tablespoon oil until lightly brown. Add tomato puree and fry 3 minutes more. Add wine and simmer on low until most of the liquid is dissolved. Add remaining ingredients and cook for 5 minutes. Add a bit more wine if needed to moisten the sauce. Pour sauce over the mahi mahi and either serve immediately or cover and chill overnight. Bring to room temperature before serving.

Serves 2

....

Mission Wines: Intoxicating Acolytes Since 1769

The first variety of wine produced in North America was made by missionary fathers and named Angelica. While grapes grew natively in California, the Native Americans seem not to have thought of fermenting them. That awaited the arrival of Jesuit and Franciscan missionaries in the late-eighteenth century, who constructed a string of missions throughout the state to minister to Indians. The Spanish crown favored these settlements, which helped establish its claim on prime California real estate; the British and Russians were already sniffing around the state and planting little yellow "Sold" signs. But austere, celibate Spaniards such as Bl. Junipero Serra had bigger things in mind than politics; they wanted to work their way to heaven, and bring along as many Indians as would join them. To do that, they needed the Sacraments, and that meant wine for the Mass. So wherever they built a mission—and they traveled the length of the state on foot establishing them—these priests planted vineyards and wineries. (On the wall of Mission San Gabriel you can still see a mural depicting the grapes and presses.) The friars introduced some European strains of grape which crossbred with the native varieties. They also planted and tended fruit trees, opened schools for the natives, and fought for indigenous rights against land-hungry white settlers. The hard-working friars set themselves to learning dozens of native languages and dialects, the better to explain Christianity to the Indians they encountered. They taught the natives how to read and write, cultivate orchards, and sing Baroque liturgical music. In much the same way depicted in the movie *The Mission*, the friars became the Indians' greatest protectors—first against the Spanish,

and later the Mexican and American governments, which were eager for Indian land. Most of the missions were seized and only a few still function today, but the exquisite buildings still stand, and the grapes the friars planted still grow in abundance.

And they're still made into wine—though most of it isn't very sophisticated. Angelica is often enhanced by stronger liquor to produce "fortified" (i.e., hobo) wine. Private companies raising the old Franciscan grapes include Robert Mondavi and Gallo. Angelica is often bought by churches for use as altar wine at Mass by priests—and at off- hours by tipsy altar boys. The delightfully offbeat vintner Bonny Doon does make a high-end dessert Angelica that will charm you as it rots your teeth. Still, for all its historic importance, Angelica wine is mostly thought of as inexpensive, inoffensive, and cheap.

How very unlike actual angels, who aren't harmless at all, but are absolutely terrifying—less like a candy-sweet glass of dessert wine than a flaming shot of 151-proof rum thrown at you from across the bar to get your attention. Except that the one who threw it at you is God. Does He have your attention now?

....

Montepulciano: Saint Robert Bellarmine, Super Tuscan

The exquisite Renaissance town of Montepulciano in Florence has a lot to boast about. The most obvious are the wines it makes, and the grapes that bear its name. There's grape called Montepulciano, which for some reason grows nowhere near the town for which it's named, but in faraway Apulia and Abruzzo. Wines made from it include Montepulciano d'Abruzzo, a bright red wine with a dry and pun-

gent taste. A simple table wine, it goes well with almost any traditional Southern Italian dish—except of course for tripe,[6] an offal dish made from any or all of a cow's four stomachs: the *rumen*, the *reticulum*, the *omasum*, and the *abomasum* (though watch out for this one, it's described by veteran diners as "kind of . . . glandular"). If you must consume a dish of tripe—let's say you lost a bet, or it's served at a wedding—it's best eaten as quickly as possible, with multiple shots of grappa. But with almost anything else, Montepulciano d'Abruzzo will do just fine.

A more distinguished wine is the varietal known as *Vino Nobile di Montepulciano,* which includes no Montepulciano grapes, but at least is grown in the vicinity of the town. Made mostly from Sangiovese,

---

[6] Wikipedia helpfully points out that another Tuscan wine, Chianti, "had a mention in a popular film *The Silence of the Lambs* in the catchphrase "I ate his liver with some fava beans and a nice Chianti." It goes on to warn aspiring cannibals "that a young wine as Chianti is an exceptional poor choice for eating entrails." Just, you, know, FYI.

these wines can be quite distinguished, and won from the Renaissance poet Francesco Redi the title "*il Re dei Vini.*" The resident winos at SeeTuscany.com say of this variety that the best wines "have a solid ruby-crimson color, a rich cherry scented aroma with accents of leather, violets, and cigar tobacco, and a rich full taste in the mouth." These wines are irresistible to those of us who love all these flavors, but for health reasons have had to give up smoking cigars, eating violets, and chewing leather.

To keep such famous wines as this tasting the same as they did during the Renaissance, in 1963 the Italian government put in place complex regulations determining how wine could be made, cutting off experimentation with different types of grape. As visceral[7] Catholics who love the lasting over the ephemeral, Italians are wedded to their culture, not their government. In fact, the only way to make sure an Italian will do something is to pass a law forbidding it. This will set off his native ingenuity looking for loopholes, back doors, crawl spaces, and bureaucrats to bribe.

Thus, Italy's strict wine laws goaded vintners into inventing new varieties—one of which they grandly named the "Super Tuscan." Now from the title, you might think these wines are produced for the tables of enormous, flying fresco painters, or poets who are also, secretly, X-Men. In fact, this term simply means a Tuscan wine made with something extra—for instance, juice from a cabernet sauvignon or merlot. These wines proved explosively popular, and included such high-priced exports as Sassicaia and Tignanello, which are often made by traditional producers of Chianti Classico. These new wines are much more complex and finely crafted— although their stingy vintners no longer throw in those nifty wicker baskets.

If there's anything to come out of Montepulciano deserving the title Super Tuscan, it's not so much a wine as a Jesuit priest, the theologian and saint Robert Bellarmine. In his time, this fierce controversialist defended Galileo (he had to back away carefully from that one), corrected a pope's dunderheaded attempts to *add stuff to the Bible,* refuted John Calvin, offended the crowned heads of Europe, and set the Jesuits on a path of resistance to secular authority that would someday get the entire order suppressed. What is more, Bellarmine set down in coherent form ideas that would someday reoccur in the Declaration of Independence.

Born in 1621 as the nephew of a cardinal who'd later become the pope, Bellarmine entered the Jesuits and quickly proved the pointiest head in that already brainy outfit. His sermons packed the churches, and his wit was so keen that the order set him the task of reading every book ever produced by any major Protestant, and debunking it. The book he produced, *Disputationes de Controversiis Christianae Fidei Adversus Hujus Temporis Haereticos,* was a big hit all through

---

[7] As opposed to say, practicing.

Europe—despite its less than catchy title.[8] As the *Catholic Encyclopedia* notes, "the blow it dealt to Protestantism being so acutely felt in Germany and England that special chairs were founded in order to provide replies to it."

But it was Bellarmine's political writings that really got under people's skins because he furthered the Jesuit theory (adapted from Aquinas) that rulers derived their authority from the people—not straight from God. While the Church supported the powers of monarchs when they ruled justly and defended the Faith, Jesuits such as Bellarmine taught that tyrants could be overthrown by consent of their subjects or deposed by popes. This infuriated aspiring tyrants such as James I of England, who wrote in response to Bellarmine that "kings are justly called gods, for that they exercise a manner or resemblance of divine power upon earth." To answer Bellarmine, the Anglican theorist Robert Filmer wrote the infamous manifesto *Patriarcha* (1680), in which he asserted that kings had all the rights over their subjects that fathers had over children. Okay, and a few *extra* rights—like the authority to execute them. This outlandish defense of absolute royal authority, which would have set medieval Englishmen laughing, was taken up by the Anglican establishment and embraced by absolute monarchs from Portugal to Austria who wished to subjugate the nobility, the peasants, and the Church. For the sin of suggesting that royal authority had its limits, the Jesuits were systematically removed from positions of influence, and targeted by Enlightenment *philosophes* who wanted to curry favor with the kings. In the end, the Bourbon monarchs of France and Spain bludgeoned the pope in 1759 to suppress the order entirely. A whole generation grew up in France without Jesuit education—and when they came of age, promptly cut off the Bourbons' heads.

In a piece of irony, it was Bellarmine's book that provoked *Patriarcha*, and *Patriarcha* in turn prompted John Locke to write his own theories of government,

---

[8] If we could have just sat down with him for a minute, the book would have got a name like *The Bad Catholic's Guide to Heresy*, and you'd be able to find it today at Books A Million.

which reflected many of the ideas favored by Bellarmine (minus the pope, of course). The Lockean contract theory, which drew on Thomas Aquinas, formed the basis of the American system of government. As Rev. John C. Rager wrote:

> The ancient Church which is often depicted as retarding modern enlightenment, liberty, and democracy, was the very agency which produced the great protagonists of democracy in the period of its greatest danger and saved out of the democracy of the Middle Ages what might be termed the seed-thought for the resowing and growth of democratic principle and practice among the nations of modern times.[9]

Of course, Father Rager was writing in 1930. If you follow the march of "democratic principle and practice among the nations of modern times" since then—and recall the savagery committed by such democratically elected regimes as, for instance, Hitler's Germany or the Spanish Republic, the persecutions of the Church conducted by France's Third Republic, and the embrace of abortion and euthanasia throughout Western Europe today—it's tempting to give poor Filmer a second look.

Or at least to look with some skepticism on today's uncritical embrace of democracy. The American Founders were, shall we say, "pessimistic" about the prospects of a purely democratic regime unconstrained by a Constitution.[10] As its main author, James Madison, wrote in the Federalist #10:

> Democracies have ever been spectacles of turbulence and contention; have ever been found incompatible with personal security or the rights of property; and have in general been as short in their lives as they have been violent in their deaths.

Signer of the Declaration (and patron "saint" of a popular microbrew) Samuel Adams agreed: "Democracy never lasts long. It soon wastes, exhausts and murders itself. There was never a democracy that did not commit suicide." In establishing a decentralized republic with a firm Constitution that constrained the will of the many, in order to protect the rights of the few, the Founders looked back to the principles of Common Law and localism laid by Catholic thinkers—such as Thomas Aquinas and Robert Bellarmine.

But we don't limit ourselves to medieval monks or Counter-Reformation Super Tuscans. One of our favorite political thinkers is the historian and economist Hans

---

[9]Rev. John C. Rager, "Catholic Sources and the Declaration of Independence," *The Catholic Mind,* XXVIII, no. 13 (July 8, 1930).

[10] For some idea of what such a regime might look like, we suggest reading today's edition of the *New York Times.* Turn to the section labeled "Washington."

Hermann Hoppe, a snarky,[11] chain-smoking Austrian anarchist who lives in Las Vegas. One of the authors once sat with him in a Zurich café arguing the merits of democracy and monarchy.

There, and in his book *Democracy: The God That Failed*,[12] Hoppe argued that what matters most to citizens is less how their government is chosen than how powerful it becomes—how much it meddles in their lives, taxes away their wealth, and goads them into slaughter on the battlefield. Hoppe points out that on all three counts, modern democracies score much, much worse than medieval monarchies. Richard the Lionheart, for instance, had little control over how his subjects lived. His serfs paid only 10 percent of their crops in tax, and only his nobles fought in wars. For all the power-grabs made by later kings, it took the democratic radicals of the French Revolution to imagine that because they represented "the people," they had the right to mold every individual unlucky enough to live in the country. These radicals invented a new religion which they tried to impose by force, stole the lands of the Church and the nobles to enrich themselves, and drafted every peasant who could walk to fight in their wars of "liberation." What's more, they set the tone for subsequent regimes from Mexico (**see Kahlua**) to Russia and China, where "people's democracies" rode roughshod over the rights of actual individuals, in the name of enforcing the General Will. Even Henry VIII (**see Gout**) didn't have the stones for that. As Hoppe pointed out over a *kaffee mit schloss*, "At least in a monarchy, you know the government is pretty much your enemy. Democracies convince their citizens that the government *is* the people. That means it can do with them whatever it wants."

Don't mind us, but we side with the Italians.

....

Loophole to the Ten Commandments #6: Thou Shalt Not Commit Adultery

This commandment is pretty stark on the face of it, and there really aren't any loopholes left to speak of. In fact, one of the many shockingly unpopular things that Jesus did during His earthly mission was to brick up the few escape hatches left behind by Moses, which had made this aspect of the Law a little less austere.

---

[11] And we do mean snarky. When he learned that one of the authors had come to do research in Switzerland but didn't speak German, he hissed with disdain. "Oh, isn't it chust great, how Amerikans can come to Eurrrr-op and eferbody speaks Eeenglish. Dat's chust great." To which this author replied, "Well be fair. If ya'll had won the War we'd all be speaking Cherman."

[12] Hans Hermann Hoppe, *Democracy: The God That Failed* (Rutgers, NJ: Transaction Publishers, 2001).

As dutiful readers of the Old Testament[13] know, the old Covenant was in some ways stricter on things like diet than it was on matters of sex. Eating shellfish, for instance, was prohibited—but not polygamy. Divorce was allowed, (Deuteronomy 24:1) and a husband could get one unilaterally by affirming that he'd found some "indecency" in his wife, and refunding her dowry to her father. This was originally meant to cover infidelity, but some flexible-minded commentators expanded the grounds for divorce to include a wide variety of faults—for instance, lousy cooking. Burnt food or burning bed, these liberal rabbis offered plenty of wiggle room for weary husbands—or those who wanted someone young and fertile to re-place the aging wife of their youth.

While such a policy and the practice of polygamy may have suited the social needs of a tribal society where the men often died fighting wars against pagan neighbors, it clearly subordinated women to men, and fell short of the imperative for justice and equality proclaimed by the Hebrew prophets. On the other hand, to modern male eyes these innovations sound mighty convenient, and point forward to the "no-fault" divorce law reforms of the 1970s.

These gaping loopholes for easy divorce were clearly abuses—as rabbis of the time recognized. Jesus was just one of many teachers to call for reform. But He went much further, proclaiming on His own authority: "Moses because of the hardness of your hearts suffered you to put away your wives: but from the begin-ning it was not so." (Matthew 19: 8) He went on to explain that when man was first created, before his Fall, he was meant to marry one woman and remain with

---

[13] i.e., Protestants.

her for life. This "original unity" of husband and wife was interpreted by the Church in subsequent centuries to mean that every validly contracted marriage was an indissoluble Sacrament—even infidelity could not end it. Of course, some popes were less than faithful to the spirit of this law, granting easy "annulments" to kings whose armies might otherwise march on Rome. Had Henry VIII reigned closer to Italy than England, a white-knuckled pope might have had to grant his annulment. England might have stayed Catholic—and the Irish therefore gone Protestant.

But the principle remained, and was almost always honored. In modern times in the West, as lifespans have lengthened, this teaching of the Church has grown ever less popular. For one thing, marriage has stretched from a ten-year jaunt that ended fairly promptly with a case of plague, to a 40- or 50-year commitment that entails joint retirement funds, Grandparents Day, and simultaneous menopause and "mid-life crisis." It's just plain much more dangerous nowadays to yoke yourself for life to someone whom you know is likely—well, to *live*. And so will you. For years and years and years. . . .

Pope John Paul II did yeoman's work in developing his Theology of the Body,[14] attempting to explain this "hard saying" of Christ in philosophical and psychological terms, making clear that the vision of human dignity implied by our Christian faith implies that the sexual union must be for life. He also cites the devastating effects on millions of children of easy divorce, who have watched their parents trade each other in for newer models, and developed lifelong phobias of commitment.

This collision between this teaching of Jesus Christ and the unexpected expansion of human life has likely been one of the reasons why Westerners postpone getting married—sometime well into their 30s and early 40s. It has also provoked the explosion of annulments, as well-meaning Church bureaucrats are overwhelmed by requests from embittered couples seeking release. Many more reasons have been adduced by Catholic psychologists and canonists for declaring, in retrospect, that this particular nightmarish marriage might not have been Sacramental. While some of these may be spurious, others are not. For instance, if either partner enters a marriage secretly believing that divorce and remarriage is really an option—that is enough to queer the deal, whatever the other partner may have believed. Given the deep-seated American attachment to serial polygamy, that probably means that a goodly percentage of the weddings you're attending are delightful pagan charades that will someday be legitimately dissolved. And no, you *won't* get back your gift.

One of the authors went to high school at a place where the deserted quarters

---

[14] This complex and sophisticated development of doctrine is best explained in laymen's terms by apologist Christopher West, in a series of popular books that unpack its many, rich implications. See *www.christopherwest.com.*

once inhabited by vanished teaching Brothers had been transformed into a postmodern, high-speed annulment factory. Indeed, the Diocese of Brooklyn in the 1970s and '80s set a record for churning out Decrees of Nullity which attracted the attention of the Vatican. The pope was . . . impressed. Even a little concerned. In 2005, a document, *Dignitas Connubii,* was released by the Holy See clarifying the grounds for Church annulments. As devout "foodies" we combed it carefully and checked with canon lawyers, only to find that "burning the beans" is not included.

Napa Valley: Waiting Out the Dark Ages

It's well known to winos like us that for the survival of wine making in Europe we have the monks to thank. When that continent was overwhelmed from two sides (**see Burgundy**)—by illiterate, beer-loving barbarians pouring across the Rhine, and abstemious Islamic armies storming through the Pyrenees—it was only the patient labors of Benedictines and other religious that nurtured Europe's vineyards through the Dark Ages. Indeed, as Desmond Seward documents in his inspiring history *Monks and Wine*,[1] these tonsured tipplers pioneered the techniques of making wine we still use today. According to the wine aficionados of Boca, Italy, whose Web site features a micro-history of wine, from ancient times wine was cultivated

> . . . using the "*to altena*" system, whereby the vine was supported from trees. The vines grew to great heights, and harvesting had to be undertaken with ladders. After about the year 1000, the Benedictine monks of Saint Nazzaro on Sesia introduced a new method of cultivation; attaching the vine to a pole that was anchored into the ground, and

[1] Desmond Seward, *Monks and Wine* (New York: Crown Publishers, 1979).

supporting the branches with sticks called "*topia*." These improvements, together with methodical pruning, improved the quality and quantity of the wine.

It's telling that deep in the most chaotic and primitive phase of European history, churchmen were pioneering new agricultural technology.

While as patriots we might prefer to deny it, an age just as dark once gripped the United States. In the wake of our blundering intervention into World War I (**see Gewürztraminer**), our nation itself succumbed to a dual onslaught of rank superstition and an invading, alien creed: Fundamentalism and Progressivism. These two movements, which stood on opposite sides of the Tennessee Monkey Trial, had more in common than most historians admit. To wit, neither had much use for Catholics, or for liquor. The Fundamentalists regarded alcohol as Satan's brew—which raises some curious issues of biblical interpretation (**see Wedding of Cana**)—while Progressivists saw it as a relic of the Old World that afflicted women and the poor. And both groups viewed with alarm the influx of Catholics whom they regarded as hapless addicts of the papacy and the grape. With a little help from their friends in the Klan—newly revived, it took up the cudgels for Temperance—these movements managed in 1919 to ban alcohol outright throughout the country (**see Temperance**).

The passage of the Eighteenth Amendment dealt a crippling blow to breweries and distilleries across the country. Even worse were its effects in Napa Valley, the California region where grapes had been grown and wines produced since 1838. In that year, reports Epicurious.com, George C. Yount took the Mission grapes first

planted by Franciscan friars (**see Mission Wine**) and tried cultivating them in a new environment. The region's rich, volcanic soils and its widely varied "microclimates" made it the ideal site for developing a sophisticated range of different wines. The region proved so welcoming to wine grapes that by 1890 more than 160 vintners had opened in the Valley.

A number of them closed in subsequent decades, during the phylloxera epidemic. This vine-killing parasite is endemic to the U.S., where our native vines are immune. But the "scuppernong" you can make from those hearty American grapes tastes pretty much like a jar of Welch's Jelly—which may explain its popularity among elderly Southern ladies with finely coiffed blue hair and a yen for gossip and canning. So the friars introduced the European species of grape *vitis vinifera* to California in the hope of producing something that reminded them more of . . . well, *wine*. When the American vine bug jumped ship in France and spread across Europe,

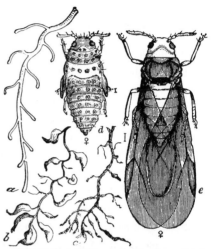

Phylloxera (*P. vastatrix*). — *a*, healthy vine rootlet; *b*, rootlet showing nodosities; *c*, rootlet in decay (natural size); *d*, female pupa; *e*, winged female, or migrant. (Short lines show natural sizes.)

it devastated wine production and boosted consumption of less healthful alternative drinks (**see Absinthe**). These nasty little aphids attacked California's imported vines, and the industry took decades to recover.

By the time the Napa wineries were back on their feet, they had to face a new and ideological pest: Prohibition. This draconian national law—written by a coalition of Bible-thumpers, dietary cranks, and eugenicists—strangled the struggling art of American winemaking in its cradle. It caused almost every winery in the United States to close, and provoked thousands of Italian immigrants to go back home, in search of a saner environment. (Mussolini was coming to power. Oops.) But a few doughty souls looked at this stifling law and found in its puritan rigor two tiny exceptions: one could still produce "medicinal" alcohol, and wine for Sacramental use.

So a dozen or so wineries soldiered on in Napa Valley, and among them some that would later become well known: Sebastiani, Beringer, Trefethen, the monastic Christian Brothers Winery, Beaulieu Vineyards, Louis M. Martini, and San Antonio. Each clung to life by selling wine to area churches for use at Mass. This must have proved a pleasant surprise to local priests, who were no doubt used to the cheap stuff used at liturgies up to then. Come the Volstead Act, they were suddenly inundated with the products of the region's best wineries, on whose products they held an unsought monopoly. Winemaker Steve Riboli, whose father named the San

Antonio Winery for his patron saint, recalled to California Country Television: "Two churches kept our doors open for 10 years. We always talk about it with tremendous pride because it's what kept us around—just two churches!" Remember that in the 1930s, no Catholic churches distributed the consecrated wine (**see Precious Blood**) to the congregation. Yet somehow, two parishes managed to keep alive an entire winery for a decade. Short of some miracle of Cana in reverse, we can only conceive two explanations. Either

> A). the priests were from Italy, so they were drinking it with dinner, or
>
> B). the priests were from Ireland, so they were trading it for whiskey.

It makes us glad to think that the Church helped her children squeeze through a loophole in an unjust law to keep alive an art form. It's just another example of the Church, almost alone, keeping lit the flame of (viti)culture. Much the same thing happened after the fall of Rome, when monks painstakingly recopied most of what has survived of the ancient literature of the West. But there's one important difference: The art of wine making in Napa Valley had its greatest flourishing after it left the hands of the Christian Brothers.[2] The rich complexity and subtlety that now mark Napa wines (rent *Sideways* to watch Paul Giamatti drink far too much of the stuff) are the results of the great culinary revival of the 1970s led by the likes of northern Californian Alice Waters, which launched the organic foods movement, the drive to revive local and "sustainable" cuisine, and any number of the trends that make contemporary life so much more pleasant. And given what has happened to our culture, we need all the help we can get.

You see, the Western civilization preserved by the monks was a rich and varied product, enhanced and deepened immeasurably by the Christian contribution. The brothers, nuns, and priests who spent their lives inscribing illuminated manuscripts held a view of the universe that was almost infinitely rich. They saw man as a creation only a little lower than the angels, watched over by a heavenly Virgin, invisibly linked by the Communion of Saints to every other soul who had ever lived, and created for life in eternity with a loving God. Nowadays we "know" ourselves as naked apes, scrabbling for survival in a meaningless universe at the whim of selfish genes and boorish memes. To modern primitives in 2007, the theology of the Church must appear as the monolith did to Stanley Kubrick's hairy Cro-Magnons in *2001*: an alien reminder of a high civilization whose ways we cannot begin to understand.

---

[2] In 1995 the Christian Brothers Winery sold their land to the Culinary Institute of America, which seems to have a hankering for churches; its East Coast campus is located in the buildings of a former Jesuit seminary, where aspiring chefs now sweat under stained glass windows depicting the seven Sacraments, and stumble occasionally over the gravestone of Teilhard de Chardin.

CELEBRATE: Try if you can to revive the exquisite, holistic worldview held by medieval man by reading deeply in the products of that world. Study the *Summa Theologiae, The Divine Comedy,* and C.S. Lewis's handy world map of the old Western mind, *The Discarded Image.*

Failing that, embrace your primate state, and assuage the soul-annihilating anxiety that attends modern life by focusing relentlessly on your physical health. Take up a starkly ascetical exercise regimen, which no one will consider unusual as long as you make clear you have absolutely no interest in spiritual improvement. You can emphasize this point by removing your scapular when you run, and wearing a profane T-shirt. Might we suggest for women the charming garment produced by Abercrombie & Fitch that reads: "Who needs brains when you have these?" On a man that message might prove puzzling, so he might instead try something like "Who Farted?" or "Porn Star." This will clear up any confusion.

Besides your strictly secular mortifications, you really ought to stop eating the rich foods recommended here for those who believe in life after death. If this go-round is all you get, then the goal is to die old, rich, and thin after spending your 1.2 children's inheritance. And you have a better chance of attaining that if you switch to spa cuisine, like the light and healthy dish we outline below—which goes very well with a high-end Napa wine such as the Riboli family vineyard's Cabernet Sauvignon. Eat foods like this almost exclusively, and you'll add to your life years and years of "quantity" time. Just make sure you never think of it as "fasting."

Vegetable Dumplings with Daikon Salad
Steamed Fish with Black Bean Sauce
Baby Bok Choy
Bean Thread Noodles
Gingered Grape Sorbet (see recipe)

Gingered Grape Sorbet

1 2-inch piece ginger	1 pound crimson grapes
4 ounces fresh blueberries	1/2 cup sugar
6 ounces fresh raspberries	1 teaspoon vanilla extract

Peel ginger and finely dice. Use a spoon to gently remove just the outer skin; the most essential oils and therefore flavor are just beneath its surface.

Rinse berries and grapes.

Toss all together and allow to macerate 1 to 2 hours.

Blend in two batches. Pass through a fine strainer and stir in 1/2 cup water.

Adjust with a bit of lemon juice, if needed, to cut the sweetness.

The end result will be very thick, more of a granita than a sorbet. For a finer texture, add another 1/4 cup water.

Turn in an ice cream machine.

Makes 1 quart

Nebbiolo: Microclimates and Micromanagement

Poets and philosophers have long seen the parallels between human culture and viticulture. Like man himself, the wines he makes are no simple product of a reaction such as your chemistry teacher might have written on the board—which you'd ignored because you copied your homework from the Asian kids in return for making them fake IDs.

No, the growth of a grape is dependent on dozens of different factors, nature and nurture, a product of soil, shade, and sun, inflected by the water that bubbles up through the stones and the pruning hands of man. One of the most complex and interesting grapes in Italy is called Nebbiolo, which is used in making the famous Italian red Barolo. As the eminently useful Epicurious.com reports, the grape takes its name from the *nebbia* (fog) "that rolls over the hills of northern Piedmont and the regions nearby [and] helps the Nebbiolo grape ripen properly, thereby creating some of Italy's finest red wines. . . . The aroma and flavor of these dark-colored wines are suggestive of chocolate, licorice, raspberries, truffles, and violets."

Sounds yummy, and it is. It shouldn't surprise the reader to learn that this grape and its attendant wines were developed first by Benedictine monks, including the brethren who founded San Martino di Marcenasco in La Morra. These monks were more than gardeners; they applied their finely honed contemplative attention to the unique particularities of this region, where the richly varied terrain creates what cork-dorks like to call "microclimates." The patchwork of widely different environments produces grapes subtly different from each other, which master monastic vintners combined to create exquisite wines. As winemaker Renato Ratti, who now tends the old monastic vineyards, explains:

> [C]enturies of work have allowed successive producers to transmit the secrets of every single vineyard. It is known, for example that some zones are more susceptible to hail, just as others might be more prone to snow, ice, wind, etc.. A classic example of microclimate is a small vineyard in La Morra called "*Conca dell'Abbazia dell'Annunziata.*"

[Seashell of the Abbey of the Annunciation] Every year at springtime, a small red flower blossoms, called "Anemone Coronaria," a one-of-a-kind rarity in the entire Langhe and Roero region. It is interesting to note that the concept of microclimates was already common knowledge to the Benedictine monks who cultivated Nebbiolo in that vineyard back in the 13th Century. . . . For example, at La Morra there are three historical vineyards . . . quite close to one another, but with different characteristics: Cerequio presents trace elements of truffle and mint, Brunate bears a greater range of spices and Rocche dell'Annunziata is reminiscent of tobacco leaf, truffle and rose.

If monks and priests were able to understand the minute particularities that make the grape and shape the wine, they have also spent centuries studying the hybrid creature who drinks it. A little lower than the angels, a mish-mash of meat and mystery that scandalized Satan, each man or woman is at once irreducibly complex, but subject to stern laws of human nature which no culture or cult can ever change. It has been the study of the Church for two millennia to make some sense out of this tangle. Where modern ideologies cut neatly through the human heart with a cleaver, the masters of the spiritual life have patiently struggled instead to understand it—and shape it as gently as a patient vintner coaxes his vines. The science of guiding individual souls within the broad guidelines laid out by the Christian faith is known as "spiritual direction." Wherever they founded their monasteries, Benedictines and other religious would invariably attract both wine consumers and ambitious

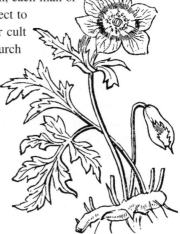

The Anemone Coronaria flower

souls who sought their advice on getting to heaven. Even hermits such as the Carthusians would attend visiting laymen through the grilles of their stony cells—serving as spiritual micromanagement consultants.

If you're an average, Sunday-and-most-holydays Catholic like us, you might be surprised at this phenomenon, but there are thousands of deeply devoted souls who take the spiritual life seriously. These people are scattered lightly throughout the Church, like peppercorns in a soup. We don't mean fanatics who follow unapproved apparitions that set a date for the Apocalypse (**see Absinthe**), or prudes who make a spectacle whenever you mention an R-rated movie. The folks we're talking about are quite different, and not all reminiscent of the Pharisees. If anything, they're more like the penitent Magdalene, who've seen through to the depths of their own weakness and worldliness, and come out of it with a rueful humility.

They're the kind of people who react to a torrent of really entertaining (i.e., malicious) gossip by smiling and talking about the weather; who greet the sight of a scantily clad model on TV with a whispered prayer of gratitude for the beauty of Creation; who stay at Mass long after Communion with their eyes closed, trying not to cry.

On first blush, of course, such people are no fun at all, and it's not surprising if you don't know any. People who won't share our vices—but don't even do us the courtesy of seeming scandalized and impressed by them—are something of a buzz-kill. At least at first. If you take the time, however, to cultivate the company of someone like this, and find it in your heart to forgive him his virtues, you might someday come to treasure him as a friend. His simplicity, kindness, and apparent lack of malignant narcissism may prove refreshing. It will at least serve as a novelty.

If you visit such a person's home, you'll probably find just a few religious objects, humble icons in questionable taste chosen for the saint they represent instead of the Renaissance Italian who painted them. If you wait till your host goes to the bathroom and start pawing through his books, you're liable to come across some marked-up manual of spirituality, like St. Francis de Sales's *Introduction to the Devout Life*, Msgr. Escriva's *The Way*, or the sermons of Cardinal Newman. When you do, take our advice: *Put it down immediately.*

For one thing, such books are full of disturbing appeals to go beyond our comfy, everyday mediocrity aimed at making the ever-popular "bottom rung of Purgatory," to embrace, instead, perfection. The same thing Jesus called for. And look where He ended up!

More to the point, if your increasingly—let's admit it—*saintly* friend is really using this book, it's probably full of personal reflections and confessions, which are none of your bloody beeswax. He'd be mortified if he came back in the room to find you leafing through his notes on "problems with purity," or "dealing with worldly friends." Such as, for instance—you. You might even find your name in there, alongside a note "remember to pray for. . . . " Then it's your turn to feel mortified. If there's one thing worse than agreeing to pray for someone, it's finding out that he prays for you.

It seems that your prayerful friend—come on, *put it down*, he just flushed the toilet—is the sort of Catholic who seeks out what is called a "spiritual director." Put simply, this is a confessor whom he meets with frequently, to unfold the struggles he encounters on the path to Christian perfection. The Church insists that every member of a religious order have such a confessor; most priests have one, as does the pope. But a surprising number of laymen, single or married, also make use of this little-known tradition to keep them from going off on some wild tangent of laxity or scruple (**see Sangue di Giuda**), or following a private inspiration that *seems* to come from God, but in fact has the whiff of brimstone. These people know, as the Church has taught them, that the spiritual life is dangerous. The higher you try to climb, the farther you have to fall. (One more reason to stick with us, down here in the wine cellar.)

This hard, cold fact is affirmed by saints such as Ignatius Loyola, who developed elaborate "rules for the discernment of spirits." Viewed most broadly, the rules the Jesuit founder laid out are meant to help us discern God's will in complex situations. But they're also baldly literal: sometimes a monk or nun (usually one who's been fasting) will find himself presented with an actual spirit, who shows up in his cell with messages "from Heaven." Since the devil himself can "appear as an angel of light" (2 Corinthians 11:14), how is the poor soul supposed to know? That's where the Church's hard-won wisdom comes in. Having witnessed over the millennia countless charlatans, lunatics, and proud souls deceived by demons who invented new heresies, conducted secret orgies, displayed fake stigmata, and generally spread bad taste among the peasantry, churchmen have developed a healthy skepticism of the supernatural. The *Catholic Encyclopedia* sums up Ignatius's wise criteria:

> [T]he evil spirit speaks only to the imagination and the senses, whereas the good spirit acts upon reason and conscience. The evil labours to excite concupiscence, the good to intensify love for God. . . . As the good angel's object is the welfare of the soul and the bad angel's its defects or unhappiness, if, in the progress of our thoughts all is well and tends to good there is no occasion for uneasiness; on the contrary, if we perceive any deviation whatsoever towards evil or even a slight unpleasant agitation, there is reason to fear.

Put more practically, Ignatius notes that messages from Heaven are always meant to help us live the vocation we have discerned, not turn it upside down. Hence a married woman who sees a spirit that tells her to leave her husband and join a convent need not feel around to find the cloven hoof.

Our favorite tale of spiritual direction concerns St. Faustina, who passed along the most important modern devotion, to the Divine Mercy of Jesus. When she first began receiving apparitions, which claimed to be Christ, her spiritual director proved cool to the idea. (As opposed to being "cool with it.") He questioned her sternly, week after week, and urged her to interrogate this unearthly figure appearing in her cell. At last, when he could not come to a decision, he hit upon the perfect question to pose to this ghostly visitor. He told Sister Faustina to ask the spirit what she'd said in her last confession. She duly did so, and returned to the priest deeply confused. The spirit had simply replied: "I don't know. I have forgotten."

The old priest's jaw dropped, as a cold chill went down his spine. Almost reluctantly, he told the anxious nun that her apparition was . . . authentic. No devil would say such a thing: Satan's very name means "the adversary" or "the accuser," and it is he who goads us to despair about our sins, and cling to them long after they have been forgiven. At absolution, Christ does indeed forget our sinfulness, and accept us as His prodigal children. That's what mercy is all about.

Similar to the monks who tend the fragile grapes in their thin soil in the fog, directors like Faustina's cultivate the sensitive souls who seek a perfection on this earth hinted at only by Barolo.[3] And that's enough for us.

The Nose of a Wine and the Odor of Sanctity

Remember fourth grade? In some ways it's the most idyllic year of school. You and most of your classmates have outgrown the most disgusting childish habits, from

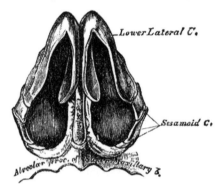

nose-picking to puking right after lunch, but you haven't yet begun the awkwardness of adolescence. For this brief, golden time most of the kids in your class have neither permasnot nor pimples, and the nightmare of sexual awakening is still at least a couple of years away. Girls are just plain *icky*, and boys are totally *gross*, so you can devote all your attention to forming single-sex secret clubs, hiding coded messages, and establishing a ruthless primate pecking order. It's also the year when you first start doing experiments in science class—easy stuff, like baking soda volcanoes and dry-ice fog machines, which don't yield results worth recording, and don't require any math. Perhaps the best of these science demonstrations involves the sense of taste and smell. This is the year in most schools where the teacher brings in pieces of apple, onion, and other foods and makes the students taste them with a blindfold and a clothespin, to prove how essential is the sense of smell to the taste of food. If you remember mistaking a clove of garlic for an anchovy, you'll recall the point your faintly sadistic teacher was trying to make.

If it's true for food, the link between smell and taste is even more important with wine. It is for this reason that wine lovers make a big to-do about swirling the wine in its glass—to oxidize the liquid thoroughly, and release its complex aroma or "nose." Conversely, it's why those—such as homeless men, high school kids, and adjunct humanities faculty—who are reduced to drinking Thunderbird knock it back as quickly as possible, sometimes holding their nose. As the helpful experts over at *www.drinkwine.com* explain,

---

[3] For instance, the 1998 Luigi Pira Barolo Vigna Rionda, at $99.99 a steal from B-21 Fine Wine and Spirits.

. . . a wine consists of over 300 different chemical compounds, many of which are identical or similar to those found in fruits, vegetables, spices, herbs, and other substances. That's why wine aficionados[4] describe a wine's aromas in terms of various fruits, vegetables, herbs and spices (e.g., apple, melon, citrus, cherry, berry, honey, peach, mint, bell pepper, grass, green olive, clove, licorice, cedar, etc.). They're not being fanciful; there actually are chemical correlations underlying the comparisons, which explains the rich metaphorical language used to describe a wine's sensory characteristics.

Of course, it's more fun to make up your own terminology when tasting wine, particularly if you're at some chi-chi restaurant where you suddenly realize you're radically underdressed, and your only choice is to sneak out or get roaring drunk. We suggest the following words and phrases, for use in lieu of fruits and vegetables, in a voice just loud enough to turn the sommelier the color of Shiraz:

- I find this chardonnay "furry."
- As with most Vino Verde, the nose is redolent of flop-sweat, with a slight *profane* afterburn.
- This Malbec is hyperactive on the palate. It has that "child- scratching-head lice" quality I adore in Argentinian reds.
- From this Retsina I'm getting a vinyl bouquet, with just a hint . . . of pine air freshener.

In fine wines meriting such scientific description, the bouquet is so indicative of quality that researchers in Australia are attempting to mechanize the process. Basing their research on the olfactory sensors found in bugs and worms, these techies are trying to build an electronic "nose" that will sniff out defects in vats of large-production wine early on in the process. This seems to us rather a waste of ingenuity. Why not save a step, and employ the actual creepy-crawlies to test the wine? Or if this sounds too distasteful, why not emulate the airport screeners who rely on the infallible noses of beagles to turn up contraband?[5]

If the nose is essential to appreciating wine, it's equally important to professional exorcists. This elite corps of specially-trained, spiritually bulletproof priests, whose job it is to muck around in the lowest swamps of preternatural evil, is the theological equivalent of proctologists or medical examiners. And they have one thing in common with those specialists: They must learn to deal with appalling smells.

---

[4] E.g., "fast-moles" (**see Late-Harvest Wines**).

[5] Which reminds us of the long-told old saw about how the inside of a dog's mouth is almost germ free. We didn't used to believe it, until one of us got a pair of beagles. Then we realized it must be true. From the smell of their breath, there's nothing that could live inside that maw. That smell (think 10,000 years of sun-baked, rotting fish) could kill any aerobic microorganism. You could no doubt use their tongues to sterilize surgical instruments. In fact, we'd like to suggest this to any surgeons among our readers.

Even though he has no body, and lacks God's power to become incarnate,[6] when Satan or one of his subcommittee chairmen manifests himself on earth, humans can sense that something's a little . . . *off*. Perhaps it's their nine-year-old daughter chanting "Death to America" in Farsi—which might make sense in Teheran, except that these people are German-Americans living in Fargo.[7] Or one of the dogs is reading the paper. Most disturbing of all, observers of the preternatural report, is the *stench* emitted by devils when they possess a person. Working exorcists have reported that the reek is sulfurous, resembling the odor of brimstone or rotten eggs. St. Teresa of Avila, one of the most productive intellectuals and poets of her century, used to complain that when the devil came to pester her, the worst thing was the smell. Since she lived in the seventeenth century—when the medieval love of bathing had given way, through fear of plague, to a modern filthiness that persisted until Pasteur—the smell must have been prodigious.

Other saints could even smell sin. The great preacher and pastor St. Jean Marie Vianney (the Cure of Ars) was renowned for his skill and persistence in the confessional. He would sometimes spend 14 hours without interruption, listening to the people who lined up for miles to tell him their sins. Even amidst this crowd of penitent, unwashed Frenchmen, Vianney sometimes got a whiff of something serious. More than once, he is reported to have jumped out of the confessional to pull from the back of the line someone whose sin was stinking up the church.

Conversely, holiness can have a scent all its own. Sometimes it smells like . . . tobacco. At least, that's what devotees of Padre Pio have said, when they reported that he appeared to them from time to time. Besides bearing the wounds of Christ, the saint had the power to bi-locate, which must have been very handy—though we're not sure it compensated for his ability to read human souls, which must have been even more unpleasant than reading Italian newspapers.

Other saints reek of roses—for instance, St. Thérèse of Lisieux, whose body from the moment when she died emitted a powerful floral aroma. What is more, Catholics around the world who have asked this beloved saint for favors have reported that when she granted them, they were doused with a mysterious scent of roses.

Thérèse was not the first saint by any means whose "odor of sanctity" was overpowering. The phenomenon is old enough that the phrase itself became a metaphor for saintliness, and was duly applied to plenty of thoroughly holy people whose bodies followed the normal course of corruption, and came to stink. Still, the notion that the body of a saint might serve as a spiritual air freshener intrigued believers, and influenced artists like Bernini. Art historian Howard Davis noted that this

---

[6] So relax, and go ahead and name your kid after Damien of Molokai if you want. It doesn't mean that Gregory Peck will have to plunge a ceremonial dagger into his chest.

[7] Of course, the Church always seeks a natural explanation. It's quite possible she learned to do this from watching Al-Jazeera, or in Social Studies class.

devout sculptor decorated the tomb of Pope Urban VIII with bees[8]—to suggest that the dead pope's holiness was so overpowering his grave smelled like a bank of flowers. This idea would have come as a surprise to some of Urban's contemporaries, who blamed the pope for spending his treasury on his fortresses and nephews, and seeming to side with Protestants during the Thirty Years' War.

Of course, the most impressive scent-events connected with saints have to do with the "Incorruptibles"—those holy men and women whose bodies have never decayed. Without any embalming, the corpses of certain saints have simply remained . . . intact: sweet-smelling, immune to damp and fungus, and unpalatable to maggots, lying in state. It took a team of grim Soviet specialists working round the clock for decades to manage the same for Lenin, but the Church makes her Incorruptibles the old-fashioned way: She earns them. Or at any rate, God provides them, without any outside intervention. Indeed, the body of Lourdes's visionary, St. Bernadette Soubirous, was buried for 30 years—then disinterred and examined: her cheeks are still pink, and the nun seems like she's taking a nap. In fact, she looks much healthier than she did while she was alive—plagued as the poor girl was by tuberculosis and paparazzi.

Other saints who exuded a beautiful aroma include the aforementioned Teresa of Avila, St. Teresa Margaret (1747–70), and the twentieth-century Spaniard St. Madre Maravillas De Jesus. One thing these sweet-smelling female mystics had in common with Thérèse is that they were all Carmelites—members of the Church's most sternly ascetical order. Apparently, it requires a lifetime of self-denial and a slog through the Dark Night of the Soul (a term invented by yet another Carmelite, the terrifying St. John of the Cross) to purge the stench of sin from the depths of the soul and replace it with roses or tobacco.

We're not sure we're up for that task of ascetic aromatherapy, but we're grateful for the saints who were, and are happy to invoke their help—to dab a little behind each ear on our way out the door in the morning.

··

The Nuns of Wine

There are many myths still floating around the mysterious subject of Catholic women vowed to celibacy, poverty, and obedience. (In case you were wondering, our friends who have worn the habit report that celibacy and poverty are a walk in the park compared to obedience.) The secular culture, which has successively demolished each sexual taboo short of incest committed with endangered species, is

---

[8] "Bees on the Tomb of Urban VIII," *Notes in the History of Art,* Vol. VIII/IX. Summer/Fall 1989.

still beguiled by the "forbidden fruit" that hides within the habits of women who've wedded themselves to Christ. Our friend Elizabeth Kuhns, who wrote a fascinating history of sisterly apparel,[9] was crestfallen during her on-line research as she discovered that a high percentage of "nuns' habits" sold today are made of leather or latex, and unzip with unseemly ease. The fetishists who wear these are not known for serving the poor, teaching children for a pittance, or making wine, and need not detain us further.

Real religious women perform all those services and more. In many areas of the world—from the slums of Calcutta to the AIDS-ridden villages of Africa—they are the front-line soldiers in the Church's war on human suffering. While active orders tend to the health and education of the laity, the contemplatives seclude themselves, the better to "work and pray" in the spirit of St. Benedict. Indeed, it was his twin sister St. Scholastica, who became the mother of Western monasticism, and passed on the same ethos to the communities she founded. Theologians speculate that the spiritual heavy-lifting done by contemplatives serves as a subsidy to the rest of the Divine Economy, making up the missing prayers unsaid by the rest of us, who are at once too lazy and busy. To make this point, Pope Pius XI named the sickly contemplative Thérèse of Lisieux patron saint of foreign missions. It's sobering to think that the prayers of solitary mystics like Thérèse silently ward intrepid Jesuits in Burma, and replenish the livers of boozy gourmets like us.

Like monks, contemplative nuns are glad to take donations—particularly in the form of isolated castles; so if you've got a spare one, here's how to unload it. But the nuns mostly live on the fruits of their own labors—and that includes tending the vineyards. The great St. Hildegard of Bingen, alongside her work as a theologian, composer, and experimental scientist, oversaw her Rupertsberg convent's production of fine Rhine Wine. As the wise lady once observed, "Man hurts men, but wine heals them."[10] Desmond Seward notes that one ancient winery, founded by Cistercian nuns in 1133 near Dijon, created in its vineyard the famous French wines Clos du Tart and Bonnes Mares, which they produced for almost 700 years—before their land was stolen during one of the following historical events (multiple choice):

[9] *The Habit: A History of the Clothing of Catholic Nuns* (New York:Doubleday, 2003).
[10] *Monks and Wine*, p. 55.

a. The French Revolution
b. The Boxer Rebellion
c. The British Invasion

The way was prepared for the attacks on religious sisters in France by slanderous eighteenth-century books from the likes of Denis Diderot and the Marquis de Sade. Their pornographic accounts of outrageous luxury and imaginary orgies inside convents found echoes in later anti-clerical writers searching for scapegoats. In nineteenth-century America, published stories about the imposter Maria Monk (who pretended to be a victim of nun abuse) helped goad the Protestant nativist mobs who plundered and burned convents in Charlestown, Massachusetts, Philadelphia, and Montreal. The French, Russian, and Mexican revolutions and the Spanish Civil War were rife with such "progressive" pogroms—which too many historians tend either not to mention, or to excuse.

Less toxic but still envenomed accounts of the good sisters are popular among Catholics of a certain age, who treasure bitterness about long-ago acts of corporal punishment. The teaching orders, which once nunned the vast network of American Catholic schools, succeeded in civilizing and catechizing hordes of newly landed Catholic peasants (**see Irish Cream**). But they were not always known for gentleness. Their methods included rote repetition, stern discipline, and a finely honed sarcasm whose echoes still ring in the heads of some 50- and 60-something Catholics.[11] In the wake of Vatican II, most sisters swapped their habits for pink Dacron, and these methods for "modern educational techniques." Anyone familiar with human nature—someone who has encountered *children,* for instance—could have predicted the results: Catholic kids who turned out much like their brethren in those red-brick government schools. They can't identify Jesus Christ on the Cross, or the United States on a map. But they're bursting with healthy self-esteem!

As these sadist-penguin caricatures fade into oblivion, they are replaced by others. Our own memories of nuns involve very few habits at all,[12] and lots of oddly applied amateur make-up on women who loathed the pope. One of us recalls:

- Watching recruitment films for the Sandinistas during religion class.
- Hearing long diatribes on the "patriarchal" nature of Polish society, which could hatch such a "sexist" cretin as Pope John Paul II.
- Being stood up in front of the class to explain how on earth, "in a starving world," he could support the Church's teaching against birth control and abortion.

---

[11] Okay, people, do you think it might be time to let those third-grade traumas go? Maybe *before* you go on chemo?

[12] Except, of course, for one habit that seems likely to endure till the Second Coming: *Lining up in height order.* For some reason, this has proved, since the early Church, to be conducive to catechesis. Researchers really ought to check the frescos in the Catacombs, where we bet they'll find this practice pictured.

- Sending detailed letters documenting each of these catechetical improvements to the relevant authorities at the Vatican.

But why dwell on such memories? This sort of thing happens to everybody in high school.

For a brief time in the late 1980s, it seemed as if dissident sisters would lead a charge to change essential doctrines in the Church. Convents, which 20 years before had devoted themselves entirely to educational and charitable work, became beehives of "reform," as the sisters jetted off to conventions at which they produced manifestos demanding the ordination of women, the neutering of God, "non-sexist" language in the Bible, still more tinkering with the already-battered Roman liturgy, and a top-to-bottom makeover of the Church's sexual teachings. The intrepid journalist Donna Steichen went "undercover," frumping herself up to look more feminist, and attended some of these heady conferences. At these meetings, she later reported,

> . . . feminist theologians anathematized all subordination, every trace of cultural, pastoral, episcopal or papal patriarchy, including the episcopally ordained priesthood, and called for a "reconstituted" priesthood of self- or community-identified pastoral and ritual leaders of either sex. They began to insist that non-marital sexual relations, contraception, abortion and homosexuality must be declared licit, even among those vowed to chastity.[13]

Let's not even bring up all the Wicca.

It's too easy to rag on these poor sisters, whose orders are dying off, as young women with a taste for sexual license, radical feminism, and witchcraft find their rightful place in college English departments. Thanks in part to such radical shenanigans, the number of women religious in America has plunged from 185,000 in 1965 to fewer than 70,000 today. The only orders still growing are those that retain the religious habit, revere their saintly founders, and cleave to the doctrines of the Church they were founded to serve. While the graying, radicalized orders can still whip out a mean press release to greet every papal visit, most Catholics who bother

Mother Angelica's Mug Shot (purchase your own at www.ewtn.com)

---

[13] Donna Streichen, *Ungodly Rage: The Hidden Face of Catholic Feminism* (San Francisco: Ignatius Press, 1992), p. 22.

to pay attention will be watching that visit on Eternal Word Television Network, founded by the cranky, black-habited Mother Angelica (pictured).

So let's not disseminate another nasty stereotype about the sisters. If we look at the women entering the religious life, and thus the groups with a future, we see a much more encouraging picture.

In the Developing World, where life on this earth has not yet become so pleasant or beguiling that it's easy to pretend it will never end, the Church is positively thriving[14]—and orders of women religious are serving their countrymen in a hundred humble ways. Most relevant to our concerns is one group of nuns from Mbarara, Uganda, who rediscovered the joys of making wine. According to *Wine and Dine* magazine, (*www.winedine.co.uk*) these nuns began collecting grapes from existing vines and pressing them into wine around 2003—using an empty garage as their impromptu cellar.

Although experts might have told them their climate is too hot to grow grapes worth fermenting, these sisters wouldn't let a little thing like weather stand in their way. They surfed the Internet in search of expertise, and soon encountered a willing wine maven, Philip Jonker of the Weltevrede wine estate in South Africa, to help them improve their output. The nuns—Sister Mary Stella, Sister Mary John Baptist, Sister Mary Elizabeth, and Sister Mary Businge—traveled to Weltevrede, where Jonker taught them the finer points of quality wine making. Said Jonker:

> In the matter of a few weeks a great relationship was formed between them, my family and my cellar team with whom they worked. The sisters were hard working, keen to learn, quick to grasp complicated aspects of microbiology and science and covered everything from terroir to malolactic fermentation. They were great fun and we laughed a lot.

As Sister Mary Stella told the *Pretoria News*, April 15, 2006, "Before, we had used a basic winemaking recipe. Although it tasted good, we only used it for home consumption and in the church. But we learned so much at Weltevrede that many changes have been made to how we make wine now. We have many plans in place and soon we will be able to produce wine we can sell." The president of Uganda, Jonker reports, likes to visit with the nuns and hoist a glass or two.

Another convent producing wine is Cremisan, near Jerusalem. In that beleaguered place, Salesian nuns operate an international school of theology and seminary, attracting students from 14 countries. (Five bishops of the Middle East received their training at Cremisan.) To underwrite the cost, the nuns run a winery founded in 1880, processing up to 450 metric tons of grapes a year, and selling

---

[14] To learn more, see Philip Jenkins's fascinating *The Next Christendom: The Rise of Global Christianity* (New York: Oxford University Press, 2002).

their wine across the region. The seminarians work alongside the nuns harvesting grapes and perfecting the wine—which in times of peace is poured for pilgrims to the Holy Land. In times of war, it's served to weary AP reporters helping the nuns pick through the rubble.

While it might seem that nowadays the Holy Spirit prefers to work only in places known for endemic malaria, the wealthy West also boasts a number of thriving female orders. Our favorite is the Sisters of Life (*www.sistersoflife.org*), founded in New York in 1991 by John Cardinal O'Connor. Besides the three traditional vows, these sisters take a fourth: to protect and advance the sacredness of human life. The order's Superior General, Mother Agnes Mary Donovan, S.V., is a one-time professor at Columbia University (another of the sisters is a former NASA scientist). Mother Agnes explained her order's mission to *America* magazine on April 1, 2000:

> Our fourth vow colors everything we do. Each human life is an intentional creative act of God, made to participate in the love of God and made for its own sake. Recognizing the great dignity that God has created in each person drives all our prayer and all our work. Our overall aim is to promote and celebrate the culture of life—to promote ways of living that attest to the dignity of each sister in our community and each person we touch in our apostolic work. In contrast to the culture of life, you see the culture of death everywhere—in the way we are tempted to cast aside not only the unborn, but the aged, the infirm and the handicapped.

To live out this vow, the sisters offer shelter to women with crisis pregnancies and newborns; healing retreats for women who have had (or men who have caused) abortions; and retreats explaining the Theology of the Body to youth. We've known personally women who'd suffered under the burden of unacknowledged guilt for years, who, thanks to these self-sacrificing sisters, found forgiveness, healing, and joy. About the only criticism we can offer of the sisters' way of life is that they have not founded a winery. We hope that, in time, some pro-life oenophile will endow them with suitable acreage where the sisters and their ripely swelling charges can pluck the sweet fruits from the vine, while the new mothers and their toddlers stomp the grapes.

CELEBRATE: It's hard outside Uganda to find convent wines (believe us, we tried), but you can honor the weary love of these hard-working, hard-praying women by contributing financially to their support. Rather than grimly passing the hat, we suggest you make this fun by holding a Nun-themed Halloween Party, where your guests are encouraged to dress in the habits of various religious orders, and write a fair-sized check, which you'll send to a worthy group. We suggest the Sisters of Life, but you might want to ease the retirement of elderly sisters left without a pension by contributing to the Retirement Fund for Religious sponsored by the U.S. bishops. (*www.nccbuscc.org/nrro*)

Here's one way to structure the party and make it fun: Set up a panel of judges, and rate each guest upon arrival for the accuracy and excellence of costume on a scale of "one ruler" up to four. The guests in the best ("four-ruler") costumes only have to pony up $20, while "one-ruler" costumes or guests in plain clothes have to pay $75. Any man who shows up in convent drag should be fined $100, and shunned. If anyone appears at your fête in fetish garb (i.e., latex or leather), follow the etiquette advice offered by Our Lord: "Bind him hand and foot, and take him away, and cast him into outer darkness, there shall be weeping and gnashing of teeth." (Matthew: 22:13) Guests who own such outfits probably enjoy such treatment, anyway.

Opus One and Opus Dei: Worldwide Conspiracy in a Glass

If there's one thing that makes people happier than finding a forgotten bottle in the cupboard or a six pack in the fridge, it's finding out that world events are dominated by an evil conspiracy. It's hard to explain why such a discovery proves so consoling, but it does: Some 35 million people shelled out cold, hard cash to buy *The Da Vinci Code*—most of them Christians, eager to read a tale that portrayed their entire religion as a scam cooked up by a Roman emperor and perpetuated by a spectral order of murderous, albino monks. Clearly, they were

not picking up this book because it depressed them. Such books give readers the free and easy feeling that they needn't lift a finger to change the world—it's all so futile anyway. ("What can you and I hope to do, against the likes of . . . Them? So let's go rent *Jackass* again.")

At the same time, however, there's a gnostic thrill that comes with finding out sordid secrets, the feeling that you are now privy to the seamy underside of life, one of only 35 million or so "insiders" who know the score. As you come across bits ofsupporting evidence, it's fun to forward them to skeptical friends, with snarky commentary like: "Oh, and I suppose *this* is a coincidence?"

In the past it was Jews, Jesuits, Masons, or Communists who bore the brunt of suspicion—though sometimes (somehow) it might be all of them at once. The Nazis persecuted all of these groups—perhaps, as evil conspirators themselves, they wanted to pre-empt the competition.

In subsequent decades, the usual suspects have sometimes come in for blame in one place or another. Sometimes a grain of truth in one allegation was built up into a mock-pearl of great price later, to wit: the fact that a few American Communists at one time both worked for civil rights and spied for Joseph Stalin[1] gave J. Edgar Hoover the license he needed to spy on the patriotic Rev. Martin Luther King, Jr.

---

[1] A close friend of the authors—a Red Diaper baby who later found Christ—recalled to us that her grandmother did both, and she later saw FBI documentation proving it.

One of the present authors grew up hearing from his mother extensive warnings about the "secret Soviet plot to seed Catholic seminaries with Communists." One evening, when he brought his co-author home for Thanksgiving, his mother regaled them both with a long lecture on why African-American panhandlers *should never be given money*. As *Mère* Zmirak explained:

> I heard this from an FBI agent on television—she was a colored woman herself. She worked for J. Edgar Hoover. She said it doesn't matter if the beggar is dressed as a priest or a nun . . . don't give them a dime. Because they are all, *all* raising money to buy guns and ammo for the Race War.[2]

An awkward dinner. The turkey was dry.

Such theories are thankfully less respectable today. Instead, the focus of suspicion has shifted to the likes of Opus Dei. A Spanish apostolate founded in 1928 in Spain by Rev. Josemaria Escriva, Opus Dei hearkened back to the theology of St. Benedict, incorporating spirituality in one's everyday life and work.[3] Having seen the effectiveness of Masonic groups in attracting people and working together—even grown boys love a secret—Escriva decided to cloak the group in a bit of mystery. His constitutions for the group ask initiates to "always maintain prudent silence about the names of other members, and not to reveal to anyone that you belong to Opus Dei." Such practices have fired the imaginations of critics ever since, as has the group's success in attracting highly educated and successful members. What is worse, the organization doggedly upholds traditional Catholic teaching, and some of its members still employ old-fashioned penances, like flagellation. All this seems terribly unwholesome to outsiders, who darkly suspect that the practice is *not* meant to generate sexual pleasure. It's all so *sick*. . . .

Da Vinci Code typist Dan Brown chose Opus Dei as the villain of his novel, rightly guessing that modern readers would thrill to read of the evil machinations of a secretive, well-funded group from Spain—Inquisitionland![4]—which carried on doctrines and customs that can only be described as "medieval." Even better if the truth these conspirators sought to suppress was that Jesus Christ was not really the founder of a Church, but merely a misunderstood male feminist, a soccer dad, Who was always supportive of His life-partner's career—in this case, as the embodiment of the Divine Feminine. It all worked wonderfully, to the point where Brown achieved the closest thing to canonization available to the living: Tom Hanks starred in the movie. To your average multiplex moviegoer, that's like making a film about the Bible where Jesus plays Himself.

---

[2] Only slightly more awkward was his attempt to take his mother along with some friends through New York's Chinatown. She refused to get out of the car, averring simply: "I haven't trusted THOSE people since Pearl Harbor."

[3] At least that's what They want you to think.

[4] Also briefly the name of a failed pre-Vatican II theme park in Ohio.

Intriguing theories about Opus Dei aren't limited to readers who revise their religious beliefs based on novels they read while "going Greyhound." A cottage industry has grown up around the group, spinning ever more elaborate and sinister webs of intrigue around these shadowy Spaniards. If you troll the Internet for half an hour, you can turn up some amazing revelations about the group.

For instance, according to Web reporter Wayne Madsen, who claims to be a former NSA analyst, Opus Dei is a "shadowy and sinister Roman Catholic group [that is] running an espionage and political assassination team in the United States." (one that apparently can't shoot straight enough to hit Dan Brown, but never mind.)

In the book *Their Kingdom Come: Inside the Secret World of Opus Dei*, British journalist Robert Hutchison calls Opus Dei "a Mafia shrouded in white." He asserts that the group assigns its members to infiltrate intelligence agencies, newspapers, banks and political parties, and cultivate connections with organized crime. This power, once amassed, will be used to stifle reform within the Church and provoke a confrontation with Islam that would culminate in a revival of the Crusades. Nice work, if you can get it.

Nor are Moslems the only target. The Opus Dei menace is homing in on gay wedding planners, according to blogger Bob Geiger of *Democrats.com*. In his article, "Is Brownback Bringing Opus Dei Into The Senate?", Geiger slams the Catholic-convert Republican Kansas senator Sam Brownback for opposing same-sex marriage with arguments drawn from the Princeton University-based Witherspoon Institute. That group, according to Geiger, is

> linked to Opus Dei, a strict, religious group that some former members have described as a cult. . . . [C]ritics in academia—which include former members who sometimes go through "deprogramming" upon exiting Opus Dei—charge that organizations like the Witherspoon Institute are just veiled attempts by Opus Dei to spread its influence in top-tier academic circles.

A think-tank trying to exert influence by giving money to professors and sending out press releases. . . . Will these monsters stop at *nothing?*

Another resolute critic of Opus Dei is Miguel de Portugal, a self-proclaimed visionary who makes it his life-work to spread apocalyptic warnings over the Internet. Among his claims is that Opus Dei is at once backing pro-life neo-Nazis in Argentina *and* selling abortifacients in Spain; infiltrating the FBI[5] to cover up its

---

[5] Okay, so that part is true: Two O.D. members include former FBI director Louis Freeh, and current jailbird Robert Hansen—who used the money he got from his Soviet spymasters to pay tuition for his daughters at the Opus Dei school, Oak Crest, in Virginia. One of us used to date a graduate of that school who knew the Hansen family. She assured us that Oak Crest *no longer* gives discounts to parents who pay in rubles.

involvement in the Anthrax attacks; and smuggling massive quantities of *ganja*. And one more thing: Remember when Pope John Paul II canonized Opus Dei founder Rev. Josemaria Escriva? To most of us that was simply (like all such canonizations) an exercise of papal infallibility. To Miguel de Portugal it was in fact the "abomination of desolation" warned of in the Apocalypse (**see Absinthe**). Just in case, you know, you were wondering.

Nor is the world of wine immune to the many-tentacled reach of global conspiracies. While it's true that octopuses cannot survive on land, and therefore rarely appear in vineyards, that does not mean that winemakers are safe. Witness the tangle of accusations that surround the vintner Robert Mondavi. A Stanford graduate with a business head, Mondavi came from a long line of Italian winemakers, and in 1966 established his own winery in Napa Valley (**see Napa**). Unlike most of his competitors, he sold his wine by *variety* (such as Sauvignon Blanc) rather than simply labeling it by *region* (such as Napa). He also strove to raise the standards of California wines to equal or rival European brands. Mondavi's innovations proved so successful that he was soon able to buy up some of his rivals, and prevail in blind-taste test competitions against the finest imports from France.

Indeed, the wines produced by Mondavi and his imitators have begun to displace the products of ancient family vineyards in France and Italy—to the outrage of traditionalists. In fine American fashion, the Mondavi winery makes use of high-tech techniques and consultants to turn out wines that suit the tastes of influential critics like *Wine Spectator*'s Robert Parker—whose 100-point wine ratings get prominent play in wine shops, and can make or break a vintage. Such wines can best be described as "big," with potent flavors and lots of "fruit." Indeed, the most overwhelming of these wines are sometimes ridiculed by cognoscenti as "fruit bombs." It was wines like this, recommended by critics such as Parker, which won most Americans away from drinking Mateus and great big jugs of Ernest & Julio Gallo.

But that doesn't mollify some critics. As *New York Times* food critic Eric Asimov has written (May 20, 2006):

> Parker's critics have asserted that his power is so great, and his taste so monochromatic, with a preference for powerfully concentrated fruity wines, that some producers around the world feel compelled to customize their wines for his palate. These "Parkerized" wines have proliferated, they say, and as a result wines from all over the world, made from different traditions and from different grapes, taste the same.

Instead of big, obvious tastes created with the help of chemists, some wine aficionados prefer the subtle, complex flavor acquired by wines made in the

---

[6] Please. You people are *so* naïve.

traditional way, where the taste is redolent not of expertise but of the sun, soil, and shade that attended the earth (**see Terroir**) where the grapes were grown. They worry that the prevalence of a narrow set of tastes will homogenize the variegated wines of the world, and reduce the ancient art of wine making to yet another scientific field dominated by Americans—who will promptly get bored and outsource the entire industry to China.

As critic James Bowman writes, a number of these wine activists have embraced conspiracy theories, suggesting that winemakers like Mondavi and critics like Parker work hand in hand, forming an axis of oenophiles to extend their domination across the wineries of the world. In the otherwise excellent 2005 documentary *Mondavino* Bowman finds a troubling political undertone:

> That the Mondavis' conspiracy against the world's wines is linked to the grand unified conspiracy theories of the left is sufficiently attested to by the fact that both Parker and the representative of the Rothschild winery of Bordeaux which is collaborating with the Mondavis on their up-market, Opus One, brand have the same photo of Ronald Reagan holding up a glass of wine prominently displayed in the room where they are interviewed.[6]

Here at last we find the smudgy fingerprints of conspiracy: The *Rothschilds* are involved. This family, which first acquired its wealth serving as the bankers to royalty, is perhaps the single most abused bloodline

in Europe.[7] Anti-Semites and Marxists alike could come together in hating this family: They are Jewish and they helped keep monarchies afloat. Indeed, as Hannah Arendt pointed out in *The Origin of Totalitarianism*, the various branches of the Rothschilds, who worked in London, Paris, Vienna, and Berlin, were often employed as unpaid diplomats by their governments—which might not trust their own ambassadors, but could rely upon the Rothschilds. The family knew that war was bad for business and frequently strove, through its various branches, to patch up quarrels among the European nations. The last such peace initiative was launched in 1914, as various Rothschilds shuttled all over Europe trying to avert the outbreak of World War I. That war brought down three monarchies that all used

---

[6] James Bowman, *The American Spectator* (May 31, 2005).

[7] One of the authors has actually dated a member of the House of Rothschild—the New York–based Gregoire de Rothschild—and found him perfectly charming, with excellent taste in wine. He never, at least in her presence, exerted undue control over world events.

to do business with the family; this forced the Rothschilds to concentrate on their vineyards—and a one-time sidelight started to turn out some decent kosher wine (**see Wedding of Cana**).

But their honest dealings never won the Rothschilds any gratitude among narrow nationalists, who suspected the loyalty of Jews, aristocrats, and clergy—each of whom had dangerously "international" connections, as Rothschild critic Myron Fagan[8] asserts:

> Adam Weishaupt was a Jesuit-trained professor of canon law, teaching in Engelstock University, when he defected from Christianity to embrace the Luciferian conspiracy. It was in 1770 that the professional money lenders, the then recently organized House of Rothschild, retained him to revise and modernize the age-old Protocols of Zionism, which from the outset, was designed to give the Synagogue of Satan, so named by Jesus Christ, ultimate world domination so they could impose the Luciferian ideology upon what would remain of the human race after the final social cataclysm by use of satanic despotism.

For instance, by making better wine. In 1978, Baron Philippe de Rothschild, owner of Château Mouton-Rothschild in Pauillac, France, met with Robert Mondavi to discuss a joint venture that would wed French tradition, American technique—and presumably, Luciferian ideology. The winery they started, Opus One, produced what was perhaps the first "ultra-premium" American wine, introduced in 1984 at $50 per bottle—more than double the price of comparable California vintages. As Steve Pitcher wrote in *Wine News* (Feb./Mar. 2000), the price reflected the work that had gone into the wine:

> Opus One is meticulously "hand massaged," with frequent topping of barrels and six rackings during its 18 months in barrel, making it extremely labor intensive. The wine is moved only by the gentle force of gravity; mechanical pumps are banned. In the first-growth tradition, the $700 French barrels are never reused. And, at a cost of more than $29 million, the Opus One Winery ranks as one of the world's most expensive single-product facilities.

The wine was an immediate and enduring success, which of course awakened suspicion. Was it merely an *accident* that a vulgar American corporation was working with scions of an ancient Jewish banking family to dominate the worldwide

---

[8] A playwright and journalist, who "launched a one man crusade to unmask the Red Conspiracy in Hollywood which had set about to produce films that would aid that One World Governement [sic] plot," according to the often surprising educational site: *http://educate-yourself.org*.

wine market? Surely, there must be more to the story than that—some Hidden Hand squeezing the grapes. . . .

And indeed there was. According to the always-informative Web resource Illuminati Today Index (*www.scoreboard-canada.com*), that Hand belongs to Opus Dei. The intrepid anonymous author of the September 3, 2006 exposé "Dorothy Bush-Koch Linked to Rothschilds and Opus Dei through Devil's Wine" reports with alarm that Dorothy Bush-Koch, sister of the president, is married to a man named Robert "Bob" Koch, himself also a president—albeit only of the Wine Institute, an industry lobbying group. But who should turn up among the members of that secretive vintners' cabal? None other than both the Mondavis and the Rothschilds. Even worse, the site reports:

> The winery itself and the name of its prime product "Blood Red" have given rise to suspicions of satanic ritualism and architecture. The Baroness Rothschild who now heads this particular enterprise also has a joint venture with the Chilean winery Concha y Toro—or Seashell and Bull—in Chile. That Winery is openly run by Opus Dei. Its favorite brand is Cassilera del Diablo or Devil's Cellar. The silver wrapping on the cork has the outline of a devil. Rather odd for a group that claims to be doing God's Work as the name Opus Dei implies in Latin. . . .
>
> A QUESTION WITH AN ANSWER WE MAY NOT WANT TO KNOW: Does the Catholic Church use Opus One for Mass?

We checked on this, and the author is absolutely right: Concha y Toro's CEO is indeed Eduardo Guilisasti, 53, of Santiago, Chile, and he does belong to Opus Dei. As to the more critical question of which parishes serve up Opus One (now $149 a bottle) at Mass. . . . We're still out there looking. If any of our readers turn up such a church, please send us the name and driving directions.

....

Organic Wines and Contraception: Washing Down "The Pill"

Here's a subject that will provoke an easy fistfight among Catholics whose cars have different bumper stickers. An increasing number of grape growers and wine makers, like other farmers, have started to eschew the use of pesticides and fertilizers and label their products "organic." While it costs a little more to grow crops this way (you have to eat some losses as the insects eat your grapes) it has certain advantages as well. For one thing, you know that you're not polluting the water table with runoffs of nitrogen and insecticide, toxic messes that someone (i.e., we taxpayers) will have to clean up down the road. One such vineyard and winery is the Abbey of New Clairvaux, in Vina, California, where 25 Benedictine monks work the land in nature's way, eschewing the intrusive techniques of high-tech agriculture. The monks grow a wide variety of grapes such as "petite sirah, tempranillo, graciano, zinfandel, barbera, viognier and

muscat blanc," reports the Associated Press (May 22, 2006). According to AP, the monks "are currently rebuilding part of an 800-year-old Spanish monastery William Randolph Hearst bought in the 1930s, dismantled and shipped to San Francisco's Golden Gate Park, where it was never reassembled." New Clairvaux monk Rev. Harold Meyer told the reporter: "There's a sacredness about working with grapes. . . . Wine is very special."

The wine made at New Clairvaux is bound to appeal to a certain type of consumer—who will pay premium prices, go to special stores, and choose from a narrower range of products, in order to "go organic." Some do this simply because they think it's healthier, or to assuage a sneaking sense of guilt about their prosperity; others because they feel responsible as stewards of Creation—whether or not they even believe in a Creator. Still others want to help keep alive family farms, a goal laid out by Pope Pius XI in *Quadrogesimo anno* (1931), and popularized in the 1973 classic *Small is Beautiful*. That insightful critique of both socialism and capitalism once lay alongside the "rolling paper" in the knapsack of every hippie in America. The book—wisely packaged with a psychedelic Gandhi cover—now sits on the leather seats of Volvo-driving vegetarians everywhere. What few of them might realize is that its author, E. F. Schumacher, was no New Leftie, but a Thomist philosopher. His goal in writing the book was to revive the Catholic social teaching pioneered by Pope Leo XIII.

But it's best not to gloat about this with the folks you meet down at Whole Foods. Chances are, they have a slightly jaundiced view of the Church, and adopt a number of practices that make even bad Catholics squirm. But look past their noserings, patchouli, and "pro-choice" tattoos, and you might find that these people are on to something. Even as they lost hold of some central truths they've clung to others, which some orthodox believers have forgotten. Just as it took Arab copyists to preserve Aristotle for the use of St. Thomas Aquinas, perhaps God entrusted to these "progressives" some fragments of the Truth which would otherwise have been lost.

What wisdom warms in the fanny packs of these suburban agrarians? The core reality they recognize is summed up best by Pope John Paul II in his encyclical *Centesimus annus* (1991). While in one sense that papal letter allowed the pope to slam shut the coffin of Karl Marx, and jump on it to dance a happy *mazurka*, it also critiqued the excesses of our technocratic, state-sponsored capitalism. As the pope wrote:

> Equally worrying is *the ecological question*. . . . In his desire to have and to enjoy rather than to be and to grow, man consumes the resources of the earth and his own life in an excessive and disordered way. At the root of the senseless destruction of the natural environment lies an anthropological error, which unfortunately is widespread in our day. Man, who discovers his capacity to transform and in a certain sense create the world through his own work, forgets that this is always based on God's prior and original gift of the things that are. Man thinks that he can make arbitrary use of the earth, subjecting it without restraint to his will, as though it did not have its own requisites and a prior God-given purpose, which man can indeed develop but must not betray. Instead of carrying out his role as a co-operator with God in the work of creation, man sets himself up in place of God and thus ends up provoking a rebellion on the part of nature, which is more tyrannized than governed by him.

Few Catholics would argue with this in principle, but there are plenty of you out there who might be getting suspicious of us right now, who might even be ready to throw our book across the room. Citing such traditional Catholic rhetoric nowadays seems to put us in bed[9] with animal rights fanatics, politicians like Al Gore, and population maniacs who want to put nine-year-olds on the Pill. As a friend once said to us, "Who cares about endangered species, when babies are being aborted?" We feel her pain, but cannot follow her logic. Just because you stop your son from removing his sister's spleen doesn't mean you have to let him shave her head.

Moral conservatives who are happy to see the transformation of our planet from a divine artwork to a traffic grid remind us of the sweet old white-haired lady we know from Latin Mass (her son's now a priest in New York). One morning, as we emerged from 90 minutes of incense and chant, she accosted us, brimming with joy. She'd turned up a secret, which she simply had to share:

> I just read an article about the environmentalist scientists. Do you know what they're planning to do? They want to reduce the population of the earth to 700,000 people—and turn the rest of the planet into a nature park.[10] And you know how they're planning to get rid of the rest of us? They're going to *clone dinosaurs*.

We were tempted to raise an objection or two. . . . But the prospect of evil ecologists scheming to let loose a T-Rex just made her so danged *happy*. So we decided to play along, telling her:

> Well you know what I found out? The Freemasons have been faking the weather *for the past 30 years*. I don't have time to give you all the details, but I'll fill you in next time I see you.

She beamed like a kid who just got her first bicycle.

This sweet old lady lives on one side of the electrified fence that divides the Church today. On the other, we find devotees of Dorothy Day with bits of tofutti clinging to their beards. Each side thinks it has the truth—and it does, or at least a jagged little piece of it. As Anne Roche Muggeridge documented in her book *The Desolate City*,[11] the controversy over birth control took the dusty mirror the Church once held up to Truth and smashed it into a pile of shards—allowing individual believers to grasp only the pieces they preferred.

Before this controversy, it was easy to find "progressive" theologians who were

---

[9] Bleech!

[10] Jurassic Park.

[11] Anne Roche Muggeridge, *The Desolate City* (San Francisco: Harper and Row, 1986). The book is at once bracingly funny and heart-wrenchingly sad. We recommend reading it in small doses in a hot bath, accompanied by large mint juleps (**see Bourbon**).

also solidly convinced of the Church's traditional teachings on sexuality, divine Revelation, and the Eucharist. At the same time, the most "traditionalist" theologian in the Church, the great Cardinal Alfredo Ottaviani (1890–1979), was a bitter critic of the bombing of Hiroshima, who condemned any use of nuclear weapons— even in self-defense. The matrix of truths and counter-truths held in the tension of orthodoxy allowed for Catholics of many political stripes to co-exist and cross-fertilize. The Church stood solidly athwart the simplistic, secular left/right spectrum, unwilling to identify with any of the political panaceas of the century.

When the controversy over birth control blew up like a humongous, pope-shaped piñata in the wake of *Humanae vitae* (1968), this fragile balance snapped. Catholics who rejected this papal teaching discovered that a whole lot of other things were suddenly up for grabs, and started tearing whole pages out of the catechism (they make great rolling paper, man!) while those who clung with whitened knuckles to the old sexual morality hopped onto a tank with Dr. Strangelove. Hippie nuns started banging on banjos with anarchists; pink-faced anti-Communist Irish-Americans waved flags alongside "speakers in tongues" whose fantasies entail flying naked into the clouds and waving rapturously down at all the Catholics who got Left Behind.

Each "side" held fast to the pieces of mirrored truth they grasped with bleeding fingers, and squinted suspiciously at those in the hands of their one-time co-religionists—now enemies. In America, "progressive" Catholics began to be infused with downright secular values, while the "orthodox" soaked in the prejudices of individualistic or nationalistic conservatives. The old bipartisanship of Catholic truth collapsed into factionalism, spawning the ecclesiastical equivalents of Air America and Fox News, of Michael Moore and Ann Coulter. So the folks who cared about ecology accepted chemical contraception as "progressive," while traditionalists who embraced Western technology's conquest of nature drew a line at the bedroom door.

It has happened throughout history that the Church has been hit blindside by a sudden social change, which made her traditional teachings hard to understand or accept. Sometimes this required what John Henry Newman called a "development" of doctrine—accompanied by theological "growing pains." This happened, for instance, on the question of extending credit. In the Middle Ages, a MasterCard in your wallet would have seemed as sinful as a condom—since all lending-at-interest was condemned as "usury." This ancient teaching was based on the old, static economies of the Hebrew and Roman worlds, where investment barely existed. In the ancient economy, loans were not financial instruments but tools of exploitation, by which the rich could take advantage of famines to cripple small farmers with debt, then confiscate their land. So the Church agreed with the Old Testament, which condemned such lending as a mortal sin. Dante put the moneylenders in Hell alongside the "sodomites"—and we've passed by upscale martini bars in New York City's Chelsea area where both groups still congregate today.

But the Western economy changed radically around the thirteenth century. Foreign trade had exploded after the Crusades, while the survivors of the Black Plague had plenty of land to go around, once they'd picked it clean of corpses. In this context, lending money to merchants and thriving farmers might well be a service to society. The Church felt compelled to re-examine its teaching, and revise it to specify that only "excessive" or exploitative interest was an occasion of sin—but it was still a mortal one. So modern bankers need no longer fear that they are on the road to Hell. As for executives at credit card companies that flood the mailboxes of eighteen-year-olds with offers of $100,000 lines of credit at 22 percent—even as they strive to "reform" bankruptcy laws. . . . You can smell just a whiff of brimstone.

In the late nineteenth century, a similar social change demanded that the Church re-examine reproduction. While artificial contraception may have been invented by nymphomaniacs and racists, it had a built-in market among the married. With the rise of hygiene, medicine, and vaccines, kids, once born, had a distressing tendency to . . . *live*. In the old days, maybe 4 out of 11 would live to adulthood. And they'd all work on the farm, marry at 15, and move down the road. You died at 50, so you didn't have to worry about retirement. Life was good, while it lasted. And even if it wasn't, you barely had time to notice.

By the end of the nineteenth century, as a result of the Industrial Revolution, most people were moving off the farms into tiny, railroad apartments with one bathroom per family of twelve. What's more, the kids all had to go to school—for years and years—and you couldn't even count on them dying in some industrial accident. Population throughout the West doubled in decades instead of centuries, and something had to give. By the 1850s or so, the Vatican approved a primitive version of "Natural Family Planning," which had every moral advantage except that (in the famous words of a Duke of Norfolk), it "didn't bloody work." We just didn't know enough about biology yet, and the method was promptly labeled "Vatican Roulette." Still, the idea that sex was for something beyond just bearing children was fully accepted by the Church—which constituted not a reversal, but a true development of doctrine.[12]

The Church's solution, because it was moderate, pleased no one. Adherents of contraception dismissed this attempt to work within the structure and "rhythm" of nature even though research showed it to be more reliable than most artificial forms of contraception.[13] It didn't help that rigorists (not popes) insisted that large families are required under pain of mortal sin. In fact, this is not the Church's teaching (**see Loophole to the 10th Commandment**).

---

[12] For the papal statements explaining this doctrinal development, see Thomas Storck's fascinating "NFP: A Defense and an Explanation," at *www.ignatius.com/Magazines/hprweb/storck.htm.*

[13] For solid statistics on the reliability of NFP, see *http://www.usccb.org/prolife/issues/nfp/myths.shtml.* Different studies turn up varying numbers, between 85 and 99 percent, pretty much depending on how often the couples using it "cheat."

Now it's tough for pragmatists like most of us to understand the difference between using chemicals to get what you want, and working within the structure of God-given nature—like those crackpot organic farmers. Once you've accepted Descartes as your personal lord and savior, it's hard to see such distinctions as meaningful. The world is here for man to dominate, from the strip mines of Kentucky to the wombs of every woman. We call this Progress.

It's a bitter irony that nowadays, the very people[14] who treasure a deep concern for the ecology of the planet and maintain a healthy suspicion of the technological designs of large corporations have embraced the use of a drug produced by pharmaceutical giants which doses a woman's womb with hormones every day—you know, the kind of hormones[15] you don't want in your chicken? That's exactly why you go to Whole Foods to buy "free-range" in the first place. . . . People who rightly don't want biomedical waste dumped in a wetland will pour it into their bloodstream. They'll make sure the skin cream they buy wasn't tested on animals—then vote for stem-cell research that aims at cloning human babies to serve as spare parts.

Conversely, the social conservatives who see the poisonous effects of scientific rationalism in the bedroom can't imagine that the same worldview might be problematic elsewhere. They don't have any issue with inhumane factory farms, they pooh-pooh global warming (and turn up their air conditioners), and warn that using Natural Family Planning is usually a sin. Anyway, Jesus will rapture us long before the icebergs melt. This guy I met at the gun show gave me this pamphlet proving it *from the Bible.*

Let's just pray that the Freemasons decide to turn down the thermostat.

....

Ouzo and Orthodoxy: The Liqueur to Soothe a Schism

It's sad to say, but most Catholics know little about the Christian East; far less than most Eastern Christians learn about the Roman Catholic Church. We know about Protestantism in all its 57 varieties, 31 flavors, and 95 theses. But the average Catholic is probably ill-equipped to explain what separates an Orthodox priest from a Catholic one. Okay, *beyond* the beard.

Each of the authors lives in a Greek neighborhood, so we're more familiar with this shade of Christianity (they're a pleasing olive, we can report). We can stop by any of their bejeweled parishes in the middle of a Wednesday to kiss an icon and

---

14 With some honorable exceptions, such as the feminist Germaine Greer, a long-time skeptic of chemical contraceptives.

15 The equivalent male hormones are called "steroids" and are deeply illegal.

wonder at the abstract angels painted on the ceiling. On weekends, we watch our Greek friends troop faithfully by in their Sunday best to catch the last five minutes of the liturgy, pick up some blessed bread, then dash out for coffee and *galakto-boureko*—a rich, creamy dessert filled with custard and best served over cigarettes.

Like Italians, the Greeks enjoy a good procession and a nice, profitable festival centered on some ancient saint who lived on a pillar or died hideously for Christ, who now presides over wheels of fortune and Tilt-a-Whirls and really strong-smelling food. Except that the Greeks drink more than wine; they also chug down the sweet-smelling, paint-stripping liqueur known, loved, and feared under the name of *ouzo*. Made from pressed grapes or raisins, ouzo is fermented and flavored with spices or herbs such as anise, cloves, or mint, then distilled in copper stills to 80 proof or more.

We first tried this stuff at Holy Trinity Cathedral's Greek Festival in New Orleans, where Creoles, Cajuns, and Hellenes intermingle promiscuously over cute little lambs on flaming spits. The liqueur wasn't sold straight, rather, in the tradition of New Orleans's beloved drive-thru daiquiri shops, it was mixed into a frozen cocktail and artificially colored blue. These drinks tasted at first like licorice rocket fuel, but somehow after five or six they grew on you. As we walked tipsily through the guided tour of the exquisite Holy Trinity, the ouzo exerted an eerie power: *It seemed to make the icons talk.* Now this was a little spooky. You really don't want your raucous Sunday of gyros and baklava interrupted by urgent messages from the Madonna of Extreme Humility. Thankfully, the pictures spoke in Greek, so we were able to stumble outside to the fair grounds and focus on hurling baseballs to Dunk the Turk.

Greeks and other Orthodox see icons as more than simple pictures; their theology teaches them that these holy images—which are properly painted by monks or nuns, who accompany each step in the mixing and application of paint with special prayers—are portals into the other world, windows on Heaven. Windows that lack, for instance, screens. This accounts for the fact that icons are often associated with miracles—for instance, when an icon of Our Lady begins to weep tears of blood. This usually presages some complete disaster: a fresh raid by the Turks, an earthquake on your island, or the fact that one of your sons will be soon horribly maimed, or marry a girl who isn't Greek.

There's one such weeping icon of the Virgin in Astoria, Queens. It used to dwell in the home of an acquaintance, but now sits encrusted in gold at a humble Greek parish on 23rd Avenue called the "Sacred Patriarchal and Stavropegial Monastery of Saint Irene Chrysovalantou." When we mentioned this icon to a Greek friend of ours, her face went white. "Those things are bad luck. No wonder they gave it to the church," she said. "You have to *get them out of the house right away.*"

More ordinary icons, which don't call attention to themselves, are welcome in every Orthodox home. They serve as sites of prayer, and often have little lamps burning before them, as reminders of the sacred and unseen. In Greek households, they're as common as bottles of ouzo—though as we have seen, it is best not to mix the two.

Ouzo is the modern version of *raki*, the favorite drink for millennia throughout the Byzantine empire. This drink sustained the people of Greece through centuries of grim repression by Ottoman Turks—who conquered the Greek-speaking world in the fifteenth century and ruled it for almost 400 years. As Islamic conquerors had done before them from Jerusalem to the Pyrenees, the Ottomans pressed the local Christians beneath crippling taxes and humiliating laws. All education beyond the most rudimentary was forbidden. Their printing presses were taken or destroyed, so no new Greek books could be printed for centuries. Their greatest churches, most prominently Hagia Sophia in Constantinople, were seized and turned into mosques. No new churches could be built, nor could old ones be repaired. No Christians could walk in processions, ring bells, or call attention to their faith. Their status as *dhimmis*, or reluctantly tolerated infidels, was reinforced at every possible occasion: and painfully, in the regular raids conducted by the Turks to kidnap Christian children, who'd be raised faraway as Moslems, then sent back home as "janissaries," fanatical soldiers of occupation.

No wonder the Greeks needed something a little stronger than Retsina. After a series of disorganized revolts, the Hellenes rose up en masse in 1820—a rebellion that attracted sympathy (but little aid) from all over Europe. The poet Lord Byron was one of the foreign volunteers who died in the subsequent fighting. In the course of the next five years, the Ottoman authorities conducted such massacres that at last the British and Russians threatened to invade, forcing the Sultan to grant autonomy to the Greeks in 1826. This was not long before the raki-makers of the island of Lesbos hammered out a new technique for using copper pots to distill a better drink, which was promptly christened "ouzo." To this day, it is the leading Lesbian export (singer-songwriters come second).

If you go to Greece on an ouzo tour, you'll find that it's usually served alongside the Greek equivalent of Spanish tapas, a series of hearty appetizers called *mezedes*. There's a spot in Astoria near the park where we go from time to time, after chasing squirrels, to tie up the beagles and chow down on grilled sardines, fried octopus, calamari, and saganaki—high protein foods that blunt the ouzo's edge and keep the icons quiet.

It is not just icons and ouzo that attract us to the Greeks. We also love their liturgy, which closely resembles that of the Catholic Eastern rites. Unless you're lucky enough to reside in a cosmopolitan city like Steubenville, Ohio, where lots of immigrants from regions like Ruthenia and Ukraine arrived in the late nineteenth century,[16] you've probably never met any Eastern Rite Catholics. These are Christians in full communion with the pope, who follow the same Byzantine liturgy used from Vladivostok to Mykonos. This rite resembles in many ways the traditional Latin liturgy of Rome: the priest faces the altar, believers receive the Eucharist on the tongue, and sacred chant surrounds the proceedings. (Instead of tamborines.) While the Latin liturgy was torn out and replaced in 1971 by a sleek, updated edition, the Eastern rites retain the gravity and reverence they inherited from the ancient Church. Many Catholics who felt unfulfilled by the *Novus Ordo Missae*—and let's face it, folks, it's pretty much like the adaptation of Shakespeare's *The Tempest* by the TV dog Wishbone[17]—find the Eastern rites a spiritually fulfilling experience. It beats spending Sundays with schismatics in crew cuts and black mantillas who loathe the pope, or driving 300 miles to the mental hospital chapel where one's local bishop permits the Latin Mass.

Perhaps the most prominent difference between Eastern Rite and other Catholics is that the former have married priests—except in the United States, whose Irish bishops considered married clergy "unapostolic" and "unpastoral," but mainly "icky."[18] In the 1920s, these bishops approached a Vatican bankrupted by feeding the refugees of World War I and offered to pay its debts—at the price of forcing celibacy on U.S. priests of the Eastern rites. The Holy See reluctantly

---

[16] They'd heard the streets were paved with gold. It turned out to be rust.

[17] This was at any rate the conclusion of Klaus Gamber's *The Reform of the Roman Liturgy* (Fort Collins, Colorado: Roman Catholic Books, 1993), which deplored many of the changes in the Mass, noting that almost none of them had been authorized at Vatican II. Then-cardinal Ratzinger wrote the preface. Scholars of the *Novus Ordo* should note that the *Wishbone* episode to which we referred was entitled "Shakespaw."

[18] One of our mothers (the Irish one, natch), on learning that the Greeks she lived among had churches with married priests, looked nauseous, muttering: "I could never take Communion from a *married man*. That's disgusting." We were tempted to dial 1-800-ANTHROPOLOGIST for an emergency consultation.

agreed, driving many Eastern Rite priests to keep their wives but hand their parishes over to the Orthodox—while others retained long and enduring relationships with their parish "housekeepers." Ahem.

But the vast majority of Eastern Christians throughout the world, including the Greeks, belong to churches that split from Rome in 1054 for mostly profane reasons. The doctrinal differences between the Eastern and Western versions of Sacramental Christianity are few and largely forgotten, except among small coteries of passionate apostates from one church or the other. Both churches share seven Sacraments, revere the Virgin Mary, invoke the saints, cherish relics, pray for the dead, baptize infants, and celebrate feast days even if they haven't bothered to fast.

The split between the churches stemmed mostly from the ambition of Byzantine emperors, who craved authority over Church as well as state. There were also profound cultural differences that had crept in between two churches which spoke different languages, used diverse liturgies, and followed divergent strains of theology. But these only made it easier for emperors to force a schism, leaving themselves as the highest authority in their half of Christendom. (Think Henry VIII, with a fistful of feta.)

Of course, over the subsequent centuries we've spent apart, some "issues" have arisen between the churches—mainly in areas where Rome felt the need to clarify some doctrinal point or other. The Orthodox object to these decisions taken in their absence—even when they accept the teaching in question. For instance, the Immaculate Conception. Since the early Church, both East and West have referred to the Virgin Mary as free of all sin. Indeed, in the exquisite Byzantine "Hymn to the Blessed Virgin," the people sing:

> It is truly proper to glorify you, who have borne God, the *ever-blessed and immaculate* and the Mother of our God. More honorable than the Cherubim and beyond compare more glorious than the Seraphim, who, a Virgin, gave birth to God the Word, you, truly the Mother of God, we magnify.

Sounds pretty immaculate to us. And yet, when Pope Pius IX proclaimed that this doctrine was infallibly a dogma of the faith, many Orthodox objected. Some even went back to see if they couldn't find some hint of original sin in the Blessed Virgin. Maybe she nagged Jesus about going to medical school. Was she an annoying yenta?

The same thing happened when Pius XII declared the dogma of Mary's Assumption (or Dormition). Both churches had always believed that Mary's body was taken up into heaven by God—as Jews believed He'd done for the Prophet Elijah.[19] But come 1950 and a papal declaration, and Orthodox suddenly developed

---

[19] The big showoff.

doubts. You can see why they felt they had to: *A pope was saying it.* And worse yet, making it mandatory. Surely, there must be something wrong with it.

For fun, we'd like to see Pope Benedict or his successor infallibly declare that Jesus actually *existed.* We want to see how many monks on Mt. Athos find a way to deny it.

What's the reason for this Pavlovian response to papal teaching? Were Orthodox clergy ever subjected to "Wire Monkey" experiments, locked in cages with enormous effigies of the pope and given electric shocks? Not according to our research. . . .

No, the papacy never played "Shock the Monkey" with the Orthodox. In fact it saved their bacon[21] on many occasions. As the great Russian thinker Vladimir Solevyev pointed out in *Russia and the Universal Church*, it was only the intervention of the papacy that periodically preserved the Eastern churches from falling into various emperors' pet heresies.

Case in point: think of those exquisite icons with the disturbing propensity to weep. Left to themselves, the Eastern Orthodox wouldn't have them—and might be praying in whitewashed cabins that resemble Calvinist meeting halls, or the Los Angeles Catholic cathedral. Beginning in 726, the Patriarch of Constantinople, under orders from an emperor,[22] systematically undertook to destroy all religious art. Countless ancient mosaics and even relics of saints were gouged, burned, or thrown into the sea. When the pope issued a protest, the iconoclast Emperor Leo III sent him a letter promising to invade Rome, destroy all of the pope's art too, and lock the pontiff in chains. This was no idle threat—Pope Gregory II lived in a half-civilized crumbling city, while Leo commanded navies. Yet the pope's support gave courage to the icon-loving monks of the East who resisted this wave of vandalism. In 787, bolstered by letters from the pope, an Eastern church council reversed this policy.

Other heresies followed a similar path—the faithful priests of the East appealing to the pope to free them from secular domination. Indeed, Catholics would argue that is one main function of the papacy—to offer a locus of authority less subject to State enslavement than an isolated bishop. However many kings and emperors have attempted to hijack the Roman Catholic Church—and they came pretty close in Avignon (**see Chateauneuf du Pape**)—the pope's authority as heir of St. Peter always helped him shake free. Thus popes faced down the armies of Napoleon.[23]

---

[20] Greeks call it "halloumi."

[21] It's not known whether he was trying to placate the local Moslems, or had been drinking too much raki, and couldn't stand the chatter.

[22] And Hitler. Those who still think that Pius XII was anything but the Führer's sworn enemy should wonder why Hitler planned to kidnap the pope and hang him—or why Pius helped the generals plotting to blow Hitler up in 1944. These facts, and the tales of the more than 700,000 Jews whom Pius managed to save, are documented in Rabbi David Dalin's *The Myth of Hitler's Pope* (Washington, D.C : Regnery Publishing,. 2005).

Not so the Orthodox, who from the day Constantine moved the capital of his empire to the city he named for himself have proved a *little* too willing to go along in order to get along. When emperors adopted heresies, all too often they'd find their patriarch compliant—or they'd toss him out on his ear, and grab another monk by the beard to fill his throne. With no higher authority to consult (after the Schism) the faithful mostly obeyed. When the Moslems conquered that Empire, they appointed the Orthodox clergy as their tax collectors, to govern the Christians on their behalf (**see Vin Santo**). Again, in Russia after the Revolution, once the Bolsheviks had given up trying simply to exterminate all the Christians—and millions of Orthodox martyrs had died in the event—the clergy were thoroughly infiltrated by the Soviet KGB, who appointed patriarchs and kept the remnant of believers in line. Indeed, when Stalin decided after World War II to wipe out the Ukrainian Catholic Church, many of these appointed Orthodox bishops collaborated eagerly—usurping the buildings and congregations as their own. And they still won't give them back.

But we're willing to overlook such sad episodes, inspired to thoughts of unity by exquisite plates of *mezze,* long nights of *rebetika*, and happy hours spent nursing Lesbian ouzo daiquiris.

CELEBRATE: Cushion your system against the alcoholic shock, and your ears against the danger of talking icons, by enjoying ouzo in the way it was originally intended—with a lavish dinner of Greek appetizers such as the *mezze* below.

Oysters in Lemon Oil (see recipe)
Feta Pancake (see recipe)
Keftedes in Tomato Sauce (see recipe)
Green Beans with Tomatoes
Fried Eggplant Slices
Salad of Cucumber, Tomato, Romaine Lettuce, Red Onion, Oregano
Fresh Fruit with Yogurt and Honey

Oysters in Lemon Oil

Ideally oysters should be shucked at the last minute and all of the juice collected. However if you are not used to the task it can be rather daunting. Most fishmongers will shuck them for you and pack it all up in plastic with shells and liquor.

1/4 cup lemon juice	1/2 cup olive oil
Pinch sugar	36 oysters
Pinch salt	2 tablespoons watercress leaves
Freshly ground black pepper	chopped, plus leaves for garnish

Preheat oven to 300 degrees.

For the sauce, combine lemon, sugar, salt, and pepper in small bowl. Whisk in olive oil drop by drop.

Place oysters on the half shell in a shallow baking pan. Sprinkle with reserved liquor. (If the liquor has been lost, bottled clam juice can be used instead.)

Roast for 5–10 minutes, the oysters should just start to set and have a hint of warmth.

Top with lemon oil sauce and watercress. Any remaining sauce makes a lovely salad dressing.

Arrange oysters on platter garnished with leaves. Enjoy!

Serves 6 as an appetizer

Feta Pancake

4 large eggs
2 cups water
1 cup all purpose flour
1 pound feta cheese

Freshly ground black pepper
2 bunches green onions,
  green part only, sliced
1 tablespoon butter

Combine eggs, water, and flour in blender. Blend smooth. Pour through strainer into a bowl and cover. Rest at least 2 hours to overnight, refrigerated.

Allow to come to room temperature before baking.

Heat oven to 450 degrees.

Butter 1 1/2-quart baking dish. Heat dish 5 minutes in oven.

Lightly stir half of both the cheese and green onions into the egg mixture.

Pour into warmed dish. Crumble in remaining cheese and top with green onions.

Bake 40–45 minutes until golden brown and puffed.

Serves 6–8 as an appetizer or light lunch

Keftedes in Tomato Sauce

3 pounds ground lamb
3 slices country bread, crusts removed
1/2 cup milk
3 medium yellow onions, grated
1 teaspoon dried oregano
1/4 cup chopped parsley
2 eggs
Salt and freshly ground pepper

1/4 teaspoon ground allspice
1/4 teaspoon ground cinnamon
Flour for dredging
1 tablespoon olive oil
1 small yellow onion, diced
2 28-ounce cans plum tomatoes,
  chopped

Put lamb in large bowl and knead with fingers to make a paste. This will create remarkably tender meatballs. Put bread and milk in small saucepan over low heat.

Stir with rubber spatula until all liquid is dissolved and bread is smashed.

Add to lamb along with onions, herbs, eggs, and spices. Mix well. If time allows, chill covered for 1 hour. Form meat using two spoons to make football shaped "meatballs."

Heat the oil in wide pan that will accommodate the meatballs in one layer. It will probably require two pans. Roll gently in flour and fry until well browned on all sides. Add the diced onion and fry 2 minutes. Add tomatoes and stir gently. Cook until slightly thickened and add up to a cup of water. (If two pans are used to fry the meatballs, make sure one is larger and can eventually accommodate everything; add the onions and tomato to the larger pan. Then transfer meat from second pan to main pan. Use water to deglaze and add to all.) Allow to bubble gently for 30 minutes.

Adjust seasoning and serve. It is impossible to determine whether Keftedes are better the first day or second. Also delightful eaten straight from the refrigerator.

Serves 6

....

Loopholes in the Ten Commandments
#7: Thou Shalt Not Steal

Here we encounter another commandment that's a no-brainer on the face of it, one easily summarized thusly:

> Don't. Take. Other. People's. Stuff.

With that, we could note that St. Nicholas is the patron saint of thieves,[23] and move on to our next liquor.

Except that it's not so simple. Like most rights, the right of property hangs in tension with other truths. Unless we have created, for instance, our home *ex nihilo*, as God made the universe,[24] our claim on it is somewhat less absolute than His.

---

[23] The very first Santa was known for convincing crooks to give back their loot. He's invoked both by nervous property owners and practicing thieves. In past centuries, pious bandits used to call themselves the "knights of St. Nicholas," and honor him by dropping unexpectedly down chimneys. They seem to have missed the point.

[24] We found Web sites explaining how to do this, but remain skeptical.

Some Catholics we have known are Seventh-Commandment fundamentalists. To them, their right of property is absolute, just like the right to life. This meant that every dime of taxes the State took from them was a theft—no better than when a pickpocket lifts your iPod, or a dingo steals your baby. Trespassers on their land could simply be shot, without a qualm. Now, as far as we know (we haven't stayed in touch) these good people never actually fired on hobos, and were much more charitable in practice. But they did express an unhealthy interest in Web-based, self-taught constitutional scholars who insist that any citizen can refuse to pay income tax. According to these libertarian activists—who for some reason tend to congregate in West Virginia—the income tax laws are riddled with constitutional loopholes. In fact, paying any tax at all is *entirely voluntary.* You didn't know that? According to these folks it's black-letter law, going back to the Magna Charta. So if you'd rather not pay any tax, all you have to do is write the IRS a detailed letter (single-spaced, please, using both sides of the paper), citing Anglo-Saxon legal precedents provided in the handy kit available from *www.whitepatriot.com* for only $17.76, payable in gold.

The last time we checked, sending this kind of letter is the one infallible way to get yourself investigated—the tax law equivalent of going to Spanish Harlem to burn a Puerto Rican flag. So we hope our old pals aren't facing 20 years in a cell with Wesley Snipes (another self-taught tax resistor).

We can't quite agree with our gun-toting friends that every encroachment on private property amounts to theft. For one thing, the Church teaches differently. As the Catechism of the Catholic Church sums things up:

> The right to private property, acquired or received in a just way,
> does not do away with the original gift of the earth to the whole of

mankind. The universal destination of goods remains primordial, even if the promotion of the common good requires respect for the right to private property and its exercise. (#2403)

In other words, unless you played a part in forming the planet Earth from cosmic dust, you're going to have to *share*.[26] Our portions of private property are goods we hold in trust, but the legal title is God's. In practical terms, this means that, as Thomas Aquinas taught, a starving man with no other recourse may justly steal a loaf of bread—though not, St. Thomas hastened to add, a flat-panel Sony Home Entertainment System. By extension, the poor of a nation may vote to establish a social safety net, so in the midst of abundance the truly helpless never need starve.

In the nineteenth and twentieth centuries, several popes deplored the side effects of a deeply imperfect capitalism—from child labor to toxic workplaces and widespread starvation wages—which disrupted traditional society, fractured the family, and fueled the growth of poisonous fantasies such as Marxism. Such ideologies hoped to force-march mankind at the point of a bayonet back into the Garden of Eden. Long before the Russian Revolution, popes foretold the building of the Gulag, and knew that attempts to enforce equality would end in universal poverty (**see Highballs**).

In response to real social problems and these utopian "solutions," a series of popes beginning with Leo XIII began to develop the Church's "social teaching" concerning the proper limits of the market, and the duties of the government to regulate private property and pursue the Common Good. These teachings were meant to debunk both burgeoning Socialism, and the crackpot pseudo-science of Social Darwinism, which embraced as the principle of human brotherhood the "survival of the fittest." (This proved a consoling thought to men with inherited fortunes, assuring them that they were the cutting edge of Evolution.) While the Marxists saw man as lumpy raw material which could be beaten into an angel, the Social Darwinists believed that we are a troop of hierarchical baboons. With her typical lack of tact, the Church disagreed with everyone—and kept her specific prescriptions for fixing social ills maddeningly vague, to the point where we are still arguing today over what Leo XIII meant in 1891 in his 70,000-word encyclical *Rerum novarum*.

Instead of the (depressingly) specific sort of teaching we're offered on matters such as sex, on social and economic issues the Church gives us mostly broad guidelines within which to form our consciences. Broadly, says the Catechism (#2425):

> Reasonable regulation of the marketplace and economic initiatives, in keeping with a just hierarchy of values and a view to the common good, is to be commended.

---

[26] This teaching helps explain the otherwise puzzling proclivity of nuns in the old days to seize some child's gum, and demand: "Did you bring enough for everyone?"

Yeah, that's pretty conclusive. It's the kind of proof-text you wheel out when you want to win an argument . . . by putting the whole room to sleep.

But there really are critical principles contained within the Church's social teaching, though they don't come in paint-by-number. The popes have taught that private property must be respected—but not enshrined, as if every stock certificate contained a piece of the Blessed Sacrament. We must run our businesses honestly and in accordance with just laws, with an eye toward protecting human dignity and the raw material which makes prosperity possible. This means that if you own a factory that's giving its workers black-lung, or poisoning the county's water supply, or paying men so little that they have to stick their wives in sweatshops and infants in daycare—you've got a problem.

The Church goes on to say that society is best served when more people own property and are economically independent—when they run their own farms or businesses, rather than toiling for paychecks issued by others, which could dry up at the drop of a stock. It's the gnawing anxiety that comes with economic dependence that drives people to vote in socialists and Communists—who attempt to impose monastic poverty and obedience at gunpoint. (They know better than to try imposing chastity.)

On the other hand, the Church has seen enough tyrants over the centuries that she knows how dangerous the government can become. Lest it turn into a giant, meddling octopus, she teaches that the State must be kept in a cozy straight-jacket. For instance, the Church insists that any social good which *can* be accomplished without coercion *must* be left in private hands. Tasks which require the State, like building roads and policing the streets, should be done by the local government wherever possible—to prevent the growth of impersonal bureaucracies. This principle, called "subsidiarity," goes back to the Middle Ages, and forms the core of Pius XI's *Quadrogesimo anno* (1931). In the midst of the Great Depression, it took a bold pope indeed to state this principle while living in Fascist Italy, whose Duce taught in his *Fascist Catechism* (an actual book!): "Everything for the State; nothing outside the State; nothing against the State." But this teaching also rankled meddlers such as President Franklin Roosevelt, who tried to impose federal price controls on pencils.

When we read the documents which come from bishops' conferences—often written entirely by staffers who used to work for "pro-choice" Democratic congressmen—endorsing higher federal taxes and welfare programs for illegal immigrants, it helps to remember *Quadrogesimo anno*—and the fact that most prelates' expertise in economics derives from paying their lawyers and betting on golf.

Papal Infallibility and Lager: Purity Guaranteed by Divine (or German) Law

Outside academia, the commonalities between the doctrine of papal infallibility and the manufacture of lager beer have been too little explored. But with the election of a pope who hails from Munich, where lager[1] beer making was perfected, these deep convergences can no longer be ignored.[2] By way of introduction to this rich vein of historical study, here are just of few of these commonalities, and some key differences:

Lager Beer	Infallible Papal Declarations
Traditionally aged for months, to clean away impurities	Confirm age-old traditions, clearing up ambiguities
Beloved for crisp, sharp flavor	Resented for brisk, stark tenor
Purity preferred to originality	Purity *definitely* preferred to originality
Guaranteed free of sugar	Guaranteed free of error
Product protected from adulteration by the Bavarian Purity Law, enacted 1516	Product protected from adulteration by divine intervention, see Matthew 18:18
Common as dirt; see Budweiser	Rare as hen's teeth; see Immaculate Conception
More popular in America than Europe	Unpopular outside the Philippines
Bottom-fermented	Top-down
German	Jewish

Why is all this important? Because when Catholics go off the rails and fall out of agreement with the Church, it usually centers on some issue of authority—most commonly the pope's. While within his own diocese each bishop shares in the teaching power called the "Magisterium", you don't find people leaving the Church when they differ with their bishop. For one thing, it's easy enough to cross state lines, and then you're outside his jurisdiction. (In fact, it's great fun to slip across the diocesan border and jeer at the ecclesiastical authorities, who are now powerless to touch you. Try it some time!)

---

[1] The term "lager" comes from the German word *lagern,* "to store".

[2] If we do, then the terrorists really will have won.

But there's no escaping the pope, who wields "supreme, full, immediate and universal ordinary power" over the entire Church (Code of Canon Law # 331), the power to "bind and loose" in Heaven and on earth (Matthew 18:18), and—just in case those don't suffice— the promise of infallibility (Vatican I, Session 4, Ch. 4). An impressive arsenal, on paper. It's easy to pretend that the pope's authority translates into worldly power, and set yourself up as David fighting Goliath. Apart from condemning sins like necrophilia or simony to which you're not remotely tempted, this is the quickest way to attain a rush of self-congratulation—and at certain colleges, tenure.

Because as modern Westerners we have been conditioned to resent the very idea of authority, it's easy for us to chafe at the notion of a teaching authority with the right to command our assent. (It's not clear who's to blame for this, though Jacques Maritain wrote a classic, *Three Reformers*, pinning it on Luther, Descartes, and Rousseau.) Instead, we internalize as core principles in the formation of conscience the favorite questions of every obstreperous four-year-old—"Why?" "Who said so?" and "Who's gonna *make* me?" So *Left Behind*-reading podiatrists serving on school boards defy biologists, crackpot Internet nutritionists defy the AMA, theologians defy their bishops, and everybody defies the pope.[3] Instead of facts and reason, each argument descends to the arena of opinion and ideology. Satirist Stephen Colbert (who teaches RCIA at his son's parish) pointed this up, when he told the Washington Press Bureau and a president:

> I'm a simple man with a simple mind. I hold a simple set of beliefs that I live by. Number one, I believe in America. I believe it exists. My gut tells me I live there. I feel that it extends from the Atlantic to the Pacific, and I strongly believe it has 50 states.

We strongly agree.

---

[3] Isn't it fun? Now let's all spin around and go *Wheeeeeeeeeee!!!*

The Church's understanding of doctrine suggests another way, proposing that we ought in general to trust those to whom the Church has entrusted the office of teaching handed on by Christ, and defer to them until we have good reason to think otherwise. In other words—and yes, guys, I'm talking to you—we should be willing *to ask directions.*

Of course, not every tenet of Catholic faith is set in stone—or written in the blood of martyrs who died rather than deny it. (Though a disconcerting amount is indeed, you know . . . written in blood. Kind of messy, come to think of it.) Indeed, many of the misunderstandings of the Church's use of authority have to do with misreadings of the teaching on infallibility—the more common kind exercised by universal councils of bishops, and the rarer, papal variety.

Those who've wandered off into theological left field have convinced themselves that few if any Church teachings are guaranteed with any certainty. Consequently, core beliefs such as the nature of Christ, the content of the Sacraments, the historical resurrection, the virginity of Mary—they're pretty much all up for grabs. Or to be more precise: they're up to academics, whose scholarly back and forth has

usurped the Magisterium of the Church. Want to know what you should believe this month? Don't bother with the Catechism; check the latest issue of *INSeCT*.[4] Of course traditional moral teachings fall into the same murk, and are subject to no authority but "conscience," informed by fashionable opinion. Read enough "progressive" Catholic publications, and you'll become unsure that anything is really sinful—except maybe racism.

Way over in the fever swamps on the far right, racism is somehow not much of an issue—though there's an abiding concern with anti-Semitism.[5] Worst of all, from a theological perspective, certain activists seem intent on proving themselves more Catholic than the pope. The most extreme among them are those called the *sedevacantists*—those who believe that the seat (*sede*) of St. Peter is empty (*vacante*),

---

[4] The actual name of a journal published by the International Network of Societies for Catholic Theology.

[5] And how to promote it.

and has been since 1962. Having convinced themselves that nearly all the decisions of a "true" pope must be prudent, all his statements perfectly clear and all his policies wise,[6] these people deny the claims of "so-called popes" such as John XXIII, Paul VI, John Paul II, and Benedict XVI—all of whom they regard as raving heretics. Since the pope has the supreme judicial authority in the Church (an infallible teaching, by the way), who judges them as heretics? Answers differ, but most on the *sede-vacantist* right fringe agree that the de facto arbiters of papal orthodoxy are rightly bloggers, Web masters, and little old ladies in the Midwest. Having cut themselves off even from other Traditionalists (such as the followers of Archbishop Marcel Lefèbvre) *sede-vacantists* often have to obtain religious or episcopal orders on the sly. In the 1970s, several of them prevailed on the periodically insane former Archbishop of Saigon, Ngô Dinh Thuc, and have been passing the orders on ever since. Sometimes the result can be less than *dignified*—notably, when six of these folks get a wild hair and decide to elect one of themselves pope (1990), or to "ordain" Sinead O'Connor as a priest (1999).

Perhaps we can help the confused souls at either extreme by pointing out the very limited nature of papal infallibility—which we think of as "a hand on the papal ticker." As Jesus promised, the Holy Spirit sticks around. It is the power that keeps the Church "on message," keeps it from making things up as it goes along, revising its beliefs to suit public opinion. While God will let popes get up to some serious mischief—from adultery committed inside St. Peter's Basilica, to making war on the rest of Italy, to really kinky stuff like digging up the previous pope and putting his body on trial—He draws the line somewhere.

Whatever they do in their personal lives, the Comforter-cum-Enforcer prevents popes from leading us astray. When they teach from the chair (*ex cathedra*) of St. Peter, invoking their full authority, as they rarely do, popes are physically prevented from teaching error. If necessary—and this is our favorite part—God will strike a pope dead in his tracks, rather than let him get away with this. God doesn't inspire the pope with magical knowledge, making him an oracle who can predict the price of gold. (If only! We could stop bothering with Sunday collections. That dollar a week is really starting to pinch.) No, God takes a more direct approach, saying: *Teach heresy, get a heart attack.*

CELEBRATE: Show your gratitude for the purity of the Church's salvific teaching guaranteed by Christ's promise of infallibility, and the clean, pristine taste of a good lager, by cooking up a festive *Ex Cathedra* Beer-Can Chicken (pictured).

---

[6] Such people were spoiled by a brief, lucky run of mostly sensible and saintly popes, beginning shortly after the French Revolution. However, a few hours spent with Google and some Renaissance and early medieval pontiffs offers another view.

Now don't get cute by trying to use St. Peter brand beer from England. All its products are excellent, but they only come in bottles. While broken glass does add texture, the taste of your own blood can overwhelm the bird's subtle flavor. Instead, celebrate Simon Peter's heritage by using an oven-safe can of fine Israeli beer such as Goldstar. The beer will evaporate, making the bird moist and succulent, and when you serve it mitred, crowned, and seated on its throne, your dinner guests will see papal authority in an entirely different light.

Ex Cathedra Beer-Can Chicken

This ingenious method of roasting chicken creates one of the most succulent birds you will ever encounter. It is not necessary to roast in cast iron but it is ideal. After roasting, a sauce can be made right in the pan from the drippings.

1 4–5 pound organic free-range chicken	Freshly ground black pepper
6 cloves garlic, peeled	1 tablespoon dried wild oregano
Salt	2 teaspoons sweet paprika
3 tablespoons organic raw apple cider vinegar	2 tablespoons extra virgin olive oil
	Juice and zest of 1 lemon
	1 can beer

Remove giblets reserving for another use. Thoroughly rinse and dry bird.

In a mortar, smash garlic and salt together with pestle. When a thick paste has formed, add vinegar, pepper, oregano, paprika, and olive oil.

Rub mixture all over and inside the cavity of chicken. Douse with lemon.

Allow to sit 2 hours at room temperature. Food should not be cooked straight out of the refrigerator. If time allows always bring meat and fish to room temp.

Preheat oven to 350 degrees.

Open the beer and drink half. Cut slits in the can, going horizontally about an inch from top. Place in center of cast iron skillet. Lower the bird onto the can so that the can fits into the cavity. The legs will act as two of the legs of a tripod and the beer can the third.

Roast until juices run clear and thigh meat registers 180 degrees on a meat thermometer.

Remove from oven and allow to rest a few minutes before carving.

Serve with roasted potatoes.

Serves 4

SERVING NOTES: Dissenting Catholics may omit beer can; sede-vacantists may omit chicken.

Pisco, Peru, and Pizarro

One of the most beloved legal[7] exports from South America is the grape brandy called *pisco*. It's a high-octane liquor made from wine grapes, which conquistadors first planted in Cuzco, Peru, in 1560. Apart from the Christian faith, grapes were one of the few good things the Spaniards brought to the region. When Francisco Pizarro landed in 1532 at the head of a small army, he found in the Inca Empire a highly developed civilization that spread across half a continent—with irrigated crops, a monotheistic faith, elaborate art works in gold, and no trace of the cannibalism which had tainted the Mexican Aztecs (**see Kahlua**). Deeply impressed, he decided to conquer the place.

To give his plan some fig-leaf of religious justification, the tin-hatted bandit announced that his sole intent was to bring the Incas the Gospel. His method was what we might call a "catechetical ambush." Now, we don't know if you've ever been ambushed by evangelists—perhaps outside your house by friendly Mormons in clip-on ties, or outside a French Quarter bar by Assemblists of God with a flashing red neon crucifix that reads "This Blood's for You." Sure, it's never much fun, but the Peruvians had it worse. Pizarro's ambush was rather literal, and involved a fair number of cannon.

On Nov. 16, 1532, Pizarro laid in wait for a procession of the Incan emperor and his court. As the historian William Prescott relates in his *History of the Conquest of Peru*:

> Elevated high above his vassals came the Inca Atahuallpa, borne on
> a sedan or open litter, on which was a sort of throne made of massive

---

[7] Another much-loved product from that continent appears on our shores, borders, and in our airports by the kilo—sometimes concealed in hollowed-out Bibles or baked into statues of the saints. The drug that novelist Jay Mcinerney termed "Bolivian marching powder" has fueled the growth of criminal gangs, the emergence of "gangsta rap," and the phenomenon of surrealist, unfunny 12-minute segments of *Saturday Night Live* which leave the viewers stunned and muttering "What were the writers *snorting*?"

gold of inestimable value. The palanquin was lined with the richly colored plumes of tropical birds, and studded with shining plates of gold and silver. The monarch's attire was much richer than on the preceding evening. Round his neck was suspended a collar of emeralds of uncommon size and brilliancy. His short hair was decorated with golden ornaments, and the imperial borla encircled his temples. The bearing of the Inca was sedate and dignified; and from his lofty station he looked down on the multitudes below with an air of composure, like one accustomed to command.

Pizarro had other, innovative ideas about who should command the Incas, which he implemented on the spot. He sent his chaplain Fray Vicente de Valverde, O.P., to confront the emperor with a crucifix and a Bible. A real linguistic whiz, Valverde had learned the Incan language, and he took this opportunity to conduct some impromptu R.C.I.A. In fact, he gave the impatient monarch a thumbnail sketch of the entire Catholic Faith, and a sales pitch urging him to convert while he still had the chance. Oh yes, and one more thing: He'd have to become a subject of the Emperor Charles V.[8] Valverde was clearly not much of a "closer," since Atahuallpa insisted on looking through the catalogue. After flipping through the Bible and not finding anything to order, he tossed the alien book aside and ordered the Spaniards out of his country.

And that's when they opened fire. The hidden Spanish troops shot a cannon, and started taking potshots into the crowd of unarmed Incas. Between two and ten thousand Indians died, Atahuallpa was conquered, and Valverde was well on the road to becoming bishop of Cuzco, the capital. It was not a great day for religious liberty.

That said, the churchmen in the midst of the gold-hungry Spaniards did their best to turn Pizarro's fig leaf into an orchard, marching through the country on foot and learning a dozen languages to preach the Gospel without the benefit of gunpowder. The Franciscan St. Francis Solanus (1549–1610), for example, won thousands of souls, and was famed for what was either an urban legend or a flashback to the first Pentecost: when he preached to mixed groups of Indians, each understood him in his own dialect.

When the priests saw the conquistadors robbing the country of everything not nailed down, and enslaving the natives to work in silver mines, they started defending the Indians' rights and organizing them on farms. Jesuits taught Indians to grow grapes and ferment them. The wine they produced was good enough that it won over thirsty exiles and Incas with a low-alcohol tolerance (Pizarro famously teased his subjects for proving "cheap dates"). Soon all the colonies were drinking it instead of the pricey bottles shipped in from Spain. Enraged Iberian vintners—don't

---

[8] This is no longer required of converts to Catholicism.

cross these people, trust us—rioted for their right to soak the colonials, and in 1614, the ever-meddling Spanish Crown outlawed the sale of Peruvian wine.

The ever-crafty Jesuits (**see Winkler Jesuitengarten**) applied their scientific training to invent a new drink which fit neatly through a loophole in the law—a brandy that was soon named for the earthenware containers which held it, *piskos*. A stronger drink that gave you more bang for the buck, "pisco" soon caught on throughout New Spain, and gave the long-suffering Indians an industry they could count on. They would need it, as the former Inca empire succumbed to civil wars, fought between nostalgic Inca chiefs and rival Spanish governors, which continued on and off for almost 30 years.

In 1812, when Spain was ruled by a puppet king with the good luck to have a brother named Napoleon, most of its South American colonies revolted. It was bad enough paying tribute to a foreign king; at least he ought to be legitimate. Even after a real king ruled again in Spain, most colonies continued their revolt, and Peru gained its independence in 1821. Of course, these rebellions were all led by men of European descent, grandsons of Spain whose descendants still hold power in these lands today. One source of the populist, bone-headedly Marxoid movement led by Hugo Chavez of Venezuela—which is spreading through South America—is ancient Indian resentment at a houseguest who just won't leave. But he also invented pisco, so he really can't be all bad.

Indeed, the Faith planted by the friars who followed behind the conquerors—muttering "Sorry about this" and trying to clean up the mess—still thrives in Peru, if in a variety of forms which might not have pleased St. Solanus. Most Peruvians are still Catholics; in the Indian regions with colorful admixtures of old pagan customs. One of these is that the native population still retains a healthy respect for *apus*—mysterious and mighty spirits said to dwell on mountain tops. The missionaries didn't try to burst their bubble, but instead taught Indians to think of these venerable snowmen as saints. Indeed, each village now embraces its local patron saint/apu, and instead of fearing him invokes his intercession—sometimes by sacrificing guinea pigs in his honor, to ensure the fertility of the llamas.[9] Elaborate celebrations mark the annual feast days of such saints, involving almost the entire population—except perhaps for the local Pentecostalists, a group that's growing in numbers, proving that Incas are still impressed by preachers who speak in tongues.

What's impressive to the outsider is the way that these villagers can make a mighty yeti out of local saints whose real-life qualities were less than mountainous. One comes to mind: the humble Peruvian saint Martin de Porres, a gentle vegetarian and mulatto slave who joined the Dominicans as a house-servant. The miracles he performed had nothing to do with avalanches, but all involved healing the sick, and he never aspired to any station higher than kitchen serf. He made of his humble galley an animal hospital, and instead of exterminating rats he persuaded them

---

[9] Did we mention that we *love* this religion?

to run away. It's a tribute to the vision of these Catholic Incas that they can see St. Martin not as he once was, but as he really is today—a towering giant of charity stalking through Heaven, winning favors for the people he left behind.

CELEBRATE: Show your respect either for the heroic endurance of the Indians, or the Machiavellian piety of Pizarro—depending on your politics, and hey, we're not here to judge—by serving up the cocktail which both Peru and Chile claim as their national drink: the Pisco Sour. (In fact, they've fought wars over the region that grows pisco grapes, and are still battling in international court over the right to trademark the stuff.) It's a potent drink, which seems in our experience to drain the body of all energy to do anything but eat. A good thing there's a dish to accompany the stuff, called *ceviche*, the South American equivalent of sushi. It's raw seafood (e.g., shrimp, fish, or squid) which is marinated overnight, "cooked" in lemon juice and spicy seasonings to a firm consistency and piquant flavor. It's the national dish of Chile. And Peru. And yes, they're still fighting over that one, too.

Pisco Sour

Shrimp Ceviche (see recipe)

Scallop Ceviche (see recipe)

Shrimp Ceviche

1 tablespoon olive oil
1 teaspoon cumin seeds
1 pound medium shrimp, peeled
Salt and freshly ground pepper
2 tablespoons lime juice
2 tablespoons orange juice

1 tomato, finely diced
1 jalapeño; cored, seeded, diced
1 mango, diced
1 red onion, finely sliced
1/4 cup cilantro, coarsely torn by hand

TO GARNISH:
Avocado slices   Corn nuts

Heat oil and toast cumin; as soon as the seeds are brown add seasoned shrimp. Cook in two batches if a small pan is used. They should cook in one layer. Working quickly, toss and cook until shrimp just turns pink on the outside. Transfer to nonreactive bowl and toss with remaining ingredients. Serve immediately with garnishes.

Serves 4

Scallop Ceviche

Make sure to inquire of your fishmonger the packing method of the scallops. Many purveyors pack them in water and a preservative, extending their shelf life but eliminating flavor and texture.

The Precious Blood: The Reason for the Squeezin'

It's obvious why any book about churchmen making wine must explore the theology of the Blood of Christ: Had Jesus not held up a cup of Passover wine at the Last Supper and consecrated it, then fed it to His apostles as His Blood, two millennia worth of monks would not have purpled their toes in the first place. In fact, to look at the whole thing from a God's-eye view, we might say that the reason He created both grapes and yeast was to make possible the Mass. Sure, that's a sticky-fingered, pious way of putting it, more suited to a sentimental priest giving a pitch to wealthy old matrons he hopes will fund his "pilgrimage" to Burgundy, but that

The Precious Blood: The Reason for the Squeezing   *219*

doesn't mean it's not true. If we really see God as a clear-sighted craftsman of the universe, He surely foresaw the use to which His Son would someday put the "fruit of the vine and work of human hands." And He planned ahead. He made wheat the staff of civilization, and wine the sauce which makes it bearable, then appropriated both as the stuff from which His priests would confect the Eucharist. It's moving to think that the evolution of *vitis vinifera* was gently guided from Above with an eye to Sacramental theology. Let's be glad that Our Lord chose wine instead of, say, prune juice. Most parishes are already short of restrooms as it is.

The use of wine in our ritual goes back to the Old Testament, of course—but not to the Temple sacrifices once performed in Jerusalem. The high priests had no need for bread and wine to serve as sacrificial species; the species *bos Taurus*[10] would do just fine. Beginning with Abraham, God's people showed Him their devotion by slaughtering beasts as "sin offerings." This practice got almost out of hand when Abraham bound up Isaac as a human sacrifice—but God stepped in and replaced the boy with a ram, as He'd someday provide mankind with a Lamb.

All of which might lead us to wonder what exactly was up with that. Why did an omnipotent Deity with at least one universe to run require a band of dusty Jews in robes to cut the throats of bulls and birds, and ritually burn their corpses? If the boys at a Yeshiva school tried that today they'd get arrested, and spend the next ten years on a shrink's couch and Ritalin. Religious doubts like this have driven countless teenage vegans on the Upper West Side into postponing their bar mitzvahs, but the Hebrew Bible offers answers, as do the thoughtful rabbis who interpret it. For one thing, it's not clear that God wanted the sacrifices for His own sake. As the prophet Isaiah reported, quoting an anonymous, "highly placed source":

> I have more than enough of burnt offerings, of rams and the fat of fattened animals; I have no pleasure in the blood of bulls and lambs and goats. When you come to appear before me, who has asked this of you, this trampling of my courts? Stop bringing meaningless offerings! (Isaiah 1:11–13)

The medieval Jewish theologian Maimonides explained that God had allowed the people to offer Him blood sacrifices because that was what they expected of any religion. The pagan cults all around them sacrificed actual humans, and the Hebrews were starting to feel left out. They sought a resonant religious symbol—so He sighed, and gave them one. St. Paul might have disagreed with Maimonides, since he taught that "almost all things are by the law purged with blood; and without shedding of blood is no remission." (Hebrews 9:22) When Jesus was born, Joseph and Mary brought Him to the Temple to consecrate their first-born to God—an echo of Abraham's sacrifice—and offer a pair of birds to "buy" Him

---

[10] i.e., domestic cattle.

back. On the Cross, His own blood shed would ransom all of us, and render the Temple sacrifice irrelevant. The Romans, soon after, would render it impossible by looting the Temple, then bulldozing the place.

When St. Paul tried to win over his fellow Jews to accept the eternal sacrifice of Christ, he employed a clever bit of rhetoric—pointing out that there was one sacrifice recorded in Genesis which predated Abraham's. Even before the shepherd Abram got religion, changed his name, and got bumped up to Patriarch, a neighboring king named Melchisedech was worshiping the one true God—and praising Him with offerings of bread and wine. It was this sacrifice which Jesus carried on, the wily Paul argued (Hebrews 5:10), in an older and purer tradition even than Abraham's. So *there*.

Not all the Hebrews were convinced.

But the devotion to the Precious Blood of Christ quickly became an important part of Christian practice. Relics which were said to contain some drops of that Blood were revered in shrines across medieval Europe—though the primitive state of serology precluded proper testing. Until 1981, that is. In that year, doctors completed a series of tests on the miraculous Host of Lanciano. It seems that in the eighth century, a monk saying the Mass had doubts about the Real Presence of Christ, which he thought was merely symbolic—like a holy card or a Jesus-fish bumper sticker. But when he raised the bread during the Mass, as he muttered the words of consecration, the host turned into a piece of bloody flesh. As he recovered from an incipient heart attack, the monk told onlookers the story of his doubts—which had curiously evaporated. But the blood never did. In 1981, medical school professors Odoardo Linoli and Ruggero Bertelli took this very old piece of meat to their testing lab, and found that it was flesh from a human heart muscle, caked with blood of type AB—the rarest variety, but the same blood type found in the Shroud of Turin. This suggests that either something miraculous really happened, or that a band of futuristic time travelers raced around medieval Italy, just to mess with us.[11]

It wasn't until after Vatican II that laymen in the Western rites began to receive Communion under both species (**see Wedding of Cana**); however, the Church has always taught that both Jesus' Body and Blood are fully present in either form of the Eucharist. Nevertheless, it may be that laymen felt kind of left out when they weren't offered the cup. This could help explain the enormous popularity of the cult of the Precious Blood, which was spread by St. Gaspar del Bufalo, an early nineteenth-century priest whom Napoleon kicked out of Rome for refusing to swear loyalty to that megalomaniacal dwarf. St. Gaspar roamed the countryside, convincing bandits to lay down their arms, stop spilling innocent blood, and instead adore the Blood of Christ. Under Gaspar's influence, the exiled Pope Pius IX made a vow to promote the Precious Blood devotion, provided he got his kingdom back. Pius soon returned to Rome in triumph, and kept his promise. The Feast of

_____
[11] Which would be just *like* those damned time travelers. We hate those guys.

the Most Precious Blood was set for the first of July. Pope John XXIII marked this feast in 1960 with an apostolic letter, *Sanguis Christi*. In it, he taught:

> Unlimited is the effectiveness of the God-Man's Blood—just as un-limited as the love that impelled Him to pour it out for us, first at His circumcision eight days after birth, and more profusely later on in His agony in the garden, in His scourging and crowning with thorns, in His climb to Calvary and crucifixion, and finally from out that great wide wound in His side which symbolizes the divine Blood cascading down into all the Church's Sacraments. Such surpassing love suggests, nay demands, that everyone reborn in the torrents of that Blood adore it with grateful love.

Further down, he quoted St. John Chrysostom, who urged Christians scurrying home after Mass:

> Let us, then, come back from that table like lions breathing out fire, thus becoming terrifying to the Devil, and remaining mindful of our Head and of the love he has shown for us . . . This Blood, when worthily received, drives away demons and puts them at a distance from us, and even summons to us angels and the Lord of angels.

These theological reflections strike our untutored minds as incredibly cool.

It's potent stuff, that mystical liquid offered to us by Eucharistic ministers in the form of treacly sweet altar wine (**see Mission Wine**), sometimes out of goofy porcelain cups that contravene canon law. Since God made the Sacraments of earthly signs that would move our hearts as well as minds, it must fill some deep psychic need to know that the spilt blood of the incarnate Son of God, poured over us like the bull's blood sprinkled by Moses on the Jews, washes away our sins. That fermented grape juice, lifted by a weary priest to the warbling of some "contemporary choir" doing tunes taken from the musical *Cats*, can redeem our scathing gossip, banish those phantom tax deductions, and clear our Internet history. It sounds at once completely crazy, and utterly right.

The eerie significance of drinking redemptive sacred blood has inspired both mystical nuns and secular singers. Take the Sister Adorers of the Precious Blood, for example, a group of contemplative nuns founded in nineteenth-century Canada with convents today across North America and Japan, who strive "that the work of the Saviour may produce its fruits of salvation and sanctification in themselves and in their brothers and sisters throughout the world." Or the songsters of Most Precious Blood, an all-vegan hardcore band whose 2003 album "Our Lady of Annihilation" included a leaflet from People for the Ethical Treatment of Animals—

longtime opponents of ritual sacrifice. Musicologists who chronicle this ensemble note in the authoritative *Grove Dictionary of Music*:

> The band's mastermind, Justin Brannan, is also a published author, painter and folk singer. Rob Fusco, the band's vocalist and front man, is a master chess player and former chess instructor, Rachel Rosen, the band's CEO, co-founder and Brannan's musical confidant for the past decade, spends her free time doing autopsies for the NYC Medical Examiner's office (Read: the morgue). Drummer Colin Kercz did time on drums with Damnation A.D. and currently lives in Australia. Bassist Matt Miller collects skateboards and has a mammoth beard.[12]

Purim: Hang Haman and Go Get Hammered

This feast is one of our favorite holy days. For one thing, it marks a glorious incident in the Hebrew Bible in which God's people avoided extermination. The tale is told in the biblical Book of Esther, a romantic page-turner rife with intrigue, violence, extensive cosmetic makeovers, and hundreds of sexy harem girls. A faithful film adaptation would surely be rated R, and should probably be directed by Quentin Tarantino. (In fact, a modest PG-13 version, *One Night With The King*, appeared in 2006, designed to appeal to the evangelical Christians who attended Mel Gibson's *The Passion* by the busfuls.)

Make no mistake: the threat to the Jewish people was all too real, and their escape a narrow one, which hinged on the brave and isolated Esther, a nice Jewish girl who was forced to marry a *goyische* king, then use her charms to talk him out of genocide.

At the time, almost the entire Hebrew population dwelled in exile—most within the Persian Empire, including Babylon, where they had been force-marched by the thousands (**see Jeremiah Weed**), and lived at the sufferance of a hostile government in the land we now know as Iraq. Afraid of insurgents, they mostly stayed in the Green Zone with the reporters.

One of these exiled Jews named Mordecai worked at the royal palace. Since he was almost 100 years old, he mostly *kibitzed* and *kvetched*, but he also kept his ear to the ground. Literally—he used to lie around outside the palace gate. It was there that he overheard some eunuchs talking in high, screechy voices about their plot to murder the king. Mordecai had no reason to love the pagan tyrant Ahasuerus, but eunuchs creeped him out, so he reported the plot and saved the king. *But did he get*

---

[12] Or was it Wikipedia? Copy ed.—please check this.

credit for this, we ask you? No, he did not. "That's okay, don't thank me," said Mordecai. "Who am I that I should expect gratitude?"

The king took Mordecai's loyalty for granted, and instead promoted a social climbing gentile named Haman who had kind of a "thing" for eunuchs. Mordecai didn't think much of Haman, and had no use for the bowing and scraping which marked this brown-nosing pagan court—so when Haman passed him on the street, Mordecai refused to do him honor. He'd just shake his head and mutter "*Fech!*"

Instead of dismissing Mordecai as just a grumpy old fart, the thin-skinned Haman decided to get even. In fine Ba'ath Party style, he opted for revenge on a massive, bloody scale: he would convince the king that the Jews were plotting against him, and get permission to order a general massacre of every Jew within the empire that spanned from India to Ethiopia—man, woman, and child. Haman won Ahasuerus over, and the king sent out orders to every corner of the empire for the killing to start on the thirteenth day of the twelfth month—Haman's lucky day. Haman even built a gallows right by Mordecai's favorite gate from which he planned to have the old man hanged.

But Mordecai smelled blood in the wind. He finagled a copy of the order and took it to his niece and adopted daughter, Esther. Some time before, after a nation-wide talent search ("Babylon's Top Model," this fall on the CW Network), this lovely virgin had been chosen to step in as Ahasuerus's new wife—and Queen of Persia. She now dwelt in the palace as in a gilded cage—without even one of those nifty parrot swings. She had limited access to the king, who didn't grant audiences to petty underlings like his wife. In fact, she could be put to death for approaching him uninvited.[13] Mordecai insisted she take the risk and convince the king to spare her people. Terrified, she refused. Appalled, he kvetched. They went back and forth like this for hours until the borscht got cold, and at last poor Esther gave in. "If I perish, I perish," she said with a sigh. Mordecai said, "*Fech!*"

Esther spent three days fasting and praying, underwent a pricey makeover, then marched off to face the king. The New American Bible recounts what happened next:

> In making her state appearance, after invoking the all-seeing God and savior, she took with her two maids; on the one she leaned gently for support, while the other followed her, bearing her train.
>
> She glowed with the perfection of her beauty and her countenance was as joyous as it was lovely, though her heart was shrunk with fear.
>
> She passed through all the portals till she stood face to face with the king, who was seated on his royal throne, clothed in full robes of state, and covered with gold and precious stones, so that he inspired great awe.
>
> As he looked up, his features ablaze with the height of majestic anger, the queen staggered, changed color, and leaned weakly against the head of the maid in front of her.
>
> But God changed the king's anger to gentleness. In great anxiety he sprang from his throne, held her in his arms until she recovered, and comforted her with reassuring words.
>
> "What is it, Esther?" he said to her. "I am your brother. Take courage! You shall not die because of this general decree of ours. Come near!" (Esther, D:1–11)

We observe from this exchange that king Ahasuerus was something of a *schmuck*. Male readers should know that if you're trying to calm down a woman when she is crying—especially if it's your fault, say, because you've ordered some general slaughter—this is not the way to do it. Try rubbing her feet, or whipping out some piece of jewelry you've saved for the occasion. But pretending to be her brother? That just makes you sound like some kind of perv.

That's how it must have seemed to Esther; the poor girl passed out cold. By the time she regained consciousness, the king was in a panic, and ready to offer her anything—if only she would "for God's[14] sake quit with the crying, already." He promised to grant her anything she wished—up to "half of my kingdom." At that,

---

[13] An archaic relationship strategy which most Catholic therapists now discourage.

[14] As a Babylonian, Ahasuerus would have invoked the idol Marduk, but you get the idea.

Esther dried her tears, took a mirror and fixed her makeup, and set out to save the Jews. She coolly arranged a private dinner for three, at which she and the king would host the hated Haman. When the dinner rolled around, as she sat with the king and the bureaucrat who planned to hang her uncle, Esther waited until her husband was a couple sheets to the wind. He started blathering on, as he was wont to do, about how much he loved her, and would offer her "half of my kingdom" if she asked. At this, Esther made eyes at the king and, "Well, there is something you could do. . . ." The king insisted she tell him what she wanted. She hesitated just long enough, until he was practically begging, then dropped her bombshell. Could the king maybe hold off on slaughtering all the Jews (especially Mordecai who had, ahem, *saved his life*), and instead punish someone who deserved it, like—well like Haman here. Why not hang him instead? It would seem a shame if that perfectly good gallows went to waste. . . .

The king went outside to smoke and think in his garden; inside Haman started groveling before the queen, grabbing her knees and begging for mercy. Haman was still kneeling in front of her when the king came back in the room. Big mistake, touching the queen.

The king flew into a rage and ordered Haman hanged from his own scaffold, and sent orders for the Jews to be spared. In fact, he told the Jews to take up arms and kill the local anti-Semites who'd been gathering for the pogrom. Which the grateful Jews promptly did. And they all lived happily ever after.

This happy story has inspired harried Jews in many lands throughout the centuries—no doubt because such threats arose to haunt them again and again. By remaining faithful to the one true God, staying out of pagan beds, and faithfully keeping kosher, these exiles had managed not to dissolve into the gentile ethnic stew (recipe not included). Of course, this ethnic separatism made their jealous neighbors suspicious. Who exactly *were* these foreigners in their midst who kept apart and called themselves the "chosen"? Where did they get all their money, why were so many of them scribes, and weren't they secretly *planning to take control*?

Audible sigh. . . . Such paranoid fears have made the chronically exiled Jews the scapegoats of Christians and Moslems alike for two millennia—until at last a neo-pagan regime which had discarded every element of Christendom *except* distrust of the Jews decided to "solve" the "problem." God help us, they nearly succeeded.

Catholic novelist Walker Percy once made a profound observation about the roots of Nazi anti-Semitism. In his novel, *The Thanatos Syndrome*, Percy suggests that in attempting to eliminate the Jews, the Nazis were trying to root out the evidence of God's intervention in history, the better to make of man a god. To the ex-believer haunted by the ghost of God,[15] the very survival of the Jews, out of all the embattled tribes of the ancient world, served as God's fingerprints. As Percy asked, "Where are the Hittites?" That much stronger and more numerous tribe was a much better candidate to survive the centuries, and end up running sewing machines in New York's Garment District. But the Hittites are history, while Abraham's seed still swims.

It's that joyously spurting seed Jews mark every year on the feast of Purim with popping champagne corks and bubbling beer. On the other 364 days of the year, Jewish custom strongly discourages heavy drinking except when accompanied by heavy eating. (Think rich, creamy blintzes, chunks of challah and steaming plates of kügel.) In decades past, Jews used to say that the "*shikker* (drunk) is really a *goy* (gentile)." To which the tipsy Irish fireman on the next barstool replied, "You're fecking right I am, ya Christ-killing sheeny!" And the fight was on.

But on the feast of Purim, Jews are commanded to drink themselves silly. Commanded by God Himself, according to the Talmud: "A person is obligated to become inebriated on Purim until he doesn't know the difference between 'cursed is Haman' and 'blessed is Mordechai.'"

As Christians we are "spiritual Semites,"[16] so we're happy to join the Semites at their spirits.

CELEBRATE: Honor the heroism of brave queen Esther and grumpy old Mordecai by making the traditional Jewish Purim treat, Hamantaschen. These little tri-corner cookies are meant to resemble the hat worn by hated Haman—and eating it is meant to mock his failure to wipe out the Jews.

We know what you're thinking just now. . . . And the answer is NO. It would NOT be a good idea to "update" this recipe for the sake of "contemporary relevance," making cookies that resemble Nazi officer's hats. Just trust us on this one, okay?

---

[15] Most leading Nazis were embittered ex-Catholics, as Marx and Trotsky were anti-Semitic ex-Jews. Hitler and Himmler rank as history's most evil ex-altar boys; Josef Stalin was the world's most resentful seminary dropout—arguably even worse than Garry Wills.

[16] As Pope Pius XI taught, rebuking the wannabe Hamans of his day.

Hamantaschen

We enjoy these cookies with a variety of fillings. Shockingly expensive but worth it are Sarabeth's™ preserves, particularly the Peach Apricot and Strawberry Raspberry– if you can stop yourself from eating it all straight from a spoon. Another favorite is a small square of highest quality bittersweet chocolate.

4 cups flour	1 cup sugar
2 teaspoons baking powder	2 eggs
1/2 teaspoon salt	Zest of one orange
1/2 pound butter, room temperature	2 teaspoons orange blossom water
1 pound cream cheese, room temperature	Fillings of choice

Combine flour, baking powder, and salt. Set aside.

Beat together butter and cream cheese with sugar.

Add eggs one at a time followed by orange zest and blossom water.

Mix thoroughly.

Add flour mixture in two additions. Scrape bowl between additions and combine thoroughly.

Dump out onto a floured surface and knead one or two strokes to form into a ball.

Divide in half, flatten each piece into a disk and chill overnight.

Preheat oven to 375 degrees.

Working on a counter sprinkled with a mixture of powdered sugar and flour, roll dough to 1/4 inch thick.

This dough is very soft, if it becomes too warm and difficult to work with pop it in the freezer for 5 minutes and resume. Cut out 3-inch circles and dab a small bit of filling in centers. Fold up three sides to form a triangular shape with an opening in the center.

Chill in freezer for 10 minutes on parchment-lined baking sheets.

Bake 25 minutes and cool on racks.

Makes 40 tiny hats

Quietism: A Heresy for Your Hangover

If you've ever wondered how a once-fervently Catholic country such as France descended into the persecuting atheism which marked its Revolution, and the snide secularism which hangs over the land at present like the smell of a stale Gauloise, it helps to know just how bonkers, out-of-control *obsessed* the place once was with issues of religion. Throughout the sixteenth century, Counter-reformed Catholics and puritanical Huguenots conducted their debates over papal authority, free will, and predestination with dagger, musket, and cannon—and occasional, judicious doses of poison. For a sexy, gory, thoroughly biased account of these conflicts, rent the racy Huguenot propaganda flick *Queen Margot* (1994). Like its British counterpart *Elizabeth* (1998), it depicts its Protestants as noble idealists besieged by scheming, oppressive papists who never seem to bathe.[1] If *Queen Margot* didn't flash so much of Isabelle Adjani's noble flesh, you might think its director was that Belfast bigot, the Rev. Ian Paisley.

With the partial victory of the Catholic party over the Calvinists, France settled into a kind of clerical Cold War, with Huguenots living in enclaves in France's southwest—the same region which once hosted its Albigensian heretics, medieval New Agers who considered Creation evil and loathed the flesh. (For a glimpse of their theology depicted in oils, see the paintings of Hieronymus Bosch whom some art historians believe was an adherent.[2]) Soon other strains of theological controversy came bubbling to the surface, in the form of the Jansenist heresy, which was essentially Calvinism dressed up in a Catholic costume. (Since these men *were* French, the costume was still quite tasteful.) As

---

[1] Film theorists of the future will wonder how the filmmakers managed it, but the Catholic characters look so filthy you can almost *smell* them onscreen.

[2] Cf. *The Secret Heresy of Hieronymus Bosch,* by Linda Harris (Edinburgh: Floris Books, 1996). A word of caution for Catholics here: This book costs 75 bucks.

we explain elsewhere (**see Winkler Jesuitengarten**), Jansenists dared to hope that almost all men were damned—with a special emphasis on the flames that await unbaptized infants.

Bizarre as it might seem to those of us who have smoked a single cigarette with a modern Frenchman, this dour heresy swept France like a fashion craze, and had to be forcibly suppressed. Ironically, it took the militaristic Jesuits to convince the adulterous King of France to pressure the pope to condemn an overly rigorous reading of Catholic morality which was sweeping the *laissez-faire* French. To all of which the modern reader can only say, "Wow. What happened to those people?" To which the obvious answer is *burn-out*. Spend enough time advocating the extreme form of any cause, banging your head against the stone walls of reality, and eventually you're going to give yourself a migraine. You'll strap on a helmet[3] and look for some nice couch in front of a TV set with a bottle of Vicodin. Which is pretty much what the French did in the wake of the low-level civil war provoked by the Jansenists.

Viewed another way, the fifteenth and sixteenth centuries all across Europe could be seen as a very long binge, in which Christians from Scandinavia to Languedoc thought entirely too much about religion—and killed rather too many fellow-Christians who disagreed with them. After the Peace of Westphalia (1648), which stopped the slaughter of the Thirty Years' War, it became unfashionable to argue too fervently over doctrine. It seemed a form of disturbing the peace. But people still craved the consolations of faith, and looked for theological solutions raising fewer opportunities for conflict. In England this would take the form of Deism, which imagines God essentially as Homer Simpson snoozing at the control panel of his nuclear plant. In Germany, Lutherans began to embrace Pietism with its heavy emphasis on emotion—for instance, the sacred sadness induced by singing lugubrious hymns—over the fine theological distinctions which had fueled the murderous Siege of Magdeburg.

In France, the same religious burn-out took a very different form—and one which is on its surface very appealing—in the heresy of Quietism. If one views the French Wars of Religion and the Jansenist controversy as a protracted Spring Break in Tijuana gorging on the Spirit in nearly lethal doses, then eating the worm, Quietism may be seen as the protracted hangover spent in a quiet dorm room listening to Enya. No loud noises, please, and no exertions, just a period of calm with lots of fluids, giving you time to commune with your deeper self and apologize to your liver.

Because Quietism is even more relaxing than it sounds. It's like a cold compress applied to the soul, an hour of Hatha yoga conducted on an isolated beach between massages. Such an Eastern allusion is apropos: The old *Catholic Encyclopedia*

---

[3] Wasn't it nice of the people at the Living Skills Center to lend you one? Looks rather jaunty. . . .

points out that the Christian Quietists were in fact striving not so much for union with God as for a secular *nirvana*.[4] Their spirituality was less a modern invention than the resurgence of ancient, Eastern pantheism, which claimed that God is an indeterminate spiritual substance, present everywhere—though in discouragingly low doses. Like the pork in a can of beans.

According to the founder of this movement, Michael de Molinos (1640–1696), for a true Christian who has advanced in his spiritual life, the particulars of doctrine were not important. Nor was meditating on any aspect of God's nature or the life of Christ. The Bible and even the Sacraments were barriers to the true, contemplative path to knowing God—which basically amounted to tuning out, turning off, and dropping out. To Molinos, the essence of Christianity consisted of annihilating the ego, the will, and even the reason, to make room for God's presence—already manifest in the soul—to fill the void. As if dumping out all the beans would fill the can with pork. In our experience—and remember that one of us is a trained professional chef—this rarely works.

To scrape out the can, he advised his followers not to fast, or pray, or read any spiritual books, to place no stress on the Sacraments—and above all not to make any acts of preparation before (or gratitude after) receiving Holy Communion. This was perhaps an overreaction against the teaching of the Jansenists, who believed that virtually anyone old enough to receive that Sacrament was already too sinful to be worthy of it. To this, the Quietists cheerfully advised the opposite error. Instead of worrying with the Jansenists that one was likely doomed to Hell, the Quietist should emulate the Jamaican mystic Bobby McFerrin, who advised his spiritual directees:

> *Here's a little song I wrote*
> *You might want to sing it note for note*
> *Don't worry, be happy*
> *In every life we have some trouble*
> *But when you worry you make it double*
> *Don't worry, be happy*

Translating from theological jargon to laymen's terms, the *Catholic Encyclopedia* explains this passage as follows:

> . . . the desire to do anything actively is offensive to God and hence one must abandon oneself entirely to God and thereafter remain as a lifeless body. By doing nothing the soul annihilates itself and returns to its

---

[4] This set the Quietists apart from the grunge-loving Loudists of the 1990s who sought not a ticket to nirvana but Nirvana tickets. The latter group's theology was comparatively primitive, and they need not detain us further.

source, the essence of God, in which it is transformed and divinized, and then God abides in it.

The niftiest implication of this doctrine, particularly for clergy vowed to celibacy, was that it rendered sins of the flesh irrelevant. It was really a moot point what one's body did, under the influence of lower carnal passions; none of these had any impact on one's interior union with God, which was purely spiritual—and spiritually pure. Molinos soon drew thousands of fans across the Catholic world, particularly in Italy, becoming that century's answer to Andrew Greeley.

Madame Guyon

You can see how this piece of modern theology was an easy sell among the French. Some well-meaning mystics adopted aspects of Molinos's creed and spread it far and wide among the still-numb survivors of 200 years of religious strife. The leader of this self-help movement was the affable, charming widow Madame Guyon (1648–1717), who'd found solace from what we'd now call clinical depression in the Quietist technique of self-annihilation—which some might consider a kind of spiritual suicide.

Guyon spread her private variety of Quietist piety through a cleverly marketed paperback, *The Short and Easy Method of Prayer*, the Baroque-era equivalent of *The Prayer of Jabez*. Her fans included the great theologian and bishop François Fenelon, and many other pious Frenchmen who viewed her message of simplicity and trust in God as a healthy antidote to the neurotic scab-picking encouraged by Jansenism. But Louis XIV's new wife, the Marquise de Maintenon—whom he'd married in secret, since she wasn't of royal blood—smelled heresy in Guyon. As Louis' chief religious advisor—hey, she was better qualified than her predecessors, his mistresses—Maintenon saw Quietism as a dangerous overreaction which could quickly break down religious life altogether. Solid theologians such as the great Bishop Bossuet saw Guyon's "method" as essentially a cheap shortcut by which lazy souls might pretend to have achieved the stern detachment attained only rarely by spiritual athletes such as St. John of the Cross. Eventually, Guyon found herself in jail for heresy. At the same time, the king pressed a reluctant pope to denounce the theological rock star Molinos. In the end, both Quietists were condemned, Fenelon burned the books he'd written defending Guyon, and her ideas were largely forgotten in the Catholic world, which was soon busy fighting off aggressively secular *philosophes* like Voltaire, whose disdainful Deism and hatred of the Church made poor Madame Guyon seem saintly by comparison. The good widow signed a creed renouncing her errors, and went on to pass a quiet retirement.

In our own day, Quietism has made a roaring comeback, as New Age ideology encourages us to ignore the God in the tabernacle, the better to massage our nebulous "gods" within. Many Catholics eager to put behind them the textbook Thomism and memorized catechisms of the past have embraced the ideas of Madame Guyon: More than a dozen of her books are now available on Amazon— while Bossuet's are mostly out of print. And we can certainly see the Quietist appeal. Those of us grey or bald enough to remember hellfire sermons and harsh treatment inside a confessional (remember confessionals? They're those funny little boxes that look like telephone booths[5]) might well crave the reassurance which comes from adopting a Buddhist detachment from ideas of sin and salvation. Quietism is a way for bad Catholics to convince themselves that in fact they're incipient saints, without all the mess and bother of . . . you know, *sanctity*. It's the espresso we chug on the way to the car that cancels out those seven tequila shots and makes us "safe" to drive. And that gas pump we plow into at 66 mph which explodes in a 33-foot pillar of fire? Well, that would be God.

Quito: Cane Liquor, Martyred Politicians, and Apparitions

The city of Quito, Ecuador, has much to recommend it to authors of a devotional dictionary of alcohol. For one thing, it begins with the letter "Q." Besides, it's the city where:

- the greatest Catholic statesman of modern times,[6] Ecuadoran President Garcia Moreno, was martyred by enemies of the Church in 1875;
- an approved, important, and ominous apparition of the Blessed Virgin took place in the sixteenth century;

---

[5] Remember telephone booths?

[6] Some readers will differ, of course, insisting on—for instance—Teddy Kennedy or General Franco, but we're going to have to insist. Indeed, Pope Leo XIII called Morenos's Ecuador "the model of a Christian state." His predecessor, Bl. Pius IX, had declared Morenos a martyr.

- a miracle-granting statue of Our Lady still resides, in the convent where she used to appear;
- a paint-stripping cane liquor called *aguardiente* (i.e., "fire-water") is distilled and sold in dangerous quantities.

It's a powerfully spiritual place.

Aguardiente de Caña is a rough-edged drink enjoyed by poor folk throughout the Andes. Made from fermented sugar-cane distilled to an incendiary proof, it's

flavored with anise seeds and often served with coconut milk, or with milk, sugar, and egg yolks in a high-protein Christmas punch called *rompope*.

Aguardiente is considered the national drink of Ecuador, a country conquered by Pizarro along with the rest of the Inca Empire (**see Pisco**) in the early sixteenth century. The proud natives of Quito greeted the conquistadors by burning the city to the ground in 1534—

leaving the Spaniards little more than scorched earth on which to build. Ecuador was catechized by friars who followed in the wake of the Spanish armies, bandaging up the Indians and trying to win their souls. These Indians embraced Christianity quickly and fervently, assisted as in Mexico (**see Kahlua**) by apparitions of the Blessed Virgin Mary. If the Indians looked at the Spanish priests with a certain caution—except for the missing tin hats, they looked a lot like Spanish soldiers—they responded warmly to the feminine side of our Faith, in the form of the Blessed Mother. Even when she came bearing really appalling news, as she did at Quito.

You know how in some families, relatives talk on the phone almost every day? Well, the Holy Family doesn't work like that. Instead, Our Lady seems to be the sort of *yiddishe mama* who only calls to report on some disaster. When you hear from her, you hold your breath. You fall to your knees. You weep. Years later, you open a gift shop.

Since Our Lady dwells in eternity with Our Lord, she's permitted to see our earthly train wrecks before they happen, and give us warnings. In every Church-approved apparition[7] that foretells looming apocalypse—war, apostasy, persecution, or the rise of immodest fashions—Our Lady suggests a remedy. It usually comes in the form of fasting, sacrifice, prayer, or some other spiritual bother for which we never find the time. In fact, in all the research we've done, we've yet to find a general catastrophe Our Lady warned about that was subsequently avoided. It's as if Our Mother were sitting in the back seat reading us directions which her Son printed out from Mapquest. But we just turn up Guns & Roses' "Paradise City"[8] and drown her out. At least she doesn't come back to say "I told you so."

Garcia Moreno

You can see why one nun in particular might have wished to switch off the apparitions. In 1582, Sister Mariana de Jesus Torres was just 18, and her life was hard enough. She had sailed from Spain at age 13 to help found the first convent in Quito. Mariana belonged to a branch of Franciscan nuns known as the Conceptionists[9] who lived a starkly ascetic life based on the Rule of the Cistercians. But God wasn't finished perfecting Mariana's soul. In 1582, she began to receive a series of visits from the Virgin Mary; each came with a call for acts of self-sacrifice which escalated from the atrocious to the appalling. According to the Web resource devoted to Sister Mariana,[10] the Blessed Mother showed the Spanish nun all the evils slated to arise in the twen-

---

[7] This doesn't mean the Church guarantees the veracity of everything the solitary nun or pious peasant reports that Mary has said. (**see Papal Infallibility**) Private apparitions are not covered by infallibility— and given what some of them contain, such as souls falling into Hell like autumn leaves, that's just as well.

[8] South of the Mason-Dixon Line, we turn up "Sweet Home Alabama" instead.

[9] Wipe that smirk off your face right now young man, or you're facing a week of Detention.

[10] See *www.ourladyofgoodsuccess.com* to read the whole story of this "victim soul" and the general catastrophe she predicted for modern times—but not without a stiff glass of Aguardiente de Caña in your hand.

tieth century and asked her to offer her life in reparation for sins that lay centuries in the future. If you've ever watched the Hitler (History) Channel, you can understand what happened: the poor girl dropped dead on the spot.

Sister Mariana's soul stood on the brink of heavenly bliss—quite a contrast, compared to the blood-soaked twentieth-century spectacle she'd just had to sit through (think of *The Texas Chainsaw Massacre*, except that it's a miniseries, and it lasts 100 years). The Blessed Virgin stopped her at the door, requesting that she return to earth to accept a life of suffering on behalf of our century's boozers and polluters, flappers and gangsta rappers, pedophiles and Bolsheviks. And here's the weird part: Mariana accepted.

She awoke again in her convent, and her anguish soon began. Our Lady kept on visiting Mariana with "flashbacks" from the future, predicting the near disappearance of the Church in a welter of blasphemy, heresy, and television. She warned that the Church would be persecuted by the Freemasons—who didn't yet exist.[11] She predicted the modern vocations crisis, the collapse of religious orders—and for all we know, the breakup of the Beatles. Another time, Mary appeared to Mariana to announce that another, rebellious nun was headed straight for Hell—but Mariana could save her soul by agreeing to suffer the pains of Hell in her place for oh . . . several years. Our Lady wasn't specific. Again, Mariana agreed. Her anguish lasted a decade.

To mark all these dire predictions, the vision asked Mariana to commission a carved Madonna for the convent. In a rare glimpse of her heavenly sense of humor, Our Lady named it "Our Lady of Good Success." By this point, Mariana was in no mood to argue. She commissioned the statue, and after (surprise!) a hailstorm of soul-crushing difficulties, it was finished and placed in the convent where it still stands today. Pious souls with nerves of steel are welcome to visit the image in Quito. Thanks, but we're sticking with Lourdes.

CELEBRATE: It's hard to imagine how to throw a party themed around the prophesied near-destruction of the Church—at any rate, the kind of party we'd want to attend. There are surely folks out there who'd make merry at this prospect, but they're not (we hope) reading this book. Or at any rate, they're missing its point. Likewise, it's not immediately obvious how to host a dinner

---

[11] This prediction, at any rate, came true. Ecuadoran President Garcia Moreno (1821–1875) abolished slavery, closed the country's brothels, cracked down on corrupt elites, put the Church in charge of education—which he made universal and free—and consecrated Peru to the Sacred Heart. Enraged anticlericals met in Masonic lodges to plot his downfall, with funding from Germany's meddling chancellor Otto von Bismarck. On August 6, 1875, on his way out of Mass, Moreno was hacked to death with a machete, and his corpse riddled with bullets. His last words were *"Dios no muere!"* ("God does not die!").

which invokes in your guests the victim-soul sufferings of Sister Mariana. (Though you might start by serving your unsuspecting guests one local Quito specialty, Bull's Penis Soup—recipe *not* included.)

Instead we suggest you mark the triumphant restoration of the Church and prosperous peace which Our Lady promised would follow the tribulations. And what better way to look forward to this restoration promised 400 years ago in Ecuador than with the native foods, drinks, and customs of the country? Invoke the new hope Mary offered by celebrating with customs from Ecuadorian New Year. (Once the Aguardiente is flowing, little details like today's date or your own last name will tend to float away. . . .) You might try recreating the following party, hazily recalled by Steve Bailey of the *New York Times* (April 14, 2002):

> After dinner, everyone went outside where effigies of men representing the old year were to be burned. We were given bags containing 12 grapes and told to make a wish as we ate each grape. A brass band loudly played for dancing and anyone standing still was at risk of being pulled into the fray. Always looking for a new partner was a masked woman dressed as the widow of the dying year; nearly every man and woman and child took a turn with her. The effigies were set afire, helped by splashes of kerosene, while the dancing was helped by slugs of the anise-flavored liquor called aguardiente, consumed from a common glass. At one point the band demanded its share. Refueled, it played on while the dancers took turns leaping over the bonfire and into the new year.

If you can't hire an authentic Ecuadorian brass band, you might want to pick up Banda Machos' CD *Rancheras De Oro*. As for that masked Incan widow . . . you're on your own.

RECIPE:

Pears Poached in Aguardiente with Sorbet

2 cups brown sugar	1 cup aguardiente
1 tablespoon star anise	Peel of one orange
1 stick cinnamon	15 forelle pears
1 cup white sugar	Juice of 1 lemon
6 cups water	

Ideally the brown sugar and spices will be combined and set aside for 2 weeks. Not to fret—the flavor will still be profound even if done last minute.

Combine sugars and water in a pot that is just large enough to accommodate pears comfortably in not more than two layers. Simmer until sugar is dissolved. Add liquor and orange peel and return to simmer.

Peel and core pears; sprinkle with lemon juice. Lower in to poaching liquid. Cover with a plate to keep pears submerged and simmer on low for 1 1/2 hours until just soft.

With slotted stainless steel spoon remove pears and set aside. Reduce liquid by 1/4, strain into a container set in a bowl of ice water. When thoroughly cold, reserve 1/4 cup and process remaining liquid in ice cream machine. Place in freezer to harden at least 1 hour.

Serve pears with scoop of sorbet and reserved liquid.

Serves 15

Drinking Song #5: A Song of Sorrow

There is much of which the Irish may justly boast (**see Irish Cream**), from the work their monks did spreading literacy and Christian faith through Dark Ages Europe to the heroic patience of New York City's long-suffering cops.[12] And boast about it they will, given a pint and half a hearing. But just for now let's speak of the harps they strike, not the Harps they drink—and address the grand tradition of Irish music. If you haven't spent as much time as we have sitting in on *seisuns* in Woodside, Queens, you might not know the enormous range of Celtic music. You'll hear samples and echoes in the albums of Sinead O'Connor (**see Papal Infallibility**) and the hip-hop band Black 47. The best modern covers of Irish folk tunes are found on old albums of our absolute favorite singers,[13] the Pogues. But the reach of

[12] NYPD officers are famously reasonable compared to those of comparably ungovernable cities—for instance, the paramilitary maniacs of the LAPD. Here's how police of this department regularly employed "pain compliance" against the pro-lifers of Operation Rescue in the early 1990s, according to the *Los Angeles Times*: "They press fingers under their noses. They dig their knuckles into protesters' necks, and torque martial arts weapons around their wrists." (As cited by civil liberties activist James Bovard: *www.fff.org/freedom/0497d.asp*). To give credit, the LAPD isn't always eager to use force. For instance, toward the rioters who burned much of the city in 1992, it adopted a Gandhi-inspired pacifism.

[13] Apart, of course, from the infamous all "male" trio The Three Countertenors, who changed our world forever with their falsetto version of "My Way."

Irish music goes much farther; for instance, the jigs and reels the Ulster "Irish" (ahem) brought to the Appalachians are still the root of American bluegrass. The rebirth of Celtic music has spread from Ireland proper to Scotland, Wales, Cornwall, Brittany, and even New Brunswick—where the great-grandchildren of fishermen still curse the Quebecois in Irish. (As in *Fhrancaigh pogue mahone*, if we have it right.)

But the Irish music that's most familiar to Americans is probably of a less authentic and complex variety. Over time spent downing pitchers at pubs with fake wagon wheels and tin pots labeled "potcheen" on the stucco walls, we're much more likely to have heard the jukebox play old, schmaltzy tunes from the nineteenth century, warbled by tenors to swelling orchestras, with perhaps a *bodhran* and a fiddle thrown in. Such music was the bane of the bard W.B. Yeats. One afternoon, the authors went to hear a vocal performance by Michael Yeats, the poet's son, who sings his father's poems to the harp music played by his gifted wife Gráinne. Before he launched into "The Lake Isle of Innisfree," Yeats told a story. As Michael Yeats recounted:

> My father firmly believed that poetry was really music, and he intended many of his poems to be set to music, hoping that they would someday become the folksongs of his country. He used to cavil at the way many folksongs were sung, complaining that it was frequently impossible to discern the lyrics. But one time, he was taken by a friend to hear a performance of the tenor John McCormack in Dublin of sentimental modern Irish songs. As he emerged from the performance my father was shaking his head and muttering to himself, "The words, the words, the appalling *clarity* of the words!"

A number of modern Irish songs provoke this reaction. If you've ever gotten stuck in a Boston pub with a bunch of Kennedy addicts[14] belting out a boozy rendition of "Johnny I hardly knew ye," you know what we mean.

However, there are some classics that stand out from the pack. No Celtic soul could fail to stir at J.K. Casey's "The Rising of the Moon," or the patriotic anthem of the 1916 Rising, "The Foggy Dew" (**see Drinking Song #9**), memorably performed by Sinead O'Connor on The Chieftains' *The Wide World Over*.

Of course, the most popular Irish song that comes to mind is "Danny Boy." No solemn church funeral of a philandering, pro-choice, big-city Democrat would be complete without this tune played by a police bagpiper in a kilt during the Elevation. But really, it's a lovely tune, with lyrics that poignantly portray the grief felt by those left behind by emigrant Irish—whose kin might never see them in this life

---

[14] If you share this disease, we implore you to seek out a local chapter of Kennedys Anonymous, where you'll find a 12-step program of spiritual recovery and a welcoming, supportive community. Step 1: Acknowledge that you are powerless over voting for Kennedys. . . .

again. In a piece of historical irony, the man who wrote those lyrics was Frederic Edward Weatherly, an English Protestant attorney. But he vividly captured the pangs of separation, and his song has been justly beloved since its release in 1913.

What few lovers of the song realize is that the tune, "The Londonderry Air," is a seventeenth-century Irish melody, whose original lyrics were even more poignant.[15] Collected by a Protestant folklorist, Jane Ross, and printed in 1855 by George Petrie, its first published lyrics were the words of a famous poem, "The Confession of Devoragilla." This song told the tale of perhaps the most maligned woman in the history of Ireland—by comparison, Maggie Thatcher is as beloved as Our Lady of Knock. The medieval queen Devoragilla (1108–1193), tradition holds, was the wife of Tiernan Ua Ruairc, prince of Bréifne. In 1152, while her husband was off on a pilgrimage to visit the body of St. Patrick, she ran off with her lover Diarmait MacMurchada, King of Leinster. This sparked a war between the kings, which ended with MacMurchada inviting in as allies the English—for the very first time in history. They apparently liked the weather, since they still haven't left.[16]

But Devoragilla repented, most sincerely—probably once she got a chance to meet her husband's Norman allies—and soon returned to her husband. He accepted her, legend tells, and she went on to lead a life of great holiness. And surely God forgave her. But the Irish haven't.

The lyrics below are an imaginary recreation of Devoragilla newly returned from her lover's arms, seeking absolution ("shriving") from a priest:

"Oh! Shrive me fa - ther-- haste, haste and shrive me,___ Ere sets yon dread and fla - ring___ sun;___ Its beams of peace,--_ nay of sense de - prive me,___Since yet the ho - ly work's un - done."___ The sage, the wand'-rer's an - guish balm - ing,___ Soothed her heart to rest__ once. more;—And par-don's pro-mise tor - ture calm - ing,__The Pil-grim told her_ sor- row's o'er.__

---

[15] For the whole story, see Brian Audley's "The Provenance of the Londonderry Air," *Journal of the Royal Music Society,* 125 (2000). This song came to our attention through the work of mezzo-soprano Julia Grella O'Connell, who sang the first performance of it in the twenty-first century in New York City in 2003, in an arrangement by Benjamin Bierman, with accompaniment on concertina by Allan Atlas. Our thanks to them.

[16] Irish historian and tour-bus guide Jim Toohey disputes the traditional tale of Devoragilla's sin in the Vol. 11, No. 4 (Winter 2003) issue of *History Ireland,* offering a revisionist account which pretty much ruins the song. So we're not buying it.

2.

The charms that caus'd in life's young morning,
The woes the sad one had deplor'd,
Were now, alas! no more adorning
The lips that pardon sweet implor'd:
But oh! Those eyes, so mildly beaming,
Once seen, not Saints could e'er forget! —
And soon the Father's eyes were streaming,
When Devoragilla's gaze he met!

3.

Gone, gone, was all the pride of beauty,
That scorn'd and broke the bridal vow,
And gave to passion all the duty
So bold a heart would e'er allow;
Yet all so humbly, all so mildly,
The weeping fair her fault confess'd,
Tho' youth had viewed her wand'ring wildly,
That age could ne'er deny her rest.

4.

The tale of woe full sadly ended,
The word of peace the Father said,
While balmy tear-drops fast descended,
And droop'd the suppliant sinner's head.
The rose in gloom long drear and mourning,
Not welcomes more the sun's mild ray,
The Breffni's Princess hail'd returning
The gleam of rest that shriving-day.

The Reformation: Mead, Lost Bees, and Missing Monks

With the coming of the Reformation to England, many things were lost. The Church, which once had counterbalanced the claims of the king's courtiers, fell under the heel of the State. The monasteries, which for centuries had nursed and schooled the poor, were raped and pillaged by Henry VIII (**see Gout**) for gold to fund a war. Most poignantly of all, for historians of tipsiness, was the fate of what had been England's national beverage, the fermented honey drink Chaucer knew as mead.

Mead is a light, sweet, tangy drink, once abundant in England. In the seventh and eighth centuries, that country was overrun by learned Irish monks, who brought Christianity to the wild Teutonic tribes[1] who'd conquered the Romanized Celts. The wars they fought were immortalized in the first Arthurian legends. King

[1] For an idea of what they were like, think of Tolkien's Riders of Rohan, which he based in part on the early Germanic-Britons of the West Midlands, whose Old English language and lore he loved and taught for decades at Oxford. Learn more from Tom Shippey's magnificent *J.R.R. Tolkien: Author of the Century* (Boston: Houghton Mifflin, 2001). Unlike most commentators on Tolkien's mythology, Shippey is fully versed in the languages his former Oxford colleague taught. Indeed, he later inherited Tolkien's old Chair of English Language and Medieval Literature at Leeds University. Which he reports was still warm.

Arthur, if he ever really lived, was really Welsh, and the invaders he fought were Anglo-Saxons—not that this has stopped their great-grandsons from adopting these glorious tales as their own.[2]

Every monastery built kept bees to supply wax for thousands of candles that lit the shrines and altars. While secular homes might use lard-sticks, only beeswax could light a church. Besides shining brighter with cleaner smoke and fewer drippings, bees' wax appealed to monks because it was made by thousands of hard-working virgins like themselves. Some theologians even cited this wax as a symbol of Christ, the Light brought forth from the body of the Virgin. Now maybe that was stretching things a bit. Viewed in human terms, a beehive is a totalitarian collective where hapless slaves work to feed, pamper, and serve a single master. It sounds less like a happy convent than like Communist North Korea.[3] But the monks had never heard of Marx, so let's cut them a little slack.

Medieval beekeeping was a major industry—with monasteries producing at once illumination and illuminated manuscripts, spiritual uplift and uplifting spirits, fermented from the massive quantities of leftover honey. These beestung celibates were highly efficient; they had to be. According to *Wine Tidings* (No. 101, March 1987):

> Before the Protestant Reformation, the chief church of Wittenburg reportedly used 35,000 lbs. of wax a year. Every church and monastery kept bees and peasants holding land under a monastery paid their yearly dues in wax. A famous story is told of a fire extinguished with mead in 1015 in the town of Meissen, Germany—the inhabitants were apparently short of water!

Further east, the Poles were so fond of mead that their Prince Leszek I refused a request from the pope to serve in the Crusades. Since there was no mead in Palestine, he was sure they'd refuse to fight.

Mead goes best with hot days and spicy foods—which makes one wonder why it ever caught on in England. Of course, the popular English way to drink it was to "mull" it by plunging a hot poker in a mug, till the beverage sizzled and burned. If you're ever at a really pretentious restaurant, and find the sommelier condescending, it's great fun to order a glass of "mulled mead." When he stares at you in confusion, explain in detail how it's made. When he stammers that he has neither the mead nor a poker, just shake your head, muttering, "And I thought you had a

---

[2] Just as American football teams take the names of conquered Indian tribes, and gold-digging wives keep the name of their first husbands if it includes a "von."

[3] But it's too easy to make fun of Kim Jong Il—and besides, *Team America: World Police* got there first. Perhaps we should say that bee society—where most females never breed, and the males are parasites who never work around the hive, but buzz around, eat, drink nectar, and hope to mate—instead evokes contemporary Italy.

comprehensive cellar. . . ." Then take out a notepad and write something down, so he thinks he's just ticked off a critic.

Mead was also popular at weddings. In fact, the word "honeymoon" may very well come from a rough and ready Anglo-Saxon custom of plying the groom on his wedding night with mugs of mead—in the hope that this would help him sire a son. Now we're not medical professionals, but we wonder how well this worked. . . .

One famous ancient mead-making site, Lindisfarne, now manufactures it once again—though it's done minus the monks. Holy Island, two miles off the coast of Northumbria in northern England, was once the religious center of the region. It was here that St. Aidan, a missionary monk of the order of St. Columba, came in 635 to found the monastery of Lindisfarne—which served for some 900 years as the hub of education and social improvement. The place hatched plenty of saints, training such early leaders of the English church as St. Chad of Lichfield,[4] saints Cuthbert, Egbert, Edilhun, Ethelwin, Oswy—and many more monks with unpronounceable names that would someday afflict little English boys in boarding school. Somehow, it's just easier to justify giving a wedgie to someone named Eg-bert. What else is one to do with him?

The first few times the monastery was destroyed it was by Vikings, who invaded in 793 and 875, to burn the buildings and slaughter the monks. This massacre is still celebrated by "black metal"[5] musicians such as Stormwarrior, Enslaved, and Dark Rites; each band has recorded songs commemorating the Vikings' efforts at preserving Nordic pagan values—for instance, theft, illiteracy, and random bloodshed.

But the monks were not so easily discouraged. The survivors, who'd carted off with them the incorrupt body of St. Cuthbert, rebuilt on the ruins the church whose ruins still stand today. There they copied and drew the magnificent Lindisfarne Gospels (pictured).

In 1082, the Benedictines took the place over, and ran it until 1536, when Henry

---

[4] A saint invoked by smart-alecks throughout the disputed 2000 U.S. election.
[5] I.e. Nazi-leaning Satanist wankers.

VIII seized the monastery. We've written elsewhere (**see Gout**) about the devastating effects of Henry VIII's attacks upon the Church—especially his looting of England's monasteries and convents, which for centuries had been the island's centers of learning. They also served as engines of technological innovation: it was monks who developed new methods of farming, and first made distilled spirits (**see Whiskey**). When the king's soldiers rounded up these unarmed priests and turned them out, their once-grand abbeys were looted and left in shambles. The lands they once held went to Henry's wealthy supporters (as happens nearly everywhere the Church is looted, **see Kahlua**), who even used the stones which once made up these houses of God to build their vast country castles. The gold crucifixes once prayed to by the poor were melted down into aristocratic flatware, and all these changes were summed up simply by historians as "progress."

As the monasteries crumbled, reformers encouraged a Calvinist "cleansing" of the churches, documented in Eamon Duffy's history *The Stripping of the Altars* (Yale University Press: 1992). Despite popular resistance, which occasionally erupted into rebellion, the king's commissioners seized from churches anything shiny that wasn't nailed down, smashed statues and stained glass windows, and whitewashed medieval murals. In essence, they set the tone for parish renovations in the 1970s, and deserve to be recognized for their eerily prescient understanding of modern liturgy.[6]

If you've ever watched Merchant & Ivory films, and wondered why England has so many grand estates, the reason is clear—they replaced those pesky monasteries. The charming, informal gardens surrounding them were once open sheep commons, where lowly shepherds could feed their smelly flocks. With Henry's reign, the oligarchs tidied things up, took the land, and hired the shepherds as butlers.

As the monks faded into memory, so did mead. Indeed, an old saying has it that "Hops, Reformation, Carp and Beer/Came into England the same year." Hop production, and the beer it was meant to make, shot up to fill the gap created by the loss of monastic mead. As a sweetener, honey was soon displaced by sugar from the New World, as England traded a product created by worker bees for one made by human slaves. So everybody won.

Apart from some recently re-founded abbeys, all England has left today of its monastic heritage are some impressive Gothic ruins—and little Victorian churches designed to look like medieval convents. You see, in the nineteenth century, appalled at the bloodbath which still raged across the Channel in France (**see Drinking Song #7**), Sir Walter Scott and other Romantic writers began to re-evaluate the Middle Ages. Compared to modernity's "total wars" and early capitalism's grinding misery, the time of friars and farming began to seem idyllic. In his best-selling

---

[6] See Michael Rose's careful study of modern church architecture *Ugly As Sin* (Sophia Institute Press, 2001). Or go see what's left of the cathedrals in Dallas and Milwaukee.

Waverly novels, Scott revived the image of chivalric knights, wise monks, and vast, green commons where sheep could safely graze. These novels crossed the Atlantic, and spread throughout the American South a fascination for things medieval. If you visit the Citadel in South Carolina, or the old Louisiana State Capitol in Baton Rouge, you'll see gothic forts erected to Scott's popularity.

In England, long-forgotten monastic ruins began to attract wandering poets and painters. Anglican clerics such as John Henry Newman started reading Augustine and Aquinas, giving birth to the Oxford Movement (**see Drinking Song #4**). Of course, some people got carried away: One baron who happened to have a still-intact medieval abbey on his property had it pulled down to make "romantic" ruins.[7] And the craze for building neo-gothic went occasionally haywire. In New Haven, the campus of Yale University boasts a medieval-looking industrial workshop—complete with gothic chimney, and a gym that looks like a church; students call it the "cathedral of sweat." In the gothic Sterling library, the phone booths look exactly like confessionals, and the circulation desk like an altar. Every year, at least one confused Catholic freshman is seen to genuflect.

There are worse reactions. Lost beauties of the past may be best viewed through a misty-eyed affection—instead of modernist scorn. It's a starved soul who (for instance) looks at the monstrosity that replaced New York's Penn Station and tells himself: "And a good thing too. The new building is cheaper to heat."

Nowadays, it is a similar nostalgia, a yearning for some *frisson* from the distant past, which drives people to hunt up a bottle of mead.[8] But it's worth the effort. Mead is a lovely drink. And there's nothing quite like plunging a red hot poker into a cup of frothing mead to set the tone for a honeymoon. Just be careful with those candles.

CELEBRATE: If you're already married, or have given up on your prospects, there's no need to despair. (Or maybe there is, but it shouldn't keep you away from mead.) Enjoy this classic British drink in a newfangled way—by whipping up a batch of Mead-flavored honey ice cream.

---

[7] The craving for things "gothic" persists among the English. According to a January 2006 report by BBC, St. Edward's Anglican parish in Cambridge hosts a weekly "Goth liturgy," with priests vested in black and music by Depeche Mode and Sisters of Mercy. (Hey, it beats the St. Louis Jesuits.) Boasts the Web site for the distinctive apostolate: "The service is candlelit with a specially written liturgy and uses a variety of modern rock and as well as classical music. The structure of the service revolves around the baptismal candle and reflects a serious engagement with the depressing and darker sides of our lives before moving towards a position of hope and happiness found in the empathy of the Lord Jesus Christ."

[8] The most evocative comes from St. Aidan's Winery on Holy Island.

Mead and Honey Swirl Ice Cream

2 cups cream	3 ounces honey plus 1/4 cup for ribbon
2 cups mead	6 large egg yolks
1 sachet mulling spices	Pinch fleur de sel

Heat cream and mead in separate pots, one of them large enough to accommodate all the ingredients. Add honey to cream and bring to a boil. Meanwhile, heat mead with spices. Do not boil.

In large bowl lightly whisk yolks. Ladle in cream a bit at a time while whisking. Add mead; minus the spice sachet.

Pour all back into larger pot. Stir with wood spoon over low to medium heat. Add salt. The custard will not get as thick as in traditional recipes because of the mead. However, it will lightly coat the back of the spoon. Strain and cool in an ice bath.

Because the alcohol has not cooked out and the fat content is low, it is susceptible to separating. It will look as though melted butter was added. If this happens, an immersion blender will correct everything.

Chill overnight, covered.

Turn in ice cream machine. Remove and pour a ribbon of honey throughout.

Makes 5 cups

Restoration from Reformation: The Wine of Buckfast Abbey

While the story of English monasticism is overall terribly sad—rather like watching a troop of army ants tear apart a puppy—there are also bright spots worth pointing out. In the nineteenth century, the Oxford Movement reawakened many in Britain to what their forefathers had forgotten: the beauty and holiness of monastic life. Abbeys and convents (both Anglican and Catholic) sprouted up across the country, some of them on the very same sites as ancient convents. The miraculous shrine of Our Lady of Walsingham, for instance, once left as a pile of rubble, now boasts both a Roman and an Anglican shrine, in friendly competition. (They even share a tourism Web site: *www.walsingham.org.uk*.) And at Walsingham, for once, the Catholic shrine's architecture is finer than the Anglican one.[9]

Our favorite restored monastic structure, however, is Buckfast Abbey, in the

---

[9] Through most of England and even Ireland the ancient churches are still in Anglican hands, while Catholics make do with structures built in the nineteenth and even (God help us) the twentieth century.

Dart River valley near Devon. Founded in the early eleventh century, it flourished for over 500 years under the Benedictine and then the Cistercian rules. But in 1539, its abbot—appointed by Thomas Cromwell, King Henry's bandit-in-chief—expelled the monks, sold off its properties to the highest bidder, then gave the building itself at a bargain price to his brother-in-law. The place would lay desolate for over 400 years—until the end of the nineteenth century, when Benedictines fleeing other persecutions arrived on English shores. In France, the Third Republic had begun its (largely forgotten) attack on the Church, which ended in 1905 with the expulsion of every religious order from France. Previously, in Imperial Germany, Otto von Bismarck had conducted a *Kulturkampf* ("culture war") against German Catholics, whose loyalty he distrusted, closing Catholic schools and associations.

Led by Abbot Boniface Natter, these refugee Benedictines reconstructed Buckfast (pictured) from the old stones, and founded a thriving community. (Visit its beautifully illustrated Web site at *www.buckfast.org.uk*). It's still a vibrant place today, with dozens of monks, a lively schedule of retreats, and a bang-up gift shop that sells the products made by the monks in the spirit of St. Benedict's "*Ora et laborens*" (work and pray): there's toffee, cat toys, candle-making kits, and chocolate.

But most importantly, there is wine: Buckfast's Tonic Wine, a sweet, fortified drink with a mighty kick (30 proof). Made since 1897 from a family recipe passed on by one of the first French monks, this elixir is a mix of wine, maté tea, coca leaves and vanilla. Like so many alcoholic concoctions created in monasteries (**see Eau de Vie, Vodka,** and **Whiskey**) this wine was originally intended for strictly medicinal purposes; as its first label read: "Three small glasses a day, for good health and lively blood." Through the late 1920s, the abbots sold the wine by mail and from their gift shop. When local bureaucrats pulled their liquor license, the monks nearly stopped production. But Providence intervened in the form of a London wine merchant

who paid a visit to the abbey, and offered to take over marketing and sales himself. He had them dilute the wine a little, so it tasted less like cough medicine, and soon Buckfast Tonic Wine was on sale all through Great Britain.

Since then, it has become a marketing phenomenon. It's especially beloved among the shiftless urban youth of Scotland. In Glasgow, its connoisseurs like to say of the wine they call "Buckie": *Made by monks, drunk by punks.* While it was intended as a "tonic" to serve after soporific English meals, "Buckie" is currently drunk straight from the bottle in paper bags on street corners all across Britain. To the horror of the prayerful monks who make the stuff, Buckfast Tonic Wine has been rechristened, variously:

- Brown Sauce
- Bottle of Beat the Wife
- Liquid Speed
- Monkey Juice
- A number of things which we can't print that rhyme with "Buckfast."

The drink's popularity with the wee ones has even led the Scottish Minister of Health, Andy Kerr, to attempt to have Buckfast banned as a "hazard to public health."

None of this is the monks' fault, of course. They created the wine for grown-ups and have done nothing to encourage its consumption by the young and the toothless. Still, we can't help seeing a bit of historical, poetic justice here: All unwittingly, the wine-making monks of Buckfast are doing to certain British cities what the Brits once did to Buckfast. . . . To all of this we can only say: Pass the Monkey Juice!

Rum: Official Liquor of the Caribbean Slave Trade

So far we've focused mainly on drinks having some monastic origin. And for a very solid reason: Sometimes a situation cries out to heaven for liquor, in large high-octane quantities. For instance when:

- You've lost a job for standing up for your beliefs—such as, "I believe I'll call in sick today, I've got a hangover."
- The hot young thing you met on a Catholic dating site dumped you because of a difference over *Mater et Magistra*;[10]
- You just heard back from auditors at the IRS. You could hardly understand them, they were laughing so hard, but you could make out the phrase, "Nice try."

At times like these it feels more wholesome to numb your cortex with a liqueur produced by Carthusians. There's something about their celibacy and poverty which helps you resign yourself to your own. Think you might go to prison? These monks' cells are about the same size as yours will be. And so on.

But there's not much to love about the origins of rum. The drink developed as a direct result of the slave trade. When European colonists conquered the Caribbean islands, they quickly learned that the Indians they found there were not much use as field hands. When Spaniards, Englishmen, and Frenchmen slapped chains on Arawaks and Caribs and set them to cutting sugar cane in the blazing heat, these natives responded by staging a large-scale "sick out": They up and died. Desperate for someone else to do the grunt work, the Europeans turned to Africa—where Moslem slave-traders had been trading in human cargo for centuries. (Indeed, the Arab slave traders of Algeria were only stopped from raiding Europe for slaves in 1830, when the French invaded the place. In recent decades, the Algerians have duly returned the favor.) By the seventeenth century, slaves from West Africa in the hundreds of thousands were transported across the Atlantic packed in the holds of sailing ships. The death rate was staggering. The majority of those who survived this horror landed in the

---

[10] Just about anybody can trash a relationship by arguing over *Humanae vitae*. *Real men* squander marriage opportunities by pounding the table over arcana of Catholic social teaching.

Caribbean islands to live out their days cutting sugar cane on the large plantations. It was one of these slaves who discovered rum in that same century. Working in a factory on Barbados that processed cane into sugar, he found a batch of the by-product molasses which had mysteriously gone "bad." It had turned into a sticky, potent drink with a dark caramel color and a rich, dark flavor—it went really well with Coke. Within a few years, this new drink—first called Rumbullion, and Kill-Divil—had replaced the comparably fragile wine and watery beer as the drink of choice for slaves and masters alike. Indeed, the owners of plantations made sure to distribute generous quantities of the stuff to all their slaves. It kept them from rising up, and contributed what happiness was available to men working in cane fields under the whip.

Soon rum became the main trade good in the Caribbean, replacing gold as the currency traded for sugar and slaves. This enterprise enriched English settlers from Jamaica to Massachusetts, where many of the rum distilleries were built. Rum soon displaced most other drinks as the favorite beverage of Colonial America. It was cheaper, stronger, and virtually never spoiled—though if you weren't careful, it might evaporate. As our friend, the Church historian and fellow tippler Charles Coulombe wrote in his delightful book *Rum: The Epic Story of the Drink That Conquered the World*, the economy of New England came to depend on the "Triangle Trade." The Yankees who 50 years later would lead the fight against slavery in the South were living off inheritances built on trading black flesh for white crystals and liquid gold.

Just as rum replaced other liquors in the Colonies, it dominated life on board the ships that plied the seas. In 1655, when the Brits conquered Jamaica, the standard ration of French brandy once issued their sailors gave way to rum—which, when combined with other maritime customs, gave rise to the saying that summed up life in the Royal Navy: "rum, sodomy, and the lash." In 1740, the British Admiral Vernon, concerned at a growing imbalance among these three, would order his sailors' rum diluted with water and lime—inadvertently protecting his crew from scurvy. This drink would become world famous as "grog," named for the admiral's grogram coat, a rough fabric of loosely woven silk and wool. Such rations (or "tots") of rum would be given to every Royal Navy sailor from the seventeenth century right up until 1970. And flogging on ships was abolished in 1879. Which only leaves. . . .

Ahem. There are many historical ironies wrapped up in the rise of rum. On the one hand, the drink accompanied the growth of modern, Cartesian philosophy (**see Loreto**), which strove to banish all sense of mystery from the world. This underwrote the cold calculation accompanying the highly profitable trade in human slaves, equating kidnapped human beings with "chattel" (i.e., cattle). Such a rational detachment reached its extreme in the English-speaking world, where slaves were forbidden to marry, and were neither taught to read nor catechized. As historian of slavery Eugene Genovese pointed out in *Roll, Jordan Roll,* in Catholic

countries the opposite was true: Slaves were introduced to the Sacraments, and the Church forbade slave-owners to break up families. Cold comfort, of course, but times were tough, and Europeans needed sugar for their tea.

The religion that became popular among "enlightened" Europeans in this period was Deism, which envisions God as an absentee Father, who spawned the world long ago and then went fishing. Indeed, we might call Deism the "masculine heresy," since it banished altogether the biblical image of God as a nurturing Presence in the world.

Conversely, in the cramped and squalid quarters inhabited by the slaves in places like Saint Domingue (later Haiti), a very different sort of religion emerged. There the polytheistic, pagan creeds of West Africa were mixed with French Catholicism to make a potent cocktail we now know as Voodoo or Santeria. Coulombe calls the resulting religions "imperfectly inculturated Catholicism," and he has a point. With its Sacramentals and rituals, and its faith that an unseen reality is more important than what we see, Voodoo is much closer to Catholicism than the dry-as-dust Deism preached by, for instance, Thomas Jefferson,[11] who had no use at all for weeping icons, bleeding hosts, or bodies of long-dead nuns that never decay—just to cite a few of our favorite aspects of the Faith.

---

[11] Indeed, while he was president Jefferson used government money to publish his own version of the New Testament. The so-called "Jefferson Bible" is a cut-and-paste job which he performed by excising all the miracles and references to the divinity of Christ. What resulted was a book in which a rabbi dispenses wildly impractical advice such as "Sell all you have, and give it to the poor"—but offers no reason at all why anyone should listen to him. Read it, and you'll want to crucify him too.

African gods such as Babalu-Aye[12] were equated with saints like Lazarus, and the statues helpfully provided by Catholic priests were employed in equipping pagan shrines. If wine was the Sacramental species for Catholics, and tea the drink for Deists, the slaves who practiced Voodoo stuck to rum. To this day, they pour it out on icons and shrines, and drink it liberally while engaging in their faith's orgiastic liturgies. Fans of the Mickey Rourke film *Angel Heart* will remember Lisa Bonet engaging in a sensual Voodoo dance to summon the gods and embarrass Bill Cosby.

If Deism is hypermasculine, the Voodoo faith runs to the other extreme, envisioning not a single, distant and dryly rational god, but a fertile explosion of passionate gods, busybodies who gossip and quarrel, take an interest in everyone's business, and get angry if you don't remember their birthdays. They seem to respond well to shiny objects, flowers, and chocolate.

CELEBRATE: You needn't be a slave owner or Santeria priest to enjoy the spiritual uplift to be found in a bottle of Coruba. (Though if you know anyone who fits either description, be sure to invite him to liven up your next fête.) Banish any lingering traces of Enlightenment with rum cocktails, and spoil your taste for tea with a platter of spicy Jamaican food. Pop in that Bob Marley (**see Tej**) CD you bought for your frat house, and serve up some chewy fried conch or blazing jerked goat. It's the only proven cure for Deism. Throw back enough Hurricanes or Mai Tais, and you'll start seeing Jah everywhere. For instance, inside the porcelain altar. . . .

Jerk Goat

JERK PASTE:

2 tablespoons whole allspice	1/4 cup soy sauce
1 small cinnamon stick	1 habañero chile, stem and
Freshly grated nutmeg	seeds removed
1 sweet onion, diced	2-inch piece ginger, peeled
6 cloves garlic	1 cup ketchup
1/4 cup green onion, green part	1/2 cup tamarind pulp
only, chopped	1 tablespoon fresh thyme leaves

GOAT:

3 tablespoons oak chips	3 pounds cut up goat meat with bones
1 bunch thyme branches	2 tablespoons olive oil

Make paste.

---

[12] Remember Ricky Ricardo pounding on a bongo and singing "Babalu"? Why wouldn't he let Lucy come to the club, anyway? No wonder she divorced him.

Over low heat toast allspice and cinnamon, add nutmeg and swirl to toast in residual heat.

Meanwhile, combine remaining ingredients in blender and add spices. Blend until smooth.

Jerk paste can be made ahead of time. Any remaining can be stored refrigerated in a glass jar for up to a month.

MARINATE GOAT:
Rinse and dry well. In a nonreactive container toss meat with enough paste to coat well.

Cover and marinate 4 to 24 hours.

SMOKE:
Smoke with thyme and oak chips 30 minutes in a stove-top smoker, or cover the bottom of a roasting pan with heavy-duty foil. Place herbs and chips on foil. Cover this with more foil and place meat on top. Cover and smoke on medium heat.

ROAST:
Remove foil and meat from roaster. Re-place meat in roaster and drizzle with olive oil.

Roast at 400 degrees 30 minutes. Reduce heat to 350 and roast for another hour.

Makes 6 small portions

....

Loopholes in the Ten Commandments #8: Thou Shalt Not Bear False Witness Against Thy Neighbor

This commandment seems innocuous enough. On its face, it only prevents us from telling malicious falsehoods damaging to others. Okay, we're not really thrilled about that—especially if we're active in politics— but we can understand it, and grudgingly agree. But like most other elements in Divine Revelation, it has grown over time and extended its reach into all sorts of analogous situations, as rabbis, then bishops and popes, strove to explore all its implications for human life. It's as if each commandment were a pebble dropped into a

pond, and our job were to trace all the ripples. But that metaphor doesn't quite work, because it makes things too easy. Ripples from a pebble flow in clear, predictable waves, and a freshman physics student should be able to account for them. The pieces of Revelation that have fallen on us from space are not inert but active, and the pool in which they plop—human life—is murky and full of dark, swimmy things. And some of them have claws. So perhaps a better image is a giant Alka-Seltzer, dropped in a swamp: *Plop-plop, fizz-fizz, Oh what a morass it is!*

This commandment especially fits that description. On the one hand, the Church teaches us in the Catechism (#2467):

> Man tends by nature toward the truth. He is obliged to honor and bear witness to it: "It is in accordance with their dignity that all men, because they are persons . . . are both impelled by their nature and bound by a moral obligation to seek the truth, especially religious truth. They are also bound to adhere to the truth once they come to know it and direct their whole lives in accordance with the demands of truth."

Catholic theologians point out that man is hardwired both to seek and speak the truth, and it's on the assumption that people's words are trustworthy that communication is predicated. Think what it would be like if that weren't true: recall that really annoying example you had to study in Philosophy 101—where a man from Crete tells you "All Cretans lie," and you have to figure out whether or not you should believe him? Remember how you reacted?[13] Imagine every encounter with other people turning into that kind of tedious brain-twister, and you'll appreciate Yahweh's point. Or let's view this thing in terms of dollars and cents. Societies which don't value straight dealing and honest business waste enormous resources on bribes, wire-tapping, bulletproof auto glass, and personal body guards named Ivan, impoverishing everyone except a tiny, corrupt elite. And if you don't believe Yahweh, you should visit New Jersey yourself.[14]

On the other hand, there's also such a thing as "too much information." For instance, when a D.A. questions a priest about the contents of a confession. Or when women arise at romantic dinners and excuse themselves by announcing, "I gotta pee!" In each case, the speaker is under a solemn obligation to withhold this information—if need be, by throwing people off the scent. The priest can say, "I do not

---

[13] "Screw this! Let's go get a keg."

[14] It was telling that in 2004, when the stench of his corruption began to crowd out the reek of the Meadowlands, New Jersey Governor James McGreevey dodged investigation for his actual malfeasances by resigning over a sex scandal. In a press conference, McGreevey dabbed his eyes and said, "My truth is that I am a gay American." As if anyone cared. What mattered was his orientation as a "corrupto-American." Now there's a persecuted minority: Even today, thousands of these fellow-citizens languish in minimum security cells all across America.

know." Or the woman could say "I need to wash my hands," and let you finish your lemon sorbet in peace.

The need for discretion arises not just from the Sacramental obligation of secrecy, or the queasy demands of courtesy. The Church sees a duty in *charity* sometimes to withhold or even cloud the truth. For instance, when one is tempted to spread ugly facts about a third party without grave and sufficient reason. Dishing the dirt about somebody just for the fun of it can actually amount to a serious sin, even—and here's the weird part—*if what you're saying is true*. We know, we know. . . .

It's hard for modern readers of the press to wrap their heads around this one—accustomed as we are to hidden cameras poking into the bedrooms of Hollywood starlets, and congressional probes into the president's pants. But this prohibition on "detraction" is reiterated in the most recent Catechism, with certain exceptions made for journalists.[15]

Theologians have argued for centuries about how to reconcile these two principles, truth-telling and charity, and have come to a wide variety of conclusions. Church Fathers Origen and St. John Chrysostom each believed that sometimes outright lying might be acceptable, if keeping silent wasn't an option and telling the truth caused greater harm than the lie itself. Historians report that Martin Luther embraced this idea, once declaring: "What harm would it be if a man told a good lusty lie in a worthy cause; for the sake of the Christian Churches?" A curious quotation, which leaves Luther looking like a Protestant stereotype of a scheming Jesuit.

In fact, the Jesuits and other Scholastic Catholics wrestled mightily with the obligation to tell the truth, since they felt bound by the teaching of St. Augustine, who rejected as intrinsically evil every kind of fib. As the 1917 *Catholic Encyclopedia* explained:

> St. Augustine held that the naked truth must be told whatever the consequences may be. He directs that in difficult cases silence should be observed if possible. . . . If a man is hid in your house, and his life is sought by murderers, and they come and ask you whether he is in the house, you may say that you know where he is, but will not tell: you may not deny that he is there.

Augustine's position here is elegant, clear, consistent—and we must add, kind of crazy. It holds up truth-telling as a higher good than life, and encourages the Christian to keep his conscience clean at the cost of another man's murder.[16] This seems strange until we consider that Augustine also taught that killing—even waging

---

[15] Because of the nature of their profession, these wordsmiths are considered essentially subhuman, and are bound only by "journalistic ethics," which are modeled on the rules governing bonobos. No throwing turds inside the troop.

[16] Immanuel Kant would later adopt the same position, keen as he was to create a system of perfectly self-consistent human Reason as a replacement for the God Whose existence he'd started to doubt.

wholesale war—could be perfectly moral, if done in self-defense, or defense of the innocent. This means that for Augustine, when faced with murderers at the door, a good Christian may never mislead them. Instead, he may shoot them.

Leading Catholic thinkers lined up behind St. Augustine in subsequent centuries, making fine distinctions about the types and gravity of lies. St. Thomas Aquinas—the Henry Ford of our Faith who liked to break things down into tiny, interchangeable parts—divided lies into three categories:

- *Injurious*, the kind of lie that leads men to Hell or gets them killed. For instance, if one were to say that Mother Teresa was "a demagogue, an obscurantist and a servant of earthly powers."[17] Or that Saddam Hussein had by 2003 amassed weapons of mass destruction which he planned to transfer to terrorists.[18]
- *Officious*, the sort of lie designed to cover one's butt or other body parts, as in "I did not have sex with that woman."
- *Jocose*, a statement which is meant as a jest, but could be taken seriously—for instance: "No, honey, you don't look fat in that dress." Which is clearly a joke. Sweetie, if you *have to ask*. . . .

The need to balance Augustine's stark position with the demands of discretion and charity grew more urgent over time. When the Protestant English kings began to persecute the Church—hunting down priests and torturing them to death—moral thinkers began to look for ways to permit laymen to effectively hide these priests[19] when questioned. Theologians, many of them Jesuits, developed the notion of a "mental reservation," which permitted someone to tell only part of the truth, in a somewhat misleading way—leaving the listener to draw an untrue conclusion. For instance, you might say, "I haven't seen any priests," while *mentally reserving* the rest of the sentence, "in the last 30 seconds."

This seems a squirmy kind of loophole through which to preserve a principle, and it certainly would not have satisfied St. Augustine. By the late-nineteenth century, some Catholic thinkers tried to formulate exceptions to the duty to tell the truth in a less back-handed way. They admitted that it is always wrong to lie, but redefined[20] a lie as an untrue statement made to someone *who has the right to the truth*. And a killer or priest-hunter at the door had no such right.

---

[17] Christopher Hitchens.

[18] Also Christopher Hitchens.

[19] Many old English homes contain man-shaped "priest holes," of obscure origin. Since England is the land of "British liberties," some have theorized that these holes are a naturally occurring phenomenon. Just like Mt. Rushmore, according to Cher. (Or so Sonny Bono claimed she believed—but then he was bitter, and a congressman.)

[20] Sometimes the Church can only break through a conundrum using this handy method, as we once redefined "usury," "religious liberty," and "baptism." But if you're hoping some pope will one day redefine, say "porn," don't hold your breath.

Back in 1917, this seemed a bold position, and the theologians editing the good old *Catholic Encyclopedia* dismissed it as having "made little or no impression on the common teaching of the Catholic schools." Then something happened; a concrete historical change requiring the quick development of doctrine. Historians call it "World War II."

With the rise of a murderous dictatorship that hunted down millions of innocents because of their race, Catholics all across Europe were faced with the same dilemma once posed, almost idly, by theologians. For yet another time in history, there were indeed thousands of armed state-sponsored murderers banging on the doors in search of innocents hidden inside. The thousands of Polish Catholics who sheltered Jews from the Germans—and Pope Pius XII himself, who arranged for some 700,000 or more persecuted Jews to be hidden in monasteries and convents—now faced the terrible choice between telling the truth and betraying the innocent. Inside the Reich, conspirators such as Colonel Claus von Stauffenberg (a Catholic aristocrat), were forced to tell hundreds of falsehoods as they plotted to assassinate Hitler in 1944; instead of condemning their efforts, Pope Pius helped them transmit messages to each other. The Frenchmen who fought in the Resistance had to deceive their occupiers and their own puppet government—and so on. The unprecedented phenomenon of a totalitarian state bent on genocide helped sweep away the squeamishness of theologians, and show the primacy of justice in defending the innocent.

In the 1994 edition of *Catechism of the Catholic Church*, this once-daring distinction found itself enshrined as follows:

> Lying is the most direct offense against the truth. To lie is to speak or act against the truth in order to lead into error someone who has the right to know the truth. By injuring man's relation to truth and to his neighbor, a lie offends against the fundamental relation of man and of his word to the Lord. (#2483)

Sounds fine to us. But then in 1997, Pope John Paul threw another Alka-Seltzer into the swamp. His revised, Latin edition of the text removed the phrase "someone who has the right to know the truth," thus reopening the question. And raising a question for us: Did Karol Wotyjla get through six years of German occupation—and take part in the Resistance—without ever telling the SS a falsehood? Should the Catholics who hid Jewish children and "lied" through their teeth to keep them out of Auschwitz have confessed this "sin"? This issue remains unresolved. Perhaps what we seek is "too much information." We'd like to continue this inquiry, but Denise has to go . . . wash her hands.

CELEBRATE: Engage in the most jocose sort of deception by serving up to your friends the deliciously misleading New Orleans specialty Mock Turtle Soup. It's just like the genuine article, except that the de-boned pieces of hacked up snapping turtle have been mentally reserved. Which is just as well, since the meat costs more than $11 a pound.[21]

Mock Turtle Soup

4 pounds meaty oxtails	2 red, 2 green bell peppers, diced
Salt and freshly ground pepper	3 ounces tomato paste
1-1/2 tablespoons grape seed oil	1/2 bunch parley, chopped
1-1/2 teaspoons butter	1 clove
3 carrots, whole	1 tablespoon black peppercorns
2 stalks celery, whole	Sprig of rosemary
2 onions, diced	Sprig of thyme
2 heads garlic, minced	1 preserved lemon
1 head celery, diced	Roux (see below)
4 large carrots, diced	

SEASONINGS:

1 cup Dry Sack Sherry, medium	Several dashes Tabasco
Splash of Worcestershire	Pinch of ground cloves, allspice,
Juice of 2 limes	and cayenne

Rinse and dry oxtail. Season liberally.

Over medium flame, heat a stew pot wide enough to accommodate all the oxtail in one layer. Add 1 tablespoon oil and 1 teaspoon butter. Sear meat on all sides to a deep brown.

Add water to cover with an inch to spare. Simmer for two hours with the 3 carrots and

2 celery stalks. Meat will be tender and vegetables will have given all their essence. Remove "scum" as it rises to the surface. Remove vegetables.

Meanwhile, using remaining oil and butter, sauté vegetables. Start with onions and salt lightly, then add garlic, celery and carrots together, and then peppers. Last, stir in tomato paste using wood spoon, and fry for 3–5 minutes. Add vegetables to pot with oxtail.

Add next 6 ingredients. Raise heat to a medium simmer. Cook for about 30 minutes. Pour in roux and mix to dissolve. Stir frequently once roux has been added to avoid flour sticking and burning. Add seasonings. Taste and make adjustments; add salt and freshly ground pepper.

Simmer another 30 minutes. Serve with Tabasco at the table.

Serves 6

---

[21] If you want the genuine article, you can get it from our favorite Baton Rouge seafood merchant at *www.tonyseafood.com.*

ROUX:

1/4 cup butter   1/2 cup plus 2 tablespoons flour

Melt butter in cast iron skittle. Add flour by letting it fall bit by bit from your hand.
   Whisk constantly until the color of the peanut butter inside a Reese's Peanut Butter™ Cup. Watch very carefully at the end – it can go very quickly from almost ready to burnt.
   The roux can be made ahead and melted as needed.

Drinking Song #6: A Love Song

It's obvious that any tome whose authors hope will be carried into bars and used as a songbook must include a heartrending love song. While it's true that the human heart is often moved to music by other matters, such as love of country, friendship, faith, and early twentieth-century Irish political squabbles, the best reason of all to launch into song is because you're in love. From Ovid's Ninth Elegy, "He Compareth Love to War," to Kiss's immortal power-ballad "Beth," the heartstrings of Western man and teenage girls have resounded to the melodies of Eros. Indeed, the

great Thomistic philosopher Josef Pieper entitled one of his most eloquent books, a treatise on beauty, *Only the Lover Sings* (San Francisco: Ignatius Press, 1990). And of course, sitting smack dab in the middle of Divine Revelation is the Song of Songs, a celebration of the sensual pleasures of marriage—which Christians have learned to see as also an allegory of Christ's marriage with the soul. So we really couldn't let this book go to press without a love song; people might think we were prudes.

   Of the thousands of love songs which have come down through the ages, the most enduring melody is surely "Greensleeves," whose tune you'll recognize from the beloved Christmas hymn "What Child is This." That tune always brings tears to our eyes as we kneel before the Knights of Columbus crèche, as it pipes out of the tape machine securely fastened behind the change box. The Knights leave the manger empty from the First Sunday of Advent through Christmas Eve, and there's nothing quite so poignant as the sight of the Virgin kneeling, the shepherds staring, the eyes of the plaster ox fixed, on a vacant cradle. It helps make up for those pre-Christmas sales which now begin on November 1—and in 20 years will start with the 5th of July.

The full title of the melody is "My Ladye Greensleeves," and legend tells that it was written by none other than England's King Henry VIII (**see Gout**). At least, we hope it's a legend. It really might spoil for us even the sound of the Christmas hymn to think that it was written by this enemy of Christ. We hope that by pointing out its possible provenance, we haven't forever linked "What Child is This" with ruined monasteries, burning Carthusians, and a series of headless wives. For if we're to trust the legend, King Henry (an accomplished musician) composed the song himself, both tune and lyrics, while married to Catherine of Aragon, for his mistress Anne Boleyn. This was the second Boleyn girl he'd bedded—for two years he'd dabbled with her elder sister, Mary—and it didn't bode well for Church or State. In pursuit of a live male heir and his passion for Anne, Henry applied for his infamous annulment from Queen Catherine—which the pope denied.[22] Enraged and afraid of the civil war that might result if he should die sonless, Henry cut England off from the Catholic Church and persecuted any who resisted him. He married Anne in 1536—and within three years grew tired of her, and beheaded her on a trumped-up charge of treason. The poor, 12-fingered girl—a whiz on the harpsichord—came to be known as "Anne of a Thousand Days." (Watch her sad tale for yourself in the 1969 film of that name starring Genevieve Bujold.)

Should the chance that this is true ruin our appreciation of the song? Should we hate Billy Joel's "Just the Way You Are" even more than we already do—if such a perfect hatred were possible this side of Hell—just because the singer who made his fortune with this paean to his wife promptly dumped her for Christie Brinkley? These are thorny questions, but as firm artistic formalists we must say, no. Some great works of art have been born in squalid contexts, churned out for ready money, or conceived for evil purposes—such as popularizing Bolshevism, extolling the "Master Race," turning kids on to heroin, or promoting vegetarianism. But that can't ruin the artwork for us—any more than the best of intentions can turn something shoddy into a masterpiece. We really don't care how sincerely pious was the person who painted that mural in Manhattan's Immaculate Conception Church—apparently by using various colors of Crest toothpaste—which depicts the angels of the Book of Revelation as doe-eyed flower children waiting for Sergeant Pepper to come command the Yellow Submarine. We're not his spiritual directors. We're his victims.

---

[22] It's a pity, historians have mused, that the United States had not yet been settled; had Henry applied for his annulment in Los Angeles, Westminster Abbey would still be in Catholic use today.

Still, if a great Christian hymn might well owe its origin to the sixteenth century's answer to Diocletian, it's clear that God can bring good out of evil. We like to think of this process as theological recycling. Likewise, in doing His work on earth, we can take works of art which began with pious good intentions but not a trace of talent and put them to good use. For instance, all those hymns the clergy have inflicted on us since the 70s. Now it's obviously true, as Thomas Day pointed out in *Why Catholics Can't Sing* (New York: Crossroad, 1992), that most of these songs have no place at all in church. Sappy, weepy, cloying, sing-song, simplistic, most of them would draw disgusted groans at a pep rally for the Special Olympics. Embryologists have employed three-dimensional imaging to detect signs of distress among second trimester fetuses at the sound of "On Eagle's Wings."

But that doesn't mean all these songs are useless. Theologians of divine providence such as Jean-Pierre de Caussade have speculated that the permissive will of God allows great evils to occur to plant the seeds of some greater good. To further that end, we'd like to propose some wholesome uses for some of these musical productions of the post-conciliar liturgical renewal and the Oregon Catholic Press:

- "Be Not Afraid." This nasal, repetitive drone is too simplistic to accompany the Teletubbies, much less the Eucharist. While its message is apparently intended to be reassuring, NIMH clinical trials have shown that it reduces serotonin levels in the brain's frontal cortex, mimicking the short-term effects of cocaine withdrawal or clinical depression. For this reason, we suggest its use is indicated on patients suffering from the manic phase of bipolar disorder, to normalize mood swings and render them compliant with hospital staff.
- "Glory and Praise." Another sing-songy brain-punisher, this tune is chipper in precisely the manner of a chatty, middle-aged Chicagoan chirping loudly about her grandchildren's potty training on her cell phone in the next booth at a diner as you try to read your newspaper. But its melody and cadence are perfectly calculated to repel invasive deer which gather outside suburban homes in search of food. (Those concerned about animal rights should use a hunting rifle instead.)
- "Here I am, Lord." This hymn depicts a human soul responding to the call of Christ—but the music is whiny and grim, evoking in most people's minds a can of rancid potted meat, being slowly spread by windshield wipers across a plate of dirty auto glass. You hear Christ calling, all right—but you feel like He's some hobo who's tapping at your window at 4 a.m. to wake you from a sound sleep so He can ask you directions to Dunkin' Donuts. You don't so much want to answer Him as clock him with a slipper. Sung in a sleepwalking, zombie rhythm, its use at Communion time produces a strikingly cinematic effect, which film critics have dubbed "The Church of the Living Dead." Here again,

we have a chance to bring good out of evil: In preliminary tests, use of this song by military interrogators has proved a successful, slightly more humane replacement for water-boarding.

- "Hosea." A bland, saccharine adaptation of a stirring Old Testament story—a prophetic humdinger in which the relationship of God and His people is presented as a marriage, and human unfaithfulness compared to prostitution. Stern stuff—here reduced by banal lyrics and anile music to a warbling monologue from a straight to video chick-flick starring Patrick Swayze. What is more, one of the song's lines is unintentionally obscene. When the cantor drones "Long . . . have I . . . waited for your . . . coming," it's impossible for any Catholic above age 11 to avoid conceiving of certain conjugal "difficulties." If you're experiencing such problems, you surely hear about them often enough; they shouldn't assault you in church. Being helpful souls, we have searched out a positive use for this terrible, evil song: Many Catholic husbands who love their wives have attended closely to the injunction of Pope John Paul II, who noted in *Love and Responsibility* that "the woman's excitement grows more slowly than that of the man. The man must take this difference between male and female reactions into account." If you're one of those husbands trying to take that difference into account, this song is for you. Hum it slowly to yourself, at crucial moments. There's no more potent buzz-kill known to man.

Reviewing the well-meaning output of the past 30 years of Catholic musical creativity is enough to make one nostalgic for a hymnist like Henry VIII.

Greensleeves

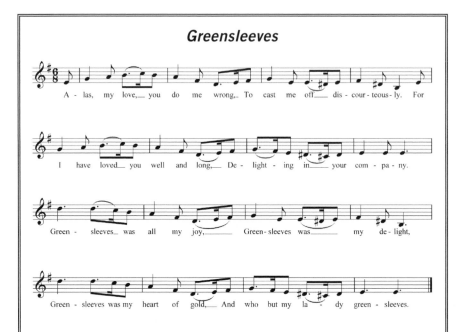

A - las, my love,__ you do me wrong,__ To cast me off__ dis - cour - teous - ly. For
I have loved__ you well and long,__ De - light - ing in__ your com - pa - ny.
Green - sleeves__ was all my joy,__ Green - sleeves was__ my de - light,
Green - sleeves was my heart of gold,__ And who but my la - dy green - sleeves.

2.

Your vows you've broken, like my heart
Oh, why did you so enrapture me?
Now I remain in a world apart
But my heart remains in captivity.

Refrain

3.

I have been ready at your hand
To grant whatever you would crave
I have both wagered life and land
Your love and good-will for to have.

Refrain

4.

If you intend thus to disdain
It does the more enrapture me
And even so, I still remain
A lover in captivity.

Refrain

5.

My men were clothed all in green
And they did ever wait on thee
All this was gallant to be seen
And yet thou wouldst not love me.

Refrain

6.

Thou couldst desire no earthly thing
but still thou hadst it readily.
Thy music still to play and sing
And yet thou wouldst not love me.

Refrain

7.

Well, I will pray to God on high
that thou my constancy mayst see
And that yet once before I die
Thou wilt vouchsafe to love me.

Refrain

8.

Ah, Greensleeves, now farewell, adieu
To God I pray to prosper thee
For I am still thy lover true
Come once again and love me.

Refrain

Bonus Drinking Song: A Sappy Hymn, New and Improved

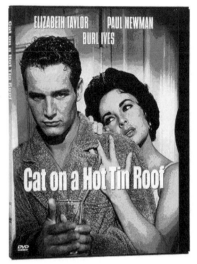

Speaking of hymns which set one's teeth on edge and make you question the existence of a benevolent God, one of the most vividly awful praise-songs in Christian history made its way into a great American film, Richard Brooks's 1958 film of Tennessee Williams's play *Cat on a Hot Tin Roof*. In that film, Maggie (Elizabeth Taylor) and Brick (Paul Newman) are trapped in a childless, sexless marriage thanks to his unspoken . . . issues concerning an old high school buddy, Skipper.

But Brick's brother Gooper has no such problems, having collaborated with his truly awful wife Mae Flynn to produce a vast, whooping brood of little blonde kids whom Maggie dubs the "no-neck monsters." In the film, Mae whips up these children into a frenzy of filial welcome to greet the return of her father-in-law, Big Daddy (Burl Ives), a cotton baron who's dying of cancer and whom she's dying to impress. As the grandchildren, dolled up in their Sunday best, welcome Big Daddy, they intone a cloying hymn, "I'll Be a Sunbeam." Written in 1900 by Nellie Talbot to music that sounds like it should play on a Merry-Go-Round, this song's lyrics are as follows:

> Jesus wants me for a sunbeam,
> To shine for Him each day;
> In every way try to please Him,
> At home, at school, at play.
>
> Refrain:
> > A sunbeam, a sunbeam,
> > Jesus wants me for a sunbeam;
> > A sunbeam, a sunbeam,
> > I'll be a sunbeam for Him.
>
> Jesus wants me to be loving,
> And kind to all I see;
> Showing how pleasant and happy,
> His little one can be.

Refrain

I will ask Jesus to help me
To keep my heart from sin;
Ever reflecting His goodness,
And always shine for Him.

Refrain

I'll be a sunbeam for Jesus,
I can if I but try;
Serving Him moment by moment,
Then live for Him on high.

Refrain

We don't know about you, but this Victorian ditty affects us just as it did Maggie the Cat: It makes us want to slap innocent children. Now, we're neither musicologists nor theologians, but we're pretty sure that's not how Christian hymns are meant to move the heart. But we really can't help it. This hymn combines a ticktock, repetitive melody with lyrics so sweet they rot your teeth. . . . It reminds us of the songs from the infamous hymnbook *Glory and Praise*[23] which the chaplain at LSU used during student services, while wearing Snoopy vestments. The only way we could sit through those creepy songs was to grit our teeth and think of Purgatory. . . .

Instead of just carping and whining, however, we've decided to do something useful, to turn this sickly-sweet lemonade back into lemons. So here's our improved version of the song, presented to you with our hats doffed to Tennessee Williams. It's at once more biblical (albeit mostly Old Testament), and a lot more in the spirit of traditional Catholic catechesis. Teach it to your little ones for the next family gathering. It makes quite an impression on guests.

---

[23] We preferred to give it the Faulknerian sobriquet "Abomination and Bitchery."

The Battle Hymn of the No Neck Monsters

Je - sus wants me for a hail - stone, To smite the hea - then horde,

To smash their Lam - bor - ghi - ni glass And bruise them when He's bored.

A hail - stone, a hail - stone, Je - sus wants me for a hail - stone;

A hail - stone, a hail - stone, I'll be a hail-stone for Him.

2.
Jesus wants me to share the wrath,
Drive men to bend their knee,
Falling like Wormwood from the Sky
And poisoning the sea.

Refrain

3.
I'll fall as fire on Sodom
Like Noah's flood, like frogs.
I'll storm the gentile's city
Like a pack of Gadarene hogs.

Refrain

4.
I'll be a hailstone for Jesus,
A warning from the sky,
An Angel of death avenging,
Reminding that doom is nigh.

Refrain

St. John: Poisoning the Bishop

Of all Jesus' Apostles, the only one who didn't die violently was Jesus' favorite, John. All the others were murdered, mostly by the Romans (though some enterprising rabbis may have tossed St. James the Lesser from the roof of the Tem-

ple in Jerusalem). Stories vary as to how John survived to become the old man who wrote the Apocalypse (**see Absinthe**). The most enduring legend tells that pagans attempted to poison the apostle's wine. But when John made a simple blessing over his cup, a serpent leapt out of his wine, winked at him, and crawled away. And here is the really telling part: *He didn't send the bottle back.* Like any connoisseur, John knew that you're only supposed to do this if the wine has been spoiled by corkage. Instead, John calmly drank the cup and walked away unharmed.

This story inspired Catholics in later centuries to make St. John a patron saint of vintners, and bless wine on his feast day (Dec. 27), with the following prayer (taken from the Roman Ritual):

> Lord Jesus Christ, Who spoke of Yourself as the true vine and the apostles as the branches, and Who willed to plant a chosen vineyard of all Who love You, bless + this wine and empower it with Your blessing; so that all who taste or drink of it may, through the intercession of Your beloved disciple John, apostle and evangelist, be spared every deadly and poisonous affliction and enjoy bodily and spiritual well-being. We ask this of You Who live and reign forever and ever. Amen.

We like to tell St. John's story to the kind of gloomy-gus Catholic who puts too much emphasis on suffering—as if the Passion of Jesus made anguish a good thing in itself. Some chroniclers of saints' lives in the past seemed to take it as a personal challenge to prove that their saint suffered more than any other in history, often piling on the tortures, persecutions, and miseries to the point where the modern reader winces—then cracks up laughing. Read enough detailed accounts of virgins who were hacked up, burned, stabbed, and fed to lions—*but still didn't die*, until they were beheaded—and pretty soon you're not so much thinking of St. Agatha as of Rasputin.

To Catholics who enjoy this sort of thing, who obsess over tales of victim-souls, we answer: If suffering is such a good thing, *why keep it to ourselves?* If it's the key to salvation, we should be spreading it, far and wide. Instead of serving as the single largest social welfare agency in the world—running hospitals, clinics, hospices, and shelters on six continents—all with the goal of *diminishing* suffering, the Church ought to be promoting it. As New Yorkers, we have some ideas on how to get this new project started. Clergy and laity could work together to encourage:

- Unjust wars, waged indiscriminately against civilians
- Sexual promiscuity, with all its attendant heartbreak
- Hasty marriage and easy divorce
- Needless and counterproductive plastic surgery
- More albums by The Three Tenors
- Fast food
- Bauhaus architecture
- Urban sprawl
- Business travel
- Houston

Much as this idea might appeal, the Church is unlikely to adopt it. In fact, Catholics are only asked to embrace suffering when it is unavoidable (or the only alternative to sin). When that happens, we're meant to unite it with Christ's, in order to find meaning in it—turning life's lemons into spiritual lemonade. But we're not supposed to look for it. As the long-suffering St. Thérèse once observed, "Ordinary life throws enough curveballs; no sense in trying to get hit by a pitch."[1] For those of us without the backbone to stand up to torture, it's reassuring that the apostle "whom Jesus loved" (John 13: 23) died peacefully in old age. We need not look for martyrdom; if we really need it, it will find us.

CELEBRATE: German-speaking Catholics still mark St. John's feast day by brewing up a tasty batch of mulled *Glühwein*, a hot, fruity drink which helps ward off the Teutonic winter. The English drink something similar, which they call "Bishop Wine," (as an apostle, John was one of the first 11 bishops). The same

---

[1] Okay, maybe this isn't an exact quote. Being French, St. Thérèse was probably less interested in baseball than in cycling. Having shut herself in a cloister, she could never realize her dream of winning the Tour de France.

drink in Sweden is called *Glögg*, and in the Netherlands *Bisschopswijn*—though the Nether folk serve it on the Feast of St. Nicholas (Dec. 6). Why not warm up your Christmas season by ladling a bowl of this concoction for your friends and family? One old custom has it that at each cup, you offer your loved ones this toast: "I drink you the love of St. John," and between the toasts read aloud a quote from St. John's Gospel, such as "God is love." (1 John 4: 8)

Depending on how you feel about your family and friends, you might prefer to offer them some reflections from the Apocalypse (**see Absinthe**) such as the following, themed according to your guest list:

- If some of your friends are cohabiting: "But I have a few things against thee, because thou hast there them that hold the doctrine of Balaam, who taught Balac to cast a stumbling block before the children of Israel, to eat things sacrificed unto idols, and to commit fornication. (Apocalypse 2: 14)
- At any gathering of bad Catholics: "So then because thou art lukewarm, and neither cold nor hot, I will spue thee out of my mouth." (Apocalypse 3: 16)
- At an interfaith celebration: "Behold, I will make them of the synagogue of Satan, which say they are Jews, and are not, but do lie; behold, I will make them to come and worship before thy feet, and to know that I have loved thee." (Apocalypse 3: 9)
- For the children: "And I looked, and behold a pale horse: and his name that sat on him was Death, and Hell followed with him. And power was given unto them over the fourth part of the earth, to kill with sword, and with hunger, and with death, and with the beasts of the earth." (Apocalypse 6: 8)

Glühwein

1 750-ml bottle red wine, preferably made by monks	1/2 cup water
	1/2 cup sugar
1 orange, sliced in rings	1 stick cinnamon
Peel of another orange	4 cloves

Combine all ingredients. Simmer 15 minutes.
  Strain.
  Serve warm.

Serves 6

Sake: The Sauce of the Hidden Christians

One of the most refreshing "exotic" drinks we've come across is sake—the Japanese rice wine which most of us have drunk steaming hot with a plate of sushi. Of course, that's usually the cheap stuff; there are dozens of different varieties of sake, some of them finely crafted and quite expensive. The best brands are complex and flavorful, and properly served cold. Still that won't stop us from scarfing down a carafe of the $9 variety on a cold December day—though probably not on December 7.

The Chinese and Japanese are still arguing over who invented sake, some time back in the third century B.C. (Indeed, so much of Japanese culture and religion comes from Chinese sources, that one can't help wondering at the *chutzpah* it took for the Japanese to conquer and enslave large parts of China in the 1930s. Then again, in 1940, the Germans conquered the Greeks. . . .) What we do know is that the first sake was made by peasants chewing up rice to break down the starch, and spitting it into a tub to ferment—a process that makes this Westerner crave some wine pressed by smelly European peasants' feet. Early sake factories must have resembled fields of cattle, clad in kimonos, chewing the cud. It took hundreds of years for a peasant whose jaws got tired to discover a handy mold which rendered saliva superfluous—and freed these farmers up to actually start eating their rice. It was only after they traded spit for mold that the sake industry really took off.

What's interesting to us about sake—beyond its potent kick and pleasant afterburn, as the perfect accompaniment to a plate full of raw sea-urchins and fiery green wasabi—is the role it played in the tangled, sometimes secret history of Christianity in Japan.

In the great age of European exploration, when advances in navigational and military technology gave nations such as Portugal and Spain the chance to assert themselves against ancient civilizations from India to Japan, Catholic missionaries tagged along for the ride. The assorted adventurers who manned the ships were hardly the cream of Europe: In fact, they were largely scofflaws, bankrupt nobles, and others who saw no future at home in Iberia. With little to lose and much to gain—for instance, great big barrels of Asian seasonings such as pepper, in Europe worth their weight in gold—they embarked on the sixteenth-century equivalent of a trip to the planet Mars. And not all the Martians were impressed. Chinese accounts of the Portuguese and Spanish they encountered show mainly scorn for men they considered barbarians, who demanded knives to cut their food—a shocking *faux pas* to the hypercivilized mandarins, who mocked the Westerners for "eating with their swords." The "long-noses," as the Europeans were called, carried shocking new weapons like rifles and cannon, and appeared to the men of the Orient as crude, rude, and on the make—like a crowd of Alabama Amway salesmen descending on Paris, armed with light sabers.

But not all the explorers who came from the West had money in mind. On the same ships, serving as chaplains for the journey, rode missionary priests from religious orders such as the newly founded Society of Jesus (**see Winkler Jesuitengarten**). The most famous was Francis Xavier, a Spaniard who in 1529 had been wowed by St. Ignatius Loyola at the University of Paris into joining the fledgling order. In 1541, Francis sailed as a missionary to India, founding churches and studying Eastern languages, in the hope of planting Christianity across all Asia. In 1549, Francis landed in the Japanese city of Kagoshima. He spent a year studying Japanese, then set about traveling the country to evangelize. He left behind several flourishing Christian communities, and Jesuits to lead them. Ever pragmatic and eager to adapt themselves to local conditions, the Jesuits inquired of the Vatican if they could use sake and rice cakes instead of (scarce) grape wine and wheat-based bread for the Eucharist. "No," the Vatican explained.[2]

As the Jesuits discovered, the Japanese warrior culture had long ago reconciled this pagan people to the necessity of suffering. Indeed, the samurai had created a kind of cult of pain, which carried over among the new Christians. The Jesuits found their freshly baptized followers all too willing to flog their own backs and

---

[2] There were serious reasons for the Holy See's refusal. Unlike some gnostic, New Age religions, the Church believes that the material world is sacred, that particulars are important, and that the historical specifics of Christ's life are decisive. He used bread and wine, and commanded us to "do likewise"—not to do something "vaguely analogous," or "curiously evocative," but the *same thing*, over and over again, in unbloody repetition of the sacrifice of Calvary. For this reason, the Church has warned that funky liturgies employing carrot-cake and Pepsi (for some reason, usually celebrated by Jesuits) are not simply inappropriate but *invalid*. If you ever find that your pastor has introduced some alien substance instead of bread and wine, show your gratitude by stuffing the collection basket with Monopoly money. And don't be stingy!

impose all manner of excruciating penances on themselves. Recalling the example of St. Ignatius, their founder—whose excessive penances had ruined his health—the priests restrained the new Christians from torturing themselves needlessly.

All too soon, the need would arise on its own. Thanks to political blunders on the part of the Europeans, Japan's warlord rulers turned against the suddenly, scarily popular priests. To the Japanese ruling class, these missionaries now seemed like a fifth column working on behalf of foreigners such as the Spanish, who by then ruled the nearby Philippines as a colony. In 1587, the samurai launched a persecution of the missionaries and their flocks, who by now numbered some 200,000. Despite this persecution, the numbers of Japanese Christians kept on growing. By 1597, the authorities began to torture and slaughter Christians wherever they found them. Dozens of martyrs whose names have come down to us—and some 200,000–300,000 others—suffered hideously for the Faith, as the pagan warlords skinned them, hung them to die slowly from trees, burned them alive or crucified them. Soon, the only Christians remaining in Japan practiced their faith in secret. And so they would stay, as *Kakure Kirishitan* ("hidden Christians") for some 250 years.

These secret Christians made a show of practicing Shintoism or Buddhism. They conducted Christian rituals in hiding, reciting liturgies from memory and snatches of prayers in Latin and Portuguese which they'd long ceased to understand. They held Communion rituals using fish and sake instead of bread and wine. In the nineteenth century, when the emperor lifted the ban on Christianity and French missionaries arrived, most of these Christians came forward—and quickly reverted to the pure form of the Faith for which their ancestors had died. But not all were willing. So much time had passed, and so fuzzy had memories grown, that thousands of *Kakure Kirishitan* refused to join the churches planted by these priests, and stayed home practicing the half-remembered faith their parents had whispered to them. As if in a game of catechetical "telephone," the details of the creed had gotten confused, and the rites of the Church transformed into something quite curious, thoroughly Japanese, and new. In 2000, Anthropologist Christal Whelan released a film *Otaiya: Japan's Hidden Christians*, documenting these ultra-traditionalists, who celebrate Christmas and Good Friday but have forgotten the feast of Easter. Their numbers have dwindled to the hundreds, and soon the group is likely to disappear entirely.

Their fate is poignant to us, because we know quite a few Catholics in the West in a similar plight. In the 1970s, as Pope Paul VI faced wholesale rebellion by progressives in the Church, he wielded his papal authority instead to persecute the small numbers of Catholics who resisted the most expansive readings of Vatican II. As a flag of resistance, these traditionalists also rejected the new, truncated liturgy—which Paul VI had imposed, suppressing almost entirely the rites which the Church had used for well over 1,000 years. In 1970, with initial Vatican approval, French Archbishop Marcel Lefèbvre founded the Society of St. Pius X (SSPX) to meet the needs of Catholics bewildered by post-conciliar changes—most of which went far beyond what was authorized by the documents of the council. Indeed, so did the liturgy imposed by Paul VI, which bore little resemblance to the reforms called for in *Sacrosanctum Concilium*—a point recognized in several books by the present Pope Benedict XVI.

It was not long before hundreds of seminarians deserted the newly radicalized seminaries of France for Lefèbvre's institute in Ecône, Switzerland, and progressive French bishops appealed to Paul VI to suppress the group. He did so in 1975—after refusing to consider Lefèbvre's canonical appeal. He soon suspended Lefèbvre and all his priests—who had meanwhile set up chapels around the world, to minister to Catholics who'd been alienated by the sudden changes in liturgy, practice, and (apparently) doctrine. Thousands of laymen who'd stopped going to Mass altogether, and gathered weekly instead to say the Rosary in their homes,[3] flocked to the chapels of the SSPX—even as their local pastors labeled them schismatics. This made traditionalists virtually the only group which Paul VI had dealt with firmly, even as bishops' conferences defied him on major issues of faith and morals, religious orders embraced Marxist theology, and pastors around the world conducted liturgical experiments that ranged from "consecrating" pizza and beer to dressing as clowns to celebrate Mass.

Recognizing the injustice with which traditionalists had been treated, Pope John Paul II attempted to win back Archbishop Lefèbvre and his followers in 1988—offering them substantial autonomy in relation to the local bishops they considered (with some reason) abusive. Distrustful, dying, and surrounded by youthful hotheads, Lefèbvre refused to make a deal, and consecrated four more bishops to carry on his group when he was gone. This won him and his bishops a decree of excommunication—but won for those willing to leave the SSPX and take the Vatican's offer the right to revive the ancient Roman liturgy, granted by the 1988 *motu proprio* entitled *Ecclesia Dei*. Those who left the SSPX, the Fraternity of St. Peter, now work throughout the world, with parishes planted wherever local bishops will tolerate the use of Gregorian chant and a reverent liturgy. Several other groups

---

[3] These folk even adopted a poignant term to describe themselves: "Home-Aloners."

have since sprung up, with Vatican encouragement, to carry on the Church's liturgical heritage. As we write, hopes are high among traditionalists that Pope Benedict XVI will extend universal permission for any priest, however squeamish his bishop, to celebrate the same rite said by St. Francis Xavier on a makeshift altar in Japan. It's widely anticipated that at some point in 2007, the pope will issue another *motu proprio* to this effect—although several bishops of France are even now helpfully lobbying to prevent it. If this document is issued, it may well reconcile the Society of St. Pius X with the Holy See, and end what some have called the first Church schism of modern times.

Of course, we pray that this happens, and look forward to the day when our parish priest will turn his back on us to pray facing the tabernacle. But even if this happy event takes place, it's certain that significant numbers of traditionalists will refuse the pope's outstretched hand. Like those traumatized "secret Christians" of Japan, they will cling to Calvary, and refuse to believe the message that He is risen.

Salvator Beer—Save Us From Lent!

This beer's name and history nicely sum up the creed and practice of beer-drinking, loophole-hunting, confessional-hopping bad Catholics like, well . . . us. It was first brewed, reports "Delicious Bavaria" (the region's official culinary Web site) in

1629, "by Paulaner monks in the Neudeck op der Au monastery on the outskirts of Munich and called 'Sankt-Vaters-Bier.'" That is, the "Holy Father's Beer." It got this name because brewing and drinking it required special permission from the pope. (And Protestants say we're control freaks. . . .[4]) You see, unlike the paler beers often drunk in the region (**see Papal Infallibility**), this beer was thick and dark, bottom-fermented to 15 proof—much stronger and heartier than Pilsners or Weissbiers. It was meant for Lent, to compensate a bit for the strictness of the monk's seasonal fast. Which makes a kind of

---

[4] In fact, the regions that followed Luther and Calvin were always far more repressed, weighed down by the millstone of a doubt-wrenched, Bible-thumbing conscience. We papists subcontract such agonizing to the specialists down in Rome. That's why nobody's ever slandered us with a phrase like "the Catholic work ethic."

spiritual sense: since these celibates wouldn't be eating very much, they wanted to make sure their drinks were . . . stronger. Ah yes, can't you picture the tipsy, half-starved monks knocking into each other in refectories across Bavaria, lapsing from their psalms into the strains of *Carmina Burana*? A better way to prepare for Easter is hard to imagine.

So it's easy to see why explicit papal permission was needed to undertake making this strong stuff, which contained more nutrients and would swell the empty monastic bellies. The monks sent a barrel of their Doppelbockbier down through the Alps to Rome, waiting nervously for a note from the pope declaring the stuff far too delicious to drink during Lent. What the monks did not count on was that once the beer crossed the Brenner Pass it would be *handled by Italians*. The barrel was greeted by bureaucrats in oversized hats insisting on piles of paperwork—or judicious bribes to speed its journey. It was redirected from warehouse to whorehouse to outhouse in a slow-moving donkey cart, as it baked in the southern sun. It bubbled and foamed and spoiled, and probably rode alongside a wheel of taleggio long enough to soak in the scent, because by the time the beer made its way to Pope Urban VIII (**see Nose of a Wine**) it stank like a barrel full of rotting badgers, but tasted rather worse. The artsy, sophisticated pontiff took a single sip and gagged—then granted blanket permission for these eccentric German monks to drink as much as they liked of this horrible stuff, as part of their Lenten penance.

The Bavarian government would like us to point out here that in 1770 the evocatively named monk Barnabas Still "improved the taste of the Doppelbock so much that it became known far outwith [sic] the borders of the monastery." Indeed, the monks would start out Lent by presenting the local prince with their very first tankard of the stuff. In 1780, the ruler Karl Theodor pronounced himself so pleased with Salvator that he granted the monks permission to sell it to the public. The brothers' brewing business grew so brisk that within 20 years the state confiscated the place and threw out the monks. (No good deed goes unpunished.) But brewers carried on the brand, which is still made today. And the custom continues of opening the first barrel as Lent begins, and presenting the first mug to Munich's mayor.

Perhaps you'll pardon us for pining for the days when Salvator was made by monks, Bavarians had a king, and new brands of beer required explicit permission from the pope. All of which made life so much more *interesting*. . . .

··

Sangue di Giuda

This rather offbeat northern Italian red wine has a pungent, off-putting name which translates as "Blood of Judas." On the face of it, this does not exactly make us want to uncork the stuff; after all, if anyone in the universe really is drinking the blood of Judas, it's probably the devil—and we'd rather not walk in his hooves. The wine critic who commended this bottle to his readers at *www.wineloverspage.com* did a little digging to find the origin of its off-putting name. As he wrote:

> Enrica Verdi, with Azienda Bruno Verdi, the seven-generation family producer . . . responded (in English, thankfully) to my E-mail question: "Local legend has it that the name . . . was given by friars who disapproved of its stimulating and aphrodisiac effects."

This explanation is curious on two counts, since the wine is only 15 proof—hardly likely to make an Italian girl who grew up quaffing Chianti with dinner drop her standards or her skirt. And anyway, Judas's sin had nothing to do with sex. Nor was it about money, as some Church fathers suggested, arguing that Judas betrayed his Messiah out of greed. Indeed, the gospel account refutes that motive pretty convincingly, depicting as it does Judas hurling the money back at the high priests in disgust. Of course, anti-Semites in latter centuries made much of the fact that Judas had turned in Christ for a bag of silver . . . conveniently leaving out the fact that he gave it back. Whatever Judas's motives, it *wasn't about the money*.[5]

The reasons for Judas's "betrayal" of his Lord remain a profound mystery, and have prompted writers great and small to speculate about what could possibly have goaded one of the twelve men in history privileged to spend three years gadding about with the Son of God to turn against Him. Perhaps the most interesting literary variation on this theme is by the great Jorge Luis Borges, whose story "Three Versions of Judas" depicts a tormented Protestant theologian who becomes convinced that Judas turned Jesus in order to save mankind—that he knew what he

---

[5] On the other hand, turning from biblical betrayal to ordinary business, it's worth remembering that whenever someone insists "It's not about the money," this is apodictic proof that it's *only* about the money. If he invokes "the principle," "integrity," or "self-respect" you should pause for a moment, nod reassuringly, and cut your offer in half. This guy is desperate, no doubt in debt to loan-sharks. If you let him hole up in your basement, he'll probably work for food.

was doing, and willingly offered up his soul to further our redemption. A twisted and unpersuasive thought, but it's just the kind of thing that sets off nineteen-year-olds smoking cloves and sipping their tenth espresso into four-hour arguments with friends, "existential crises," or the ill-advised decision to attend grad school in the humanities. You have been warned.

What interests us more is the sin which damned Judas in the end. It wasn't betrayal. In a lesser way on the same night, Peter also denied His Lord, and also wept bitter tears. But as theologians have taught for centuries, Judas responded not with genuine repentance but *despair*. He decided that his sin was too great for even God to forgive, and went off to hang himself. (If you follow Mel Gibson's version, he was goaded to it by a band of Italian urchins with Martian ears, but this detail might be apocryphal.) By exalting his sin over God's mercy, Judas essentially died of pride—choking to death on healthy self-esteem.

In the way each one responded to the fact that he'd betrayed the Lord, these apostles were true to form. Judas, the cautious accountant who'd worried about the penitent woman "wasting" her perfume on Jesus' feet, and Peter, the dopey fisherman who'd assured Jesus not three hours before that he had no fear of martyrdom. In fact, each apostle spent the night of Holy Thursday relapsing into his own besetting vice:

Scrupulosity: Judas's sin, which exaggerates harmless actions into sins and real sins into monstrous crimes, and convinces the sinner that his misdeeds are so massive and grandiose that even God cannot forgive them. The result is *despair*, and in Judas's case suicide. Martin Luther also suffered from this spiritual illness, and spent years tormented by the fear that his sins rendered him unworthy to say Mass. He found an answer—and no, we're not making this up—in an apparition of Satan, who argued Luther into denying the Catholic teaching on the Eucharist. This soothed Luther's conscience, and convinced him that the Mass was a "false blasphemous cult." (NOTE TO SELF: When a theological argument is posed by the Father of Lies, it might be best to seek a second opinion.)

Laxity: Peter's problem, which turns great sins into peccadillos, small sins into charming character traits, and leads the sinner to blithely trust in God's mercy without all the bother entailed in actually repenting. This leads to *presumption*, and dunderheaded behavior such as Peter exhibited . . . well, throughout most of the gospels. It took the crowing of mocking cocks to awaken Peter's conscience. In his case, it was only his deep-rooted humility—acquired over three years of blundering—that saved him from following Judas to the noose. Fittingly, Peter's sin has afflicted many popes. Laxity and presumption were the sins responsible for most of the corruption in the Renaissance Church, which gave Luther the fodder for his 95 Theses (1517). Drunken, adulterous pontiffs who were better at leading armies than shepherding souls, who presumed that their office would knock down the door to Heaven, are every bit as responsible for the sundering of the Church into hundreds of fragments as the tormented German monk is—who at least meant well.[6]

So we see how these seemingly opposite vices can work in tandem. Call it "sinergy," if you like. In our experience, few people are overpoweringly either scrupulous or lax. Instead, most people's consciences are a weird mixture of both. We tend to adopt a stern scrupulosity about sins which do not tempt us, or which we've already

licked—like annoying "dry drunks" who want to close all the bars—while extending an easy laxity to those we haven't conquered and hope never to give up. For this reason, many conservative Catholics give an easy pass, for example, to racist jokes, while professing shock and awe at the sight of porn. As for progressive Catholics— the converse is true. We each do a little victory dance over things that no longer (or might never) trouble us, and extend the healing hand of compassion to the sins we hope to fondle for decades to come. C.S. Lewis pointed this out in *The Screwtape Letters*, and must be chuckling even today, in Purgatory's well-appointed Anglican Quarter, at the sight of one sort of priest thundering to Latin Mass parishioners about Freemasonry, while another warns his left-leaning, guitar-banging flock against Halliburton. It's the well-trained homilist who will tick off his congregants by addressing the sins they actually, probably *commit*. And he will soon find himself transferred to a different parish. This practice is what certain bishops refer to as being "pastoral," and derives from a variant edition of the New Testament employed at Bishops' School. We feel it's time someone pointed it out: Our Lord did *not* say "Eat my sheep." (John 21:16) That must have been a typo.

....

Satan, Duvel, and the Augustinian Concept of Evil

Belgium is a quirky country, rife with paradox. A small, neutral nation with a famously do-nothing army,[7] it once ran the harshest European colonial empire (the British ruled Bermuda; the Belgians ran Rwanda). Its nineteenth-century ruler, King Ludwig I, held the whole of Congo as his personal property, where he forced

<hr/>

[6] Yeah? Well so did Woodrow Wilson (**see Gewürztraminer**).

[7] Belgium boasts the world's only unionized army.. This might explain the 1940 Blitzkrieg, when that land's heavily fortified frontier collapsed to the Nazis in something like 20 minutes. The army must have been "on break."

the natives at gunpoint to gather rubber to make—well, *rubbers*. The country's population is also anomalous, the result of a shotgun marriage between the Flems and the Walloons. Who held the shotgun? Successively, each of Belgium's neighbors, from the conquering Germans and the revolutionary French to the easygoing Dutch. The only nearby country that has never at any point tried to rule Belgium is tiny Luxembourg (**see Willibrord**), whose turn is coming up soon. What united the Belgians despite their linguistic differences was for centuries their Faith. Belgium was founded in 1830 as a kind of refuge for the Catholics of this region, where they might rule themselves free of Calvinists and Jacobins alike. But this Faith, once the nation's *raison d'etre* (or in Flemish: *bestaansrecht*) is fading.

What is a country to do without its *bestaansrecht*? It can make chocolate and cheese, and the Belgians do an excellent job of both. Maredsous's washed-rind monastic cheese is justly famous for its scent—which evokes a fresh, sunny battlefield such as Ypres. Callebaut chocolate is our favorite ingredient for baking. But even the cheaper Belgian brands such as Leonidas—in Antwerp the equivalent of a Hershey bar—are good enough for export.

And the country can churn out theologians. The elite Catholic University of Louvain (with its Flemish sister school Leuven) each year turns out a fresh crop of dissenters to torment the Holy See. Without that school, such papers as *The Wanderer* would run short on their whine supply. Unlike other modernist exegetes, these Louvain grads emerge with a comprehensive knowledge of beer. That's the country's most famous export, and the Belgian paradox extends even into this fundamental realm.

When you first hear the words "Belgian beer," you're liable to think of brews produced at abbeys (**see Trappists**) such as Chimay or Orvel, by men consecrated to God. In the Benedictine spirit, they see their work as prayer, and you can taste their celibacy in the beer.[8] On the other hand, a disconcerting number of Belgian

---

[8] Our favorite beer commercial promotes one of our least favorite beers, the thin, yellow fluid called Coors. This famous ad shows a sturdy ram standing in a crystal-clear fast-flowing river, while the narrator promises "You can taste it in the beer." And indeed, you can.

beers have names which evoke another spirit altogether: the Father of Lies, the Lord of the Flies, the Prince of Darkness, the "devil who is a murderer from the beginning." (John 8:44)

It's unclear why you'd name a bubbly, recreational beverage after the enemy of human souls, whose hatred and envy seeks to drag every man, woman, and child who attains the age of reason down screaming into the abyss where the "worm dieth not, and the fire is not quenched," (Mark 9:48), and God's eternal absence ensures that "there shall be weeping and gnashing of teeth" (Matthew 24:51). Not to put too fine a point on it.

We have to wonder what's going on here. Have renegades from Louvain who decided to switch "teams" infiltrated the brewing industry? Are they now serving Satan—in blatant violation of both their baptismal vows and their non-compete agreements? Or perhaps Belgium has seen a re-emergence of the ancient heresy of Dualism, which posits that evil in the universe is the creation of a second, evil god. That god, according to Zoroastrians, Manicheaens, and other Dualists, is every bit as ancient and as powerful as the good God—so even if you don't serve him, you'd better try not to tick him off. This heresy once cropped up among the Troubadour love poets of southern France. Has it returned among Belgian brewers? If so, is it safe to drink these demonic beers—or is it, like playing with a Ouija board, an invitation to possession? Hey, we've read *Hostage to the Devil*,[9] and seen clips from *The Exorcist*; no beer is worth having to spew up that much pea soup—especially if it includes chunks of ham (see recipe).

A little research turns up an answer that's less unsettling. It seems that the first Belgian beer to adopt a diabolical title was Duvel, produced by the Moortgat Brewery in Breendonk. It was founded not by a band of Satanists, but by Jan-Leonard Moortgat, in 1871. The Moortgat brewery actually makes beer on behalf of the Maredsous Abbey, so the monks can concentrate on putting the stink into their cheese. But Moortgat's most famous beer is a golden ale, brewed from Scottish yeasts, developed during World War I. That conflict devastated Belgium—which had made the mistake of locating next door to Germany—and the brewers at first gave their beer the wistful name "Victory Ale."

According to legend, a local connoisseur once called this beer "a devil (*duvel*) of an ale," and after the war, the brewery adopted this as its name. Michael Jackson, the pope of beer, calls Duvel "devilishly deceptive, drinking far lighter than its 8.2 per cent." On his Web site, *Beerhunter.com*, he notes that "the Belgians serve it lightly chilled, in a Burgundy sampler, as an aperitif. I like it after dinner; its flavours remind me of the brandies made from the Williams pear in Alsace."

It's a heady brew—literally. If you pour it slowly as the Belgians recommend, you'll find yourself sipping beer through a four-inch pile of froth. It's a crisp, clean

---

[9] Malachi Martin's extremely informative and thoroughly alarmist memoir of his days as an exorcist. Use it to scare your family members away from Reiki.

drink, which goes well with chicken or fish, and has proved so popular that it spawned a host of imitators. Two of them highlight their similarity to Duvel by adopting cognate names: There's a Lucifer beer, and another called Satan. Like the original, they are crisp, light beers that go well with *moules frites* or mac and cheese.[10]

We're happy to know that there's nothing explicitly evil behind this trend of Satan-themed beers, though we wince a little at such willingness to render evil trivial. It reminds us of the short-lived Bombay restaurant witlessly named for Hitler, or the innumerable noise bands with names like Godless, Ritual Carnage, and Dissection. In point of fact, eternal damnation is as serious as cancer, and calling cigarettes "coffin nails" doesn't make them any less dangerous.

On the other hand, the devil is an ass, and richly deserves to be mocked. He blew an eternity in paradise for a moment's hissy fit—and now wastes his enormous angelic intellect steering teens to fetish Web sites. (You'd think he'd find something more interesting to do—if only playing Sudoku.) Besides, such mockery helps us put evil into perspective, to see that the devil is no way an equal, opposite force to God. In fact, he is a kind of cosmic parasite, a flea on the Mystical Body of Christ, entirely dependent on God for what being he retains (**see Zima**). St. Augustine, himself a member of Manicheans Anonymous, shook off the Dualist illusion and formulated the Church's definition of evil, which has stood ever since: Evil is simply the absence of the good. An evil man has twisted the goodness given to him by God, and the devil is nothing more than a twisted angel, whose being itself is good—though he makes bloody poor use of it.

Photo credit:
http://en.wikipedia.org/wiki/Image:
Kwak.jpg

This principle can be nicely demonstrated by serving Belgian beer. As you might know, every brand has its own special glass. Duvel's is a wide-mouth sort of brandy snifter. But an even more delightful beer called Kwak—from Gheel, hometown of our home girl St. Dymphna—is served in a funky beaker, which cannot stay up on its own but requires a wooden stand (pictured). If you decide some Halloween to serve up a satanic Belgian beer, we recommend pouring it in the Kwak glass—which illustrates the fact that evil has no standing of its own, but must lean on the goodness of God. Make this catechetical point to your dinner guests as they finish their green pea soup.

---

[10] We're not kidding; the excellent NYC Belgian bistro Petite Abeille serves a crispy baked casserole of "*macaroni jambon fromage au gratin*" which we've washed down with glasses of Lucifer—though not without reciting the St. Michael prayer.

CELEBRATE: Serve up Duvel without serving Satan by pouring it into the orthodox Augustinian Kwak glass, alongside this delicious, exorcism-themed green pea soup.

Split Pea Soup ala *The Exorcist*

This soup is very rich and needs very little accompaniment other than a modestly dressed salad and a glass of wine.

2 small ham hocks	3 stalks celery, diced
3 leeks (white part and green tops separate)	Salt and freshly ground pepper
	1 tablespoon cumin; toasted, ground
1 teaspoon black peppercorns	4 baby new potatoes, small dice
1 bay leaf	Zest of 1 orange
1 pound dried green split peas	2 pounds smoked pork butt, large dice
1 tablespoon olive oil	1/2 cup orange juice
4 carrots, diced	

In large soup pot cover ham hocks with plenty of water to cover and bring to a boil. Include leek tops, peppercorns, and bay leaf. Simmer for 1 to 1 1/2 hours until meat is falling from bone. Remove hocks and set aside until cool enough to handle and pick off the meat; discard leek tops.

First rinse and pick through peas then add to broth. Simmer 30 to 45 minutes.

Meanwhile, clean and slice white part of leeks. Heat oil in sauté pan and add leeks, carrots, and celery. Season with salt, pepper and cumin; cook until deeply browned. Toss in potatoes. Add vegetables to peas along with orange zest. Stir and bring back to a simmer. Now add both pork butts as well as reserved meat. There will be very little meat from the hocks, but they will have offered flavor to broth.

Cook for another 30 minutes. Potatoes will be soft and peas mostly dissolved. Adjust seasoning and stir in orange juice.

Serves 6

Stout: A Beer that will Serve as Breakfast

Devout drinkers of beer need no introduction to stout, which most of us know from long nights downing foamy pints of Guinness while cheering on *seisun* bands made up of illegal Irish aliens and off-duty cops, while ogling the pink-cheeked barmaids and trying to avoid slipping on the floor or into a fistfight. The Irish do know how to party. They call a good time *craic*, and for a certain percentage who can't hold their liquor, it seems that *craic* is what they've been smoking. One of the authors remembers a musical evening at a pub in midtown Manhattan where an aging football hooligan stood two feet from the stage and menaced the singer—a soft-voiced young man who tried to croon a lilting melody accompanied only by a guitar, over this man's sodden shouts of:

> That's not an Irish song!
> *(Prolonged belch.)*
> Get him the f—k outa here.
> That's not an Irish song!
> *(Hacking cough. Spit.)*
> Get that feckin' dago off the stage. . . .

And so on. The author tried to intervene, and soon found himself in a half-nelson, getting dragged out by two overgrown altar boys in boiled shirts (bar staff) who threw him face first onto the Third Avenue cement. When he sought an explanation, a pretty dark-haired girl with crooked teeth and azure eyes blew out a puff of smoke with a little shrug, "He must be a reg'lar. Can't afford to piss off your bread and butter." So as far as we know, that old heckler is still in there today, threatening the bands and picking fights as the last bits of his liver trickle slowly down his leg. Even today, this author can't pass O'Neill's without wanting to hurl a cement block through the plate glass window, and he tells all his Irish friends that the place is owned by the British Crown. It's not easy being Irish—not by half.[11]

One spot from which neither of us has yet been expelled is Paddy Reilly's on 28th Street and 2nd Avenue. It has hosted dozens of well-known bands over the years, including the hybrid Irish/hip-hop group Black 47, whose raucous songs take old Irish folk tunes and add an "urban" groove, with lyrics inspired by the Marxoid faction of Sinn Fein. To a driving beat, they belt out crackpot rants about the "international solidarity of workers and small farmers" which in Belfast would get the singers shot at by both sides. But their songs are a lot of fun, once you look past the fact that their singer can't actually *sing*, but instead brays like a traditional Irish donkey. We own several of their albums.

Paddy Reilly's brands itself as "New York's Only All-Guinness Pub." Of course

---

[11] Especially when one's other half is Croatian. It's like being part nitro and part glycerine.

it sells other beers, but foaming black Guinness is the only brew it keeps on tap. Besides its delicious flavor, the stuff is nutritious and filling, obviating the need for food. Devout Guinness drinkers like to explain that *food is empty calories*—it gets you fat, but doesn't get you drunk. And in the hazy atmosphere of Paddy's, if we squint, we can see their point.

Don't tell the old bedwetter who's heckling the band, but "stout" is of English origin, a strong form of porter. It was first made in London in the 1730s, where breweries sold it from their very own pubs—as Germans still do today. The beer made its way to Ireland in 1759 "when Arthur Guinness bought an abandoned brewery at St. James Gate in Dublin in 1759," according to beer critic Sara Doersam at Sallysplace.com. As Doersam describes its taste,

> [T]he classic Irish-style dry stout includes a malty, caramel flavor up front with a distinctive dry-roasted bitterness in the finish. There should be no perceptible hop or fruity aroma or flavor, but it should display a rich, creamy head and rich character with medium to full body.

Besides being the first to develop the distinctive Irish style of stout using black malt, Guinness established its dominance over other excellent brands such as Murphy's by promoting the beer as a health tonic. Doctors were even then prescribing stout porters for athletes and nursing mothers (and laudanum for infants), and it wasn't hard to make the case that something tasting as hearty and wholesome as stout must somehow, please God, be actually *good* for you.

Long before it became a nice way of saying "fat," the word "stout" used to mean "strong," and Guinness commissioned posters making the most of the association— suggesting that a strong-bodied beer would make the drinker strong. By this logic, pure ethanol drunk straight out of the beaker should render one invincible—and a nice pint of Rubensesque Haagen-Dazs might make of a porky woman a painter. As Michael Jackson discovered, in the 1920s a British advertising agency quizzed Guinness drinkers about why they preferred the brand, and the most popular answer was "It does me good." It does us good, too.

Guinness became and remained the most popular stout in Ireland, despite one well-known fact about the brewery: Unlike competitor Murphy's,

Guinness was owned by Anglo-Irish Protestants. Indeed, in researching the beer we turned up the following posting on a listserv evocatively entitled "Alcohol, Health and Heresy":

> Arthur Guinness was Protestant, God save him! I believe however the Lord will count the great good he did for humanity to make up for his heresy!

The writer went on to explain that

> . . . Irish Catholics in Ireland at one time were suspicious of drinking Guinness because they believed pages of the Protestant bible were purposefully added to the mash in order to force Catholics to ingest it!

This creative piece of paranoia highlights one long-standing difference between Protestants and Catholics—their attitude toward the Bible. It's an old canard that Catholics are suspicious of the Bible and never read it. Of course, there's a slight kernel of truth behind such accusations. Columnist Joseph Sobran admits:

> As a Catholic, I take my hat off to these "Bible Christians." We Catholics keep Bibles on hand in case we really need them, but it must be admitted that we can't hold a candle to these folks. They can quote rings around us, Scripture-wise. What do we know? When they cite a verse like Second Ben-Hur 26:19, we can only take their word for it.

And it's true that Protestants are much more likely than Catholics to have their memories stuffed with "proof-texts" supporting the doctrines in which they believe. Even though the particular teachings of each religious tradition—be it Methodist, Baptist, or Pentecostalist—were hammered out over decades or centuries of debate among authorities of those churches and enforced by internal discipline, the average American Protestant is likely not to know this. Instead, he will treasure an inchoate sense that the tenets of his distinctly Moravian, Anabaptist, or Arminian faith reflect the plain sense of Scripture—as any literate Inuit or Zulu would discover, if only he had a Bible. And so, over centuries, Protestant Bible societies have shipped them out, by the crateload, to seven continents in hundreds of languages.[12] As the *Catholic Encyclopedia* (the old, orthodox, snarky one) pointed out, the results were not always what the well-meaning missionaries had hoped:

> In China, India, and elsewhere, they either altered the Catholic versions or wrote new ones in various dialects before they had acquired real knowledge of the language into which they were translating; these they

---

[12] When those Antarctic bibles written in Penguin didn't really "move," they got put on ice.

scattered broadcast, without explanation. Educated natives declared that in many cases the translations were so bad as to make absolute nonsense and in other cases were even blasphemous. They derived from them nothing but contempt for Christianity. Moreover, the way in which these sacred books were distributed shocked all, especially the Mahommedans, who declared nothing would induce them to give the Koran to anyone unless they were certain it would be treated respectfully. These Bibles were often used as wrappings for drugs and other merchandise, wallpapers, or covers for [bullet] cartridges.

There are good historical reasons why Protestants do not forefront the role of human expertise and church authority in interpreting the often-puzzling lines which fleck the Bible like habañeros in the pudding. In 1517, when founding Protestant Martin Luther rejected the authority of popes and councils, he developed an alternative support for his readings of the Bible: The sincere believer who asked the Spirit for guidance could interpret Scripture unaided by outside authority. God Himself would guide the believer, infallibly, to each verse's real, inspired meaning. This theory held up for exactly eight years—at which point several of the dozens of fractious factions of "Reformed" Christians enthralled by Luther's revolt against Church authority proclaimed that the Holy Spirit had "inspired" them to abolish secular authority as well, and turn Germany into a communist utopia. This they pursued by starting a vicious civil war. The resulting "Peasants' Revolt" tore the country apart, inspiring Luther to urge the princes:

> Whosoever can, should smite, strangle, and stab, secretly or publicly, and should remember that there is nothing more poisonous, pernicious, and devilish than a rebellious man. Just as one must slay a mad dog, so, if you do not fight the rebels, they will fight you, and the whole country with you. ("Against the Murderous and Thievish Bands of Peasants," 1525).

To guide his own religious movement, Luther quickly reasserted the importance of traditional scriptural scholarship, and of the precedents set by Fathers of the Church—especially St. Augustine. The notion of "Protestant orthodoxy" came to dominate German universities, as Reformers like John Calvin began to emulate the Inquisition by persecuting heretics such as Michael Servetus, who was burned alive outside Geneva in 1553. In the U.S., the Southern Baptist Convention seems to be inspired by Calvin's example.

Nevertheless, the notion that the believer may safely look unaided to the Bible for answers to theological questions became deeply rooted in the practice of Protestant believers, especially in denominations we'd today call "evangelical." Instead of catechisms and theology books, the average evangelical Christian seeks answers to religious questions in the "literal" lines of Sacred Scripture, guided in his interpretations solely by the Holy Spirit. He hopes.[13]

Instead of the messages from Fatima or the legend of St. Hubert (see **Jäger-meister**), the American Evangelical looks for guidance on everyday decisions to the example of prophets like Jeremiah, judges like Jepthah, and ass-whooping heroes like Sampson. Unless he knows better, he counts on the Spirit to make sense of inspirational verses such as the following—wrenched out of their Old Testament context to appear on the T-shirts of stoner wiseguy secularists manning used-bike shops across this great country of ours:

- O Daughter of Babylon, doomed to destruction, happy is he who repays you for what you have done to us—he who seizes your infants and dashes them against the rocks. (Psalm 137: 8–9)
- Hath he not sent me to the men which sit on the wall, that they may eat their own dung, and drink their own piss with you? (2 Kings 18:27)

And the ever popular:

- There she lusted after her lovers, whose genitals were like those of donkeys and whose emission was like that of horses. (Ezekiel 23:20)

Real funny, guys—now toddle on back to your Narcotics Anonymous meeting and go cash that fraudulent disability check so you can buy some cigarettes at the co-op.

Educated Protestants do in fact rely on Bible commentaries and the implicit authority of elders in their church—past and present—to make sense of the complex, exquisite tapestry that we call Sacred Scripture. Like Catholics, they regard certain traditional readings, canonized by earthly authority, as normative for faith. They just don't like to admit it. But then Guinness & Co. still won't admit to poisoning our ancestors with pages of Protestant Bibles, so what else should we expect?

CELEBRATE: Take full advantage of the nutritive, health-giving properties of the King James Bible by serving up this delicious chocolate cake, laced with generous quantities of Guinness Stout.

---

[13] To the anti-Catholic fundamentalists who cite Galileo, Torquemada, and Alexander VI, we shoot back: John Brown, Mary Baker Eddy, Tammy Faye Bakker and Jim Jones. That usually sends them back into their minivans.

Guinness Chocolate Cake

The use of a starter adds a bit of lightness and tang to an already intense cake. You absolutely must use the Billington's sugar called for in this recipe. This sugar is so good you will want to eat it with a spoon.

STARTER

1/2 cup warm milk   1/4 teaspoon active dry yeast
1/2 cup cake flour

CAKE

1 cup Guiness Stout   2 eggs, room temperature
10 tablespoons butter   1 vanilla bean, seeds scraped,
16 ounces Billington's Dark Brown   pod saved for another use
   Molasses Sugar   2 cups cake flour
3/4 cup cocoa   2-1/2 teaspoons baking soda
3/4 cup sour cream   1/4 teaspoon fine salt

FROSTING

10 ounces Cream Cheese   1/2 cup cream
1-1/4 cups confectioner's sugar

TO MAKE STARTER:

Pour milk into a small bowl. Add flour and yeast. Mix well. Cover well and let ferment 8-10 hours at room temperature.

TO MAKE CAKE:

Preheat oven to 350 degrees. Butter and line with parchment paper a 9-inch springform baking pan. Butter the parchment paper, then dust with cocoa.

Heat Guinness in saucepan and add butter. Melt butter and add sugar and cocoa. Stir until smooth and remove from heat. Transfer to a mixing bowl.

Meanwhile combine sour cream, eggs, and vanilla. Add to beer mixture.

Add starter and combine thoroughly.

Combine flour, baking soda, and salt and whisk lightly. Add to above mixture in 2 additions, stirring between each addition.

Pour into baking pan and bake 55-60 minutes. A toothpick will just start to come out clean. The batter may cling a bit—this is a moist cake.

Allow to cool on rack in pan.

Remove from pan and place on platter.

TO MAKE ICING:

In stand mixer combine cream cheese and sugar. Beat out all lumps. Lightly whip cream. First add 1/3 of whipped cream and gently combine to lighten frosting. Add remainder of cream and gently combine. Pile on top of cake.

For absolutely best results serve the cake the next day.

Serves 12

Evangelical Exercise—Confuse an Anti-Catholic!

All this talk of biblical authority, the role of the Church in interpreting it, and mugs of foaming stout, brings to mind the perennial experience of Catholics living in such a profoundly Protestant country as ours; a wit once said that in Italy even the Jews are Catholics, while in the U.S., even the Catholics are Puritans. There's more than a little truth to that; no religious group can dwell for centuries as a minority without soaking in quite a bit from its environment. Apart from an inborn individualism that makes us resistant to any authority figure—from the traffic cop we'd like to punch to the pope whose teachings most of us ignore—we have also drunk in with our mother's Prozac the notion that all our religious beliefs must somehow be derived from the pages of the Bible. This principle is central to Protestantism, and dates no farther back than Martin Luther. To the Greek Orthodox and other churches which split from Rome in earlier centuries, such a notion would seem impossible. Because, in fact, it is.

This is something we like to explain when confronted by anti-Catholic fundamentalists. In fact, we've done so more than once—sometimes with large Hurricanes in our hands at the curb outside a Bourbon Street pub. In his grad school days in Baton Rouge, one of the present authors was moved to take on these would-be apostles in a more public forum. Back in the early 1990s, when Jimmy Swaggart Bible College was still a going and growing concern—before its founder's chronic wardrobe malfunction[14] discredited him—seminarians at the school used to take road trips across town to the campus of LSU to "witness to the heathen," by which they principally meant Catholics.

The most memorable of these evangelists were a pair of snow-blonde male identical twins with vaguely Neanderthal brows, matching polyester suits, and Christmas ties. Let's call them the Harpers.[15] These brothers—who had somehow escaped from the pages of Flannery O'Connor's *Wise Blood* to prove by their appearance the theory of evolution—would appear on campus once a week, at the gathering spot by the Student Union called "Free Speech Alley." This spot got its name because anyone who stood up there and tried to make a point would be

---

[14] A falling zipper.
[15] Their real names, of course. Let 'em sue.

shouted down instantly by stoners, jocks, and "bow-head" Tri-Delts—leaving it essentially "free" of "speech."

Except when the Harpers rolled in. Their distant ancestors must have parted company with other proto-humans before our species developed the chromosome for shame, because these brothers would take turns standing atop a cement bench, King James Bible in hand, and spit out brimstone speeches to the jeering crowd. They would shout, and cry, close their eyes and speak in tongues: the whole Swaggart repertoire, which they were learning from the master. Best of all, they'd pause periodically to single out a passing girl in a short skirt, then point at her and shout, "Look at that SLUT! She is drawing every man who sees her into sin, and they will fall into the FIRE with her, lest she REPENTETH." Or if a guy passed by with an unfamiliar haircut, or a Depeche Mode T-shirt, they'd offer him a friendly warning: "SODOMITE!"

Most of the kids in the crowd these preachers addressed had been through Catholic schools where catechesis after Vatican II had collapsed into damp, gray puddles of Kumbaya, so the fundamentalists had a distinct advantage: They knew something about Christianity. Heck, they knew more about distinctly Catholic doctrine than the average graduate of Bishop Sullivan High School—and they came prepared to attack it. So bemused undergrads who vaguely regarded themselves as somehow Italian, Irish, or Cajun (and hence Roman Catholic) were subjected outside the Student Union to elaborate, Bible-based critiques of Catholic tenets with which they themselves were quite unfamiliar. This resulted in inter-religious dialogues such as the following:

> Harper #1: "How much do you Roman Catholics even *know* about your own religion? Did you know that your priests take little pieces of bone from dead so-called saints and rub them and carry them around for special blessings?"
>
> Jock: "What?"
>
> Harper #2: "They call 'em 'relics.' They got knee bones, thigh bones, skulls encased in gold and crusted with shiny jewels. . . ."
>
> Bowhead: "Eeewwww. Gross."
>
> Harper #1: "They take little babies and dribble water on 'em, and that's supposed to make 'em into Christians. They don't even know nothin'—they're just kids!"
>
> Bowhead: "I was godmother to my niece, Evangeline, last week."
>
> Harper #2: "You're helping send that little girl to *Hell*. . . ."
>
> Bowhead: (flouncing away) "Shut UP! You crazy redneck."
>
> Jock: "Yeah, leave her alone."
>
> Harper #1: "And ya'll worship the Virgin Mary—that's just fertility goddess *paganism* ya'll took from the Babylonians. You know who

you Mexicans and Eyetalians are praying to? Not the Mother of Jesus, but the goddess *Semiramis!*"

Stoner: "Dude, we studied that in English class. The Hebrews were totally patriarchal, and goddess worship had to go underground. . . . In Catholicism, that same patriarchal structure forced the common people to express their relationship to the feminine aspect of the Divine. . . ."

Harper #1: "Sodomite!"

Stoner: "Uh, no. . . ."

Jock: "Yeah, sodomite. Heh-heh."

Harper #1: "We challenge any of you Roman Catholics here who claim he's a Christian to debate the Word of God with us—anytime, anyplace."

Harper #2: "Ya'll don't even *read* the Word of God. You let those so-called celibate priests read it for you and tell you what it means. For hundreds of years they wouldn't even let ordinary Christians touch the Bible, much less read it."

Stoner: "Ordinary people couldn't read at all. The striations of the feudal class structure. . . ."

Harper #1 (perking up at the sight of hot girl passing in jogging shorts): "Harlot! WHORE!"

And so on.

Fun as it was, the present author saw here a source of scandal, and decided to do something about it. Together with a friend he accepted the Harpers' challenge. They arranged a debate, sponsored by the college's Religious Studies department, in the university's theater, against the Harpers. The event, well-advertised, drew almost 400 people. Presided over by the erudite chair of the department—a tolerant, slightly weary Episcopalian—it allowed the author and his friend to face off against the twins in a relatively sober environment. In the course of it, the Harpers rattled off every talking point they'd learned from Jack Chick comic books, and the Catholics in response were able to make the following points, which the reader might find useful in dialogues with anti-Catholic evangelists:[16]

- The New Testament itself was created by the Church, not the other way around.
- There were dozens of books floating around, claiming to be "gospels," full of every kind of crackpot anecdote about Christ—including a few which portrayed Him as a wicked prankster Who performed malicious

---

[16] If you ever have the chance to debate species-atavistic identical twin fundamentalists, we recommend arming yourself beforehand with one of the many excellent books explaining the Church's relation to the Bible, such as the eloquent Pat Madrid's *Where Is That In the Bible?* (Huntington, IN: Our Sunday Visitor Press,1999).

miracles. Each time another of these third-century fantasy novels pops up, such as the "gospel" of Judas, it makes the cover of *Time*.

- It took over 300 years of debate among the Fathers of the Church to decide which books were authentically inspired.
- The bishops who discerned which books were really the Word of God were all in union with the bishop of Rome.
- These bishops baptized infants, venerated relics, prayed for the dead, gave absolution for sins, filled their churches with religious art, used incense at Mass and believed in the Eucharistic presence of Christ. Their churches venerated Mary as a Virgin. Most of their liturgies referred to her as "immaculate," spoke of her assumption into Heaven, and implored her intercession. These beliefs are older and more apostolic then the canon of the New Testament itself.
- These bishops based their decisions on which books were inspired largely on which ones had been used at the Catholic liturgy in major cathedrals around the world—and on which ones accorded with the oral Tradition of interpreting Christian doctrine handed down from the apostles.
- In other words, the infallible word of God was compiled, edited, and fixed in its current form by a bunch of heathen, papist idolaters.
- And you still believe in this book?

The debate went rather well. The Harpers never came back to campus again, leaving LSU safe for "idolaters," "harlots," and "sodomites" alike. The Catholics who'd come to the debate formed a campus club devoted to spreading solid information about the Church, and the students went right back to drinking Dixie and singing Kumbaya.

Tej: Faith and Fermented Honey

If you live in a major city which happens to be blessed by immigrants from Ethiopia, you may already have been exposed to a little of that country's fascinating culture and cuisine. One of the African nations with the oldest continuous literate culture, it is also one of the two countries that first embraced Christianity; Ethiopia competes with Armenia for the title of oldest and the longest-persecuted Christian church. Like Armenia, Ethiopia was largely converted to Christianity in the fourth century, and spent most of its history surrounded by hostile, non-Christian neighbors. Keeping the faith in each of these countries was a slow and painful battle, generating dozens of saints and martyrs whose names have come down us—but which, sadly, we cannot pronounce:

Krikor Loosavorich *(Armenia)*
Ewostatewos *(Ethiopia)*
Vartanantz *(Armenia)*
Gabra Manfas Queddus *(Ethiopia)*
Mesrop Mashtots *(Armenia)*
Takla Haymanot of Shoa *(Ethiopia)*
Vartan Mamikonian *(Armenia)*

Try to read off a litany of these saints really quickly, especially after a few glasses of the Ethiopian honey wine tej, and you'll appreciate one of the difficulties Christians in these countries endured. Oh yes—and both nations were surrounded by aggressive, Islamic neighbors. That never helps.

Tej is a form of fermented honey drink similar to English mead (**see Reformation**), flavored with ground up leaves of the *gesho* plant. In its native land, tej is served at bars called *tej abet.* It's spicier and often drier than mead, but sweet enough to serve as a counterbalance to the hot cuisine that Ethiopians enjoy. If you've never eaten with Ethiopians, you'll benefit from this little dining tip: Wash your hands before eating, because they're what you'll be using. Like Europeans before Marco Polo, the Ethiopians eat with their fingers—and their mothers don't rebuke them, because it's the custom. All food is served as dollops of meat or vegetables doused with piquant sauces, arranged on large, flat pieces of spongy bread called *injera,* made from an African grain called *teff.* You grab a piece of the bread, wrap it around some of the entrée, and pop it in your mouth. Then, since it's quite spicy enough to burn an American palate, you douse your mouth with a sip of refreshing tej. Repeat the process, trying a variety of dishes such as *doro wat* (chicken stew with hard boiled eggs), *sega wat* (diced lamb), or our favorite Ethiopian dish, *kitfo* (raw steak, ground with cayenne pepper, served with farmer's cheese—see recipe). As you might guess, in the case of kitfo, freshness is important; best not to use old, scavenged carcasses of cattle you found by the side of the road in preparing this one. Save that for a good, old-fashioned American shepherd's pie.

We're told that in Ethiopian homes, a hostess traditionally balls up the food for each of her guests and pops it in his mouth. Since we've never traveled to that ancient, war-ravaged country, we haven't experienced this ourselves, but we imagine it has important implications for etiquette, and might prove handy when entertaining contentious guests. How many of us have wished, while serving dinner to various crank friends we've collected like lint balls over the years, that we could interrupt someone's monologue about the Middle East, Vatican II, or the "corpses of aliens frozen in the cellars of the Vatican" (a favorite of our old acquaintance Malachi Martin[1]) by stuffing their thundering pie hole with a bread roll. Well, in Ethiopia, *you can!* So perhaps the next time you find yourself faced with hosting cantankerous cousins, or conspiracy theorists from your charismatic choir, you should announce: "Tonight, we're eating Ethiopian style." Confiscate the silverware, and hover around the table with the platter, feeding guests whenever they need to be silenced. This may make you feel like a mama bird facing a nest full of chirping chicks with gaping mouths, but resist the atavistic temptation to chew the

---

[1] We'll never forget the lunch at Manhattan's Mon Petit Café, at which Martin whispered to one of us the "secret" that because of defects in the post-conciliar rite, no priests had been successfully ordained in the West since 1971. He said it with a wistful gleam in his eye. . . .

food first and regurgitate it into their mouths. In Ethiopia at least, this simply *isn't done*.

Ethiopia stands out from other African countries in that it alone was never colonized by Europeans. Because the place was already Christian, they lacked the requisite fig leaf to justify an invasion to bring the Gospel to the natives—who already had it, albeit one written in the (now-dead) liturgical language of Ghe'ez. The country has links to the Bible which long predate the arrival of the Ten Commandments in Europe; its native histories claim that the Queen of Sheba came from Ethiopia, and that from Jerusalem she sent one of her sons sired by King Solomon back to the homeland to serve as their king, and convert the nation to Judaism. Likewise, the locals assert that after the Babylonians sacked Jerusalem (**see Jeremiah Weed**), the Jewish high priests smuggled the Ark of the Covenant to Ethiopia, where it still resides in the monastery of the Church of St. Mary Zion in Axum. We can't judge the truth of this, since only a small number of monks are allowed into the shrine to see the Ark—though the modern Israelis clearly don't believe it, or else they'd be trying to get it back. (Israel did, however, make heroic efforts in the 1970s and '80s to rescue the Ethiopians who still practice Judaism—the Falasha—from the tyranny and famine imposed by the country's then-Communist regime.)

Even after their conversion to Christianity, the Ethiopians carried on a number of distinctively Old Testament customs, rejecting various foods as "impure" and celebrating the Sabbath on Saturday, instead of Sunday. Ethiopian religious art—which we mainly know from the walls of restaurants in the Adams Morgan neighborhood of D.C.—features far more references to Solomon and the Queen of Sheba than to Christ or the Virgin Mary. The Coptic Orthodox Church, to which most Christians in that country belong, stands at odds with Catholic doctrine on one important point of doctrine: it accepts the ancient heresy of the Monophysites. Unlike most heresies, this one is not named for its founder. There was no deacon named Monophysos running around the Mediterranean sowing confusion; this heresy's name comes from its claim, namely, that Jesus did not possess both a divine and human nature, but had only one (*mono*) nature (*physis*)—which was somehow both divine and human at once, without confusing the two. Are you confused yet?

So are we. Since this is primarily a bar guide and not a monograph on Christology, we won't presume to attempt explaining the convoluted, fourth- and fifth-century arguments among dozens of theologians who tried to square the circle and account for Jesus' Incarnation. We leave this one to the experts. And we can't blame the poor Ethiopians for getting it wrong—particularly since they spent 1,000 years surrounded by hostile Islamic countries, isolated from the rest of the Christian world, beginning with the Moslem conquest of Egypt, until the arrival of Portuguese traders in 1508.

And we can't deny a certain fondness for one of the founding Monophysite fathers, Severus, Patriarch of Antioch (+538). Born at Sozopolis in Pisidia (love them names!) he followed the local custom of delaying baptism until he could grow a beard. (This patriarchal tradition was hard on the female Christians, as one might imagine.) Severus became famous as a teenager for smashing idols and chasing out wizards. Then once his beard came in, he was duly baptized—and, according to the *Catholic Encyclopedia*, vowed never to bathe again. So that new beard must have had quite a pretty smell—a combination of man-sweat, old hummus, and garlic— by the time Severus was elected Patriarch of Antioch in 512. On entering his palace, the compulsively filthy bishop ordered its baths torn out and fired all the cooks. He wrote extensively and eloquently against the orthodox doctrine of the Incarnation, and for his efforts was deposed within six years. For some 20 years Severus continued to write, and reek, as the *Encyclopedia* reports:

> He died, 8 February, 538, refusing to take a bath even to save his life, though he was persuaded to allow himself to be bathed with his clothes on. Wonders are said to have followed his death, and miracles to have been worked by his relics.

For instance, we're willing to bet that the scent of his discarded clothes would keep Antioch free of hyenas.

But apart from these differences about the natures of Christ, the Ethiopians kept up most of the doctrines and practices familiar to Catholics and Orthodox, albeit in

exotic, ancient forms: seven Sacraments, reverence for Mary, prayers for the dead, and a long, arcane liturgy conducted in a dead language that includes the use of drums. (Though parishioners might be forgiven for going out to smoke during one of the deacon's interminable drum solos.)

Perhaps the most interesting aspect of the Ethiopian religious tradition to modern Americans is the outrageous form it took in Jamaica, where followers of the Rastafarian faith revere the last emperor of Ethiopia, Haile Selassie, as a messianic figure. In fact, the Rastafarians believe that he was the reincarnation of Christ—reborn to lead all the Chosen People (Africans) back to the Promised Land (Ethiopia), once they have smoked enough *ganja* (pot) to attain *irie* (beatitude). Have you got all that?[2]

That's a rough summary of the creed professed by the brilliant musician Bob Marley for most of his life,[3] and propounded to the Southern white frat boys of the

---

[2] Dude, it made so much more sense last night, around the bong. . . .

[3] He left Rastafarianism for the Coptic Orthodox Church before his death, taking the name Berhane Selassie.

world in his reggae albums. For instance, the song "Exodus" imagines a worldwide reverse- migration of the African Diaspora:

> We know where we're going, uh!
> We know where we're from.
> We're leaving Babylon,
> We're going to our Fatherland.

Thinking about how segregated most frats still are, you can see why they love the song.

Haile Selassie was at best ambivalent about the notion that he was the universal messiah of black people around the world. Himself an Orthodox Christian, he made no claims to divinity, and had enough problems on his hands with poverty, Communist rebels, periodic famines, and the after-effects of Mussolini's brutal invasion of his country (1935–36), during which the Fascist troops used airplanes and poison gas against his soldiers (some armed with spears), and took the skulls of slain Ethiopians back to Rome as trophies. (That showed those African "savages" didn't it?) When Selassie made a state visit to Jamaica in 1966, his plane was promptly surrounded by some 200,000 dredlocked Rastafarians, smoking spliffs and bowing deeply to worship him. Selassie, quite sensibly, refused to get off the plane.

When local believers finally managed to coax the frightened emperor onto the tarmac, he was greeted by Bob Marley's wife Rita—who promptly told the world that she had seen on his palms the stigmata, the nail wounds of Christ. Selassie never returned.

CELEBRATE: Because of ongoing political problems in that country, it's almost impossible to buy tej directly from Ethiopia—though we hope this will change soon, since that impoverished land would benefit from more international trade. But fine American versions are widely available, for instance Saba Tej from New Jersey's company of that name. We suggest serving it up to your bemused guests as they stare suspiciously at a plate of kitfo. This dish of heavily spiced raw beef on a plate of spongy bread is especially appropriate for a bachelor entertaining a lady guest at home for the first time. There's nothing quite like the look on a woman's face the first time you ball up raw meat in injera and pop it in her mouth. It makes for an evening she will *never* forget. Or repeat.

Kitfo

Berbere is a hot pepper seasoning essential to most Ethiopian dishes, available at African and Middle Eastern stores.

SEASONED BUTTER:

1/4 cup clarified butter	4 crushed cardamom pods
2 tablespoons onion, finely chopped	1 stick cinnamon
4 garlic cloves	2 cloves
1 1-inch piece fresh ginger, minced	1/4 teaspoon freshly grated nutmeg
1/4 teaspoon turmeric	

BEEF:

2 pounds filet mignon	1/4 teaspoon ground cardamom
1/4 cup grated onion	1/4 teaspoon cayenne pepper
1/2 teaspoon fresh ginger, finely chopped	1 teaspoon berbere

Make seasoned butter by combining all ingredients in small saucepan and simmering very low for 30 minutes. Strain through cheesecloth and set aside.

Finely chop beef. Add seasoned butter to pan and warm, add onion and cook until dissolved. Add remaining spices. Add filet and cook on low, stirring constantly just until raw color is gone – about five minutes.

Serve with injera (Ethiopian bread), farmers' cheese, and sautéed collard greens.

Serves 4

....

The Templars: the Secrets, the Scandal, the Dessert Wine

In the history of the Church, no group has given rise to as many fantasies as the Knights Templar.[4] Dozens of books claim to "unveil" the "mysteries" uncovered by these esoteric warrior monks—"secrets" the Church has tried to cover up ever since. Goofball titles include *The Templar Revelation: Secret Guardians of the True Identity of Christ, Holy Blood, Holy Grail*, and of course *The Da Vinci Code*, by former joke-book author Dan Brown.[5] According to Brown, the Templars' long jaunt in the Middle East exposed this French-founded order to the "inside story" concerning Jesus and Mary Magdalene; namely, that he was *not* the Son of God, but that she *was* some sort of goddess—an emblem of the "sacred feminine,"

---

[4] Unless you count informal groups such as "Catholic school girls."

[5] One of Dan Brown's old friends revealed to us over lunch Brown's main source for *The Da Vinci Code:* literary agent Albert Zuckerman's paint-by-number guide, *Writing the Blockbuster Novel*. If this book contains secrets that the Vatican has been trying to cover up, we couldn't find them. It's not even on the Index of Forbidden Books (we checked).

whatever that is.[6] Armed with this knowledge, the Templars returned to France, where they passed the secret on by encoding it in the architecture of Gothic cathedrals. For instance, they built round churches instead of cross-shaped ones, and included a "long hollow nave as a secret tribute to a woman's womb . . . complete with receding labial ridges and a nice little cinquefoil clitoris above the doorway." In her highly entertaining book *The Da Vinci Hoax* (Ignatius Press, 2004), medieval historian Sandra Miesel scours Brown's novel and his source texts for any trace of documentation or proof, and comes

up empty-handed. Whatever assertions Brown did not pilfer from nineteenth-century hoaxes and discredited urban legends, he seems to have pulled from . . . a very different bodily orifice. For one thing, as Miesel points out:

> The Templars had nothing to do with the cathedrals of their time, which were commissioned by bishops and their canons throughout Europe. They were unlettered men with no arcane knowledge of "sacred geometry" passed down from the pyramid builders. They did not wield tools themselves on their own projects, nor did they found masons' guilds to build for others. Not all their churches were round, nor was roundness a defiant insult to the Church. Rather than being a tribute to the divine feminine, their round churches honored the Church of the Holy Sepulchre.

It's not clear why anyone would suspect the Templars of uncovering secret knowledge; they weren't exactly trained as archaeologists, or even theologians. Few of them even knew Latin. Because their job consisted of manning forts and killing Moslems, the order didn't bother much with education, beyond the catechism and swordplay.

---

[6] Modern-day Wiccans, whose creed was dreamed up by nineteenth-century British dilettantes, claim that goddess-worship leads to pacifist, egalitarian, and eco-friendly societies. Tell that to the victims of human sacrifice killed in the name of Kali in India or Artemis in Greece—not to mention the thousands of infants slaughtered in Carthage to sate the goddess Tanit. If such "goddesses" were real at all, they were doubtless demons taking on female form. To our mind, the only goddess figure with any plausibility in the Western tradition is actress (and fellow Yalie) Jennifer Connelly.

Founded in 1118 as a brotherhood to protect Christian pilgrims, the Templars had morphed into an order devoted to fighting in the Crusades. Sponsored by St. Bernard of Clairvaux, they combined military skill and monastic vows, developing a theology of warfare which eerily mirrored Islamic *jihad*. Growing quickly in numbers and wealth, the Templars also became the bankers of Europe—loaning and storing treasure for most of the continent's kings. Like guilds of masons and other craftsmen, the Templars adopted elaborate initiation rituals, which members swore to keep secret. This sort of hazing must have been a great deal of fun for the upperclassmen—oops, we mean "master Templars"—but it sowed suspicion about what kind of secrets the Templars were keeping. As with the secretive Yalie society Skull and Bones, rumors spread far and wide about what *really went on* behind closed doors among all those cloistered men, and what exactly they had to hide.

Enter King Philip IV of France. This grandson of a saint (Louis IX) was something of a very different sort. In a few short years on the throne, Philip had bankrupted his kingdom in useless wars, stolen half the Church's income, despoiled and expelled his country's Jews, been excommunicated, kidnapped a pope (Boniface VIII) then held him hostage until he died, then subjected that dead pope to a rigged trial for sodomy. He would later cage the papacy itself at Avignon (**see Chateauneuf du Pape**), where it rotted for almost 70 years. We hate to sound harsh, but there's really no other word for Philip than "modern."

In 1307, as King Philip still schemed to have the dead Pope Boniface VIII condemned for heresy, he learned of dark rumors about the Templars from disgruntled former knights. Now, Templar secrecy may have had its uses when it came to combat morale, or it may have amounted to little more than the predilection boys have for keeping elaborate, silly secrets. But Philip claimed it covered something *really* dark and terrible: that during their long service in the Middle East, the Templars had gone native. They had secretly abandoned Christ, adopted worship of a local pagan idol named Baphomet, and lapsed into widespread sodomy. Acting without warning, Philip ordered every Templar in France arrested immediately, and their wealth impounded.

Most onlookers were skeptical. Pope Clement V, the French pope who moved the Vatican to Avignon, observed that the charges Philip brought against the Templars were eerily similar to . . . the charges Philip had brought against the previous Pope Boniface. What is more, all his evidence came from confessions of guilt by Templars who'd been hideously tortured, sometimes for months before breaking. Historians still debate how much merit there was in the accusations against the Templars. It's probable that some of the abuses reported did occur, in one Templar outpost or other. But the notion that the entire order had transformed itself into a secret, homosexual pagan conspiracy seems about as likely as . . . most of the assertions in *The Da Vinci Code*.

But Philip was the most powerful man in Europe. He'd already brought the

papacy to its knees, and the wealthy Templars had few allies willing to defend them. The pope tried repeatedly to spare the Templars from torture and unjust trials, but after five years of relentless pressure from Philip he agreed to disband the order—transferring its lands, much of its wealth, and the knights who weren't already in Philip's prisons, to the rival Knights of St. John. Philip burned the other Templars at the stake—some 114 in all—for "heresy." Which is what he might have done to Pope Boniface VIII, if he'd gotten the chance.

Given the secrecy once surrounding the Templars, the lurid nature of the rumors that brought them down, and the sadistic frenzy with which they were persecuted, it's probably not surprising that their story still fascinates us today.

Eccentrics of left and right have adopted the Templars as their heroes. For instance in France, bands of dotty, impoverished noblemen or antiquarian geeks have formed esoteric clubs, dressed up in medieval garb, and claimed that they were the "authentic" heirs of the Templars. (One such group included the filmmaker Jean Cocteau.) Satanic pansexual occultist Aleister Crowley (1875–1947) once led a group calling itself the Order of the Oriental Templars, which to this day performs orgiastic black masses, all in the name of the poor, burned Knights. Old Templar churches today draw hordes of American tourists with digital cameras and highlighted copies of *The Da Vinci Code*, in search of spiritual endarkenment.

But sometimes the joke turns sour. Around the year 1900, an Austrian Cistercian defrocked for "perversion" named Lanz "von" Liebenfels[7] founded "The Order of New Templars" devoted to Aryan supremacy. They camped out in a ruined castle, played with swords, and beginning in 1905 published a virulent racist, anti-Semitic journal sporting a swastika called *Ostara*—it was the favorite magazine of another demented young Austrian—16-year-old Adolf Hitler. And the rest is history.

Conspiracy-minded writers have for centuries peddled one theory or another about what "really" happened in 1307. The rather infamous Nesta Webster—whose ideas far-right Catholic cranks[8] still smoke like crack—asserted in *Secret Societies and Subversive Movements* that the Templars were *guilty, guilty, guilty*. In fact, she wrote, the Templars had absorbed esoteric revolutionary ideas from the sect of the Assassins and the Jewish Talmud, which they passed on (via the Rosicrucians and Freemasons, of course) to the architects of the French Revolution, Bolshevism, International Finance Capitalism, and the Shriners. Thus the Templars lay at the origin of most modern evils, and burning was far too good for them. If you find this theory attractive, you'll love Mrs. Webster's self-help book, *The Need for Fascism in Great Britain* (1926). Download the audio version for your iPod, and listen to it the next time you "forget" to take your meds.

Of course, for Dan Brown, the Templars' secret theology is a force for liberation. It exposes the tyranny of a 1,000-year conspiracy masquerading as a religion, led by a small minority of wealthy, highly educated men wearing robes and beards to dominate the world. This theory in no way mirrors historic anti-Semitism. Nope, not at all.

Of course, what interests us in the Knights Templar is not their role in losing the Crusades, preserving the secret identity of Mary Magdalene, or selling books for Random House. The most enduring legacy of the Templars lies in the vineyards they planted and operated all over France and throughout the Mediterranean. So fond were the Templars of wine that Frenchmen who downed too many cognacs were often accused of getting "drunk as a Templar."

Wines from their old estates include Château Templier, Commanderie de Peyrassol, Price Clos des Templiers, and Château les Templiers—among many others. Our favorite Templar vintage is Commanderia de la Bargemone Rose, a light and fruity pink wine which serves well in summer. It's made in a vineyard whose main building is a 1,000-year-old former Templar command. Dessert wines are still produced in Cyprus in former Templar vineyards. The wine-style Commandaria is named for the Knights' headquarters on that island. Made from grapes that have dried into raisins, Commandaria is heavy, rich, and sweet enough to compete with

---

[7] His real name was Adolf Josef Lanz; as Hitler's real name was Schickelgruber. The two men met at the editorial offices of *Ostara* in Vienna after Hitler became inflamed with Lanz's ideology. Must have been quite a conversation. Read more at *www.intelinet.org/swastika/swasti14.htm*.

[8] We used to have brunch with these people after Latin Mass, but they really are bad for the digestion.

your baklava. Perhaps the real secret of the Templars is how they could fight after drinking this stuff. . . .

CELEBRATE: Honor the courage of the Templars who fought to save the Holy Land, and who stood up for their innocence under torture, by serving up this tasty Greek cake made with the dessert wine they developed, Commandaria. Light your oven with a shoplifted copy of *Secret Societies and Subversive Movements*, or *The Da Vinci Code*.

Commanderia Cake

The sesame oil used in the cake is not the dark toasted oil used as a flavoring agent in Chinese cuisine. Unprocessed sesame oil is a fragrant cooking oil with a pronounced sesame flavor. It adds depth to this cake and lends a wonderful flavor in sautéing.

CAKE:

2 cups ground almonds	1 cup sugar
2 cups semolina	1/4 cup sesame oil
1 teaspoon cinnamon	1/4 cup grapeseed oil
1/4 teaspoon salt	Zest of 1 orange
6 large eggs, separated	1/2 cup fresh squeezed orange juice

SYRUP:

1-1/2 cups Commanderia wine	1/2 cup water
1/2 cup sugar	2 tablespoons almond liqueur

Preheat oven to 350 degrees.

Combine almonds, semolina, cinnamon, and salt. Set aside.

Beat yolks and 1/2 cup sugar until thick, and ribbons form when dropped from beater. Add oil and zest. Add 1/2 of the dry ingredients then 1/2 of the juice; combine; then add remaining juice and dry ingredients.

In clean dry bowl, beat whites with whisk attachment. Add a pinch of salt. Beat until soft peaks form and whites just begin to pull away from sides of bowl. Rain in remaining sugar and beat until dissolved.

Fold 1/3 of the whites into the cake batter, then gently fold in remaining whites.

Turn into a greased 9x13x2-inch pan. Bake 45 minutes or until a toothpick inserted comes out clean.

Meanwhile prepare syrup. Combine all the ingredients and simmer 3 minutes. Pour syrup over cake and allow to cool. Cut into diamond shapes.

Best if allowed to sit overnight before cutting.

Makes about 24 diamonds

Tequila—and Blood—on the Altars

For almost 500 years, the national drink of Mexico has been tequila, the premium version of the traditional liquor mezcal.[9] Both tequila and mezcal are made by fermenting the juice of the agave plant, sometimes stretched with corn or sugar cane liquor. The best tequila is made without these mixers, and labeled 100 percent agave. Because these drinks draw on native ingredients used to make beverages long before the arrival of Cortes and his friendly conquistadors, they're a vivid reminder of Mexico's Aztec past. To some of the Spaniards who arrived, these Aztecs appeared as barbarians, especially because of their bloody-minded religion, but in hindsight we can see that the Aztecs displayed many of the features of an advanced, modern civilization:

- A small, ruling class of intellectuals dominating society
- Rigid laws and bureaucratic schemes directing the economy to benefit the men on top
- An abstruse ideology used to justify the mass killing of innocents
- Harsh regulations concerning the use of alcohol[10]

It all sounds so positively *twentieth century*. One has to wonder if modern dictators took a page from the Aztecs in designing their modern "utopias."

---

[9] Yes, that is the liquor with the worm in the bottle. To *yanquis* like us, this is a mark of authenticity. To the Mexicans who make the stuff these *gusano rojo* larvae are a sign that their agave plants are infested, and it's time to apply insecticide—or at least collect the worms and sell them to one of the many restaurants that serve them as a delicacy. These worms may or may not change the flavor of the mezcal, but they certainly do appeal to male undergrads who like to "eat the worm" to impress their pals or gross out their dates. The Mexicans throw them in as a sales gimmick, and we Americans eat them up. A few mezcals are sold with a poisonous scorpion in the bottle, but these are marketed primarily to idiots.

[10] Only the powerful and well-connected were permitted to drink the fermented juice of the sacred agave plant.

But in one area the Aztecs were well behind: they had not yet discovered distillation (**see Vodka**), the method for making the hard stuff. The only alcohol consumed in Aztec Mexico was *pulque*, a weak beer made from the agave plant—discovered, legend tells, around 200 A.D., when a bolt of lightning sent by the goddess Mayahuel split a plant in half and gave peasants the idea to ferment its sap. The nurturing Mayahuel boasted 400 breasts, each yielding not milk but *pulque*—which made her understandably popular. Most other Aztec deities demanded human sacrifice, without which, the rulers and priests insisted, the gods would die and the universe would implode. The flesh from these sacrifices, which bloodied the great ziggurats of Mexico for hundreds of years, was the main source of protein for the ruling class—another modern touch.

According to tequila historian Ian Chadwick,[11] the first mezcal and tequila were probably produced in the 1520s by conquistadors or the friars who followed them, using techniques carried over from Europe. The first reference we have to them is found in a letter from the Franciscan priest Torbio de Benavente mentioning a drink he called "mexcalli." Within a few years, Chadwick reports, the Iberians were making an industry out of it:

> Don Pedro Sanches de Tagle, Marquis of Altamira, the "father of tequila," established the very first tequila factory in his Hacienda Cuisillos, in 1600, cultivating the local agave for distillation. . . . In 1608, the governor of New Galicia imposed the first taxes on mezcal wine. By 1621, "wines of mezcal" were being regularly supplied to nearby Guadalajara and the first references to an "abundant" mezcal harvest appeared in local records.

The newly developing industry quickly fell into the hands of local elites, descended from Spain—as did most of the land, apart from those held by the Church for the Indians to farm. The next centuries saw a constant struggle between the white aristocrats and the clergy over the rights and claims of the native population, with the Church generally championing the Indians, and almost always losing. As "enlightened" ideas filtered into the Spanish colonies, they became weapons in the hands of the wealthy who wished to dispossess the priests and Indians alike (**see Kahlua**). Even as the white landowners shook off their ancestral faith in favor of the French-inspired atheism promoted in Masonic lodges throughout Mexico, the mostly Indian masses clung to the Church fervently—despite the best efforts of the educated classes to wipe out "superstition" in the name of "modernity" and "progress."

This conflict between a dominant, secular elite which has captured control of the State, and a deeply religious majority was mirrored across the world—from the

---

[11] See his fascinating online series "Tequila: In Search of the Blue Agave" at *www.ianchadwick.com*.

Bolshevik regime in Russia, which murdered tens of thousands of priests and transformed historic churches into "museums of atheism," to the Third Republic in France, which expelled the clergy, seized Catholic schools, and forbade women to vote until 1944, out of fear that pious ladies would turn the anti-clericals out of power. Liberal historians like to justify such measures as necessary steps to strip the clergy of their accumulated influence in these societies—using arguments that mirror those of anti-Semites over the centuries, who have defended pogroms against Jews by pointing to their intellectual prominence and allegedly disproportionate power. As we've pointed out elsewhere (**see Göttweig**) the Nazi euphemism for stealing property from Jews, "aryanization," is an adaptation of the "Enlightened" code word for theft committed against unarmed monks and nuns, "secularization."

Catholic Cristero rebels, who fought from 1926–1929.

In Mexico, this tension between a pagan State and a Catholic people took the form of a civil war—which began, we hasten to point out, over mezcal. In 1924, one of the most viciously anti-Catholic politicians in Mexico, Plutarco Elías Calles, came to power. He began to enforce the more draconian articles of Mexico's militantly secular 1917 Constitution—which outlawed Catholic schools, monastic orders, and religious garb, confiscated Church property, and denied the clergy the right to vote or even speak about politics. Eager to cut his bishops off from Vatican support, Calles appointed an excommunicated priest as "patriarch" of a "patriotic" church, which abandoned wine at Mass in favor of the local drink mezcal—thereby invalidating its liturgies. The Church responded with peaceful resistance, a suspension of all religious services in the country, and a boycott of most industries. None of this worked, and the government only tightened its grip, ordering all priests to marry on penalty of imprisonment.

After two years of persecution, Mexican Catholics began an uprising on August 3, 1926—barricading themselves in the Church of Our Lady of Guadalupe in Guadalajara, Jalisco for a shootout with federal troops. The "Cristero" rebellion rapidly spread, as pious peasants and disaffected soldiers—in a few cases led by priests who (tsk, tsk!) carried rifles—managed to keep up the fight against the government's well-armed military for three years. The war made headlines all over the world, with atrocities on both sides. Pious women took up arms, forming the Joan of Arc brigade to fight, smuggle weapons, and care for the wounded. The government avenged itself on Mexico's Catholics by arresting and executing dozens of priests and laymen unconnected with the rebellion, including the Blessed Miguel Pro, S.J.—who was stood before a firing squad on November 23, 1927 and shot without trial. His last action was to stretch out his arms like the crucified Christ, and his last words were *"Vivo Cristo Rey!"*

Evelyn Waugh's classic travel book, *Robbery Under Law*, and Graham Greene's novel, *The Power and the Glory,* each chronicle this conflict, which claimed 90,000 lives and ended with an unhappy compromise between Church and State: The anticlerical laws stayed on the books, and the stolen Church property stayed in government hands, but the Church would be granted limited freedom to minister to her flock as long as bishops stayed out of politics. That didn't stop laymen, though, and the remnants of the Cristero movement would later give birth to the Party of National Action (PAN) which in 2000 finally displaced the corrupt, autocratic Party of Institutionalized Revolution (PRI), and repealed the harshest of the anti-religious laws. The Church thrived in Mexico despite its official status as a pariah institution—and perhaps because of it.

Indeed, the story of the Church in Mexico illustrates the paradox of Christian faith in an often hostile world. That country's political elite spent the better part of the past 150 years attempting to extirpate the Church—and instead, only confirmed the mass of people in their Faith. In equally Catholic Ireland, by contrast, since independence in 1926 (**see Drinking Song #8**), the Church has snuggled close to the State, gaining privileges and extra-legal protections—with the outcome that the common man has begun to drift away from the Sacraments. If our Lord described faith as a mustard seed, it appears that in practice it more resembles other plants. When coddled by the authorities, it tends to fester like a lily cosseted in some dowager's greenhouse. When faced with persecution, however, it's impossible to kill—like the kudzu swallowing schoolhouses in Georgia. Church Father Tertullian once wrote that "the blood of the martyrs is the seed of the Church." That said, we're just as glad we're not the ones watering the garden.

In 2000, Pope John Paul II canonized some 25 martyrs of the Cristero rebellion—including several laymen who took up arms in self-defense. And this makes us really, really happy. Sure, it's edifying to read tales of innocent virgins who fed the lions in the Colosseum rather than marry some senator.[12] But there's something bracing about the stories of martyrs who went down fighting. It helps banish any taint of Gandhi-style pacifism—an attitude that has nothing to do with Christianity,

---

[12] The legends of early Christian martyrs are often encrusted with extraneous details and pious accretions which detract from their religious significance. So if you care to meditate on the courage of St. Agnes or St. Lucy, we suggest you bring the story up to date. Imagine that the saint was a young girl from Boston's Southie, directed by Act of Congress to marry Senator Ted Kennedy—and the girl gladly chose death instead, and was fed to the pandas at the National Zoo, to cheering crowds, presided over by the president. We hope this proves more useful grist for prayer and reflection.

which is in fact a heresy, exuded by a contempt for the created world. This sort of other-worldliness makes us queasy. As we see it, each of us will be in the Other World all too soon; no sense in rushing the process. While it's true that this life is a waiting room for the next, that doesn't mean we're justified in letting people wreck the place. Hotel rooms are temporary, too: Is it okay for Christians to trash them? Not unless you're in a British hair-metal band. . . .

CELEBRATE: We won't take this opportunity to offer a Mexican recipe, and we think everyone pretty much knows how to use tequila (or better, a smoky mezcal) to make a margarita. And we regret our last book's activity suggestion for May 25 (the feast of the Mexican martyrs), which entailed thanking the Masonic lodges that led that persecution by dumping trash on the steps of your local Masonic temple. That was bad advice. Please don't do it. To find a Masonic temple near you where you should *not* pile the steps with the trash from a festive Mexican meal each year on May 25, see *www.freemason.org*.

Instead of avenging yourself on some harmless, English-speaking Masons (who aren't even on speaking terms with the anti-clerical Grand Orient Lodge which dominates France and Mexico), why not learn the words to a classic song of the Cristeros, most recently recorded by the raunchy ranchero singer Vicente Fernandez, "*El martes me fusilan*," here translated by Daniel Muller, and reprinted with his kind permission. We'd hoped to provide the sheet music, too, but record-keeping in Mexico is not quite up to *norteño* standards, and it proved impossible to track down.

El Martes Me Fusilan

They will shoot me on Tuesday
at six o'clock in the morning
For believing in the eternal God
and in the great Guadalupaña [Virgin of Guadalupe].

They found a holy card
of Jesus in my hat;
That is why they sentenced me:
because I am a Cristero.

That is why they will shoot me
on Tuesday in the morning;
They will kill my useless body
but never, never my soul.

I tell my executioners
that I want them to crucify me;
And, once crucified,
that then they use their rifles.

Farewell, highlands of Jalisco,
Michoacan, and Guanajuato,
Where I fought the government
which always fled running.

They caught me on my knees
adoring Jesus Christ;
They knew that there was no defense
in that sacred place.

I am a peasant by inheritance
Jaliscan from birth;
I have no other god but Christ
because He gave me my existence.

Killing me will never end
belief in the eternal God;
Many remain in the strife
and others are yet to be born.

That is why they will shoot me
on Tuesday in the morning.
Vivo Cristo Rey!

....

Temperance: When Less is More

If you've read this far, you realize that we're no party-poopers. You know—the kind of people who when they walk into a cocktail event, everybody cleans up his language, stands up straight, or checks her bra-straps. Your address book surely contains a few folks like this—whom you dismiss as prissily pious or dourly devout. But chances are, when you really need prayers, you fish out these people's numbers—figuring that they're probably "really close to God," or else "Not doing anything else on a Saturday night." Either way, you want them to join you in hammering on God's door until it opens.

Neither of us fits this description. When people come to us with requests, it's usually not so much for prayers as "ten extra guests for our Mardi Gras party" or ideas for borderline-illegal practical jokes.

Nevertheless, even we recognize that when it comes to alcoholic beverages, sometimes *less is more*. Any readers of Celtic or Slavic heritage (or God forbid, both) will recognize that moment in a night on the town when you know you've

had quite enough—that one more capari-hna will push you "over the edge." Do not dismiss this momentary epiphany. It is what theologians call an "actual" grace, to be resisted at your own risk. Instead, switch immediately to water and drink it by the gulpful, to avoid the otherwise inevitable reflux, fistfight, or hours at home spent morosely smoking in your chair, listening to Pink Floyd albums.

Remember the old proverb which describes the Five Stages of Drunkness as "verbose, jocose, lachrymose, bellicose . . ." then "comatose." It's best, in our sodden experience, to stop at "jocose." And if "amorous" is one of the stages you experience, it's probably best to stick with tonic water—to avoid the phenomenon that some ancient Greeks[13] first dubbed "coyote sunrise."[14] Chewing off your arm to escape waking up that stranger with whom you staggered home is really no part of an orderly Christian life.

In fact, recent scientific studies have revealed that it is actually possible to *injure your health* by drinking too often or too much. Employers[15] tend to frown on workers who show up reeking of gin and, in a slurred voice, telling filthy jokes whose punch lines they've forgotten. And more than a few marriages have been impaired by the combination of blurred logic, hysterical weeping, and alcoholic impotence. Go figure.

If any of these symptoms sound familiar, you may have a problem—and there's nothing funny about it. One modern doctrinal development which we applaud is the realization that some conditions once called "vices" are usually symptoms of illness. What moralists used to denounce as "despair" we now recognize as depression; people addicted to alcohol are not dismissed as sinners with no self control, but treated as patients suffering from a disease—one which is often hereditary. Some might fear that removing the moral stigma from this condition would eliminate the spiritual element essential to repentance and recovery. In fact, the opposite has happened—largely because the organization with the highest success rate for

---

[13] The Tulane DKE graduating Class of 1948.

[14] To be evenhanded, we should note that women have their own term for this experience: The "walk of shame." It's amazing just how *unattractive* one feels in the cold light of morn hobbling home in last night's cocktail dress.

[15] For instance, school bus companies. But even airlines are cracking down. . . .

helping people overcome the effects of addictive drinking, Alcoholics Anonymous, was founded on the practice of penitence and humility before God. Co-founders Bill W. and Doctor Bob counted among their early advisors Sister Ignatia, an Akron, Ohio, nun who circumvented the moralistic rules at her hospital to win admission for alcoholics in need. Sister Ignatia used to give her patients upon leaving a Sacred Heart medallion as a symbol of their commitment to sobriety—a custom which AA adopted, in the form of poker chips given out to commemorate days achieved without drinking. At the core of "recovery," according to A.A., is admitting one's "powerlessness" over addiction, and turning to an ecumenically titled "Higher Power." Cultivating a relationship of loving dependence on that Power of mercy and redemption is the tough spiritual work A.A. members set for themselves. Another of the founders' associates, Rev. Edward Dowling, S.J., looked at the principles which the men had drafted and assumed that they must have based A.A. on a reading of St. Ignatius's *Spiritual Exercises.* The two men—neither of them a Catholic—assured the Jesuit they'd never heard of the book. So Father Dowling decided that the work of A.A. must be divinely inspired. Having known recovering alcoholics who credit the fact that they're still alive to the group's healing influence, we agree.

So if you're a social drinker, employ moderation and pray for the virtue of temperance to make sure you stay that way. Or else, by abusing the God-given privilege of the grape, you may find yourself transformed over time into an anti-social drinker. Instead of tippling moderately with groups of friends, you'll find yourself alone on a park bench draining bottles and complaining about the Freemasons. A sobering thought.

Terroirists and the War on Terroir

Unless you happen to be a cork-dork, you might not know that there are such things as "wine controversies," or that seemingly mild-mannered, well-bred men have come to blows over issues like the influence of regional soil qualities on the flavor profile of a given Merlot. We've seen tastings get tense and hostile, especially once those well-coiffed connoisseurs stop spitting in the silver bucket, and begin throwing back whole glasses of Pinot Noir. Tempers flare, fine distinctions go out the window—and pretty soon a room full of closeted metrosexuals are taking off their blazers and staring each other down, strutting like gamecocks and channeling Robert DeNiro's taxi driver in the voice of Niles Crane.

"I believe you were addressing me?"

"I'm afraid not."

"Well there doesn't happen to be anyone else here. So, in fact, you must have been addressing me."

"You are mistaken."

This can go on for hours, since no one has the nerve to throw a punch, and it's never pretty.

Perhaps the most inflammatory issue animating oenophiles is the question of *terroir*. Sure, on the face of it, this is merely a term for "soil." But keep in mind that it is a *French* word, which means that it is fraught with dozens of connotations, weighed down by millennia of history, and often pronounced with an annoyingly correct Parisian accent. It's a fighting word.

Indeed, in 2004, documentary filmmaker Jonathan Nossiter wrote and directed a feature-

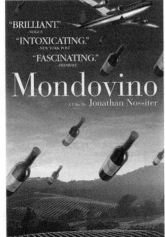

length (and then some—159 minutes long) film about the bitter disputes dividing the world of wine lovers on the importance of *terroir*. Called *Mondovino*, it's an engagingly partisan look at the conflict roiling winemakers between food science and tradition. The film shows the Great Divide between:

- The makers and lovers of New World wines, which are made with varieties of grapes uprooted from all over the globe, transplanted to alien climes and soils, and engineered using high-tech methods to achieve a basically uniform, simple, highly fruity taste. Showy, dramatic "fruit-bombs" produced by publicly held companies, and marketed using number ratings granted by highly paid experts, they're the liquid equivalent of Steven Spielberg films. In a word, one might call them "American."

And

- The partisans of Old World wines, who insist that the complexity, beauty, and uniqueness of the drink arises from the intricate interplay between soil, clime, weather, and the strain of grape which has evolved to thrive among them. (Some of the most famous varieties of grape were planted 1,000 years ago by the monks who first tended these vines. **see Burgundy**.) This quality, the unique outcome of natural interactions and human craftsmanship, the winemakers sum up with the word *terroir*, which takes on for them a slightly mystical quality. These wines are mostly produced on smaller plots, by families who have made them for centuries according to fiercely guarded recipes. The vintages which result are idiosyncratic, complicated, less predictable and slower to win over the casual drinker. Think of a French art house drama with tiny subtitles, or a Latin Mass you have to follow with a missal. You don't get much Older World than this.

This conflict is of obvious interest to Catholics, drinkers, and especially Catholic drinkers. Jesus' first miracle was an act of wine making. The greater miracle that is the Eucharist depends on *un-making* wine. Most of the joyous moments in life involve a glass or two. (How many of us would otherwise never have been conceived?) If the global market does indeed threaten to crush family vintners and make all wines taste the same, we ought to sit up and take notice.

The filmmaker has an obvious point of view, as some conservative critics have pointed out (**see Opus One**), comparing director Nossiter to the likes of Michael Moore. But this is hardly fair. In *Fahrenheit 9/11* and his other documentaries, Moore plasters his moochy face all over the screen, grandstands in front of grieving mothers at war memorials and hogs the soundtrack with his voice, narrating for the audience a Special Olympics summary of what the movie means—as if, when Moore drives a steamroller for the fifty-seventh time over the same dead horse, it really were possible to miss the point. One can hear his poor mother saying, many times, long ago: *We get it, Michael—now for love of God would you please let us get some sleep? Your dad needs to get up for work at five in the morning. . . .*

Nossiter is much stricter with himself—and therefore kinder to the viewer. He clearly has an agenda, and it's a controversial one, but he makes his points indirectly, allows the targets of his satirical camera to critique and undermine themselves—while granting them equal time to make their case. Equally, he asks tough questions of the men and women he clearly admires, and probes them for hypocrisy. The resulting film has all the complexity and texture of real life, honestly observed. Or of a glass of well-made wine—which is what the film's all about.

It took one of the authors to goad the other into seeing this film. While John is an enthusiastic drinker, his wine palate centers more on quantity than quality. But Denise is an impenitent wine snob. (And food snob. And salt snob; she has 12 varieties of crystals in her kitchen, hailing from the beaches of Brittany, the slopes of the Himalayas, and volcanic salt-flats of Molokai.) And at first, you might think Denise is the only sort of person who'd care about the questions that *Mondovino* covers, the shifting alliances and changing tastes that prevail in the global wine market. To your average recreational tippler who is lucky to remember the difference between Burgundy and Côte du Rhône, this can all sound pretty heady and irrelevant—like the quarrels between vegetarians and vegans, which really should be settled with chainsaws.

But once we sat down to watch it, we were equally fascinated. The film depicts the conflict over high-tech wine production deftly, cutting back and forth between dispassionate interviews with figures who stand on either side of (and sometimes straddle) this oenological divide. Ironically, perhaps, the most vivid representative of the New World, scientific approach to wine making is a bearded, chain-smoking Frenchman; and the most eloquent defender of Old World techniques is an amiable Jewish guy from Brooklyn who yearns for the cream sodas of his childhood.

Michel Rolland, the French wine consultant, is shown tooling around the countryside of Burgundy in a chauffeured car, chatting endlessly on a cell phone, pausing to recount how he flies all over the globe, teaching winemakers (some of whose families have been crafting wines for centuries) the secret of high-tech flavor enhancement. The secret is chemistry, he tells us—very much in the spirit of his countryman, Descartes (**see Loreto**). Over and over again, after tasting a vintage, Rolland turns to the vintners and with a flourish gives the same advice: "Microxygenate!"

As if in response, one immigrant winemaker from Haiti explains the importance of *terroir* in terms of fruit (he remembers that grapes are a fruit): "You take one mango from a tree that grows in the sun, in a certain kind of soil—and it tastes totally different from another tree's, which grows in the shade ten feet away." That's the key to complexity and subtlety in wine—attending to, respecting, and working with the way natural forces interact.

Other figures appear throughout the film, presenting a mosaic of perspectives. One elderly French grape-grower explains why he had to vote for a Communist mayor—who was the only politician to oppose American conglomerates buying up small French farms and denuding the nearby slopes to put up billboards. As he says of wine: "It is a kind of Sacrament. It unites what is in the air, in the ground, in the water, with the work of man's hands, and across the centuries. . . . It is not just some product, to be branded and mass-marketed."

Across the globe, in California, a likeable but clueless couple who made their millions in software show the filmmakers around their shiny new estate and winery—designed as a replica of a Spanish colonial chateau, complete with a dining table "modeled after that famous one," the wife says with pride, "the one in *Godfather II*." The director cuts from a family of charming Italian aristocrats who blithely acknowledge their past support for Mussolini, to a desperately poor Brazilian grape farmer, who takes in the camera crew and insists on serving them the wine he made from the grapes he planted, grew, and picked. His proud smile as he pours it outshines the Renaissance paintings in the Italians' Florentine *palazzo*.

There are many similar contrasts in the film, which is dryly hilarious. But the director doesn't squeeze them for advantage, or try to make the New World wine folks look ridiculous. The film acknowledges the complexity of the issues involved; however Sacramental a business wine making may be, it is still a business, which must produce enough income to support the men and women who plant and harvest, craft and bottle it—and sufficient capital to improve facilities, promote and advertise the product. (These realities of the market economy were recognized in Pope John Paul II's great encyclical *Centesimus annus*.) The old Frenchman who waxes so eloquently against the expansion of California's Mondavi wine empire is shown at the end cozying up to Gerard Depardieu, who opens a vanity vineyard down the road.

Even the film's best stand-in for a villain, Robert Parker, is treated rather fairly. This critic's personal taste in wines (he likes them big and fruity) is shown in the film as one of the most pernicious forces in the industry. Using a 100 point system, Parker ranks wines for a major trade magazine—and his ratings can make or break a wine. He keeps a close friendship with Rolland, whose specialty is making wines "Parker-friendly," that is, remaking them to suit Parker's taste and guaranteeing them a high ranking—and sales. Between the two of them, these men, the film suggests, are doing to the wines of the world what Americans did for cheese. Yet Parker is not demonized; he's shown as a self-made man with strong personal preferences, which happen to mirror those of his audience—Americans who didn't grow up drinking wine, but acquired the taste later in life. The New World also has its rights.

The problems arise when our simpler, streamlined ways steamroll over everything else on the earth—teaching Frenchmen, Austrians, and Africans to prefer McDonalds, "Big Brother," and backwards baseball caps to the products of their own, ancient cultures. The world that results is monotone and dismal—even to us Americans. Because it takes account of the various points of view, the film's message comes across all the more credibly at the end—just like an essay that has anticipated and answered criticism, or one of St. Thomas Aquinas's proofs, which always make the best case possible for a heresy before refuting it. *Mondavino* leaves the viewer with a profound sense of sadness at how much modern life manages to shield us from reality. Or rather, how we seek through technology to homogenize and sanitize the world, so it preserves our dulled sensibilities. How many of us grew up eating beef for years before we ever touched a cow? Eating eggs without ever chasing a chicken? How many of our sprawling exurban cities look exactly, precisely alike—down to the very last detail prescribed by the corporate officers at Wal-Mart, Subway, and Appleby's? How many hideous modern office buildings and churches resemble space ships sent from the same alien planet—one that is clearly hostile to our species?

Why *have* we moderns learned to prefer what is dull and predictable to what is different and complicated, to wish that even our glasses of wine never surprise us? Perhaps it flows from the undue exertion of human power over life—even human life, and a desperate, almost demonic impatience with limits. We have orthodox Catholic friends who've resorted to *in vitro* fertilization, rather than struggle against infertility or risk adopting someone else's unwanted child. We know liberals who drink only organic milk, but flood their wombs with contraceptive hormones (**see Organic Wine**). Millions of Christian folk are fleeing the complexity of multicultural cities to inhabit homogenous, pre-fab subdivisions in what used to be virgin land—so that each year, the earth shows less and less of God's own handiwork, and ever more of man's. Indeed, we know pro-lifers who advocate explosive population growth, and would happily see the entire earth as densely settled as Hong Kong. "We can grow our food hydroponically," as one of them explained to us after church with a beatific, "I drank the Kool-Aid" smile.

And so it goes, as Kurt Vonnegut liked to say. From left and right alike, we all agree on one thing: We want the fruit of knowledge, and we wish to be like unto gods. As the great novel *Brave New World*—read it again; you may have skimmed it in high school, but if you're like us, you didn't understand it—makes clear, this habitual choice renders us gradually less human, and ever more like the robots we're constructing.

Tipsiness vs. Drunkenness

In developing the Church's moral theology, thinkers such as St. Thomas Aquinas had to take account of many competing, seemingly contradictory injunctions and impulses in Scripture, infusing them with the insights of reason—including pagan philosophy. Rev. Paul Murray, O.P., wrote in his essay "Drinking in the Word: Dominicans and the New Wine of the Gospel," that St. Thomas himself described his task in terms of making wine. Aquinas described the teachings of Christ as wine, and the wisdom of secular sages as water. Instead of watering down the Gospel, he said he sought to imitate Christ at Cana—and turn the water into wine.

One of the controversies with which Aquinas wrestled was the proper use of intoxicating tonics. The Scriptures offered mixed messages—in one place, condemning drunkenness (Gal. 5: 19–21) and at another enjoining, "Be no longer a drinker of water, but use a little wine." (1 Tim. 5: 23) Likewise, the Socratic philosophers spoke of the "divine frenzy" that could be brought on by the grape to inspire men with love for the Good, while Stoics deplored the loss of moral accountability and rational control. With his typical subtlety and good sense, St. Thomas weighed the competing claims of reason and revelation, grace and nature, and offered not a compromise but a synthesis. It was good, he wrote, to use a thing that is given to us by nature—but only within the limits of our own nature, which we discover in reason and in the laws of God. Since the Scriptures encourage wine-drinking (and Jesus Himself undertook a miracle to make great big cisterns of the stuff) it must be in itself good; only its abuse was evil. Even the founder of Aquinas's order, St. Dominic, served wine at gatherings with his nuns, as Rev. Murray reports, enjoining "Drink up, my daughters!"

So how do you discern the line between wine's use and abuse, particularly when your vision might be getting a little blurry? Distilled[16] from St. Thomas's Scholastic language and the debating-notes format in which he developed his theology, his position comes down to this: One may and sometimes should drink to the point of tipsiness, but not to drunkenness. The former shades into the latter gradually, of course, but there are points on the slippery slope where a well-meaning sinner can

---

[16] All our puns are intentional.

gain a foothold. If you drink enough that it encourages you to commit a sin, or lose the rational faculty that tells you right from wrong, you've had too much. And that is in itself a sin. Being a philosopher and not a self-help author, Aquinas did not offer many practical hints on how to discover when you were "crossing the line." So we're here to help. The following is a list of Temperance Tongue Teasers, which you can clip and laminate, to keep in your wallet when you go out. If you're in doubt about whether it's safe to consume another round, take out this card and try to recite these phrases to your companions. Go as slow as you like. If you can't manage them, it's time to switch to tonic water and call a cab.

Temperance Tongue Teasers

Peter poped a pack of papist prelates.
St. Cyprian sifted syntheses for the synod.
The Reign in Spain slays Saracens on the plains.
Rose of Lima used raw lye to scour her lovely skin.
Modalists, Montanists, and Monophysites may never be mollified.
Saints Agatha, Agnes, and Anastasia are invoked against euthanasia.
On the Feast of the Circumcision, it's rude to start a schism.

Trappists and their Ales

Let's start with a definition. An "ale" is a strong-tasting beer fermented a little more quickly and at higher temperatures than an ordinary lager, brewed from hops and malt, with a smooth texture, a dark amber shade, and a fruitier, sometimes more bitter flavor. Ales may be too assertive for some people's tastes, but a good ale is never dull, and makes as fine a companion to food as a well-chosen wine.

Some of the richest, most luxurious ales on earth are crafted by some of the poorest, hungriest men—who lead sexless, meatless, mostly silent lives, work long hours, awaken in the dead of night, and are mostly forbidden to drink them. Should you feel guilty enjoying these ales? Maybe start a boycott and work for government sanctions, until working conditions improve?

Doesn't sound like much fun—and it wouldn't do much good, since these men chose this lifestyle voluntarily, and wouldn't leave if you asked them to. (And the soldiers of the French Revolution "asked" with bayonets.) The Trappist monks, also known as the Order of Reformed Cistercians, follow perhaps the most austere monastic discipline in the Church. (Discalced Carmelites might disagree; there is a kind of competition, incomprehensible to the likes of us, among religious orders to see which can lead the most unearthly life. Give them time, and some religious order will eventually be established on the Moon, and attempt to subsist entirely on meteorites.)

Though they are part of the great family of orders which began with St. Benedict's famous Rule, the Trappists are a reform branch of a reformed branch—which leaves them hanging out on a limb, dangling dangerously on the edge of impossibility. But with God, all things are possible—and He seems to favor the improbable—so the Trappists have flourished over the centuries. Founded in the seventeenth century by the Abbot de Rancé at the Abbey of La Trappe, the Reformed branch was intended to restore the primitive austerity of the Cistercian order, which had gradually dissipated over the centuries—to the point where some monks were actually, for instance, frying eggs and eating meat! Such clerical corruption appalled the more idealistic monks, who decided at La Trappe to get back to their roots (and vegetables). As the 1907 *Catholic Encyclopedia* says of these admirable Trappists: "Too much credit cannot be given to these noble bands of monks, who by their lives demonstrated to a corrupt world that man could have a higher ambition than the gratification of the mere natural instincts of this ephemeral life."[17]

Such stern other-worldly abbeys as these were not the sort to attract the sons of spoiled aristocrats, or extensive land-grants by friendly dowagers, so the men had to work for their living. In classically paradoxical Catholic fashion, many of them devoted themselves to making beer. And happily for us, they applied to their ingredients, process, and equipment the same rigorous eye with which they examined their consciences. Both the spirituality and the spirits found at Trappist abbeys are of almost ethereal quality. The ale-making abbeys did not survive in France;

---

[17] If any of you discover what it is, please write us care of the publisher.

repeated anti-Catholic governments expelled religious orders, most recently in 1905. Instead, the Trappists reward the people of Belgium with their brews. The brands currently made are Chimay, Orval, Rochefort, Westmalle, Westvleteren and Achel. Some Trappists market their products only to pilgrims, while others distribute them commercially in America. And a good thing, too—since the closest most of us are likely to get to the Trappist spirit is to pop a cap and pour.

CELEBRATE: Honor the spirit of the Trappists by serving some Trappist spirits, preferably alongside a traditional Belgian treat.

Shellfish and Chimay Stew

1 tablespoon olive oil
1 tablespoon butter
2 small yellow onions, finely chopped
5 cloves garlic, sliced
4 stalks celery, diced
1 green bell pepper, diced
6 carrots, diced
1 13-ounce package andouille
   sausage, quartered lengthwise
Salt
Freshly ground black pepper
Cayenne pepper to taste
3 sprigs thyme
1 bay leaf

2 750-ml bottles Chimay Premiere
   (red label)
6 small Yukon Gold potatoes, well
   scrubbed and thinly sliced
1 pound green beans, trimmed and
   cut in half
1-1/2 pounds large shrimp, shells on
2 pounds small clams, well scrubbed
4 Alaskan King crab legs,
   cut into thirds
1 pound boiled crawfish, if available
   and desired
4 green onions, green part only,
   thinly sliced

Heat oil and butter in pot large enough to accommodate all the ingredients.

Sauté onion until soft and translucent. Add garlic, followed by celery, bell pepper and carrots; stirring between each addition. Allow the vegetables to cook together for a few minutes and the temperature to recover before adding sausage.

Add and give it a good stir. Cook for five minutes.

Season with salt, pepper, and cayenne. For precise portion control, use the point of a sharp knife to dispatch the red pepper from its container. Also add thyme and bay.

Pour in Chimay. If more is needed to cover aromatics as well as the seafood-in-waiting please add. The cook should have several bottles stashed for serving with dinner. Cover and bring to a low simmer before adding potatoes. When these are mostly cooked but still resistant to the point of a knife, add the green beans. At this point the stew should still be at low simmer. Cook for 5 minutes until the beans have turned bright green.

Taste broth and adjust seasoning. Now comes the seafood. First the shrimp. Cover two minutes, then stir until all the shrimp turn red. Next the clams. Cover again and cook three to five minutes. Then add the crab and crawfish. Cook until heated through.

Garnish with green onions and serve with plenty of Chimay.

Serves 6–10

Ugni and the Armies of Allah

The region of France with the oldest claim to civilization is Provence, whose Mediterranean coast was honeycombed with Greek colonies as early as 600 B.C., of which the most important was Massalia (later Marseilles). The Hellenes brought with them the written alphabet, diverse and (ahem!) innovative sexual practices, philosophical discourse, and the art of making wine. Since these are precisely the cultural attributes about which Frenchmen still boast today, it behooves us as residents of the Hellenic colony of Astoria, New York, to remind the Frogs where they learned it all—from the Greeks. It was Grecian colonists who introduced the rude, blue-painted Celts to techniques of cultivating vineyards, planting the grapes which would thrive there for the next 2,600 years.

One of the oldest varieties in Europe, the Ugni grape dates back to the first Greek settlements—and still forms the backbone (if not

quite the taste bud) of wine making. The most widely planted white grape in France, it also accounts on its own for a third of Italian white wine—filling carafes of $8 Trebbiano for impecunious college students on first dates even today. As you may have gathered, Ugni is not the finest or most interesting grape. It's beloved by winemakers for its hardiness in bad weather and tendency to grow abundantly even in bad conditions. When one's most delicate grapes wither and die, he can count on the Ugni to keep springing up and keeping the barrels full. Its plain, almost neutral flavor makes it useful as the base to which other, more flavorful varieties can be added, and also lends itself to distillation. Juice from Ugni grapes forms the backbone of many cognacs and brandies, and at least one brand of vodka—Ciroc, whose producers boast they still employ the techniques introduced by tenth-century Benedictines of the Abbey of St. Michel.

The Greeks did more than teach the Gauls how to plant the grape. They inducted the Gauls into the vast, pan-Mediterranean economy of trade, which linked in a web of growing prosperity the forests of Scotland with the granaries of Egypt, the purple factories of Tyre, and the spice merchants who carried their wares along the great Silk Road from Asia. This benevolent globalism is the single factor which, according to historian Henri Pirenne, allowed the Mediterranean region to become the most prosperous and advanced culture in the world. The wealth that resulted from this web of complementary trade is what lifted all of Europe and the Middle East from the Iron Age, and made possible the empires of Persia and later of Rome. If a metaphor helps, imagine the Mediterranean as a vast octopus of prosperity, with its head somewhere near Crete, tentacles reaching to Portugal, Scotland, Morocco, and India, exuding instead of ink the many varieties of worldly goods which traversed the wine-dark sea.

So how did this vast, mutually beneficial system of trade give way to the chaos and near-starvation which marked the Dark Ages? Traditionally, historians have pointed to the fall of Rome, the collapse of central authority and the incursion of vast numbers of untutored tribes of barbarians into Gaul and even Italy. Indeed, the sniffy Whig historian Edward Gibbon faulted the Christian Church for the empire's collapse, and hence the next 700 years of relative darkness. But Pirenne offers another explanation, and one we like much better: He blames the Moslems.

Okay, he doesn't really *blame* them. When an army of theologically motivated conquerors try to bring down the "infidel" civilization of their enemies, who can really blame them? Our own Puritan founders did the same favor for the Indians, and the Spaniards for the Aztecs. It seems to arise from a basic human urge to *obliterate otherness*, and far be it from us to moralize about this sort of thing. Nevertheless, as partisans of European civilization and peoples (we like to root for the underdog), we can't resist pointing to Pirenne. In his ground-breaking history *Mohammed and Charlemagne,* Pirenne argues from archaeological and documentary evidence that the fall of the Roman empire was not in fact a catastrophe, that the disruptions of order which accompanied the fall of Rome were not sufficient to wreck the ancient economy. He shows the continued use of currency, the widespread trade and relative prosperity which continued under "barbarian" rulers who claimed continuity with Rome, learned to read and write in Latin, and quickly adopted Catholicism. To most residents of the old Roman empire, Pirenne argues, between the fifth and seventh centuries, the switchover from rule by Roman generals commanding barbarian armies to barbarians commanding themselves was not all that traumatic. In fact, life went on much as before.

So what happened to turn wealthy sixth-century Gaul into the howling wasteland it would become just a hundred years later? According to Pirenne, it was the Islamic conquest of the Middle East and North Africa, which cut Europe off from the ancient centers of grain production in Egypt, and Asiatic trade in Syria and Persia. Returning for a moment to our metaphorical cephalopod, it's as if the tentacles of the Mediterranean octopus reaching into Europe had been hacked off. One of the first measures the new Islamic occupiers of these still mostly Christian regions took upon conquering the countries was to cut off all trade with France, Italy, and any other region inhabited by infidels. This draconian economic boycott had devastating effects, Pirenne reports—helping within a century or two to virtually destroy urban civilization in Europe, whose towns could no longer sustain their populations. He documents how cities such as Rome and Marseilles dwindled in size and wealth, ceasing to be cosmopolitan centers of trade, and shrinking into feudal forts surrounded by struggling farms. Instead of exporting wine to Africa and importing grain from Egypt, the Christians of regions such as Provence were reduced to a simple, subsistence economy. Those in Spain were simply conquered by Moslem invaders, and subjugated for 700 years. While this meant religious persecution, it at least entitled them to take part in the vast Islamic economy—which helps explain the so-called "golden age" of medieval Spain.

As for the winemakers, Islamic invasion frequently meant the end of their industry. As Desmond Seward notes in *Monks and Wine*:

> In the tenth century, much of southern France was ravaged by Moors, whose unwelcome presence is still commemorated by the Montagnes des Maures. True to their prophet, they uprooted the heinous vine wherever they met it; according to the Koran, "there is a devil in every berry of the grape." (p. 47)

These vines, which had flourished for over 1,200 years, were painstakingly replanted in most cases by Benedictine monks (**see Burgundy**), the only men educated and organized enough to undertake this delicate task. In the Bandol wine region near Marseilles, the monks of the Abbey of St. Victor in the eleventh century restored the vineyards which produced Clairette, Sauvignon, and of course the Ugni grape.

The Abbey of St. Victor was an ancient center of Christian preaching in Provence. It was founded by the important theologian St. John Cassian in the 400s in an abandoned quarry that had been turned into a secret Christian cemetery. From the Church's earliest years, Christians had made a practice of conducting the liturgy on the tombs of holy people and venerating the relics of the dead. This gave rise to the custom, current today, of placing in every Catholic altar a saint's relic. Indeed, priests who are traveling in hostile regions without access to such altars carry an "altar cloth" with the bones, hair, or other relics of a saint sewn into the fabric, so they can make an altar out of any flat surface at need.

This abbey contained, most famously, the body of St. Victor (hence its name), a Roman officer executed in the second century for refusing to worship the emperor. It also boasted, tradition tells, fragments of the cross on which St. Andrew was killed, the clothes of the Virgin Mary and St. Mary Magdalene, and even the coffins which held the Holy Innocents slain by King Herod. Okay, so sometimes "tradition" likes to fib.[1]

This abbey was destroyed several times by invaders during the chaos and poverty that descended on the region in the wake of its artificially induced economic collapse. The Benedictines built a new abbey on the site in the tenth century, which quickly became a center for evangelizing the region. With an eye to the still-rampaging Saracens, Vikings, and even Magyars,[2] the monks prudently built around their chapel an enormous fortress—just in case. The abbey became famous for its faithfulness to the Benedictine Rule, and its monks helped reform dozens of other monasteries throughout Europe. Two former abbots of St. Victor rose to become popes—albeit Avignon popes.

The abbey was destroyed, like nearly everything else of value in France, during the Revolution (**see Drinking Song #7**)—whose partisans tore down hundreds of historic churches, including the enormous Abbey of Cluny, one of the greatest cultural centers of European history, an exquisite building almost the size of St. Peter's in Rome. It was blown up, and a highway built through its ruins.

As the post-Christian French—to the horror of the faithful remnant among them—complete the deconstruction of their Christian heritage, the heirs of the Moors and Saracens who once again populate Provence and other regions in prodigious, fertile numbers, meekly wait their turn to inherit the earth. If and when they do, we expect that the vast, green fields of Ugni grapes will once again be torn up and burned. So drink the stuff while you can.

CELEBRATE: There is something of a mild baby boom occurring among the Christian French, and a stirring of Christian practice. Besides the admirable bands of Traditionalists who have kept alive the ancient liturgy of the Church and

---

[1] In reality, this was the site where Jesus and Mary Magdalene honeymooned, before taking off to found a goddess religion and sire a race of bumbling Merovingian monarchs. We know this for a fact: We read it on the beach.

[2] Perhaps you haven't dealt with many Hungarians, but if you have, you know they do still sometimes revert to type—unlike the poor Scandinavians, who seem to have entirely lost their "edge." As for the Saracens. . . . Check today's newspaper.

the cultural heritage of France, lay movements such as the Emmanuel and the Bethlehem communities are reviving an interest among the young in the faith of their grandfathers (or more likely, grandmothers). Toast their efforts with a bottle of Bandol *blanc*, over a steaming plate of the delicious dish from southwestern France, cassoulet. It's a complex, exquisite concoction of duck fat, white beans, and pork skin—a batch takes two days to properly make and a solid week to finish eating. It's perhaps our favorite dish in this book.

WARNING: This dish is not *halal*.

Cassoulet

As in so many other things with much debt to Paula Wolfert, our culinary heroine.

DAY 1

2 pounds dried white beans	3 carrots, cut in rounds
3/4 pound fresh pork skin	8-ounce piece of pancetta
Salt and freshly ground pepper	1 head garlic, whole
4 pounds bone-in pork shoulder, cut for stew	1 tablespoon tomato paste
5 tablespoons goose fat	2 quarts chicken stock
2 onions, chopped	Sprig parsley, thyme, bay leaf, and celery tied together

Rinse and pick through beans for any foreign rocks or debris.

Soak for 2 hours.

Tie pork skin in a roll and simmer 20 minutes in enough water to cover. Drain.

In large heavy stew pot heat duck fat. Season pork shoulder and brown on all sides. Add onions and carrots. Cook 5 minutes. Add pancetta. Cook another 3 minutes. Add garlic and tomato paste; stir 1 minute. Add stock, pork skin, and herb bundle. Simmer 1 1/2 hours.

Drain beans and add to pork ragout. Simmer 1–1 1/2 hours until beans are done, depending on the freshness of beans. Cool. Skim off fat that has risen to surface and reserve.

Refrigerate overnight.

DAY 2

6 duck confit legs	1/2 cup fresh bread crumbs
1 pound fresh garlic pork sausage link	

Heat ragout gently on stove to just warm. Remove pork skin and set aside. Remove any bones that are free of meat as well as large pieces of fat. Remove herb bundle and discard. Remove garlic and squeeze back into ragout.

Steam duck legs in a colander over boiling water. Remove meat from bones and set aside.

Preheat oven to 325 degrees.

Unroll the pork skin and cut into strips. Line 2 3-quart ovenproof bowls with the skin— fat side down.

Add 1/2 ragout to bowls. Scatter duck meat over and cover with remaining ragout. Swirl in reserved fat from Day 1.

Taste and adjust seasoning.

Bake 2 hours.

Brown sausage in skillet and cut into 4-inch pieces.

Reduce oven to 300 degrees.

Place sausage on top and gently press into beans, stirring top level of beans. Cover with bread crumbs.

Cook 1 1/2 hours until bread crumbs are browned.

Remove from oven and rest for 20 minutes.

If desired, sprinkle with a tablespoon of melted duck fat.

Serve with a green salad and crusty bread.

Serves 10–12

Drinking Song #7: A Song of Resistance

Remember when the 1992 Los Angeles riots spun out of control, and engulfed the whole United States? The key moment, historians agree, occurred when police and Army commanders became caught up in the revolutionary fervor and changed sides—throwing their support to the Committee for Public Safety, led by Tom Hayden, Noam Chomsky, Ward Churchill, Michael Moore, and Edward Said. Of course, Hayden quickly fell from power and was executed, to be succeeded by D.C. Mayor Marion Barry. It was Barry who insisted that President G. H. W. Bush and his wife Barbara be tried for treason. Their conviction was a foregone conclusion. Those two executions may have shocked the world, but they sparked wild celebrations in Washington, as the First Couple's severed heads danced on poles in daylong parades. A crack whore was duly enshrined in the National Cathedral as the Goddess of Reason.

In time, Marion Barry himself was unseated, and executed in due course, and replaced by the "incorruptible" Dennis Kucinich. The ensuing Reign of Terror Kucinich launched killed tens of thousands—including corporate executives, Indian software engineers, Korean grocers, many harmless courtiers and celebrities such as Liz Taylor, Goldie Hawn, Bill Cosby, and Adam Sandler, and unnumbered professors, priests, ministers, and cloistered nuns, all accused of "subversion."

Outraged Christians rose up in Texas, Louisiana, and other regions, but the radicalized Army crushed these counterrevolutionaries, crowding hundreds of thousands of their supporters and family members onto rafts on the Mississippi, then sinking them. The Terror only ended when General Louis Farrakhan used a "whiff of grapeshot" to cow the mob. After he proclaimed himself Emperor, his ruthless secret police calmed the chaos at home—ended the church burnings and massacres, for instance—but his foreign policy adventurism sparked wars with Mexico, Canada, Great Britain and finally Russia, which ended only with his ignominious defeat and exile to Staten Island.

But all this is ancient history now. The Revolution and its wars have ended, at a cost of over 20 million lives, and the U.S. standard of living now approximates that of Kazakhstan. Was it all worth it?

That little thought experiment, which tracks the major events of the French Revolution and imagines them happening in America, should give the modern reader an idea of what the French Revolution was really like—a digestive explosion of all the basest instincts in society, led by ideologues drunk with power and thirsty for blood. It was utterly unlike the American rebellion against the English colonial officials—which amounted to a regional secession, led by the responsible members of the educated class. And for that fact we should be forever grateful, as should other countries which emulated the American model of political reform (such as Canada), rather than the French (such as Cambodia).

Of course, apologists for the Revolution will point to the inequalities and injustices of the *Ancien Regime* as justification for the bloodbath which occurred. So do revolutionaries justify every excess: Congresswoman Maxine Waters defended the L.A. riots as an "uprising" and a "rebellion" against the misery, squalor, and stagnation lived by so many members of the urban underclass.

But this claim cuts both ways. Looking back, we see that slaves in America at the Founding lived much worse lives than did poor Frenchmen at the time, and had vastly fewer rights. In fact, they had virtually none at all. Would that have justified a massive slave rebellion, ending with the murder of George Washington, Thomas Jefferson, and every other slave-owning aristocrat?

Some professors on American campuses argue just this. Their position is not some private perversity, but the logically consistent outcome of the conventional wisdom that the French Revolution was a justified, progressive event in history. If you think French peasants had the right to guillotine King Louis, then you must say that American slaves had the right to hang George Washington. To accept the American Revolution, you must reject the French.

Moving forward, the gap in wealth, privilege, and power between a third-generation welfare mother in Compton and, say, a 1992 Hollywood movie executive, was probably greater than that separating a French peasant from a 1789 aristocrat. Would that justify throwing George Lucas into jail, then guillotining him? Not even Jar-Jar Binks merits that. Probably.

Speaking of films, there is one by the French master-director Eric Rohmer depicting the reality of the Revolution much better than we can, and without using belabored historical metaphors, as we must. In *The Lady and the Duke* (2001), Rohmer adapts the memoirs of Grace Dalrymple Elliot, a kind-hearted conservative English lady caught up in the nightmare that was revolutionary Paris. A former lover, and still a friend of the squishy aristocrat, the Duc d'Orleans, Grace watches in horror as the radicals take over the city, imposing upon the cosmopolitan capital of Western culture a xenophobic, totalitarian state—complete with secret police, greedy informers, passbooks, political prisoners, and executions of the rich, the foreign, the dissenting, and the merely unlucky. "Death to the Austrian woman," the blood-crazed rabble cried, marching through burning streets to demand the murder of a queen.

Have you ever wondered why the mob demanded the death of the powerless Marie Antoinette? (Here's a hint: She never said "Let them eat cake"—that urban myth had been invented 100 years before, to defame another foreign Queen of France.) The lovely, brave, devout Marie Antoinette—who as a girl had flirted with the boy Mozart while he played the piano—would be caged like an animal for months, watching her maltreated boy, Louis XVII, die slowly of disease. Then she was dragged off to be beheaded. Her main crime? Being foreign, and having had more wit than her husband, enough to try to resist the collapse of her adopted country into subhuman chaos. But most aristocrats depicted in Rohmer's story display no such good sense.

At the heart of this exquisite film is the relationship between Grace Elliott and the Duc d'Orleans. The latter is a pampered, ambitious, cousin to the tragic King Louis XVI, a duke who throws his weight and wealth behind the revolutionaries, in the hope that they will place him on the throne. D'Orleans spouts the new rhetoric of hysterical, xenophobic nationalism, which you taste in the fevered lyrics of the revolutionary jingle *Le Marseillaise*:

> To arms, oh citizens!
> Form up in serried ranks!
> March on, march on!
> And drench our fields
> With their tainted blood!
> Supreme devotion to our Motherland
> Guides and sustains avenging hands.

The "tainted blood" of class and racial enemies would indeed flow, as the revolutionary leaders slaughtered aristocrats, priests, cloistered nuns, and "suspicious" foreigners. In the film, the Duc d'Orleans defends the Terror, as necessary to "purge" the French nation of impurities and treasonous elements; that is, of anyone who refused to march behind the totalitarian leaders of the Revolution, who refused to subsume his individuality in the "general will" of Jean-Jacques Rousseau—the theologian of society-as-anthill. (For *Star Trek* fans, Rousseau's political philosophy can be summed up in two words: The Borg.)

Grace Elliott was appalled, but kept alive her friendship with the duke in order to exert some influence on him, to urge him and his other "moderate" revolutionary allies among the aristocracy and the army to crush the rebellion before it turned on them. Even as Orleans voted for the judicial murder of his own cousin, the King, Grace risked death to save the life of a hunted stranger—simply because it was the Christian thing to do. The moral contrast between this pious English émigré and the scheming, foolish duke points up the contrast between the aristocrats who led the American Revolution, and those who launched the French.

As Russell Kirk documents in *The Roots of American Order,* the founders of the United States were sound, sober, cautious and moderate, grounding their grievances against the British king in English Common Law, the rights of local governments, and countless carefully reasoned judicial and legal precedents. The French aristocrats who voted with the ideologues and the mob to murder their king were irresponsible, frivolous, and finally cowardly—and most of them ended up on the scaffold, like the poor Duc d'Orleans. Every radical revolution eats its young, as the intellectuals of France, then Russia, Germany, and China (to name a few) would come in time to learn.

There were reasons why the French upper classes were so irresponsible, and they went back to the seventeenth century. Even as British kings were forced by Parliament and people to revive and respect the medieval privileges of local liberty and limited government, King Louis the Fourteenth, the "Sun-King"

- Trampled and crushed local elites,
- Took away the actual administrative and military duties of aristocrats and herded them into Versailles,
- Persecuted religious minorities,
- Defied the Pope,
- Squashed the liberty of the French church, and
- Gathered all power to Paris, into the hands of an absolutist executive.

Louis XIV turned the once rich and complex political fabric of France, celebrated by Montesquieu, into a brittle autocracy which would collapse at the first hammer blow. That blow would come when his descendant King Louis XVI (**see Bourbon**) bankrupted his kingdom—ironically, by financing the American Revolution. By then, the upper classes of France had been *dilettantes* and parlor *philosophes* for generations, and were utterly unsuited to embark on moderate political reform. They were the prototypes for the generation of 1968, who manned the barricades and burned the colleges on both sides of the Atlantic.

Ironically, the best source for learning about what went right in America, and wrong in France, is the work of a French aristocrat, Alexis de Tocqueville. He understood better than any U.S. native the roots of our liberty, and he looked across the ocean with jealous admiration. Reading him, and studying other works depicting the Revolution and its horrors, has forever spoiled for us the sight of the Tricolor, and the sound of Le Marseillaise—at least with its original lyrics.

But it's a fun and catchy song, with a rousing melody that can move a mob into action. It seems a pity to waste it. So we present it here in another form: a parody written by the Catholic peasants of the Vendée and Brittany who rose up in 1791 and fought a three-year war in defense of King and Church. In the end, they were crushed by overwhelming force, and massacred in the hundreds of thousands. Indeed, the revolutionary government decreed a policy of deliberate genocide against the regions—a fact considered unmentionable in France to this day; one historian told us that she dared not write about these events for fear of "never working in France again." Alexander Solzshenitsyn was willing to point it out when he came in 1993 to mark the opening of the Vendée Memorial.

The heroic resistance of these lightly armed farmers against a professional army helped unseat the atheist radicals in Paris, vault Napoleon Bonaparte into power, and force Napoleon to make a peace treaty (a "concordat") with the Church. Like their heirs in twentieth-century Mexico (**see Tequila**), these peasants put a stop to persecution. In their honor, we present the song which roused them as they marched into battle—with a translation by our good friend Charles Coulombe.

EXECUTION IN LA VENDÉE.

Al-lons ar - mé - es ca - tho - li - ques Le jour de gloire est ar - ri - vé! Con - tre nous de la ré - pu - bli - que L'é-ten-dard sang-lant est le - vé L'é-ten- dard sang-lant est le vé En-ten-dez-vous dans nos cam - pag - nes Les cris im-purs des scé - lé - rats? Qui vien - nent jus-que dans nos bras Pren - dre nos filles, nos femmes! Aux ar - mes ven-dé-ens! For - mez vos ba - tail - lons! Mar - chez, mar - chez, Le sang des bleus Rou - gi - ra nos sil-lons!

II

Quoi des infâmes hérétiques
Feraient la loi dans nos foyers?
Quoi des muscardins de boutiques
Nous écraseraient sous leurs pieds? (Repeat)
Et le Rodrigue abominable
Infâme suppôt du démon
S'installerait en la maison
De notre Jésus adorable

Refrain

III

Tremblez pervers et vous timides,
La bourrée des deux partis.
Tremblez, vos intrigues perfides
Vont enfin recevoir leur prix. (Repeat)
Tout est levé pour vous combattre
De Saint Jean d'Monts à Beaupréau,
D'Angers à la ville d'Airvault,
Nos gars ne veulent que se battre.

Refrain

IV

Chrétiens, vrais fils de l'Eglise,
Séparez de vos ennemis
La faiblesse à la peur soumise
Que verrez en pays conquis. (Repeat)
Mais ces citoyens sanguinaires
Mais les adhérents de Camus
Ces prêtres jureurs et intrus
Cause de toutes nos misères.

Refrain

V

Ô sainte Vierge Marie
Conduis, soutiens nos bras vengeurs!
Contre une sequelle ennemie
Combats avec tes zélateurs! (Repeat)
A vos étendards la victoire
Est promise assurément.
Que le régicide expirant
Voie ton triomphe et notre gloire!

Refrain

I

Let us go, Catholic armies
the day of glory arrived!
Against us, the republic
Has raised the bloody banner. (Repeat)
Do you hear in our countryside
the impure cries of the wretches?
Who come—unless our arms prevent them—
To take our daughters, our wives!

Refrain

To arms, Vendeans!
Form your battalions!
March, march,
The blood of the blues [revolutionaries]
Will redden our furrows!

II

What of the infamous heretics
Would make the law in our homes?
What of the mercenary cowards[3]
Who would crush us under their feet? (Repeat)
And abominable Rodrigue[4]
Infamous henchman of the demon
Who would settle in the house
Of our adorable Jesus?

Refrain

III

Tremble you perverse and timid,
Before the bonfires of the adversaries.
Tremble, your perfidious intrigues
Shall finally receive their due. (Repeat)
All are raised to fight you
From Saint Jean d'Monts to Beaupréau,
From Angers to the town of Airvault,
Our lads want to only fight.

Refrain

IV

Christians, true sons of the Church,
Reject your enemies and
The weakness and the servile fear
Which you see in a conquered country. (Repeat)
But these bloody "citizens,"
These allies of Camus,[5]
These treasonous and imposed priests[6]
Are the cause of all our miseries.

Refrain

---

[3] "Muscardins de boutiques," literally "dormice of the stores."

[4] Antoine Rodrigue, a local bishop who defied papal authority to cooperate with the Revolution.

[5] No, not the philosopher. . . . Armand-Gaston Camus, Secretary of the Revolutionary Convention, who led in the move to seize Church property and execute the king.

[6] This refers to the "Constitutional" priests who had sworn loyalty to the government over the pope, and were rewarded with the parishes of priests who refused; the latter were considered heroes.

> V
>
>   O Blessed Virgin Mary,
> Lead and support our avenging arms!
> Against an enemy gang,
> Fight alongside your zealous warriors! (Repeat)
> To your standards
> Is promised certain victory.
> The regicides' death
> Shall be your triumph and our glory!
>
> Refrain

Loopholes in the Ten Commandments
#9: Thou Shalt Not Covet Thy Neighbor's Wife

Here's one that is a bit of a puzzler. It's hard to think of any exceptions to such an all-encompassing and manifestly sensible rule as this commandment, which if it were obeyed would spare individuals and society the phenomenon of adultery, and associated social evils such as:

- Secret trysts at tawdry motels with creaky bedsprings, leering bellboys, and itchy, poly-blend sheets.
- Surprising genital discharges on the part of the innocent spouse, from the social disease they just *can't understand* how they caught. (HINT TO ADULTERERS: Thanks to improved understanding of public health, "You must have gotten it from a toilet seat" is probably no longer convincing.)
- Breathless, lurid articles in *Cosmopolitan* entitled "Have a Steamy Affair with Your Personal Trainer—and Get Away with It!" written by undersexed 22-year-olds fresh out of Wellesley who get most of their impure thoughts from Jane Austen novels.
- Cascades of increasingly implausible lies, for instance, to the spouse: "I got injured during my pedicure, and had to go to the *hospital!*" or "Honey, there was this fishing accident. . . ." Or to the paramour: "I'm gonna leave her . . . after our anniversary, okay? I *promise!*"
- Protracted divorce proceedings and the enrichment of attendant attorneys with monies once wistfully referred to as "the kids' college fund."
- Tedious battles over which parent will get stuck with custody of the bawling, hysterical children (and end up paying for their therapy).
- Seedy second weddings where the groom wears a blush, and the bride

wears beige, and the teenage daughter who got pressed into playing maid of honor to the person she now calls "my whoring mother" or "pervert dad" downs a whole bottle of Xanax during the tacky "Venetian Hour" and has to have her stomach pumped. Then she decides to "become a lesbian, I swear to God!"

- And so on.

On the other hand, living as the authors do in a blue-collar, ethnic neighborhood where spouses seem to gain 50 pounds or so in the course of their wedding reception, we can't see how "coveting" married people would be much of a temptation. But perhaps our experience isn't universal. Adultery is probably more of a problem in social milieus where wedded folk frequent the gym.

While the myths of the Greeks depicted their gods as tipsy philanderers straight out of *The Ice Storm*, the Old Testament took adultery seriously. Seeing it as a fundamental threat to the unity of the family and the solidity of the social order, the lawgivers of Leviticus made this sin punishable by stoning.[7] In His teaching, Our Lord firmed up this commandment, and added a new dimension, telling His disciples: "Every one who looks at a woman lustfully has already committed adultery with her in his heart." (Remember Jimmy Carter's *Playboy* interview? And centerfold?) This divine precept made it clear that the internal life of the mind, as well as the actions of the body, must be conformed both to the faculty of reason and the dictates of divine Revelation. Concupiscence, "the lust of the flesh, lust of the eyes, and the pride of life," (John 2: 16) must be disciplined for the sake of the soul. Later theologians and Church authorities extended the prohibition on lustful coveting to the unmarried as well. Pope John Paul, in his ground-breaking Theology of the Body, rooted these teachings in the notion of a divinely granted and guaranteed human dignity.

All of which, from a secular perspective, it must be admitted, pretty much *blows*. Especially if, like one of the authors, you happen to be a guy. The way men are constructed, their sexual response is primarily and powerfully *visual*. In gen-

---

[7] Of course, in the 1960s the Sexual Revolution reversed the order, generally urging newly "liberated" spouses to get stoned as a prelude to adultery, rather than the converse.

eral, men are drawn to learn more about a woman by physical beauty, youth, and subconscious cues that suggest health and fertility. While some of this may have been exaggerated by the effects of Original Sin, it seems fidestic[8] and gnostic[9] to suggest that the whole of masculine sexual response is the fruit of the Fall. In the text of Genesis 2, depicting the creation of Eve, Adam's delight and excitement at his newly crafted bride arises (ahem) the moment he *looks* at her. Her response to Adam is not recorded, but we suspect that her own interest in him grew more gradually, as she learned to trust him, saw that he was a decent provider of fruits and berries, decided he was "funny" and "not an a—hole," someone who'd persuasively feigned interest as she talked (in detail and at great length) about all the little animals and plants she'd encountered during the day. . . .

On the other hand, it doesn't take a prude to observe that the sexual instinct has become disordered. Anyone with Internet access could prove that point in oh, about, five seconds. While there is some genuine reproductive purpose—which has been explored by evolutionary biologists—underlying the preference men have for young, fertile-looking women, it's quite a long way from that to pervy middle-aged dads trolling Google for images labeled "barely legal." And that's just one of the mildest examples of what's out there on the Net. What sociobiological justification can we offer for all those videos on YouTube of college girls French-kissing each other, while their boyfriends look on, leering triumphantly? What is it these guys really think they're accomplishing? These are mysteries too profound for us to plumb. . . .[10]

Since the early Church, when Christians confronted a Roman Empire whose leading form of entertainment consisted of pornographic "snuff" shows in the Colosseum—usually starring young, Christian women and bored, overfed lions—believers have struggled with balancing the realities of sexuality and the divine limits which God has placed upon it in the interest of human dignity. And let's face it, we haven't done very well. In general, we have lurched from one extreme to the other—from half-naked art models appearing at the banquets of Renaissance popes, to fanatical monks like Savonarola burning piles of Botticelli paintings—usually not even pausing momentarily at any sane middle ground between the prurient and the prudish. This is not the fault of Christianity, but of humanity—and the extreme difficulty of the questions entailed in harmonizing male and female

---

[8] "Fideism" refers to the tendency to banish rational discussion and the evidence of secular sciences from the study of theology. It is common to fundamentalists, lazy seminarians, and pious souls whose IQ is outpaced by their ambition.

[9] Gnostic theologies, which proliferated in the third and fourth centuries like mosquitoes in a stagnant motel pool, imagine that the Fall so disfigured Creation that we can learn virtually nothing of God's original intent from the world as it now exists. Some Eastern Fathers of the Church were prone to this tendency, and theorized that sexuality itself—even the existence of man's sexual organs—was a punishment for Original Sin. To which we Westerners can only say, "Thank you, Lord, may we have another?"

[10] And why is it, exactly, that there aren't many videos of college *girls* looking on proudly as their boyfriends kiss? Just asking.

sexuality, the desires of the heart and the demands of family life. Other cultures have either draped women in shrouds or displayed them as concubines—sometimes doing both at once, albeit to different women. It's all too easy for men to divide various women in their minds into stark categories of "whore" and "Madonna,"[11] all of which is manifestly unfair to women and destructive to matrimony. It's not easy, as weary marriage counselors will tell you, to teach men once they're wed how to integrate these two, sundered halves of the feminine so they can appreciate and love an entire, intact wife. As far back as the seventeenth century, wise Jesuits confronted the fact that worldly courtesans were far more interesting company than the naïve, convent-trained virgins whom men were willing to marry. This resulted in tedious, loveless marriages, from which men drifted into adulterous liaisons with the witty denizens of the *demimonde*. In response, the Jesuits (and their female counterparts, the Madames of the Sacred Heart) started schools for girls which would train them in literature and the arts, the better to keep the interest and hold on to the hearts of their future husbands.

Today, as the wise writer Maggie Gallagher has noted[12] we face a culture which has embraced as its paradigm the sexual response of a horndog 16-year-old boy—and attempted to discipline all of us, regardless of age or sex, to live up to that standard. Women are urged to show off their belly buttons and butt-cracks, and adopt the readiness to rut of lonely lads drunk on testosterone. Men are subject, thanks to the Internet, to the sexual equivalent of hot and cold running heroin—and then expected to be tender and faithful lovers once they're married. All this after years or maybe decades of solitary fantasies about innumerable unclothed strangers who never gain weight, get pregnant, send you out on pointless errands, or insist you listen empathetically as they talk about "what I did today." The increasing incidence of impotence and plummeting birth rates in the West should come as no surprise. In fact, we're impressed that anyone gets born at all.

As to the content of this commandment, we once received excellent advice about how to follow it from a smart, holy priest of the New York Archdiocese. He told us about the "challenge" he faces when good-looking women come up to kneel before him for Communion—sometimes displaying a little more *décolletage* than he might prefer. "I don't pretend it's disgusting, or get angry at them for being 'immodest,'" he confided to one of us over lunch. "Instead, I notice their beauty, look away, and immediately give thanks to God for the glory of His creation. I pray for the woman's holiness and happiness," he said. "Then I go out and play racquetball, or something. That seems to help."

---

[11] Women rarely make this precise distinction concerning men, preferring, when they stereotype, to break men down into "losers" and "jerks." Should they decide that the man they'd married is one of the former, they cheat with one of the latter.

[12] See her fascinating, persuasive *Enemies of Eros* (Chicago: Bonus Books, 1989).

Velletri Wine: The Sauce of the Popes

One of the most ancient wine-producing regions in Italy is Velletri, northeast of Rome, which yields both reds and whites of distinction, and for centuries served the popes as their personal vineyard. The region's winemakers were the first to tie grapevines to neighboring trees, to keep the grapes from rotting on the ground. This seems to have worked, because, as *ItalianMade.com* reports:

> Throughout history, the vineyards of Velletri have served as a great reservoir of wine to be continuously tapped to satisfy Rome's requirements. In the 16th century, more than half of the wine consumed in the city came from the Velletri area.

This means that Velletri wines served as the primary lubricant of the Council of Trent (1545–63), the Church gathering that cleaned up all the confetti and broken piñatas left over from the Renaissance, and fixed Catholic practice in the form it retained until Vatican II—which smashed the piñata all over again.

During the fifteenth century, the Velletri area became part of the Papal States, the region in central Italy long controlled by the Holy See, which popes for centuries guarded fiercely as the "patrimony of St. Peter." At one point during the French Revolution, the citizens of Velletri rebelled against the pope, but after watching the anti-clerical outrages of the Jacobins (**see Drinking Song #7**), they repented and joined the papal armies fighting off Napoleon's siege of Rome.

Since Velletri was essentially the wine cellar of the Papal States, this seems like the right place to discuss the role of that vanished country in the history of the Church, and the courage of the men who fought for the popes over the centuries. Few of us remember even the name "Papal States" today, but in the nineteenth century Catholics around the world viewed the fate of the Papal States with the same intense personal concern that many Jews today regard the state of Israel.[1] Catholics lobbied their governments to protect the tiny, beleaguered religious state, surrounded by hostile and populous neighbors who claimed its land, encouraged terrorist attacks, and threatened to wipe the country off the map. Most Catholics agreed with popes such as Pius IX, who saw the territorial sovereignty of the Vatican as the best guarantee that secular governments could never again turn the pope into their puppet or prisoner. The universal ruler of a world-encompassing faith needed independence from the whims of foreign monarchs—a lesson driven home by the 70-year captivity of a series of popes at the hands of the kings of France (**see Châteauneuf du Pape**), which led to intractable schisms and at last the ludicrous spectacle of three men claiming at once to be the "real" pope.

The Papal States were ill-equipped to defend themselves, and reliant on the good will of allied governments such as France and Austria to guarantee their independence in the face of rising Italian nationalism. Apart from small papal armies (swelled by intrepid Catholic volunteers from around the world), the only force protecting the person of the pope from rebellious mobs and foreign invasion was the Swiss Guard, a mercenary force founded in 1506 by the warrior-pope Julius II. While we think of the Swiss today as peaceful, neutral cheese-eaters endowed with complicated pocket knives, that country's history tells a different story. The fiercely independent-minded farmers of Switzerland were in fact the first people to practice democracy in Europe,[2] and they defended their local liberties in a long series of wars against imperial invaders such as Austria. A mountain folk not known for their horsemanship, the Swiss used long, pointy pikes to knock down the armored knights who rode against them, and by the fifteenth century were renowned as the most viciously effective infantry in Europe. For centuries thereafter, one of the main industries in Switzerland was the export of mercenary soldiers, who served as elite bodyguards to the kings of France as well as the pope. There's an exquisite monument in Luzern to the Swiss Guards who attempted to protect poor Louis XVI when all his own men had abandoned him. These faithful soldiers were butchered by the mob in 1792 at the Tuileries Palace. They are commemorated in Lucerne by Bertel Thorvaldsen's sculpture of a dying, wounded lion—at which one of the present authors paused in summer 2000, en route to visiting the tomb of Hans Urs von Balthasar, to pray for these fallen soldiers, and all the heroes who have fought over the centuries to suppress revolutions and keep popes and kings on their thrones.

---

[1] In his chilling novel which depicts the rise of the Antichrist and the "end times," *The Lord of the World* (1907), Robert Hugh Benson shows how much the question of the Papal States was still in the mind of Catholics in his day, imagining Italy reconfigured as a kind of new Holy Land, ruled over by a saintly pope.

[2] The oldest democratic institution in Europe today is the *Landsgemeinde* which governs the Swiss cantons of Appenzell Innerrhoden and Glarus; every citizen appears once a year to vote in person, by show of hands, for local officials.

The Swiss Guards serving the popes have suffered their own share of casualties, as scholar Robert Royal notes in his fascinating history *The Pope's Army* (New York: Crossroad, 2006). The bloodiest encounter they faced in defending a pope took place on May 6, 1527, when a renegade army nominally loyal to Emperor Charles V sacked the city, looting palaces and churches, committing rape and murder on a scale not seen in Rome since the fifth century. But the Swiss Guard stood by the pope. Hopelessly outnumbered by largely Lutheran invaders—who'd been taught to view the pope as the Antichrist—the Guards held back the rampaging mercenaries long enough for Pope Clement VII to flee through a secret passage way (the *Passetto*) to safety in the impregnable Castel Sant'Angelo. There he would wait seven months for the siege to end. The city would not recover for decades, and the assault put an end to the Renaissance in Rome—sending the artists and humanists who'd beautified that city fleeing all over Europe.

Some 147 Guards died that day, defending the main altar of St. Peter's Basilica. In honor of those brave men, on the May 6 anniversary each year, inside the walls of the Vatican, the Swiss Guards repeat a solemn ritual—the swearing in of new soldiers. There before dignitaries and military commanders of a hundred nations, the Princes of the Church (cardinals), and the pope himself, each new recruit will grasp the Guards' banner and vow:

> I swear I will faithfully, loyally, and honorably serve the Supreme Pontiff [for instance, Benedict XVI], and his legitimate successors, and also devote myself to them with all my strength, sacrificing my life to defend them if necessary. . . .

The next time the Guards would prove their importance was at the Battle of Lepanto, in 1571. This great naval conflict was a turning point in the war between Christendom and an expansionist Islam. Turkish armies had already conquered Constantinople, Greece, Bulgaria, Romania and Hungary, and threatened to spill over into a divided Germany and Poland. Meanwhile, across the Mediterranean, Turkish fleets and pirates raided Christian cities, robbing, burning, and kidnapping thousands of "infidels" into lives of slavery. One Sultan vowed to stable his horses in St. Peter's Basilica. But on Oct. 7, 1571, the Holy League organized by Pope Pius V, consisting of fleets from Spain, Venice, and other Italian city-states and commanded by Don John of Austria, confronted a larger and better-equipped Turkish fleet off the coast of Greece. In what observers considered a miracle, the Christian fleets were triumphant—losing only 70 ships, while destroying 15 and capturing 177 of the Turks'. Swiss Guards fought on the ships, representing the pope who'd organized this effective, historic defense of Christendom. The pontiff, who'd begged Catholics around the world to say the Rosary before the battle, gave credit for the success of the Guards to the Virgin Mary, proclaiming the date of the battle (October 7) the Feast of Our Lady of Victory.

The Swiss Guards would once again fight for the Faith in the wake of the French Revolution. After provoking war with most of Europe, the French revolutionary regime determined to capture and control Pope Pius VI. General Napoleon Bonaparte invaded Italy in 1793, and in 1798 ordered his commander to seize control of Rome from the pope. The Swiss Guards resisted valiantly but in vain—and were briefly sent home by the French. Pius VI died a prisoner. It was only with Napoleon's defeat that Rome was freed and the Swiss Guard reconstituted in 1814. The Guards subsequently helped protect popes such as Pius IX from attacks by revolutionary mobs—and only reluctantly laid down their arms in 1870 when Pius ordered them not to resist the forces of the invading new Kingdom of Italy, which put an end at last to the temporal sovereignty of the popes—and forced the First Council of the Vatican to disperse, one step ahead of the invaders.

For 59 years after that, popes dwelt in a kind of mourning, refusing to set foot outside the papal palaces, considering themselves "prisoners of the Vatican." No Catholic was permitted to take part in the politics of the Kingdom of Italy which still squatted on papal land, on pain of excommunication—until in 1929 Pope Benedict XV concluded a treaty with Italy, guaranteeing a certain independence for the Church with a tiny patch of land (109 acres) under papal sovereignty which we now call Vatican City. It is the smallest independent nation-state in the world today. This nominal independence served Pope Pius XII well during World War II, when dictator Benito Mussolini threw an unready Italy into war as Hitler's ally. For the duration of the war, it would only be the Swiss Guards and other papal defense forces which marked off the tiny, independent Vatican City from the rest of fascist-controlled Rome.

Outside the perimeters of Vatican City, Jews and anti-fascists were herded up and sent to concentration camps. Inside, countless Jewish and other refugees were sheltered in monasteries, convents, basements—even the papal wine cellars were crowded with anti-fascist resistance leaders, and Jewish citizens whom Pius XII provided with kosher food. In Rome and elsewhere, according to Jewish historian Rabbi Pinchas Lapides, Pius XII was personally responsible for saving more than 700,000 Jewish lives—a fact quickly obscured by Communist propaganda after the war, and more recently by hack historians like Garry Wills and Daniel Goldhagen.

Today, the Guard functions more like the U.S. Secret Service. Though many Swiss Guards—a force of about 110 men—still wear the Renaissance-era uniform designed by Michaelangelo, they are all trained soldiers, veterans of the crackerjack Swiss Army. Behind those in costume, who essentially serve as decoys, plainclothes soldiers carry firearms like the Swiss-made SIG 9mm, and other automatic weapons. In 1981, it was Swiss Guards who accompanied John Paul II—a pope so determined to draw near his flock that he exposed himself to danger. When a modern Turk, Mehmet Ali Agca, tried to assassinate the pope, inflicting a near-fatal gunshot wound to the heart, the Swiss Guards could not stop the attack, but they did prevent a riot among the hundreds of thousands of pilgrims who filled St. Peter's Square that day. In subsequent years, the Swiss have schooled themselves in security and anti-terror tactics. They're the ones who even today protect the Vatican from terrorist strikes and the pope from assassination attempts. In 2005, as Royal notes, they performed one of the greatest feats of crowd control in history—directing, protecting, and supervising the millions of pilgrims who came to witness Pope John Paul II's funeral, and the election of Benedict XVI.

And the fine folk of Velletri? They're still making the wine that supplies the city of Rome, the city-state of the Vatican, and the Guards who protect it. The popes may no longer be "prisoners of the Vatican," but there are some prisoners in the region who are now taking part in Velletri's wine industry. In 2002, inmates in Velletri's jail started their own wine label. With the encouragement of the authorities and the help of marketer (and former inmate) Marcello Bizzoni, the prisoners are now being trained as vintners. On March 14, 2005, the Associated Press reported on this curious venture in rehabilitation, which generates 45,000 bottles per year of wines with names like *Fuggiasco* (fugitive) and *Sette Mandate* (Seven Turns of the Key).

As bad (if not quite arrestable) Catholics ourselves, we're happy to see that the spirit of penance and forgiveness is being turned to the making of spirits—and the spiritual rebirth of prisoners now learning an ancient and honorable trade.

Vin Santo: Dessert Wine of the Fire-Proof Monks

One of our favorite Italian wines is Vin Santo, a rich dessert wine made in Tuscany and other parts of northern Italy from grapes dried into raisins to concentrate the sugars. Then they're pressed and fermented in wooden barrels, and aged—sometimes for as long as six years—to produce a sweet, golden wine that caps off a Tuscan dinner of *coniglio ripieno* (stuffed rabbit), *peposo* (spicy stew) or *polpettone e polpette* (Florentine meat loaf). Like so many of the wines we have discussed, Vin Santo was first made by monks—who replanted the ancient vineyards of Tuscany, which had reverted to wastelands during the Dark Ages (**see Ugni Grapes**).

"The Merciful Knight," by Edward Burne-Jones, courtesy of *www.artrenewal.org*.

One monastery famous both for its Vin Santo and its holiness is Badia a Coltibuono. The place was founded in the eleventh century by St. John Gualbert (985–1073), a choleric nobleman whose family (the Visdomini) was engaged in one of the blood-feuds which have marked Italian politics since—oh, the time of Romulus and Remus. (Things seem to have been pretty peaceful before that.) When one of the Visdomini was murdered by a rival clan, as is customary in the course of such affairs, John was obliged to do his part by hunting down the killer. He tracked the guilty party to an alley, threw him down and raised his stiletto. . . . Had he simply plunged it straight into the killer's heart, John's life would have gone on as before—a festive round of banquets, jousts, and military campaigns, punctuated by the periodic assassination. But something strange happened in that narrow, stinking alley. Instead of fighting back, the killer threw out his arms in the shape of the crucified Christ and begged for forgiveness. John was moved to mercy—an unfamiliar sentiment for a Dark Ages warlord in mid-vendetta. He pardoned his cousin's killer, and let him go. Confused and almost ashamed of what others would call an act of weakness, John found his way to the Benedictine Church of San Miniato. It was there that the second miracle happened that day: As he faced the crucifix to pray, John saw the carved wooden figure bow its head in gratitude, and reach down to embrace him (as pictured in the Burne-Jones painting reproduced here). At this moment John knew he had to leave behind his armor for the habit of a monk.

Finding the local Benedictine congregation appallingly worldly—perhaps they ate too many cucumbers during Lent—John resolved to found a more ascetical group. He went off on his own to Vallombrosa, where he collected local penitents into a reformed congregation that would take its name from the place, the Vallambrosan monks. These brothers took the rather sensible Rule of St. Benedict and ratcheted up the severity by several notches: Any breaches of the Rule would be punished by scourging, the monks would live in total silence and utter poverty, and would spend all the day in prayer, instead of work. The only times the Vallambrosans allowed themselves to speak was in public—to denounce the laxity of other monks, and bishops who'd bought their dioceses on eBay.[3]

These scorching speeches naturally made the re-forming monks wildly popular, and led to the order's long-standing connection with fire—for instance, supporters of rival Black Friars burned the Vallambrosan's second convent of St. Salvi to the ground. On another occasion, when a Vallambrosan named Peter Aldobrandini accused the Archbishop of Florence of selling church offices and parishes, an angry mob gathered to demand he undergo a trial by fire—in the most literal sense. The archbishop's supporters built two enormous bonfires, between which Peter would have to walk. If he came through unscathed, they would take it to mean that God had intervened to protect him, and that Peter was telling the truth. After saying Mass, Peter emerged in his vestments, and before a leering crowd of thousands, walked calmly through the flames—to emerge without even losing his eyebrows. This "proved" he was telling the truth, and gave Pope Alexander II the pretext he needed to depose the corrupt archbishop. Peter received the title "Igneus" (fiery), and was later named a cardinal himself, and canonized a saint.

The Vallambrosans were famous for their piety and strictness—which also kept down their numbers. Even in the pious Middle Ages, few men felt called to such a stark monastic life. The wars that raged across a disunited Italy destroyed more than one of their monasteries, and in the early nineteenth century when Napoleon invaded Tuscany, his troops plundered Badia a Coltibuono. The monks tried to make do in the ruins, until the anti-Catholic government of the Kingdom of Italy seized the land in 1866. (Four years later, the same kingdom would invade and annex the Vatican; **see Velletri**). In a lottery, the Italian state sold Badia a Coltibuono to the family of Guido Guintini, which still tends the vines and makes the

---

[3] The sin of "simony," or obtaining religious offices for money, was named for Simon Magus, a third-rate magician who approached the Apostles, (Acts 8: 9–24) asking them to share their power to work miracles for a price. The practice of simony plagued the Church up until the Council of Trent, despite the best efforts of dozens of popes and the reforming monks of Cluny.

wines. The old monastery still produces Vin Santo and many other varieties, and hosts the cooking school run by Lorenza di Medici—famous cookbook author, and scion of that ancient family of Florentine oligarchs and popes.

And the name of this lush dessert wine still hearkens back to its ecclesiastical origins. According to legend, the wine's title dates to the Council of Florence in 1349, which the learned Byzantine theologian and humanist Johannes Bessarion attended in the hope of reuniting the Greek church with Rome. The last emperors of Byzantium and the popes struggled mightily to overcome the centuries of division between the churches (**see Ouzo**), partly in order to motivate Western kings to join in yet another crusade against the aggressive Ottoman Turks. After months of tedious debates over abstruse differences in Trinitarian theology, Bessarion certainly needed a drink. It is said that when some Italian cardinals served Bessarion a glass of the local dessert wine, he exclaimed that the wine was familiar—he'd tasted it in Xanthos, a Greek city in Asia Minor. The Italians thought he'd pronounced the wine "santo," that is, holy, and to be polite—since they weren't giving ground on purgatory, papal primacy, or the *filioque*[4]—they started calling that variety of wine Vin Santo.

The attempt to reunite the churches failed; the Greeks did sign an agreement with Rome but could not enforce it at home—indeed, the men who'd made the deal had to flee their enraged co-religionists one step ahead of the lynch mob, and ended up dwelling in Italy; Bessarion would spend the rest of his life there, honored by the pope with the title of cardinal, with ample access to the wine he may have named. On paper, the Byzantine emperor remained loyal to the agreement—and in 1453, when the Turkish armies at last overwhelmed the walled city of Constantinople, the churches they looted and the patriarch they deposed, Athanasios II, were still in union with Rome.

The man the Turkish sultan chose to replace him, Gennadius II, was a bitter enemy of Rome, as were most of his successors—though today's Patriarch of Constantinople, Bartholomew I, is more ecumenically minded, and eager to extend his influence beyond the few thousand Greeks left in his archdiocese after decades of persecution. Indeed, the refusal of the Turkish government to grant full religious freedom to Christians is one of the issues blocking its entry into the European Union—thank God.[5]

And what of the poor Vallambrosans? This order, which monks first founded to

---

[4] This is the word added during the Middle Ages by Latins to the Apostle's Creed to clarify the issue of the procession of the Holy Spirit and guard against the popular Eastern Trinitarian heresy of . . . oh, never mind. The Council of Florence couldn't resolve this, and neither can we.

[5] Admitting Turkey into the EU, observers such as then-cardinal Josef Ratzinger have noted, would put the final nail in the coffin of Christian Europe, extending the frontier of the EU to the uncontrollable borders Turkey shares with Iran, Iraq, and Syria. Migrants who evaded Turkish Minutemen could hop on the next train, for instance, to Tuscany—and given the instability that American policies have stoked in the region, millions would. The old division between Catholics and Communists would in time be long forgotten, as cities such as Florence divided themselves into Sunni and Shi'ite sections. And given the fate of Christian wine merchants in "liberated" Iraq (they all live in Syria now, dreading the next liberation), we don't expect they'll be producing much Vin Santo. Instead, think: Tuscan hookah pipes.

persecute themselves, was duly hunted down by rival orders and secular rulers over the centuries, tossed out of most of its monasteries and driven nearly to extinction. But we're happy to report that a few men are still attempting to carry on the spirit of St. John Gualbert and St. Peter Igneus. At the venerable monastery of Passignano founded in 890—though many times dispersed, conquered, and confiscated— in 1986 a group of monks joined the Cardinal Archbishop of Florence to reestablish a Vallambrosan abbey on that site. While they're no longer making wine, to this day they still sing the Office, welcome guests in the spirit of St. Benedict (**see Hospitality**) and invite young men who wish to consider a vocation to their order. Those interested may contact the monks at *info@passignano.org*.

CELEBRATE: Even if you don't discern for yourself the stern vocation of a Vallambrosan, you can pray for their success as you savor the wine their order used to produce. Make that your silent intention as you dunk one of these delicious Tuscan biscotti, called *cantucci*, in a rich glass of Vin Santo produced on one of the old monastic estates. The cookie is as hard as the life of a Vallambrosan, but it's softened by the spirit.

Cantucci

2 cups all purpose flour
Pinch salt
1/2 teaspoon baking powder
3/4 cup sugar
3 eggs, white of 1 reserved for wash

1 teaspoon vanilla extract
Zest of 1 orange
1 cup almonds, toasted and
    coarsely chopped

Preheat oven to 350 degrees.
    In mixing bowl combine flour, salt, baking powder, and sugar.
    In center of flour mixture place eggs, vanilla, and zest.
    Mix until combined. Mixture will be somewhat crumbly. Dump out onto counter and knead with hands until smooth. Knead in almonds thoroughly, sprinkling counter with flour. Knead efficiently, so as to not overwork the dough.
    Divide in half and form into logs 1 1/2 inches wide. Place on baking sheet lined with parchment paper. Brush with reserved egg white mixed with a drop of vanilla extract.
    Bake 35 minutes.
    Remove from oven and reduce temperature to 325 degrees.
    Cut logs diagonally into 1/2 to 3/4 inch slices and lay them on the sheets.
    Return to oven for 15 minutes. Remove from oven and turn each cookie over. Cook another 5 minutes.
    Cool on rack.

Makes 24 cookies

Vodka: The Highest Aspiration of the Spirit

It's hard for thirsty Slavs like us to believe, but vodka hasn't been around for ever—nor rum, gin, or even whiskey. In fact, no one in Europe knew how to make anything stronger than wine until the twelfth century. Natural fermentation tops out at 14 percent alcohol (28 proof), after which the intoxicating by-product kills off the yeast, in much the way that rock bands often break up after their first gold record. Think of distillation as a way of going for the platinum.

The distillation process takes advantage of the different temperatures and rates at which water and alcohol evaporate, "reducing" the grape juice, corn mash, or fermented potato juice in much the way you'd "reduce" a sauce by leaving it on the stove. This procedure was unknown in the ancient world and medieval Europe. It was Arab and Persian alchemists who invented the technique of distilling liquids (not just wine), in their quest to transform base metals into gold. And in a way, they succeeded, because various forms of high-octane alcohol (**see Rum**) would some day be seen as liquid gold, in some countries replacing currency. In other lands, they serve as a mainstay of the economy (Scotch) or the best argument against suicide (Finnish vodka). It's easy to forget that the word "alcohol" is of Arabic derivation, though it was first applied to spirits worth drinking by Renaissance magician Paracelsus—who thought the stuff pretty magical. Before that, liquors were called in various languages "water of life" (**see Eau de Vie** and also **Whiskey**) or "fire water."

Ironically, the Islamic scientists who invented the procedure really couldn't benefit from it, strong drink being forbidden by the Koran. It was only once—you guessed it—Christian monks got their hands on the equipment that alcoholic drinks began to appear across Europe. At first, they prescribed the tonics they created as "strictly medicinal." Pretty soon they were writing prescriptions by the barrel-full.

This history lesson reminds us just how "handy" Europeans have proved at making ruthlessly practical use of things discovered by other people, such as tobacco, gunpowder, printing, and America. As Tom Standage observed in his excellent *A History of the World in Six Glasses*, distilled drinks caught on most quickly in lands north of the "wine line," where it's too cold to grow grapes. These wintry folk learned the skills to make delicious, complex drinks out of whatever grew in those brief weeks when it wasn't hailing. It's for that reason we urge the reader to steer clear both of Italian "Scotch" and Icelandic "wine". Just trust us on this one, okay?

Which brings us to vodka, the *ne plus ultra* of distilled beverages. Over the centuries, a variety of ingredients have been rendered into vodka:

- Potatoes, apples, plums (Poland)
- Grain (Russia)
- Paper mill residue (Sweden)
- Sugar beets (Scotland)
- Maple syrup (Vermont)
- Grapes (France)
- Coal, chickens (the Soviet Union)[6]

Perhaps the only unfortunate side-effect of the fall of Soviet tyranny—apart from the wholesale plundering of the country by oligarchs who now sit on their ill-gotten wealth in foreign capitals like London, scheming against their motherland in the name of "democracy," by which they mean "kleptocracy"—is the decline of chicken-based vodka. After a prolonged search, we have reluctantly determined that this distinctive drink has gone the way of Aeroflot and the Komsomol. The closest a nostalgic Slav can come is to whip up chicken ala vodka, but that isn't really the same thing, now is it?

Different countries take credit for inventing vodka. One story has Russian monks learning the technique of distillation from visiting Italian missionaries in the sixteenth century, and using it on native ingredients such as potatoes and grain. As Russophiles, we hate to disagree, but it appears that these monks must have stopped over in Poland along the way: Historians point to documents from the Polish town of Sandomierz in 1404, which make reference to a strong, highly distilled potato drink. The monks who first made the stuff intended it as a medicine, but it was quickly adopted as a means of stiffening oneself to go out and plough in the snow. And to this day, it serves as an excellent fuel for any snow plow, human or mechanical. (Warning to Russians: This does NOT mean that the fuel drained from

[6] Don't ask.

the gas tank of your neighbor's snow plow can serve as an excellent vodka. This is not what logicians call a "symmetric proposition.")

Whatever its origins, vodka is in a sense the purest form of alcohol, which no doubt gives rise to brand names such as Skyy, Cristall, and of course, the Swedish brand Absolut. Indeed, this last brand evokes some complex theological questions—and has provoked widespread popular confusion—which cry out for clarification.

Philosophers who attempt to reason about the mystery of God's nature teach us that while we are relative, dependent creatures composed of mixed elements (body and spirit, reason and emotion), God the creator is "absolute." According to the *Catholic Encyclopedia*, the Absolute "signifies (1) that which is complete and perfect; (2) that which exists by its own nature and is consequently independent of everything else." In such discussions of God, we hope to capture something meaningful about the ultimate, ineffable mystery by referring to positive human attributes, taken to the greatest degree imaginable. Such reasoning is called "positive" theology, since it entails positing things about God, based on analogy from the lower things of creation.[7] This kind of thinking leads us to say that God is "all-powerful," "all-good," "all-wise," "perfectly just" and absolutely "simple"—with no admixture of lower elements, and no moving parts.

St. Anselm of Canterbury (1033–1109) defined God as "that being than which nothing greater can be conceived." He even regarded this definition as a proof that God *must* really exist, since if He didn't, then we could conceive of something greater—namely a God who did exist. . . . (*See what he did there? Pretty clever, eh?*) It's a brain-teaser worthy of freshman philosophy class, and St. Thomas Aquinas (1225–1274) didn't buy it. But Aquinas did carry on the tradition of conceiving of God as the consummate perfection of every quality of being. Given the way our minds work—we start with particular things we've seen, tasted, or touched—this could lead us to conceive of God as a vast collection of really pleasant and positive things, piled up and waiting for us in heaven like a divine buffet. But this is only because we are looking through the wrong end of the kaleidoscope; in fact, all the glorious complexity of the universe can be traced back to a pure, spiritual Source, one infinitely perfect and simple being.

Which brings us back, of course, to Swedish vodka. As a liquor, vodka has always puzzled us a little, since by general agreement, the better a vodka is *the less taste it has*. If, as Walter Pater wrote, all art aspires to the condition of music,[8] then all vodkas distill toward the flavor of moonshine. If you read the ad copy touting

---

[7] Philosophers and mystics also use what is called "negative" theology, pointing out how God is *unlike* us and our limited reality. Hence, God is "uncaused," "immortal," "unlimited," "independent," "un-created," and non-material, etc. Don't take this too far, of course. When drawing up your own lists of negations at home, leave off such terms as "unemployed," "undocumented," "disinterested" and "unsweetened." They really don't apply.

[8] It doesn't.

various vodkas, or the tasting notes compiled by connoisseurs, you'll be struck by the weirdly *theological* impulse that seems to animate them. Instead of talking about flavor, the writers brag of its absence—of the "purity," "simplicity," and "starkness" you'll find in the clear glass of almost tasteless, fiercely alcoholic liquor. The ad campaigns, which for decades touted Absolut, made the most of this, punning ruthlessly on the brand's evocative name, and inserting the vodka, Zelig-like, into virtually every life situation[9]—as if the grain liquor itself were the Uncreated, perfectly simple and self-subsistent Cause which underlay and guaranteed the existence of all lower, contingent beings. But we're pretty sure that isn't true. . . .

Okay, we did some research, and we've compiled a list of important differences between Absolut vodka and God. The following checklist should help contemporary believers keep the distinction clear in their minds:

God	Absolut Vodka
Uncreated spirit	Pure, distilled spirit
Absolutely simple	Stark, almost flavorless
Omnipotent	Powerful (80 proof)
Omnipresent	Ads are omnipresent
Perfectly free	$7.00 a shot in Manhattan
Mysteriously became incarnate	Mysteriously used in Cosmopolitans
Jewish	Swedish

CELEBRATE: Since at the Incarnation, the Absolute Spirit condescended to incarnate Itself in the sweaty flesh of a tiny boy, we are unashamed to adulterate the pristine purity of Absolut by pouring the stuff into a cookpot full of boiling lamb. The result is unfathomably delicious, and hearty enough to sustain a long day's philosophizing, plowing, or pillaging.

Absolut "Lamb of God" Stew

1 tablespoon butter	14 lamb shoulder chops
2 medium onions, diced	1 clove
4 carrots, diced	1 bay leaf
3 celery stalks, diced	1 teaspoon black peppercorns
2 parsnips, diced	1 bunch parsley, chopped
1 turnip, diced	2 cups premium vodka
1 pound baby white potatoes, quartered	Salt
	Freshly ground white pepper

---

[9] Just about the only pun the company didn't use was "Absolut Power," with a picture of Stalin on the bottle. That campaign "didn't test well" and was reluctantly abandoned.

In large soup pot heat butter and add vegetables minus potatoes. Cook 10 minutes. Season and add potatoes. Lay lamb on top and cover with water. Add clove, bay leaf, and peppercorns. Bring to a slow simmer for 1 hour. Then add 1/2 parsley and vodka. Cook another 30 minutes to an hour. Stir in remaining parsley and adjust seasoning.

Best if made a day in advance. When chilled the fat will rise to the top and can be easily spooned off. Reheat and serve with buttered noodles.

Serves a crowd

Drinking Song #8: A Song of Mourning

We offer here for your edification yet another moving song which marks the centuries-long Irish battle for independence from Britain. We hope we aren't overloading you with Hibernian songs. It's not some ethnic nationalism on either of the authors' parts (though there's some of that—as in John *Patrick* Zmirak), but rather the intrinsic qualities of these lilting, mournful songs:

- They're powerfully melodic, and easy to sing while tipsy—in fact, they're best sung that way.
- They bring a tear to the eye—and often help calm down drunks who might otherwise pick a fight.
- They commemorate the struggle for freedom of an ancient Catholic people—indeed, the race which converted the rest of the British Isles to Christianity in the first place.
- They're in English—no irritating foreign words, diacritical marks, or explanatory footnotes.
- They're in the public domain. No pesky lawsuits.

To other ethnic groups who might feel a bit left out, we'd like to point out that while we may not have included any Ethiopian, Greek, or Maltese songs, at least we showed the good sense not to include any Irish *recipes*. We like to highlight a people's strong points. . . .

"The Minstrel Boy" is a moving tribute by an Irish patriot, Thomas Moore (1779–1852), to several of his old friends who died in the course of abortive revolts against Great Britain. Set to an old Irish folk melody, the lyrics commemorate the uprisings attempted in 1798 and 1803 by the ecumenical nationalists of the United Irishmen—a group which briefly united Catholics and Protestants in a move for a unitary, independent Ireland. As one of the first Catholics ever admitted to Trinity College, Dublin, Moore had befriended a number of Protestants who also resented

English domination over their homeland—including the harsh "Penal Laws" depriving Catholics of civil rights and centralizing authority over the island in the hands of the British Parliament.

For centuries, the British crown had maintained its authority over lands from Ireland to India through a policy of "divide and conquer," pitting ethnic and religious groups with ancient grievances against each other, and presenting itself as the only force which could keep peace between them. United Irishmen leader Wolfe Tone, a Protestant, called attention to this strategy in September, 1791 in the tract called "Argument on Behalf of the Catholics of Ireland." Here Tone pointed out that the anti-Catholic laws imposed by Britain were effectively repressive of Protestants as well, intended as they were to play off "the one party [against] the other, plunder and laugh at the defeat of both."

Presenting themselves as champions of both Catholics and Protestants with grievances, the United Irishmen attracted some 100,000 members by 1797, and threw a scare into the British government—whose hands were full attempting to contain the chaos unleashed by the French Revolution on the Continent. Forced underground by act of Parliament, the United Irishmen began to plot an armed revolt, coordinating their efforts with the radicals then in control of France. Unable to face the full force of British arms alone, the rebels hoped for a landing of French regular troops and arms that would even the odds. In 1796, Wolfe Tone returned from France with a naval force containing 15,000 French soldiers—which could not land, thanks to typical Irish weather. Tone glumly sailed back to France with the troops, bitterly commenting "England has had its luckiest escape since the Armada."

Preparing for the inevitable revolt, the British government had stoked suspicions among the Protestants of Belfast that this revolt was really a plot by "papists" to take over the island, and won the support of Irish clergy by permitting—for the first time in centuries—Catholic education in Ireland, establishing Maynooth College in 1795 for the training of priests. It didn't take much to turn Irish clergy against an invasion backed by the revolutionary French, who had spent the better part of 1793–1795 conducting a genocide against the peoples of the Vendée and Brittany, who'd resisted a savage persecution of the Church (**see Drinking Song #7**).

Frustrated after years of empty promises from the French, and threatened with martial law, the United Irishmen launched their rebellion in May, 1798, intending to capture Dublin. However, informers of both religions united to tip off the British authorities, who were well-prepared for the rebels: Nearly everywhere, their poorly armed troops faced dug-in, veteran British regiments, and by July 14 (the great holiday of their far-off French allies), the insurgents knew they were beaten. A few remained in the field to join the paltry force of 1,000 French soldiers who landed on August 22, only to succumb on September 8 after the Battle of Ballinamuck. Massacres had taken place on both sides, claiming along with the combat some 15,000–30,000 lives. British penal laws on the Irish were clamped down tighter, and not loosened until after the defeat of Napoleon in 1815.

It was friends who died in the 1798 rebellion, and in an even more abortive uprising in 1803, whom Thomas Moore remembered in the moving words of "The Minstrel Boy," a song whose popularity quickly spread across the Atlantic—and was sung by Irish soldiers fighting on both sides of the War Between the States. Indeed, a third stanza was written during the war, a plea for peace which we have included here. And there's no denying that the song is haunting, and commemorates brave and patriotic men.

Still, we can't help feeling glad that Irish independence was not won with the help of the Revolutionary government that butchered peasants, burned churches, and waged war against most of Europe in the service of fanatical nationalism. While we can't exactly blame the United Irishmen for seeking allies where they could find them, it's hard to mourn the failure of Jacobin troops to land on Irish soil. For all its flaws, Great Britain during the wars against the French Republic and then Napoleon was the champion of sanity, gradual reform, and comparative religious freedom—against a series of brutal and expansionist regimes led by ideologues. The Irish who welcomed the aid of the men who'd blown up Cluny, beheaded contemplative nuns, and enshrined a whore in Notre Dame were making, almost literally, a deal with the devil. And they got burned.

Ironically, one of the best recordings of "The Minstrel Boy" was made by civil rights activist and famous bass singer Paul Robeson. Enraged by the harsh discrimination suffered by blacks throughout a segregated America, Robeson became a lifelong Communist, making tours through Stalin's Russia—which he proclaimed a beacon of civil rights for ethnic minorities. His rightful indignation at Jim Crow laws and lynchings led Robeson to accept the Stalin Peace Prize in 1952, and in 1953 to eulogize the architect of the Ukrainian famine and the Gulag as a man of "deep humanity" and "wise understanding." Sad to say, but we think Robeson picked the right song to record.

Whatever the moral compromises made by the men who inspired or later performed it, "The Minstrel Boy" is a masterful song whose haunting melody will move listeners long after the historical events which surrounded it have faded—like the Soviet Union—from memory. We have it on no less authority than *Star Trek* (both *Deep Space Nine* and *The Next Generation*) that hundreds of years from now, crewmen of Federation starships such as Miles O'Brien will be singing "The Minstrel Boy" [10] to cheer themselves up in the face of the Romulans.

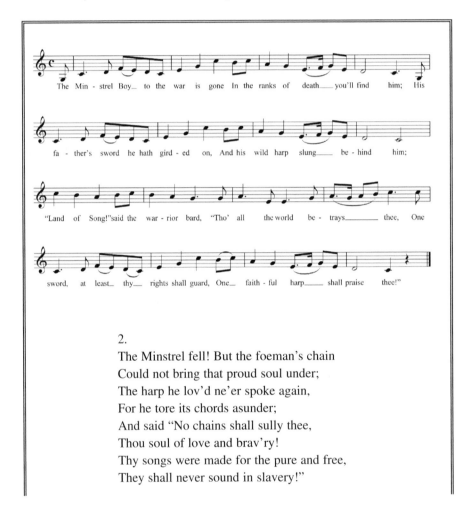

The Minstrel Boy to the war is gone In the ranks of death you'll find him; His father's sword he hath gird-ed on, And his wild harp slung be-hind him; "Land of Song!"said the war-rior bard, "Tho' all the world be-trays thee, One sword, at least thy rights shall guard, One faith-ful harp shall praise thee!"

2.
The Minstrel fell! But the foeman's chain
Could not bring that proud soul under;
The harp he lov'd ne'er spoke again,
For he tore its chords asunder;
And said "No chains shall sully thee,
Thou soul of love and brav'ry!
Thy songs were made for the pure and free,
They shall never sound in slavery!"

[10] Memory Alpha, "a collaborative project to create the most definitive, accurate, and accessible encyclopedia and reference for everything related to *Star Trek*," catalogues "The Minstrel Boy" as "an Earth song that Chief Miles O'Brien often used as his 'happy thought' in dire situations. His one-time captain, Benjamin Maxwell, was also fond of the song. A Paradan replicant of O'Brien was programmed to know the song." (TNG: "The Wounded"; DS9: "Whispers") Oh, and one more thing: "The tune of 'The Minstrel Boy' is played in the soundtrack of *Star Trek: Deep Space Nine*'s final episode 'What You Leave Behind.' It can be heard playing during the scene where O'Brien takes one last look at his quarters and finds the figurine of William B. Travis." Just in case, you know, you were wondering.

3.

The Minstrel Boy will return we pray
When we hear the news, we all will cheer it,
The minstrel boy will return one day,
Torn perhaps in body, not in spirit.
Then may he play on his harp in peace,
In a world such as Heaven intended,
For all the bitterness of man must cease,
And ev'ry battle must be ended.

The Wedding of Cana:
Serve Bum Wine at Your Reception

This incident in the New Testament (found in John 2) is one of our favorites. Of course, it is Jesus' first miracle, and the first instance of the Virgin Mary interceding with her Son on our behalf. What a cheerful way for Jesus to begin His ministry—by helping a band of Jews get tipsy at their wedding. (In our experience, they rarely require assistance, though we pitch in when we can.) It's fitting that the public life of Christ began with a solemn nuptial, since the reason He came was to re-establish a

relationship of love between God and His people, a nuptial union linking God the Father with His bride—which is how the Prophet Hosea described the people Israel, and how the Church conceives of herself. Likewise, the Song of Songs—besides making for really *steamy* bedtime reading at the honeymoon—serves as an allegory for the cosmic reunion of Creator and Creation.

The events at Cana also put paid to the sort of Protestants that claim teetotaling is called for in the Bible, who use little cups of grape juice instead of Communion wine. To them we respond, "So you're saying Our Lord was a bootlegger? Okay, but we believe in the Imitation of Christ. . . ." However, the Methodists who pioneered this oddly sober Sacramental practice meant well—they were trying, quixotically, to sober up the Welsh. Between them, the Welsh and the Methodists created some of the greatest English language hymns, from the hopeful "Come, thou long expected Jesus" to the less upbeat "Tis Finished! The Messiah Dies." So we ought to cut them a little slack.

What is more, from the early Middle Ages up until quite recently, the Western rites of the Catholic Church did not share the Communion cup with the laity. (Something to do with spreading the Black Plague.) While this had no theological significance—the body and blood of Christ are fully and equally present in both species of the Eucharist—it did create an emotional deficit which some laymen felt rather strongly. The Hussite heresy, which bedeviled fifteenth-century Prague, made a great issue of this; the followers of Jan Hus allowed laymen to drink from the chalice, which they emblazoned on the flags they carried into battle against their bishops. As late as the 1950s, orthodox liturgists such as Louis Bouyer wrote poignantly about how restricting the cup to the clergy impoverished the symbolism of the Mass. Conversely, traditionalist writers such as Michael Davies would argue that distributing the Precious Blood to the laity was a needless concession to Protestants. While Catholics are still arguing over this one, the Vatican has granted broad permission to bishops to offer both species to the laity, confident that this probably won't turn them into medieval heretics or Bohemians. Time will tell.

CELEBRATE: If you or one of your children are planning a wedding, we suggest you emulate the example of Cana, and invoke some other biblical precedents which can make the whole event more sacred and meaningful. For instance, the king who put on a wedding feast in Jesus' parable announced, "my oxen and my fatlings are killed." This suggests that vegetarian weddings are unbiblical, and your vegan guests should be left to munch on the centerpiece. It also seems that Our Lord believed in a firm dress code. So make sure to station large, hulking ushers near the doors of your reception, with instructions to eyeball everyone who shows up. Anybody whose clothes don't measure up—we're thinking polyester here, too-tight dresses, or ugly ties—should be asked, "Friend, how camest thou in hither not having a wedding garment?" (Matt. 22:12) Your bouncers will then "bind him hand and foot, and take him away, and cast him into outer darkness, there shall be weeping and gnashing of teeth." (Matt: 22:13)

Once your party is mercifully free of badly dressed vegetarians, it's time to get your groove on. Follow the precedent set at Cana by serving the worst wine first. For even more authenticity, make sure the wine is kosher. Here's a list of vintages which would have passed muster at Cana, in the order in which you should serve them:

- **Mogen David 20/20.** This beverage, usually called "Mad Dog 20/20," is the choice of kosher hobos across the world. At $4 per bottle, and 36 proof, you really can't go wrong. The connoisseurs at *Bumwine.com* say of its flavor: "Some test subjects report a slight numbing agent in MD 20/20, similar to the banana paste that the dentist puts in your mouth before injecting it with Novocain. . . . Available in various nauseating tropical flavors that coat your whole system like bathtub scum." Serve this stuff instead of champagne for the bridal toast, and your wedding will be the talk of the town!

- **Kedem Concord Grape**. This one's a little pricier—$7.50 per magnum. But this syrupy purple vintage follows in the tradition of Mad Dog, whose makers boil the grape juice, killing most of the flavor. They don't do this to be sadistic; by cooking the wine this way, it stays kosher even when opened and poured by "idolators" (i.e., gentiles). If you're running a *kashrut* restaurant, this can prove important, since most waiters you're able to hire seem to be 18-year-olds from Ecuador. (The Jewish teens are off at Habitat for Humanity, building homes for Ecuadorans.)

- **Noah Tevel Merlot**. By this point in the wedding, people are probably pretty tipsy, so it's time to break out something drinkable. This $15 bottle comes from Israel, where it's produced near the tomb of Abraham and Sarah. Ababanel Wines, which distributes Noah Tevel, says that this medium-bodied wine "opens with rich, ripe and concentrated aromas and flavors of juicy plums, currants and black cherries." Open it around the time the band starts playing old Billy Idol songs.

- **Capcanes Peraj Ha'abib Flor de Primavera 2003**. This fine $40 Spanish vintage comes from Priorat, where rabbis persuaded the local grape cooperative to raise their standards and produce a top-notch kosher wine. As wine maven Sandra Silfven wrote of this wine in the *Detroit News*: "You can almost chew the aromas, which explode with spice, tar, blackberries, cedar and smoky oak." By the time you serve this exploding wine, your guests should be finishing their overcooked steak or undercooked chicken, and nosing around for an extra piece of cake.

- **Noah Winery-Hevron Heights, Special Reserve (Judean Hills), 2001.** This $65 wine is what you'll serve last, to the boozehounds who steadfastly refuse to leave the reception, long after the bridal party has tumbled into the stretch-humvee white limos and fallen asleep.

Now you might be a little skeptical here—suspecting that Jesus might not appear at your reception to transform the cisterns of water at the door designed to wash guests' feet (why *did* you let the wedding planner talk you into those cisterns?) into Chateau Mouton Rothschild. To this we answer: Have faith. Getting married in the first place is a leap into the abyss, a venture so risky that no one should undertake it without a firm belief in miracles. Start small, by serving box wine with the canapés. As Christ said in the parable of the talents, "Thou hast been faithful over a few things, I will make thee ruler over many things." (Matt 25: 21) Maybe even your spouse.

Weissbier and the Franciscan **Nouveau Pauvre**

Almost from the day they were founded in 1209, the Franciscan friars (the Order of Friars Minor) have attracted people like a cold keg on a hot day. When the young rake Francesco Bernardone renounced his father's wealth—dramatically stripping himself even of his clothes in the presence of a disapproving bishop— he embarked upon a romance with "Lady Poverty" which won him followers from across the continent. Rival orders accused the Franciscans of drawing in students by giving them "apples and beer," reports Franciscan friar William Short, OFM.[1]

There must have been more to Francis's appeal than that—since even the beer-resistant Moslems of North Africa whom Francis visited to accost with news of Christ admired his self-forgetful zeal, and declined to martyr him. In the midst of the first economic boom in Europe since the Black Plague, Francis drew thousands to turn their backs on the *nouveau riche*, and join the *nouveau pauvre*. The saint imitated the heroes of courtly love tradition by casting off every attachment to earthly goods in favor of a single-minded love—in Francis's case, of Christ, especially as personified in the poor ("the least of my brothers," Matthew 25:40). By the time he died in 1226, there were as many Franciscan friars and sisters in the world as there are today.

Millions more preferred to admire Francis from afar. Not everyone, thank God, is called to practice poverty, chastity, and obedience—particularly in the strict sense Francis embraced. Indeed, his own order split immediately and repeatedly over how to interpret his stark commands. New Franciscan groups determined to revive his "primitive" poverty arose as recently as the 1990s—and no doubt will keep on cropping up. We guess (with apologies to Cameron Diaz) there's just "something about Francis."

And it's something that makes worldly folks like us want to be associated with him, however distantly. It could be a statue of St. Francis in your front yard—or a DVD of *Francesco* (1989, starring *Mickey Rourke*) in your library. Some laymen join the Franciscan Third Order, promise to keep up a life of prayer, and wear its scapular—two bits of brown cloth that symbolize a friar's habit. Others go a bit further—for instance, various European kings who became full-fledged Franciscans in their old age or on their deathbed, so they could be buried in Franciscan habit. Charles V, who once reigned over most of Europe and Latin America, ended his days as a humble friar.

---

[1] This according to the University of St. Francis (Joliet, IL) newspaper, which calls itself *Apples and Beer*.

Or maybe you're running a brewery or pub, and you like the association between jolly friars and foaming mugs. (Capuchin Franciscans are beloved in Bavaria for serving the poor both bread *and* beer.) Burp Castle in New York City—one of our favorite haunts—made its name by dressing its staff in the brown habits of friars, decorating its walls with murals of Franciscans brewing beer, and playing only Gregorian chant. Of late, the place is under new management and the staff has stripped off their habits—which makes us feel as if the Reformation has swept through the place. But you can still order a chanted Mass with your Franziskaner.

Perhaps you're Philip Zang, a nineteenth-century Protestant brewer, and the Rocky Mountain Franciscans ask you to build them a bell tower. You agree, on the condition that the bell is cast not to ring as "clang, clang," but "zang, zang." (We're not making this up—though maybe the Archdiocese of Denver's Webmaster is.)

In Dublin, the Franciscan Well Brewery operates "on the site of a 13th-century abbey with a holy well," according to beer authority Michael Jackson. It's a microbrewery with limited exports, so we can't evaluate the taste, but we invite readers to try it themselves and send us reports. Of course the most famous Franciscan-scented beer is Franziskaner Weissbier, a light and frothy lager produced in Munich at a brewery which has sat since at least 1363 *across the street* from a Franciscan convent on the Residenzstrasse. In 1935, when symbols of Christian faith were scorned by a neo-pagan government, the brewery adopted a monk as its emblem on the label. The gesture might seem quaint or commercial to us today, but at the time it was countercultural, like the proud public Catholicism of many Bavarians—including the family Ratzinger, whose son became the first German pope since the eleventh century, Benedict XVI. The photo on this book's cover dates from one of his visits, while still a cardinal, to a Bavarian brewery. And the drink in his glass looks suspiciously like a Weissbier.

Willibrord: The Vintners' Saint
and His Dancing Procession

If you've read this far, first of all—congrats. Not all book buyers have proven so sturdy. Close friends of ours have tossed this book across the room in outrage at our "tendentious" account of the origins of Calvados. As your reward for slogging through to "W," we'd like to tell you about one of the most delightful Catholic customs in the world: the Dancing Procession of Echternach, conducted annually to the embarrassment of sniffy skeptics and the glee of eagerly credulous believers in miracles—like us.

The procession honors St. Willibrord, the eighth-century missionary who brought Christianity to the region. Trained—like most anybody who learned to read in those days, by Irish monks—Willibrord preached to the Frisians, founding the diocese of Utrecht and an abbey at Echternach. When a pagan king conquered the region and destroyed most of the churches Willibrord had built, the intrepid missionary kept sneaking into Frisia to encourage his converts, who welcomed him back at the warlord's death. Willibrord traveled the countryside digging "holy wells," where peasants could draw potable water, which had the added advantage of being blessed. This might sound superstitious to moderns like us, who prefer to have our magic water flown in from Fiji for $1.95 a bottle.

Willibrord was acclaimed as a saint as soon as he died, and his body duly chopped up into pious relics—of which a voting quorum remained at Echternach, attracting pilgrims who associated the saint with cures for epilepsy, convulsions, and the disease known as St. Vitus's Dance. Most pertinent for our purposes, Willibrord became the patron of the winemakers of Luxembourg.

These vintners are known among those who look a little further than France for fine vintages of Riesling, Pinot Gris, Pinot Blanc, Auxerrois, Pinot Noir, Rivaner, Elbling and of course the beloved Gewürztraminer. The Moselle River, which waters some of the finest vineyards of Germany, flows through Luxembourg first, creating a comfy microclimate where an even, annual rainfall helps vintners produce wines of consistent character. What's more, if you're serving one of these wines to friends with an average American's knowledge of geography, they will never have heard of Luxembourg. So you can tell them all about the place—and what you don't know, you can invent. They won't know the difference, so you might as well "educate" your friends about the unique attributes of the Grand Duchy of Luxembourg:

- It was originally settled by a race of diminutive bakers called "Der Kieblers," who gave rise to the legend of the Keebler Elves.
- The country is ruled by a Grand Duke, selected quadrennially on the basis of height; the current Grand Duke, Henri, is 17′ 3″ tall.
- By edict of the European Union, all dentures produced on the Continent must originate in Luxembourg.
- The U.S. Army in 1944 did not have Luxembourg on its maps, so they forgot to liberate it from the Germans, leaving them in control of the country until 1962, when President Kennedy came across it on a British atlas and ordered in our troops, who encountered no resistance.
- In Luxembourg, thanks to some quirk of nature, water flows down drains not clockwise, but diagonally.
- Owning dogs in Luxembourg is punishable by death—except for pugs, which are mandatory.

And so on. Just keep pulling stuff out of various bodily orifices until one of your friends expresses skepticism, at which point you should roll your eyes in exasperation, tell him: "Look it up!" and hand him this book. By the time he makes it to "W" and catches on, your evening will have drawn to a happy close. Better yet, admit that you were "making all of it up," that Luxembourg doesn't really exist, and you made the wine in your bathtub.

Of course, the country of Luxembourg is perfectly real, if not particularly extensive (at around 1,000 square miles), and it does make excellent wines. The nation is historically Catholic, and we're happy to report that its largest daily newspaper, *Luxemburger Wort* (circulation ca. 80,000), "belongs to the Catholic Archbishop of Luxembourg and has close links with the dominant political party, the Christian Social Party (CSV)," according to European Media Landscape. The country *was* occupied by Nazi Germany during World War II, and liberated by

Grand Duke Henri of Luxembourg, 17′ 3″ tall.

Allied forces in 1944.[2] As a peaceful, tolerant Catholic monarchy, the place embodies our political ideals better than most nations in the world, so we really don't mean to make fun of it.

For centuries, anti-clericalist snoots have been laughing at the expense of the Luxembourgers for their devotion to St. Willibrord—as expressed in their Dancing Procession. Held every year on the Tuesday after Pentecost, the procession begins in the morning with a homily at the bridge on the river Sauer, then tolling of an enormous bell in the abbey church. Local bands play a Renaissance jig on mandolins, fiddles, and flutes, as pilgrims, bishops, and priests walk arm-in-arm, five abreast, dancing three steps forward then two steps back—which means that it takes most of the morning to proceed less than a mile from the river to Echternach's basilica. (This is the "modern" version of the procession, which once featured cowbells, walking on one's knees, and crawling over stones.[3]) Once inside, the dance continues around the tomb containing the remainder of St. Willibrord, then settles down for a prayer service, which ends with Benediction of the Blessed Sacrament.

This procession has been suppressed by anti-Catholic emperors, forbidden by invading French revolutionaries, and explained away by post-Catholic snobs. But no one can keep the dancers down. Dozens of stories have come down over the centuries of Echternach pilgrims who danced in this procession, then received miraculous cures for epilepsy or related illnesses. One year, the procession averted the Plague. Even today, thousands of tourists descend upon Echternach every year to swell the pilgrims' ranks—ensuring that the procession will be continued in that town as long as Americans carry cameras and insist on trying to "track down those Keebler elves."

··

Whiskey: The Water of Life

As even bad Catholics know, the water that gives eternal life is the slightly oily stuff drizzled at baptism from a cruet onto our heads. Right up through the 1960s, most theologians believed that infants who died before they reached the font would never see God, but spend their eternity watching Teletubbies in a rather cushy

---

[2] The local Church, engaged in Resistance activities, was subject to significant coercion by the Nazis, who imprisoned many of its priests in camps. For a true story of the heroic resistance of a Luxembourg bishop and priest to the neo-pagan occupiers, see Volker Schlöndorff's powerful 2005 film *The Ninth Day*, which depicts a curate who must choose between fostering collaboration with the Nazis, or returning to a prison cell in Dachau.

[3] "Progress"—how we loathe it!

waiting room called Limbo. (The place was named for the popular dance, which some speculated was practiced in the afterlife, by souls hoping to some day squeeze under the gate into Heaven.) No less an authority than St. Augustine saw in the crying and fussing of infants the aftereffects of Adam's rebellion and original sin. (Modern theologians call it "colic.")

So people rushed their children to baptism, typically on the eighth day after their birth—corresponding to the day when Jesus was circumcised. (It's surprising that the Holy Family could book a rabbi on New Year's Day—but then, they had Connections.) Old-fashioned believers still lovingly refer to their newborns as "little pagans," and often request that the priest use the old (pre-Vatican II) baptismal rite, which includes an exorcism prayer. The cleric breathes three times on the squalling infant, saying "Go forth from him (her), unclean spirit, and give place to the Holy Spirit, the Paraclete." The water poured onto the baby's head constitutes a symbolic death to original sin, and rebirth in the supernatural life. This sign is somewhat more vivid among the Eastern Orthodox and various Protestant sects, which completely submerge a child or adult, and raise him up sputtering and coughing.

Which is exactly what happens the first time most people drink whiskey. Perhaps it was this coincidence that inspired Irish monks in the Middle Ages to call the strong stuff they'd concocted from malt, wheat, or rye *uisge* (<whiskey) *beatha*, or "water of life." (**see Eau de Vie**.) And for many of us, our first experience with whiskey did mark a whole new period in life, when we put away childish things like schoolwork and began the serious business of joining (or dating) garage bands, growing hair in places we'd never before thought possible, and driving loud, ugly

cars. Of course, one has to be careful, lest enthusiasm for the "water of life" end in a brief one. It's important to cultivate virtues such as moderation and discretion—as well as at least one nerdy, shy, or ultra-pious friend who'll serve as designated driver.

It shouldn't be surprising that in the mists of history, behind your bottle of Macallan or Jameson's, there stands a bald celibate in a scratchy robe. All across Christendom, the monks and friars served as the intellectual class—as well as the transmitters of technical innovation. To neighboring farmers, a monastery was sometimes a strict landlord, but more often an agricultural extension station, dispensing better seeds, inventing superior ploughs, and instructing the local peasants on how to spare the soil by rotating their crops. It was also a package store, since monks were busy concocters of ever more forms of liquor. Benedictines, Carthusians, Trappists, and Brigittines worked in their labs with beakers and vials, distilling grains, fruits, herbs, and other gifts of the earth into potent drinks that could warm the heart on a snowy day. One of the best of these warming-up drinks is still called "Akvavit," the Danish word for "water of life." Swedes and Norwegians continue to use this monastic name for their tangy distillations of potatoes flavored by caraway, dill, coriander, or cloudberry. (Millions of Icelandic-Americans simply call it "Sterno on the rocks.") And the French still serve after dinner little glasses of *eau de vie*, pungent and tasty liqueurs made from currants, plums, cherries or (our favorite) pears. There's nothing like a glass of Poire William to wash down a guilty plate of *foie gras*—though it won't do much to rinse off Original Sin.

CELEBRATE: Make good use of the Water of Life by whipping up an utterly unhealthy, lavish dessert which if eaten more than once a month could hasten an early death. These rich custards are good even without the burnt crust. But what is more fun than firing up a propane torch after dinner?[4]

Whiskey Crème Brulee

3 cups cream	2 tablespoons whiskey
1 cup milk	12 egg yolks
1 bay leaf	Turbinado sugar
6 ounces Billington's™ dark brown molasses sugar	

Preheat oven to 300 degrees.

Heat the cream, milk, and bay leaf just to the boil. Turn off heat, cover with plastic wrap and steep 30 minutes. Add sugar and whiskey and bring to a boil.

---

[4] Answer: Taking an old Christmas tree out on the New Orleans levee and loading it up with all the fireworks you can find, lighting it on fire, then phoning Fox News and reporting a terrorist strike. Careful, though—they might believe you, and call for a U.S. invasion of Santo Domingo.

Ladle cream into yolks while continuously whisking. Strain.

Pour into 12 ramekins in a hot water bath. The simplest way is to arrange the ramekins in a roasting pan and add half of the mixture. Top off before adding boiling water halfway up the sides of dishes. Carefully place in oven.

Bake 40 minutes. Remove from water with the aid of an offset spatula. Cool for 30 minutes.

Cover with plastic wrap and chill for a minimum of two hours.

Cover with turbinado and torch.

Makes 12 custards

Winkler Jesuitengarten: The Jesuits vs. The Jansenists

One of the great religious orders to undertake the art of the grape has been the Society of Jesus, known as the Jesuits. Among the important German vintages created by this order are Winkler Jesuitengarten and Förster Jesuitengarten—the vineyards of which the priests ran for centuries until secular governments stole their land. The Novitiate Winery in Los Gatos, California made wine until 1986, when it began to run out of novices. But Jesuits still stomp the grape today; their modern vineyards include the Sevenhill Cellars in Australia's Clare Valley, which produces altar wines—plus a range of top-notch vintages for the table. Its Shiraz has "powerful minty/eucalyptus-like aromas" and an "attractive soft and savoury palate with a slight minty edge," reports *Winestate* magazine (May/June 2006). Sevenhill also makes a "complex, old fashioned" Merlot, as well as an appropriately named 2002 St. Ignatius, which *Winestate* praises as "perfumed and spicy."

If you are indeed a bad Catholic—and not some saintly soul taking time off from her heroic exertions in mystical self-abandonment to see how the other half sins—then you have reason

to love the Jesuits. Here's a religious order which for most of its 460-plus years has heroically served the Church—the whole Church, sinners, scoundrels, and all. Not just the spiritual elite, but people like us: folks who often drag themselves to Mass and sit there feeling guilty for being bored, then seek out confessors who aren't quite fluent in English and say their penance on the subway.

Someone once said that the Church, like the U.S. Navy, was a machine designed by geniuses so it could be run even by idiots. Or built by saints to be run by sinners. If this is true, then Ignatius Loyola qualifies both as a genius and a saint. He founded the Society of Jesus in 1540 as a kind of crusade, intended to win back the errant souls who'd followed Luther and Calvin into heresy. A militaristic order, it nevertheless encouraged its highly intelligent recruits to pursue advanced studies in sciences and the arts, and employ all the latest technology (from illustrated books to elaborate baroque theater[5]) to win back souls to Christ. Because it meant to preach to the worldliest souls, the Society molded its priests through a stark spirituality founded on self-sacrifice and absolute obedience. If you've ever been to a serious Jesuit retreat, you will have encountered this militant spirit. If you're anything like us, you will have muttered, "Er, thanks but no thanks. But keep up the good work!"

One central experience in Jesuit spiritual training concerns what Ignatius called the "Three Degrees of Humility." These lessons are taught at any solidly Ignatian retreat on the very first day:

1. First Degree: You are willing to give up any good thing—such as wealth or even health—rather than commit a mortal sin.
2. Second Degree: You are indifferent as to whether you have a happy life or a sad one, whether you're rich and healthy or poor and sick, so long as you're doing God's will.
3. Third Degree: You actively prefer to be poor, sick, and unhappy, so you more closely resemble the suffering Christ.

---

[5] Scholars report that hundreds of dramas were composed in many languages by Jesuit playwrights exploring modern spiritual questions, some of them considered in their day the equal of Shakespeare's plays. Sadly, few of them have survived, so we'll never know. Unless they receive a revival run at the General Resurrection. . . .

If you're like us, when the retreat master announces #1, you're pretty much on board. When he gets to #2 you're squirming in your seat. And at #3 you're on your way to the parking lot, headed for a Will Farrell movie.

Ignatius may have been fervent, but he was no fool. He knew that most of us would react this way, which is why he reserved this kind of training for student priests and the most pious laymen. Such spiritual severity formed the elite cadres of the Jesuit order, who proceeded to honeycomb secular societies (such as seventeenth-century France) with schools and colleges designed to lead mediocre souls like ours, by patient baby steps, ever closer to Christ. If we don't get all *that* close . . . well what else is Purgatory for?

By contrast, the enemies of the Jesuits despised such compromise. The followers of the austere bishop Jansenius (1585–1638) believed that only the tiniest sliver of human beings had ever been meant for Heaven—a spiritual elect who were chosen by God before the dawn of time, predestined to eternal salvation. They held that divine Grace is impossible to resist and impossible to attract; God alone decided who would be saved or damned. In fact, when sinners who are not predestined to salvation try to *mimic* the actions of the Saved—for instance, by serving the poor or receiving the Sacraments—God views this as a blasphemy, and will punish them for it *more severely than their sins*. The greatest of the Jansenists, the philosopher Pascal, wrote a series of scurrilous pamphlets against the Jesuits,[6] accusing them of accommodating sinners and offering false hope of salvation to the mass of sinners who were predestined, doomed, and damned.[7]

In response, the Jesuits urged on their worldly parishioners frequent Confession and Communion, devotion to the Sacred Heart, and other external practices loathed by the Jansenists—who regarded most people's confessions as insincere and their absolutions as invalid. The Jesuits begged the Holy See to condemn the Jansenist heresy—and at last the Holy See did, declaring in a series of papal statements that divine Grace can be resisted, that our good works can attract God's further graces, and that salvation hinges on our own response to Grace. The Jansenists went underground, and continued for centuries to spread their gospel of *Schadenfreude*: Even today, some neo-Jansenists run a Web site which claims that unbaptized infants burn in Hell, and condemns the "heretical" popes who have taught otherwise. As to *why* any soul would want to spend eternity with

---

[6] Pascal was echoing a theme long popular among Protestants, who accused the group of secrecy, craftiness, and fanaticism. So many anti-Jesuit pamphlets were written in English that their assertions entered our language; one of the meanings given in the 2006 Random House Dictionary for the word "Jesuit" is "a crafty, intriguing, or equivocating person." (In fact, this should probably read "priest with tenure.") The harmless, bourgeois devotional group Opus Dei has also spawned a cottage conspiracy industry—though the only "alternative" usage of their name came in the album entitled "Opus Dei" by the Slovenian industrial band, Laibach. We're not sure why they used the name, but the album is awesome. . . .

[7] To learn more about Pascal and his campaign against the mercy of God, see *God Owes Us Nothing* by Leszek Kolakowski (Chicago: University of Chicago Press, 1998).

a "God" who tortures infants and aborted fetuses forever for Adam's sin . . . the Web site is less specific.[8]

The victory of the Jesuits over the Jansenists made it possible for the Church to flourish for centuries, and established an easy truce between the tiny splinter of genuine saints and . . . well, the rest of us.

For centuries, your average, everyday sinner would stumble along through life, well aware that the Church held high ideals and cleaved to quite stern rules of behavior. And he knew he had not a prayer of living up to them. But he acknowledged them as true, admired those whom he suspected of sanctity, and was humbled by his own wretchedness. So he confessed his sins early and often, wore a brown scapular, and if he happened to strike it rich he'd pour his newfound wealth into Catholic schools or charities. This formula worked well for hundreds of years: All those yellow-brick grammar schools once run by nuns weren't built by men in vows of poverty, but by hard-nosed Irishmen with dirty hands, shrewd Italian-American contractors with shady connections, and penitent "burlesque" dancers with stretch marks who'd married money. Indeed, the spiritual mediocrity and Catholic guilt of bankers like the Medicis helped pay for things like the Sistine Chapel. A cozy *modus vivendi*, whereby a small minority within the Church did all the spiritual heavy lifting, while the rest of us footed the bill. This division of labor and metaphysical outsourcing proved highly efficient, generating a few hundred saints every century, but thousands and thousands of solid, earthly Catholic institutions—from missions throughout the Third World, to hundreds of perfectly orthodox (if sometimes mediocre) universities.

As we've said elsewhere (**see Gout**), the Council Fathers at Vatican II weren't happy with this arrangement. In the idealistic spirit of the'60s, they called upon all Catholics to embrace the same sanctity long prescribed to clerics, cloistered nuns, and little old ladies with too many holy cards and cats. This they termed the "universal call to holiness." If you've looked around the Church of late, you'll see it hasn't quite worked out as planned. For one thing, the radical change in the Catholic liturgy—apart from its appalling ugliness—was designed to force the average believer to take a lively part in the proceedings. Instead of kneeling quietly and watching a formal rite in a foreign tongue ringed round with incense and mystery, the average guilt-struck sinner was now enjoined by a grinning priest to come up into the sanctuary and join hands around the altar with the nuns who now wore blue jeans and banged on banjos. The altar rail was gone, and the porcelain crucifix his grandmother saved her pennies to pay for was covered by a green, felt banner with the stark demand: "Rejoice!" It's enough to send you slinking out into the vestibule.

---

[8] Since Jansenists believe that some of the joy felt by the saved comes from watching Divine Justice enacted on the Damned, perhaps the spectacle of these infants roasting forever is part of Paradise—like throwing another "shrimp on the barbie."

This shouldn't have surprised anyone. When you impose a single standard on a vast group of people with widely differing capacities, only two things can happen: the elite will be dumbed down to the lowest common denominator, or the great mass of weaklings will leave. To the consternation of several popes, these twin disasters happened at once: the fervent cooled and the tepid froze.

Meanwhile, to those of us who had, er, a little *trouble* with the Church's teachings on sexuality—which men in particular found much more practicable when folks got married around age 15—the post-conciliar era offered a whole new option. It was called "dissent." Thanks to this bold innovation, instead of stumbling into the confessional every week or so to recite the same dreary list of fumbling sins, we could pick up a slim and slickly written book by a priest with a long string of academic titles and a hipster haircut which argued that the fault was not with us but *with the Church*. We could claim that our conscience commanded we refuse the medieval strictures imposed by a sclerotic, monarchical Church,[9] and go ahead and do . . . pretty much what Kevin Spacey did in *American Beauty*. Indeed, we might call the post-conciliar chaos the Church's mid-life crisis. Minus the red sports car.

Ironically, it was a self-styled Catholic conservative who helped make dissent fashionable. In 1961, when Pope John XXIII issued an encyclical on economics (*Mater et Magistra*), which displeased William F. Buckley Jr, he wrote a column called "Mater Si, Magistra No," explaining how Catholics could pick and choose which Church pronouncements to obey. Suddenly, for Buckley, the banquet of Catholic truth had become a breakfast bar. We could concentrate on the bacon, and skip all that oatmeal and those pesky slices of fruit. Renowned dissenter Garry Wills, then Buckley's protégé, has traced his own liberation from "mindless" obedience to the Church's teaching authority to Buckley's famous column.[10] Many others followed suit, and soon in Catholic circles a hundred flowers bloomed like Morning Glories. Which, it turns out, are hallucinogens.

---

[9] Bookstore shelves soon groaned with paperbacks sporting self-congratulatory titles like *A Modern Priest Looks at His Outdated Church*—which is, we're not kidding, *an actual book.*

[10] See Wills's *Why I Am a Catholic (Why I Am also the Queen of Spain)*, Mariner Books, 2003)

Xarel-lo: Catalan Grapes and Saints

This variety of grape forms the backbone of the Spanish Champagne industry. Oops! We're not allowed to used that name for sparkling wines from anyplace outside one region in France, so we fully expect that agents of *La Direction Générale de la Sécurité Extérieure* (DGSE) will arrive sooner or later to blow up our Greenpeace boats. That's if we aren't garroted first by members of the Catalan Red Liberation Army (ERCA), who'll hunt us down for referring to their nation as part of Spain. It's a risky calling, writing about the bottle. Regional patriots cling to their local spirits as flags of resistance to central authority, especially those whose lands have long been subsumed by larger, more powerful states. We've seen bloody bar fights break out between Manhattanites and residents of Bensonhurst when the former offhandedly called Brooklyn Brown Ale "a New York City beer." It didn't help that the latter had light-heartedly dubbed the former "a bunch of faggots."

Photo by Montrealais, courtesy of Wikipedia.

A similar tension obtains in Catalonia, the region where Xarel-lo grows, and is made into *cava*, the Iberian equivalent of *spumante* and Champagne. Some worthy brands of *cava* include Castell d'Olerdola, Albet/Noya, Marques Monistrol, and the ever-popular (with lovestruck grad students and religious publishers) Cordoniu and Freixenet.

If you're an aspiring connoisseur of Spanish wines, it's important that you avoid some fundamental mistakes often made by novices. First of all, nail the geography; study a map of Spain which marks its historically fractious regions. Learn the difference between Spanish Galicia, land of Spanish-speaking Celts who play bagpipes and eat potatoes, and Polish Galicia, whose Galicians play accordions and use their potatoes for vodka. Get the knack of distinguishing between a French and a Spanish Basque (**see Izarra**); the former wear their jaunty little berets cocked to the left.

And be careful not to confuse the grape called Xarel-lo with Xarrelo, the

Russian rubber tire conglomerate. This Moscow-based exporter of tires and tubes for "passenger cars, light trucks, trucks and buses, agricultural farm tractors, industrial vehicles, aircrafts, bicycles and motorcycles" either operates or outsources from the following facilities:

- Yaroslavsky Tire Plant (Yaroslavl)
- Omskshina (Omsk)
- Voltire (Volzhsky)
- Uralshina (Yekaterinburg)
- Nizhnekamskshina (Tatarstan) and
- Belshina (Republic of Belarus)

Yes, their names sound similar, and are disconcertingly *foreign*, but in fact the products of Xarel-lo and Xarrelo are markedly different. According to the critics of *Winegeeks.com*, while Xarel-lo forms the base for most brands of Spanish sparkling wine (or *cava*), it is also "used to produce still wines that are crisp and fresh, with notes of stone fruits, cream and a sometimes vegetal quality." In contrast, the aficionados of *Moderntiredealer.com* describe Xarrelo's products as somewhat "vulcanized," with "notes of tread, and a durable consistency."

When they aren't bottling creamy, stony fruit wine that tastes like vegetables, the Catalans are busy trying to make the point that they aren't Spaniards. Or at least that they're *more* than Spaniards, as heirs to one of the first Iberian kingdoms to kick out the Moors (in 732, as opposed to 1492 in Granada). The wealthy Kingdom of Aragon would quickly become the commercial powerhouse of the peninsula, and its sway would extend as far off as Sicily. Things started to go wrong for the Catalans in 1469, when their ruler Ferdinand II married Queen Isabella of Castile—the sturdy, rural, honor-obsessed kingdom based in Madrid, which would quickly set the tone for the

unified Crown of Spain: dogmatic, bureaucratic, and plodding. Lots of long, formal receptions conducted by men in black clothes with enormous white ruffs and women with dwarves; imagine an entire kingdom inspired by *The Addams Family*—with an Inquisition run by Uncle Fester.

While the Spanish Empire, through a series of happy accidents, would soon span the globe from Hispaniola to Manila, it would be governed not by Aragonian entrepreneurs, but Castilian commissars—who were always ready to sacrifice the prosperity of other regions for the benefit of the top-heavy court in Madrid. Rigid restrictions on trade, elaborate quotas concerning who might emigrate where, and intrusive regulations concerning most areas of ordinary life would flow in reams of finely written documents from Madrid to the four corners of the empire, strangling its economic potential even as the English pirates and Puritans prospered. Had Aragonians ruled the Spanish empire instead of Castilians, the Rio Grande might well feature a border fence facing north, to keep out the "wetback" Texans.

Things got worse when the Bourbon monarchs took over from the Habsburgs,[1] and adopted the Enlightenment mania for centralization and anti-clericalism. In 1700 the Catalans fought a war on behalf of the last Habsburg claimant to the throne, who promised to respect their local privileges and culture. They were beaten, with the help of France's Louis XIV (**see Bourbon**), and subject to martial law. Things got worse after the Spanish Civil War, when Francisco Franco attempted to impose cultural uniformity on the country, banning even the use of the Catalan language. The region only re-gained a little of its medieval autonomy in 1979, from King Juan Carlos's newly democratic (if sadly secularizing and de-populating) Spain.

On top of its long history as perhaps the most innovative and creative region on the peninsula (and now the Basque ETA will come and try to kill us), Catalonia may boast one of the greatest artistic geniuses of the twentieth century—who is also an incipient saint—Antonio Gaudi. The visionary architect's office buildings, apartments, and parks can best be described as a kind of hallucinatory Art Nouveau, a material precursor to Salvador Dali's self-proclaimed "Paranoiac-Critical Method," which also depicted objects in the process of dripping and flowing into one another. Gaudi is most famous, of course, for his Cathedral of the Holy Family (*La Sagrada Familia*) in Barcelona—and that is precisely what Gaudi would have wanted. The architect was a deeply pious, ascetical Catholic, who experienced at age 31 a conversion, shortly after he began work on the Cathedral. According to Rev. Lluís

Catalan architect, Antonio Gaudi (1883-1926), a fervent believer whose process for beatification is now under way. It may be completed before his cathedral, *La Sagrada Familia,* in Barcelona.

---

[1] An historical note: Things always get worse when the Habsburgs leave. Cf. Croatia, Slovakia, Bosnia, the Ukraine, and of course, Austria.

Bonet i Armengol, vice postulator for the cause of Gaudi's beatification, the architect moved from the blithely secular world view of an avant-garde artist to a profound spirituality—principally under the influence of Rev. Enric d'Ossó, a founder of several religious orders, whom Pope John Paul II would canonize in 1993. Gaudi started reading the Scriptures and going to Mass every day, and steeped himself in the riches of the Church's prayer tradition by studying Dom Guéranger's *The Liturgical Year*—a book which has served as the bedside reading of many modern saints, including Thérèse of Lisieux. In his newfound faith, Gaudi discovered the deeper explanation for his strangely organic style of building; lost in admiration for the natural world as God had created it, he wanted his own works to mirror the organic forms of animals and plants, the better to "extend and cooperate with" Creation.

Though he was the most famous architect in the wealthy city of Barcelona, Gaudi began to dwell among the poor, wearing shabby (but always clean) clothes and spending all his waking hours at work on the Cathedral. He fasted and lived like a strict Franciscan, taking no money for his work on the Cathedral, and even making the rounds of his former patrons to beg for funds to help finish the church. Like most of Europe's famous cathedrals, Gaudi knew it would take decades, if not centuries, to finish. He told skeptical friends, who thought he'd lost his mind, "My Client is not in a hurry." In conversation with a friend, Gaudi once explained his creative ethos:

> Life is a battle. In order to fight, one needs strength and the strength of virtue and this force is only sustained and increased with the cultivation of spirituality, that is, with religious practice. Life is love and love is sacrifice. In any circumstance, one can observe that when a house flourishes, it is because there is someone who sacrifices him or herself. This someone sometimes is a servant, a housemaid. When it is two who sacrifice themselves, the life of the whole becomes brilliant, exemplary. A marriage in which the spouses have the spirit of sacrifice, has peace and joy, and this is so with or without children, with or without wealth. If there are more than two who are sacrificing themselves, the house radiates with a thousand lights which dazzle everyone who approaches it.

And that's the effect the *Sagrada Familia* still has on visitors today, who watch as Gaudi's successors painstakingly extend and fulfill his plans. Except for the college students who come there stoned. The cathedral is more likely to strike such observers as "trippy," "totally Dali," or "a rip-off of Peter Jackson's set design for Rivendell."

CELEBRATE: Tip your Basque beret to the rich history of Catalonia by serving up the Catalan menu below, which is a perfect complement to a bottle or two of cava (per guest!). To make the experience complete, get hold of the fascinating 1984 documentary *Antonio Gaudí*, a loving exploration of the artist's life and work.

Plenty of cava

Catalan Tomato Bread with Jumon Serrano

Oyster Gelee

Monkfish with Romesco (see recipe)

Roasted Red Potatoes

White Asparagus

Bunyols with Strawberries and Almond Milk Sorbet

Monkfish With Romesco

Romesco is one of the glories of the Catalan kitchen. There are infinite variations and applications. The sauce is also delicious spooned on bread. This recipe will make plenty and will keep up to one week.

2 monkfish tails, filleted	2 tablespoons hazelnuts
Salt and freshly ground pepper	Chopped parsley
Flour	Romesco (see below)
Olive oil	

Season monkfish and dredge in flour. Heat olive oil in sauté pan.

Cook on each side 3 to 4 minutes, until browned. Place on paper towels.

Chop hazelnuts in half then roast in 1 teaspoon olive oil.

Spoon Romesco onto center of plates, place monkfish on top and garnish with nuts and parsley.

Serves 4

ROMESCO:

1 ancho chile pepper	1/4 cup almonds
1-3/4 pounds plum tomatoes	1/4 cup hazelnuts
2 red bell peppers	1 slice firm country bread
3 heads garlic	1/4 cup chopped parsley
1 Spanish onion	1 tablespoon sherry vinegar
Olive oil	1 teaspoon sweet paprika
Salt and freshly ground pepper	

Stem and seed the ancho then tear into small bits. Cover with boiling water and let steep for one hour, strain, and set aside.

Preheat oven to 400 degrees.

Prepare the vegetables. Core the tomatoes and slice in half; score each end with a sharp knife making a cross. Core and seed peppers, slice in half. Leave garlic heads whole and slice through the middle. Quarter the onion. Toss all in olive oil and generously season. Roast on lined baking pan about an hour—until everything is soft. When cool enough to handle, peel tomatoes, squeeze garlic, peel peppers and onion. Add to the bowl of a food processor along with the ancho, and puree.

Meanwhile roast almonds, then hazelnuts over medium heat with a touch of olive oil. Transfer to a mortar and pestle. Grind.

Add more olive oil to pan and fry bread. Grind coarsely with nuts in mortar and pestle.

Add nuts and bread to vegetables in processor along with parsley. Pulse several times to combine.

Add vinegar and paprika. Pulse.

Water can be added to adjust consistency in increments of 1 tablespoon.

Adjust seasoning.

....

Drinking Song #9: A Song of Freedom

Apart from our court-challenge-friendly parody of a Monty Python song, this tune is the most recently written drinking song we have to offer. We have mostly selected songs which have stood the test of centuries and helped hallow many an evening of tossing back the pints. This fact demonstrates the authors' pious reverence for tradition, and their publisher's abiding respect for copyright lawyers. However, "The Foggy Dew" is a little fresher, depicting as it does events which took place in 1916, in the abortive Easter Rising conducted by a small group of Irish nationalists in Dublin.

Great Britain was at the time distracted and bogged down in a war against Germany that it might very well lose,[2] and its fleet busy patrolling the North Sea to enforce the blockade it hoped would starve German civilians into surrender. The Kaiser's submarines and ships occasionally attempted to land arms in Ireland,

_____

[2] If only it had. Counter-historical speculation is always risky, but it's a safe bet that if Kaiser Wilhelm II had defeated the corrupt and anti-Catholic France of the Third Republic, the world would never have heard of Hitler or Stalin—and some 60 or 70 million people would not have died in wars and concentration camps. Indeed, it's hard to imagine how the twentieth century could have turned out any *worse* than it actually did—barring an invasion by the Klingons. Of course, we can't *prove* this wouldn't have happened. . . .

hoping to divert British attention with squabbles in a province it had occupied by force for 400 years. But few of those ships landed, and the Irish rebels were poorly armed and few in number—only 1,250 men, none of them soldiers. (Of course, there were tens of thousands of Irish Catholics under arms—in far-off Belgium and Northern France, fighting for their occupiers.)

Besides, we're talking about Irishmen, which means that the rebels were bitterly split among themselves: Put three Hibernians in a room, and you'll end up with four political parties. Abiding distrust divided Catholic nationalists such as Pádraig Pearse from secular socialists such as James Connolly, and both groups from the moderates who preferred to wait until the end of the war to see what crumpet crumbs of self-rule the Brits might throw them. ("Home Rule" for Ireland, proposed before the outbreak of the war, had been indefinitely postponed, and was fiercely opposed by armed Protestant mobs.) The moderates found encouragement in the clergy, who'd ceased to resent the British occupation once the laws affecting the Church had been repealed. Indeed, many clerics enjoyed the convenience of a British passport, and sang "God Save the King" in an ecclesiastical brogue. Likewise, too many bishops throughout Europe snuggled closely up to whatever governments were in power, advising their flock to obey "legitimate" authority and blessing the French and German armies that marched into the trenches to kill each other. Not one of the Church's shining moments.[3]

---

[3] At least the Vatican tried to prevent the war—then intervened repeatedly throughout the conflict to attempt a negotiated peace. It's widely believed that Pope Pius X died of grief because of the Great War; in 1917, his successor Pope Benedict XV worked with St. Karl I (**see Drinking Song #1**), the Austrian emperor, attempting to end the slaughter. These popes' efforts were scorned as naïve by the hard-headed pragmatists who prevailed in Berlin and Paris and the self-anointed messiah who reigned in Washington. But when the war ended, three of the six regimes which had entered the war had collapsed, and two of the survivors were bankrupt and traumatized. The Church still stood.

Nor was this rebellion a great moment for Ireland—at least at first. On Easter Monday, 1916, small companies of rebels seized several strategic points in Dublin, including the General Post Office. It was there that the bookish schoolteacher Pádraig Pearse read the resounding "Proclamation of the Irish Republic," which to this day graces the walls of some 79.3 percent of the bars between New York and Boston. It began:

> "IRISHMEN AND IRISHWOMEN: In the name of God and of the dead generations from which she receives her old tradition of nationhood, Ireland, through us, summons her children to her flag and strikes for her freedom.

At this point, Pearse was almost drowned out by the laughter of scornful old ladies—an occupational hazard of living in Ireland. But he soldiered on:

> We declare the right of the people of Ireland to the ownership of Ireland, and to the unfettered control of Irish destinies, to be sovereign and indefeasible. The long usurpation of that right by a foreign people and government has not extinguished the right, nor can it ever be extinguished except by the destruction of the Irish people. In every generation the Irish people have asserted their right to national freedom and sovereignty; six times during the last three hundred years they have asserted it to arms. Standing on that fundamental right and again asserting it in arms in the face of the world, we hereby proclaim the Irish Republic as a Sovereign Independent State, and we pledge our lives and the lives of our comrades-in-arms to the cause of its freedom, of its welfare, and of its exaltation among the nations.

To this bold declaration of independence from the world's most powerful empire, the public response was cool. The (ironically named) *Irish Independent* called for the British to invade and put the rebels in front of firing squads—in particular James Connolly, who'd led a strike against the newspaper's owner. *The Irish Times* pleaded with its readers to stay home and read Shakespeare until things calmed down. And the British government swung into action. Some 17,000 of "Brittania's Huns" landed within the week and assaulted the hapless rebels with machine guns and artillery. The Rising soon collapsed, in apparent disgrace, having achieved little more than turning large sections of Dublin into rubble. The surviving rebels were spat on by Irishmen as they marched off to jail.

It was then that the usually wily British lost their cool. For centuries, the British empire had succeeded not so much through force of arms as judicious bribery. Its statesmen's skill at co-opting local elites, and convincing them to run entire continents on Britain's behalf, had spread the Union Jack from Hong Kong to Gibraltar.

But with hundreds of thousands of men already dead on the Western front, and the outcome of the Great War still in doubt, British officials overreacted violently. They arrested hundreds of nationalists—many of whom had opposed the Rising and never carried a gun. Instead of imprisoning the rebel leaders, the British judged them guilty of high treason during wartime and ordered them shot. Some 15 rebels were stood before a firing squad—and another, Sean MacDiarmada, who was too seriously wounded to stand, was strapped in a chair and killed.

This singular act of tactlessness turned Irish opinion on its head. Almost overnight, the malcontents and "traitors" who'd brought down ruin on Dublin were transformed into martyrs, and most Irish Catholics turned against the British government. By the time the war ended, the militants who demanded full independence from Great Britain such as (New York-born, half-Spaniard) Eamon de Valera[4] had won the hearts of the Irish nation. Led by the brilliant guerilla fighter Michael Collins, they began a war of attrition against the war-weary British which won Ireland independence (give or take 16 counties) in 1922.

It's said that "The Foggy Dew," which is set to the tune of an old folk song, was written in 1919 by Fr. Charles O'Neill—though others insist it's the work of Peadar Kearney, author of the Irish national anthem. Whoever wrote the song, it's a stirring and moving tune, well-suited to hoisting a Magner's at any of the 125,000 or so pubs that keep it on the jukebox. Like Yeats's famous elegy "Easter 1916," it's a fitting tribute to the men who led the quixotic attack on the windmill that was Britain—and by the manner of their deaths, knocked it down.

---

[4] De Valera was baptized at our favorite parish in New York City, St. Agnes.

2.

Right proudly high over Dublin Town
They flung out the flag of war
'Twas better to die 'neath an Irish sky
Than at Suvla or Sud-el-Bar
And from the plains of royal Meath
Strong men came hurrying through
While Britannia's Huns with their long range guns
Poured hell through the Foggy Dew.

3.

The night fell black and the rifle crack
made perfidious Albion reel
Through the leaden rain seven tongues of flame
shone out o'er the lines of steel
By each shining blade a prayer was said
that to Ireland her sons be true
And when morning broke still the war flag shook
its folds through the Foggy Dew.

4.

The bravest fell and the requiem bell
rang mournfully and clear
For those who died that Eastertide
In the springing of the year
And the world did gaze in deep amaze
At those fearless men but few
Who fought the fight that freedom's light
Might shine through the Foggy Dew.

5.

'Twas England bade our Wild Geese go
That small nations might be free
But their lonely graves are by Suvla's waves
Or the fringe of the great North Sea
Oh! had they died by Pearse's side
Or fought with Cathal Brugha
Their graves we would keep where the Fenians sleep
'Neath the shroud of the Foggy Dew.

6.
Back through the glen I rode again,
My heart with grief was sore
For those gallant lines of marching men
I never would see more
But to and fro in my grief I go
I kneel and I pray for you
For slavery fled O most glorious dead
When you fell in the Foggy Dew.

Yeast: Fermenting the Fertile Crescent

We're not sure when it first happened, but at some point after his expulsion from Eden, early man happened upon a reminder of Paradise. It came in a piece of fallen fruit or a slurry of grain which transported him from the grim, daily grind: "Hunt, gather, repeat. Hunt, gather. . . ." It sparkled in his mouth, tickled his throat, and helped him get his mind off tracking buffalo and planning for an early death. It reminded him not to neglect his avocations: "I really do need to get back to cave-painting," he tipsily thought, "I was pretty good, back in the day." This early man had discovered fermentation—the process by which yeast acts on sugar, producing the beloved by-product alcohol.

The first attempts to ferment beverages on purpose took place in the Fertile Crescent, the cradle of agriculture which hosted the first human cities. As Tom Standage reports in *A History of the World in Six Glasses*, brewing beer began as a means to keep the nutritive value of grain long after mere wheat would have spoiled, or bread turned into stones.

However primitive those men may have been, they weren't stupid. They knew a good thing when they tasted it. Brewing and drinking beer became the anchor of community, as festive residents of a Fertile Crescent city gathered around the vat of unfiltered, sparkling lager, to sip the beverage through straws. Beer turned into a major commodity in ancient Egypt, and its consumption was seen as what marked the "civilized" from the roaming tribes of pastoralists who periodically descended upon the hapless wheat-eaters with fire and sword. Of course, the Bible sides with the shepherds over the farmers—it is Cain who presents to God a half-hearted sacrifice of sheaves (he must have been holding back a bit to brew some beer), and

murders the sheep-tending Abel. Then Cain stalks off to found the world's first city, snorting, "Am I my brother's keeper?" (A true big-city attitude.) We hear in this allegory the first strains of the suspicion most rural folk have always treasured toward the snooty, urban and urbane—which makes Abel and his metaphorical heirs the forerunner of today's country music singers and comedians like Jeff Foxworthy. So remember this, New Yorkers and Los Angelenos, the next time you scoff at one of Toby Keith's patriotic songs: The first redneck was Abel. And God was on his side.

Handy Checklist for Pastors

The following quiz will tell you whether you're on Cain or Abel's side:

You may be a shepherd if. . . .

Your sacrifice to the Lord is not a bundle of sheaves, but your finest spotless lamb.

You would lay down your life for your sheep.

Your first instinct when seeing a flock of sheep is not to call the kids over because they're so cute, but to choose the fattest lamb for slaughter.

You avoid major urban areas, in favor of regions with good pasturage.

You do not plan your residential choices based on the best school districts or public transit, but wander from place to place, following a herd of dumb animals.

You think the grass is always greener on the other side of the Euphrates.

You find yourself outside the city walls, clad only in a goat skin, and feel the urge to scrawl insulting graffiti to confound the idolaters within. Except that you're illiterate.

You prefer sheep's milk cheese to slices of individually packaged American.

Your most significant religious experience was following some angels to a manger.

When you hear the biblical description of men as "them that pisseth against the wall" (1 Kings 14:10), you take it literally.

CELEBRATE: If you passed this test, and turn out to be a shepherd on the side of the Abels, take full advantage of your status by enjoying some delicious lamb, cooked up in this country Italian style.

Lamb Galette

This house favorite is based on a lamb pie recipe by Giuliano Gugialli found in *Foods of Sicily & Sardinia and The Smaller Islands* (New York: Rizzoli, 2002). FYI, to you grain-farmers out there, Pecorino is a peppercorn-studded sheep's milk cheese. And yes, you are your brother's keeper.

CRUST:

1 1/2 cups all purpose flour	1/2 cup lukewarm water
1/4 cup semolina	8 tablespoons butter, room temperature
Pinch salt	

FILLING:

2 pounds ground lamb	4 eggs
1 cup chopped parsley	Salt and freshly ground pepper
4 cloves garlic, finely chopped	1 tablespoon butter
6 ounces Sicilian Pecorino, grated	Egg wash

First prepare the crust. Mix together the flour, semolina, and salt. Place water and butter in center of flour. With a wooden spoon stir ingredients to incorporate the butter. Turn onto a well-floured counter and knead lightly until smooth. Wrap in plastic wrap and chill for a least an hour.

Preheat oven to 400 degrees.

Combine all filling ingredients and mix well.

Bring dough to room temperature and knead briefly on a floured counter. Roll out to 1/4-inch thickness, into an oval. Transfer to a parchment-lined sheet pan. Place meat in center of dough and fold up the sides over the top. Leave a circular hole on top. Pinch dough around to form a rim. Top with dots of butter.

Brush with egg wash and bake for 1 hour.

Serves 8

....

Loopholes in the Ten Commandments
#10: Thou Shalt Not Covet Thy Neighbor's Goods

The previous commandment, which forbade coveting "thy neighbor's wife," seemed to be aimed straight at the heart of our entertainment industry—without all that exposed and jiggling flesh, those filmmakers might actually have to hire (and we're sorry, but we must resort to archaic industry jargon here) actual *writers*, to create engaging *plots* with complex, sympathetic *characters*, played by *actors* capable of reciting *dialogue* that conveys *emotion*. . . . It's all just too much work. Far better to simply position Jessica Simpson next to Tom Cruise (poised on a cinderblock so he seems taller) and arrange for a series of high-tech explosions to gradually rip off each actor's

clothes. It's quick, comprehensible to audiences of all ages, and won't require dubbing when you release the film in Malaysia.

However, this, the last of the Ten Commandments, is in some ways even more disturbing, since it seems to target something larger than Hollywood—namely, our economic system. After all, isn't the motive force of capitalism the desire to "keep up with the Joneses," to make sure that your own income outpaces that of your neighbors? Incessant advertising informs us of all sorts of human needs we never knew we had, such as robotic floor washers, remote-control golf balls, sonic toothbrushes, Blackberries for toddlers, and "collector's edition" complete DVD-sets of *F-Troop*. Not to mention *tai-chi* classes and multicultural sensitivity training for each of our kids above the age of 4. To acquire such necessities, we strive against our colleagues for advancement, our companies fight for higher profits than their competitors, and in general we try to buy low, sell high, and keep as much of the take as possible off the books and away from the taxman. Is all this compatible with Christianity?

Various saints over the centuries have thought not, or at any rate reacted strongly against the excesses of the profit system. St. Francis, whose father made a fortune selling high-dollar items retail to the "affluent" market, turned against the materialism and radical class inequality he saw overtaking Italy as it bounced back after the Black Plague. Francis embraced a radical poverty as a route to spiritual liberation, and urged others to emulate him. Some of his followers (the bad Catholics among them) got worn out and started looking for loopholes in his Rule—while others overreacted, and tried to impose their own vocation on all Christendom. The "Spiritual Franciscans," who expected the Holy Spirit to descend any minute now and establish Heaven on earth,[1] declared the ownership of private property a mortal sin. They insisted that every Christian must live like a

[1] We're still waiting, guys. . . .

monk, and when they ignored a series of warnings from several popes they were excommunicated as heretics.[2] The Church, in her wisdom, could hold up Francis as an heroic example whose life was a prophetic protest against materialism, without endorsing coercive political utopias, or branding as sinful the drives which God implanted in every man—including the "sensitive appetite," which according to the Catechism of the Catholic Church

> . . . leads us to desire pleasant things we do not have, e.g., the desire to eat when we are hungry or to warm ourselves when we are cold. These desires are good in themselves; but often they exceed the limits of reason and drive us to covet unjustly what is not ours and belongs to another or is owed to him. (#2535)

This invites the question, of course: what are "the limits of reason." Is there some bare human minimum required for survival, on top of which anything else we might crave is a sinful luxury? Thankfully, no. As Leo XIII explained in *Rerum novarum* (**see Highballs**), we are each expected to live "becomingly," in accord with the country and social class in which we dwell. The essential thing is not to fetishize material wealth and well-being, to the point where it leads us to act unjustly, or neglect our duties to the needy—for instance, to the spouse or child who *needs* to see us in the flesh once in a while, except that we're working 80-hour weeks trying to make partner so we can finally afford those Botox injections and that *pied-à-terre* in Paris. . . .

More serious than the simple temptation of greed is the darker passion of envy. The difference between these sins is stark: The greedy man wants the same thing as (or maybe just a little more than) his neighbor. He looks down the street at the shiny new Lexus that parallel parks itself, and he goes into credit-card debt to buy it—then curses his "rotten luck" every month when the bills comes in.

The envious man, on the other hand, would be just as happy to see his neighbor's fine new car destroyed in some freak accident—like an unexplained fire, or an Improvised Explosive Device that somehow turned up in the driveway, just by chance.[3] As the Catechism points out, "St. Augustine saw envy as '*the* diabolical sin.' From envy are born hatred, detraction, calumny, joy caused by the misfortune

---

[2] These well-meaning fanatics remind us of certain right-wing Catholics we have met who counter the heresy which accepts artificial contraception by asserting that Catholics are morally obliged to produce large families, and may only employ Natural Family Planning to avoid imminent maternal death or starvation. There's just one problem with this: It is not the Church's teaching, as the text of *Humanae vitae* makes clear, advocating (section 10, p. 16) the use of NFP when parents must limit their family size for reasons which are "*iustae*" or just. Not "*gravis*" (grave), but "just." Those who argue that parents should neglect the virtue of prudence in this one area of life—fertility—are the modern-day heirs of the Spiritual Franciscans. Trying to avoid one heresy, they have gone out and invented another.

[3] Hey, it could happen. . . .

of a neighbor, and displeasure caused by his prosperity." (#2539) There's a word for this in German (of course): *Schadenfreude*, which is impossible to translate literally. The closest English equivalent is "Jerry Springer."

If the envious man sees some good thing which he cannot possess, he hopes that others will be deprived of it as well. If he is unsuccessful in his economic ventures, he embraces some form of socialism (for instance, anti-Semitism, the socialism of the stupid). If he's lonely and can hunt up some religious excuse, he may well become a Puritan, deploring the "scandalous promiscuity" and "shocking, immodest dress" of the women who won't return his calls or even meet his long, disturbing stare—probably because they remember him as "that guy who *everybody knows* blew up his neighbor's Lexus. Right there in the driveway. I swear to God."

Zima and Other Culinary Inventions from the Devil

We all know, of course, that evil has no independent existence, and subsists solely as a parasite on the Good. To attribute to Satan an equal and opposite potency to God is to embrace the error of Dualism, which once beguiled Augustine—who later comprehensively refuted it (**see Satan**). As the great bishop of Hippo (and we always like to picture him riding into battle against heretics mounted on a hippo) explained, existence itself is good, while evil is merely an absence, perversion, or misdirection of the Good. Everything that is, from the Devil himself to the rankest smelling restroom in the lowest pit of Hell, was either made directly by God or fashioned by one of His creatures out of other stuff He'd already made. Whatever is evil comes from creatures misusing the raw materials He gave them, especially themselves. There may be poisonous chemicals, but there are no evil chemicals. People may embrace evil, but their existence itself is still good.[1] That doesn't mean it's always wrong to kill them—let's say, if they're coming at you with a whirring electric knife, or tyrannizing your country. Because (and here's the tricky part) killing them won't *put an end to their existence*, but simply transfer them to another, probably hotter place.

It's sometimes hard to remember this fundamental principle of ontology, the goodness of existence itself, and the axiom that evil has no positive reality, when faced with some of the darkest, most inherently perverse works of fallen man—such as nerve gas, frozen French toast TV dinners, Lunchables, and bizarre, high-tech malt beverage beer substitutes such as Zima. Let us explain.

Back in the late 1990s, before they discovered their vocations as apologists and bad Catholics, the present authors were working on several prospective literary projects. Their first manuscript was a unique attempt at satire called (with a tip of the hat to *The Twilight Zone*) *To Serve Man: A Guide to Cooking Vegetarians.* This Swiftian recipe book was aimed not at Hindus or health buffs, but at animal rights activists who assert that animal life is morally equal to human. For instance, Princeton University philosopher Pete Singer, who rejects as "speciesism" any

---

[1] Yes, even Adam Sandler's.

distinctions made between humans and animals, whether in the kitchen or in . . . the bedroom. Yes, that means what you think it means. For any of you who are considering sending your kids to Princeton, keep in mind that Prof. Singer teaches *ethics* there.[2] And keep an eye on Fido.

To satirize Singer and his doe-eyed, bushy-tailed followers, we proposed that diners take such "pro-choice" vegans at their word. To anyone who believes that his own life is no more sacred than that of a cow or chicken, we said:

> We agree. We will honor your values and stop eating cows and chickens. We will eat you instead. And here are the recipes we'll use. And these are our favorite cuts.

Replacing animal protein with that derived from vegetarian sources would spare the lives of innocent animals, and grant thousands of young, lean idealists the chance to make the ultimate sacrifice on behalf of their furry friends. It would also honor the personal lifestyle choices of carnivores. We considered this "win/win" solution an instance of "ethical synergy," and included dozens of winning dishes such as "Paté Singer," lavishly illustrated, with tips for hunting and carving. (Note to law enforcement authorities: These recipes were tested using organically-raised, grass-fed, free-range beef—not vegans.)

Paté Singer, with cornichons and toast points. Image courtesy of Princeton University Residential Food Services

Oddly enough, no publishers were interested in this book. In fact, it frightened our agent, an old hand in the business who thought he'd seen it all. Till then. He chuckled nervously as he flipped through the detailed drawings, then quickly slid the manuscript back to us and ordered a stiff gin & tonic. "Never show this to anyone," he advised. "Not even your friends."

So that project was scotched. Our next attempt to craft a manuscript was equally

---

[2] Singer also teaches that the life of a healthy young chimp is worth more than that of a second-trimester fetus, or a newborn retarded child. We counter that this is only true at Princeton, and only if the chimp has tenure.

protein-centered, but focused rather less on satirical cannibalism[3] and more on tasty desserts: We tried to write a cookbook of desserts which were compatible with the Atkins Diet. This was back in the middle '90s when that diet was only just taking off, and about to become an enormous fad. At one point, both the authors were attempting to follow Dr. Atkins's advice to avoid nearly all carbohydrates in favor of protein and fat. They both lost weight, got grumpy, and developed that curious ketone breath, which during the dot-com boom filled the martini bars of New York's Silicon Alley with a curious, chemical smell. It's hard to describe . . . something like a Hackensack benzene plant after a thunderstorm.

Since one of the authors is a trained pastry chef, this idea seemed like a slam-dunk. All we had to do was come up with a collection of tasty, traditional desserts such as she used to make at New Orleans's Louis XVI Restaurant—and replace all the carbohydrates with other ingredients. As we researched the project, we realized that we needed low- or zero-carb substitutes for such essential dessert components as:

- Flour. We tried using soy flour, which when baked turned into small bricks suitable for building a front-yard Marian shrine. Then we used wheat gluten, which assumed in the oven the consistency of Styrofoam packing peanuts.
- Fruit. Since such natural treats as raspberries, cherries, and apples were laced by the Creator with high-carb fructose, we attempted to liven up our inert desserts with artificially flavored, zero-cal syrups. This gave the soy bricks and gluten peanuts the nostalgic flavor of Moon Rocks™ ("Just Add Water!"), and the smell of our old Mr. Wizard Chemistry Set.
- Sugar. This was the obvious problem—the search for an artificial sweetener that wouldn't make the crème brulee taste like an oncologist's petrie dish. We tried carcinogens, neurotoxins, and chemically engineered near-sugars designed to be indigestible to humans.[4] We stirred in saccharine, NutraSweet, Splenda—you name it, we tasted it. Each one was disgusting in its own uniquely man-made way. In a last-ditch attempt to use something natural, we ordered the herb-based sweetener stevia—made from a South American plant which is at once both sickeningly sweet and bracingly bitter—like a spoonful of sugar that has been soaked with iodine.

At last, the chef called a halt to the project. Eager as she was to put out a uniquely profitable cookbook and retire to Dubrovnik, she found she could no longer

---

[3] Of course in the manuscript, we distanced ourselves from this term, which we labeled as "hate speech" and referred to throughout as "the C-word." We insisted instead on happy-face euphemisms like "succulent humanist" and "philanthropist"—the latter referring to anyone who loves man, especially in a nice cream sauce.

[4] Yum!

continue attempting to adulterate dessert by turning it into an entrée. When pressed by her preternaturally persistent co-author, at last she exclaimed: "I just can't do this—these foods are . . . from the DEVIL!"

Did she mean that, for instance, the chemical compound sucralose (i.e., Splenda) was in fact an ontological evil, created by some dark Demiurge who mars Creation by exuding a force contrary to God's generative power? Well, yes—at first, she did. But a quick lesson in Augustine cleared up that mistake, and led to a fascinating discussion of the ways in which man can pervert the very best aspect of the world as God made it, in pursuit of shortcuts, easy outs, and cheap thrills. Sometimes we crave sex without a lasting relationship, or food without the calories, or dinner without the work. So we try to "cheat" a little. Depending on the moral significance of the phenomenon whose rules we're trying to bend, this can result in something as serious as a mortal sin, or as ugly as smooshy, canned peas. Not all technological "fixes" for natural problems we encounter in a fallen world are morally questionable, of course; we have no quarrel with toothpaste, vaccines, anesthesia, or deodorants. But sometimes the attempt to get around the structure of reality backfires, and "destroys a village in order to save it." Remember, the next time someone argues in favor of, say, stem-cell research[5] that the very first sin was presented to Adam and Eve as a tool of knowledge:

> Then the serpent said to the woman, "You will not surely die. For God knows that in the day you eat of it your eyes will be opened, and you will be like God. . . . (Genesis 3: 4–5)

That's why, as we explained elsewhere (**see Loreto** and also **Organic Wines**), we retain a certain skepticism when faced with human efforts to "improve" upon God's handiwork. Because according to the Owner's Manual,[6] that can sometimes void the warranty.

CELEBRATE: Throughout this book, we've recommended healthy, natural, mostly organic-based dishes that celebrate the intrinsic perfection of God's Creation. Just this once, to help the reader appreciate the positivity of the Good, we're proposing a menu of thoroughly synthetic, high-tech, chemically tarted-up food and drink that would have warmed (and after death, artificially preserved) the hearts of a couple in the early 1960s—when we all still believed that Science was unambiguously our friend, that someday each of us would live for 500 pain-

---

[5] That is, storing frozen humans as embryos, then defrosting them and killing them to use as spare parts to replace, for instance, the livers of middle-aged, alcoholic rock stars.

[6] Here's its Amazon listing: *Catechism of the Catholic Church: Second Edition* (Hardcover) by U.S. Catholic Church (New York: Doubleday, 2003).

less years, buzzing around like the Jetsons in personal rocket packs, eating astronaut food prepared for us by robot-chefs named Rosie. The menu below serves up to six friends (or better yet, enemies). It was inspired in part by one of our favorite humor books, James Lileks's *The Gallery of Regrettable Foods*, which one might justly call *The Gulag Archipelago* of the kitchen.

A Dinner from the Devil

Zima
Serve great big, glistening cases of the stuff. Drink as cold as possible. Use liquid nitrogen to attain a potable temperature, if you have the equipment.

Fat-Free Pringles with Olestra. The intestine-loosening salty snack that helped put more Boomers in slim, hip-hugging diapers than any other major food product apart from heroin.

Armour Potted Meat. Rife with enough preservative chemicals to embalm your entrails before dinner, it features such ingredients as Partially Defatted Cooked Pork Fatty Tissue and Sodium Erythorbate. Serve icy cold, straight from the fridge. Guests may serve themselves with handy plastic sporks.

Salad of Iceberg Lettuce and California Winter Tomatoes Smeared with Walden Farms Zero-Carb Ranch Dressing.

Gluten-Burger Loaf, Garnished with Tofurkey Bacon. Cook up the "bacon" in vegetable shortening (hmm… love those transfats).

Green-Bean-and-Canned-Fried-Onion-Rings Casserole. This dish is really from the devil. The Evil's One's signature? You top the casserole off with condensed soup. (See recipe.)

Instant Mashed Potatoes. Serve glistening with heart-clogging margarine.

Sugar-Free Jello with Nutrasweet™ with Sugar-Free Baby Marshmallows. Serve in a brain-shaped mold (pictured, available from *www.egeneralmedical.com/ braingelmol.html*).

Instead of letting people enjoy a smoke after dinner, hand out pieces of nicotine gum.

RECIPE:

Green-Bean-and-Canned-Fried-Onion-Rings Casserole
Courtesy of French's Web site (*www.frenchs.net*).

INGREDIENTS:
1 can (10 3/4 ounces) CAMPBELL'S® Cream of Mushroom Soup
3/4 cup milk
1/8 teaspoon black pepper
2 packages (9 ounces each) frozen French-cut green beans, thawed
1 1/3 cups French's® French Fried Onions, divided

Combine soup, milk and pepper in a 1 1/2 -quart baking dish; stir until blended. Stir in beans and 2/3 cup French Fried Onions.

Bake at 350°F for 30 minutes or until hot. Stir. Sprinkle with remaining 2/3 cup onions. Bake 5 minutes or until onions are golden.

Serves a small gathering.

Zinfandel: Not Just for Junior High School Anymore

One of the most widely planted grapes in California is Zinfandel, a red-skinned grape that is used in many of the "big" tasting "fruit bomb" wines beloved by the critics such as wine pope Robert Parker. It also provides the juice for those sickly-

sweet pink Zinfandels (**see Grapes, God, and the Vines of Sodom**) beloved by middle-school girls in the suburbs, weepy poetesses in MFA programs as they read each other their reams of Plath *manqué*, and dipsomaniac journalists at press events to which they haven't *officially* been invited. Because it ripens quickly and unevenly, a single bunch of Zinfandel pulled from the vine can include grapes which are still unripe, and others which are sickly-sweet and shriveled (**see Late-Harvest Wines**). It takes a careful vintner, willing to sort the fruit by hand, to craft some of the better Zinfan-

dels, which now compete with the best Cabernet Sauvignons from France—sometimes besting them in blind taste tests, to the impotent fury of the Frogs, who retaliate by selling advanced weapons systems to Arab countries.

The success of Zinfandel can inspire Europeans to irritation or emulation, depending on their temperaments. What rankles especially is the fact that for over 100 years Zinfandel has been marketed as a uniquely American wine. Which isn't exactly true, though it took a decade of DNA research to uncover it, and waft away the clouds of mystification and PR which have long attended Zinfandel's history.

In the mid-nineteenth century, pioneering vintners (**see Agoston Haraszthy**) saw in California a potential paradise: a mild, predictable climate, rich and diverse soils, and plenty of willing agricultural workers—such as disappointed miners drifting back from the played out Gold Rush, émigré Italian peasants, and thousands of conquered, leftover Mexicans. Grape vines planted long ago by Franciscan friars to purple their altars (**see Mission Wines**) flourished wherever mission bells chimed (**see Napa**). However, most of the grapes which grew across the state were a hybrid of the finer European varieties (*vitis vinifera*) and the hardy, blunt-

tasting native grape, the Muscadine (*vitis rotundifolia*). The resulting wine was perfect for sipping in tiny quantities at Mass—or in unconsecrated form, for intoxicating altar boys.

It took entrepreneurs such as Harazthy to introduce grapes derived from pure European sources which could produce finer wines. Harazthy brought more than 100,000 cuttings with him from Europe, plants he grew himself and sold to other vintners. The Zinfandel grape, it has long been believed, was one of these elite European varieties—and that's how California winemakers marketed it for almost a century, as a noble grape whose origins were shrouded in mystery, carried over from Europe by the dashing Hungarian count who died while boating through the South American jungle, eaten (it's said) by a crocodile. That makes quite a story, and it helped sell the wine.

In recent years, the truth about Zinfandel came gradually to light—but relax: it still involves monks. Researchers undertook genetic comparisons between the American grape and various European varieties which they suspected might be its ancestor. This paternity test turned up positive for Primitivo—a long-dismissed Italian grape that got its moniker from the Benedictine brothers who raised it in the southern Italian region of Puglia.[7] While its name suggests that the wine is rough-

---

[7] This region, which lay for longer than most of Italy under the control of the Byzantine Empire, still shows traces of Eastern influence—for instance, the Eastern-Rite Catholic churches (in full union with Rome) of the Italo-Albanian Rite. Fleeing the ravages of liturgical reform upon the Roman Rite, the authors used to attend one of these parishes in New Orleans, St. Nicholas of Myra. Founded by some of the many Sicilian immigrants to that city (who also invented its storied sandwich, the Muffaletta), the parish is mostly attended by liturgical refugees—though the last time we went there, there were still a few elderly Sicilians praying in the back, for the sake of authenticity. The parish's chapel was flooded during Hurricane Katrina, but it's in the process of rebuilding.

hewn or unsubtle, in fact "Primitivo" simply refers to the fact that it ripens before other varieties, making it the first (*primo*) grape which the monks could harvest.

But these grapes were never planted under that name in America; our first record of them in the U.S. appears in an ad for "Zinfandel" grape cuttings which was published in 1832—long before Harazthy left Hungary—for plants from the Austrian imperial collection, grown in greenhouses on New York's Long Island.[8] It pleases *mitteleuropean* New Yorkers like us to know that the backbone of the California wine industry came to that state from the Kaiser's own vineyards, via the Hamptons. Further research has turned up the fact that Primitivo grapes had originally carried across the narrow Adriatic by Benedictines from Dalmatia—where a genetically identical grape named Crljenak Kaštelanski has grown for centuries,[9] though only a few vines still remain today.

All of which goes to show the importance of name and reputation. Can you imagine Michelle Pfeiffer, in 1983, sidling up next to Al Pacino at the bar at the Beverly Hills Hotel to order a glass of "pink Crljenak Kaštelanski"? Somehow, we can't. To create the California marketing phenomenon which is Zinfandel, it took decades of careful cultivation, a romantic air of secrecy attending the origins of the grape, and above all a name that blonde actresses could pronounce. The technical (indeed, sometimes chemical) expertise of American vintners has turned that obscure Balkan grape into an international sensation—to the point where Italian vintners are renaming their Primitivo wines "Zinfandel" to boost their sales. And Californians are going to court to try to stop them.

One of our favorite producers of Zinfandel is the Coturri Winery of Sonoma, California, which carries on the tradition of Enrico Coturri—an Italian who came to San Francisco in 1901, in hopes of watching an earthquake. As Tony Cotturi told us in an interview, "My grandfather Enrico was born in a little town of Farneta outside of Lucca. The legend in the family is that he was educated by the monks in the nearby monastery and they taught him winemaking." Those would have been the Benedictine monks of the Farneta Abbey, located on the site of an ancient Roman temple near Cortona.

Enrico Cotturi worked as a barrel cooper, but began to make wine on the side, using the ancient techniques which the "black friars" had used for centuries (**see Burgundy**). He taught the craft to his son, Red,[10] who made Zinfandel for home use and to sell as Sacramental wine during America's brief flirtation with totalitarianism (**see Temperance**). In 1979 Red founded the current Coturri Winery, where he now raises grapes without use of pesticides (**see Organic Wine**) to make a wide

---

8 "Zinfandel," by Anita Tepsic, TED Case Studies # 662 (January, 2002).

9 "Looking for Zinfandel in Croatia," by Prof. Carole Meredith, *Zinfandel Express* (January, 2002).

10 No, he didn't have brothers named "White" and "Rosé." We checked. Though we are acquainted with at least one Italian-American seminarian named Primo, whose imaginative parents named his four brothers Secondo, Terzio, Quarto, and Quinto. We're disappointed they didn't have a sixth child and christen him Basta, then a seventh named Troppo.

range of highly rated, Parker-friendly Zinfandels, as well as Syrah, Pinot Noir, and other varieties. Indeed, the winery likes to boast that Coturri's Zinfandel was served to Pope John Paul II, alongside beef tenderloin stuffed with truffles, when the pope visited San Francisco in 1987. How was this wine chosen for the pontiff? The winery doesn't say, but it does admit that five years before, *Osservatore Romano* gossip columnist Fr. Guido Sarducci (aka Don Novello) had scouted out Coturri Wineries, sampling their wares. He must have liked the wines, since he kept coming back—and brought along John Belushi.

About the Authors

John Zmirak's work has appeared in *USA Today, Investor's Business Daily, Commonweal, The Weekly Standard, The New Republic, The Atlantic, The American Conservative,* and *First Things*. He has served as senior editor at *Faith & Family* magazine and as a reporter at *The National Catholic Register*. He is currently a contributing editor to Godspy.com and editor of the biannual guide *Choosing the Right College*. His dogged research for this book resulted in extensive liver damage, so he hopes you will buy multiple copies for friends to help fund his upcoming transplant.

Denise Matychowiak, who created the recipes for this book, has worked as a cook and pastry chef at Louis XVI Restaurant in New Orleans and La Caravelle in New York City, and served as food editor at *Faith & Family* magazine. She has served as a private chef to numerous New York-area celebrities and V.I.P.s, but if we told you who they were, we'd have to kill you.

Of Related Interest

THE BAD CATHOLIC'S GUIDE TO GOOD LIVING

*A Loving Look at the Lighter Side of the Catholic Faith,
with Recipes for Feasts and Fun*

Text by John Zmirak and recipes by Denise Matychowiak

*Celebrate the Feast Days of the Saints —
and don't forget your trampoline!*

Jump right into this hilarious book on enjoying and celebrating Catholicism in a whole new way! Both a comical read and an indispensable resource for observing the Feast Days of the Saints, *The Bad Catholic's Guide to Good Living* is for anyone who is interested in celebrating the history and humor behind the Catholic Faith. Consisting of selected monthly historical sketches of the feast days, as well suggested activities for celebration, this book serves as a must-have for every happy Catholic! Written by a Catholic journalist and a four-star chef, it's an entertaining guide and guerilla catechism.

"Imagine Mel Gibson crossed with Monty Python — a hilarious, in your face, Late-Nite Latin Mass."

— Angelo Matera, Publisher, Godspy.com,
former CEO of the *National Catholic Register*

"Their sharp-witted irreverence seldom fails to amuse — because they know the Church so well, and love her so dearly."

— Thomas McArdle, White House speechwriter, former communications
director, the Catholic League for Civil and Religious Rights

0-8245-2300-8, paperback

crossroad

Of Related Interest

George William Rutler
COINCIDENTALLY

From the Da Vinci Code and Roswell to E Pluribus Unum and the pyramid on the back of every dollar bill, we all are fascinated by secrets, codes, and coincidences. George Rutler — EWTN speaker, *Crisis* magazine columnist, and reigning Catholic wit — offers his reflections on the coincidental links that connect the most far-flung parts of our worlds. Topics cover the gamut of human life, from Louis Farrakhan and Edgar Allan Poe to Benjamin Franklin and the propensity of Scottish physicians to dominate the Nobel Prizes for Medicine.

Fr. George Rutler is best known as the host of a weekly program on EWTN and the pastor of Our Saviour in midtown New York City, where he lives. A convert from Anglicanism, he has published a number of books that were enormous successes in non-trade markets.

0-8245-2440-3, hardcover

Check your local bookstore for availability.
To order directly from the publisher,
please call 1-800-707-0670 for Customer Service
or visit our Web site at *www.cpcbooks.com.*
For catalog orders, please send your request to the address below.

THE CROSSROAD PUBLISHING COMPANY
16 Penn Plaza, Suite 1550
New York, NY 10001

crossroad